The International Law Commission

THE
INTERNATIONAL
LAW COMMISSION

By HERBERT W. BRIGGS

Member of the International Law Commission
Membre de l'Institut de Droit International
Goldwin Smith Professor of International Law, Cornell University

CORNELL UNIVERSITY PRESS
Ithaca, New York

Copyright © 1965 by Cornell University

CORNELL UNIVERSITY PRESS

First published 1965

Library of Congress Catalog Card Number: 65-11870

PRINTED IN THE UNITED STATES OF AMERICA
BY VAIL-BALLOU PRESS, INC.

ONULP

Preface

THE International Law Commission created by the United Nations has now functioned for sixteen years. The interest of the author in the purposes and activities of the Commission goes back to its beginnings. Most of the research and much of the writing of this volume were completed prior to the author's election to membership on the Commission in 1961, although the study has been made current as of publication.

Information about the International Law Commission is scattered in hundreds of documents consisting of thousands of pages, some of which, appearing in mimeographed form, have never been printed or published. Commencing in 1956, the United Nations has published in the *Yearbooks of the International Law Commission* most of the documentation and summary records of the Commission, but a study of the Commission involves consultation of hundreds of documents not appearing in that series.

The original intention of the author to present, in addition to what appears in this volume, a critical legal appraisal of the results of the Commission's work, was set aside when he was elected to the Commission. The volume here presented therefore involves an examination of the drafting of the Commission's Statute and of its application and evolution in practice and is intended to facilitate an institutional study of the objects, organization, methods, procedures, and activities of the International Law Commission in undertaking its important responsibilities in the field of the codification and progressive development of international law.

The utility of a study of the Commission which is largely organized as a legal commentary on the meaning of the provisions of the Commission's Statute, with elaborate citation of precedents in their application, has appeared to the author to out-weigh a perhaps more readable approach. It is the author's hope that in addition to providing a comprehensive study of the Commission in action, such an approach will facilitate reference and consultation and thus provide a convenient handbook for members of the Commission, for members of the General Assembly and its Sixth Committee, for legal advisers of foreign offices, and for scholars. Much light on the process, and the difficulties, of the codification and progressive development of international law may be gleaned from a study of the Commission's careful resolution of the problems, political as well as legal, with which it has been confronted. Indeed, implicit or explicit in debates on questions of procedure and method are to be found comments which provide useful insights into the nature of international law, its substantive rules, and their development to meet the emergent needs of an expanded community of States.

Aside from the documentary sources and periodical literature cited in the footnotes to this book, the bibliography on the International Law Commission is scanty. Occasional notes or articles on the work of the Commission have appeared in international law journals and annuals but no book appears to have been devoted to the Commission. On the early years of the Commission the authoritative studies of Dr. Yuen-li Liang, Secretary of the International Law Commission, have been most useful. The study "The International Law Commission, 1949–59" by Ambassador Shabtai Rosenne, now a member of the International Law Commission, which appeared in the 1960 *British Year Book of International Law* provides the most comprehensive analysis of the Commission as an institution and has been most helpful to the author.

As the beneficiary of a Rockefeller Foundation grant, the author had the opportunity of working in the United Nations archives in the Palais des Nations in Geneva during the academic year 1960–1961 and of observing the 13th Session of the International Law Commission. He has since participated as a member of the Commission in its 14th, 15th, and 16th Sessions in 1962, 1963, and 1964. The information and insights gained from contacts with members of the Commission and its experienced and able Secretary, Dr. Liang, have contributed immeasurably to his understanding of the institutional role of the Commission.

There remains the pleasant duty of expressing appreciation to Mr. Dean Rusk and Mr. Kenneth W. Thompson for the Rockefeller Foundation grant which was so helpful to the author; and to Mr. A. C. Breycha-Vautier, Mr. Badr Kasme, and Mr. J. Higham of the Palais des Nations library for their many courtesies; and to the Cornell University Center for International Studies for assistance in the distribution of this book to United Nations delegations and to legal advisers of Member States.

HERBERT W. BRIGGS

Ithaca, New York
August 7, 1964

Contents

PART III
THE COMMISSION IN ACTION

Note on United Nations
Documents and Abbreviations

THIS study is based primarily on documentary sources for which standard forms of classification and citation have been established by the United Nations. Except where otherwise indicated, citations are to United Nations documents and it has not been deemed necessary here to preface each such citation with "U.N. doc."

The United Nations symbol A/CN.4 designates the International Law Commission (Assembly/Commission 4). A/CN.4/ 1 ff. refers to the documentary series of the International Law Commission; and A/CN.4/SR.7, for example, refers to the Summary Record of the 7th meeting of the Commission. Issued first in mimeographed form, these documents and summary records of the Commission have largely been reissued in the printed *Yearbooks of the International Law Commission* with different pagination. Except for 1949, the *Yearbooks of the International Law Commission* (A/CN.4/SER. A) have appeared in two annual volumes: Volume I contains the Summary Records of a session; and Volume II contains accompanying documents and the annual Report of the International Law Commission for a particular session. For convenience of consultation, citations in this study are made to the Summary Records and documents as printed in the Commission's *Yearbooks* and are designated as "Yearbook, ILC," with number and date of session. However, occasional references will be found to the A/CN.4 mimeographed records where portions of them have been omitted in the Yearbooks.

Documents of the United Nations General Assembly most frequently cited in this volume include:

A/	numbered Assembly documents
A/PV.	numbered *procès-verbaux* or verbatim records of plenary meetings
Agenda item	numbered collection of documents pertaining to a particular topic on the agenda of a session
A/C.6	numbered documents of the General Assembly's Sixth (Legal) Committee; similarly, A/C.5 for Fifth (Administrative and Budgetary) Committee
A/C.6/SR.	summary records of the Sixth (Legal) Committee
A/AC.10 and A/AC.10/SR.	documents and summary records of the Committee on the Progressive Development of International Law and Its Codification
GA res.	General Assembly resolution
GAOR	Official Records of the General Assembly

Standard citations have also been employed for documents which are not United Nations documents. For example:

A.B.A.J.	American Bar Association Journal
A.J.I.L.	American Journal of International Law
B.Y.I.L.	British Year Book of International Law
U.N.C.I.O.	Documents of the (San Francisco) United Nations Conference on International Organization, 1945

Since frequent citation is made to the texts of resolutions adopted by the General Assembly, there is appended for convenience a table of symbols designating documents containing the collected resolutions of a particular session of the Assembly:

Session	Document	Session	Document
I 1946	A/64	X 1955	A/3116
II 1947	A/519	XI 1956	A/3572
III 1948	A/810 (Part I)	XII 1957	A/3805
	A/900 (Part II)	XIII 1958	A/4090
IV 1949	A/1251	XIV 1959	A/4354
V 1950	A/1775	XV 1960	A/4684
VI 1951	A/2119	XVI 1961	A/5100
VII 1952	A/2361	XVII 1962	A/5217
VIII 1953	A/2630	XVIII 1963	A/5515
IX 1954	A/2890		

Attention may also be called to "The United Nations International Law Commission: A Guide to the Documents: 1949–59," prepared by J. Higham of the United Nations Library, Palais des Nations, Geneva, and published in 36 *British Year Book of International Law* 384–397 (1960).

PART I

CREATION OF THE INTERNATIONAL LAW COMMISSION:

THE DRAFTING AND IMPLEMENTATION OF ARTICLE 13, PARAGRAPH 1 (a), OF THE UNITED NATIONS CHARTER

The Drafting of Article 13, Paragraph 1 (a)

Article 13, paragraph 1 (a) of the Charter of the United Nations provides:

1. The General Assembly shall initiate studies and make recommendations for the purpose of:
(a) promoting international cooperation in the political field and encouraging the progressive development of international law and its codification.

Considerations involved in the drafting of this clause throw light upon the functions conferred on the United Nations by its provisions.[1]

The Dumbarton Oaks Proposals for a General International Organization,[2] dated 7 October 1944, contained only one reference *in expressis verbis* to international law: the provision,[3] later abandoned in the drafting of Article 2 (7) of the Charter, that international law should be the criterion for determining whether or not a matter was solely within the domestic jurisdiction of a State.

The failure of the Dumbarton Oaks Proposals to "mention the principles of International Law as being the basis of the new Organization" or to provide "some special agency" to "further and develop International Law" was the subject of some criticism in the comments submitted by governments on the Proposals.[4] It was, indeed, remarkable that proposals for a general international organization whose purposes, principles, and functions embraced the maintenance of international

[1] See also Yuen-li Liang, "The General Assembly and the Progressive Development and Codification of International Law," 42 A.J.I.L. 66-97, at pp. 66-68 (1948).

[2] United Nations Conference on International Organization, San Francisco, 1945, III, 1–23, Doc. 1, G/1. Cited hereafter as U.N.C.I.O.

[3] Chap. VIII, A, 7.

[4] The quotations are from the comment of the Egyptian Government, U.N.C.I.O., III, 447, 448. Doc. 2, G/7 (q), April 16, 1945.

peace and security, the proscription of the threat or use of force, the pacific settlement of international disputes, and international cooperation in political, economic, social, and humanitarian matters of international concern should be so barren of reference to international law as to convey the impression that the drafters of the Proposals foresaw no continuing relation between the progressive development of international law and the functioning of the Organization.

This deficiency in the Dumbarton Oaks Proposals is even more surprising when examined in the light of earlier drafts prepared in the United States Department of State prior to the Dumbarton Oaks Conference. In a "Memorandum for the President," dated 29 December 1943, certain "basic ideas" on a postwar international organization were transmitted to the President. Among the recommendations appeared the following: " (2) That there should be a General Assembly, composed of all member states, whose principal functions and powers should relate to the setting up of a general framework of policy, the development of international law, and the promotion of international cooperation in general." [5] In the attached "Plan for the Establishment of an International Organization for the Maintenance of International Peace and Security," dated 23 December 1943, it was provided in Section IV on the General Assembly: "3. The General Assembly should initiate studies and make recommendations concerning (a) the interpretation and revision of rules of international law. . . ." [6] A "Topical Outline," based upon the "Plan" but which contained no reference to international law, was submitted to the British and Soviet Embassies in Washington, on 19 February 1944.[7] However, the subsequent State Department draft of a "Possible Plan for a General International Organization," dated 29 April 1944, in dealing with the powers of the General

[5] *Postwar Foreign Policy Preparation, 1939–1945.* U.S. Department of State, General Foreign Policy Series 15 (Washington, 1949), 576.

[6] *Ibid.,* 580. President Roosevelt gave his general approval to the Plan on Feb. 3, 1944. *Ibid.,* 256.

[7] *Ibid.,* 257. For text of "Topical Outline," *ibid.,* 581.

Assembly, provided in II, B, 2, c, (2) that "2. The principal powers of the general assembly should be . . . (c) to initiate studies and make recommendations for: . . . (2) the development and revision of rules of international law. . . ."[8] This provision was retained verbatim in the final United States draft prior to the Dumbarton Oaks Conference which was labeled "Tentative Proposals for a General International Organization" and which was dated 18 July 1944, and conveyed to the British, Soviet, and Chinese Governments on the same date.[9] It thus appears that the United States entered the Dumbarton Oaks Conference favoring the initiation of studies and the making of recommendations for the development and revision of rules of international law as one of "the principal powers" to be conferred on the proposed general assembly.

For reasons lying quarantined in the still unpublished records of the Dumbarton Oaks Conference, the provision did not survive the first phase of Soviet-British-American conversations and does not appear in the Dumbarton Oaks Proposals. However, during the Chinese-British-American phase of the Dumbarton Oaks Conference, the provision reappeared in a Chinese proposal that: "2. The Assembly should be responsible for initiating studies and making recommendations with respect to the development and revision of the rules and principles of international law."[10] Because of a decision during the Chinese phase of the conversations not to modify the phraseology of the Dumbarton Oaks Proposals already agreed upon during the Soviet phase, the above Chinese proposal was presented in a separate document to the San Francisco Conference by the Chinese Government with the sponsorship of the United States, the United Kingdom, and the Soviet Governments.[11] The same four sponsoring governments also made the following joint proposal of amendment to Chapter V, B, 6,

[8] *Ibid.*, 584.
[9] *Ibid.*, 597, 276, 282. The identical provision in the "Tentative Proposals" was also numbered II, B, 2, c, (2).
[10] U.N.C.I.O., III, 25, Doc. 1, G/1 (a), May 1, 1945.
[11] *Ibid.* See also *Postwar Foreign Policy Preparation, 1939–1945*, 332–333.

of the Dumbarton Oaks Proposals: "6. The General Assembly should initiate studies and make recommendations for the purpose of promoting international cooperation . . . and also for the encouragement of the development of international law." [12]

Prior to the San Francisco Conference, or at the Conference, more than a dozen States proposed amendments to fill the "international law gap" in the Dumbarton Oaks Proposals. The most extreme of these was the proposal of the Philippines Commonwealth delegation to add the following to the chapter on the functions and powers of the General Assembly:

9. The General Assembly should be vested with the legislative authority to enact rules of international law which should become effective and binding upon the members of the Organization after such rules have been approved by a majority vote of the Security Council. Should the Security Council fail to act on any of such rules within a period of thirty (30) days after submission thereof to the Security Council, the same should become effective and binding as if approved by the Security Council. In the exercise of this legislative authority the General Assembly may codify the existing rules of international law with such changes as the Assembly may deem proper.[13]

The Ecuadorean delegation proposed conferring the following power on the General Assembly:

The power to establish or progressively amend the principles and rules of law which are to govern the relations between the States lies with the General Assembly, through a two-thirds majority of its members. The instruments embodying those principles and rules shall only come into compulsory effect for all members of the Organization when they are ratified by a number equivalent to two-thirds thereof.[14]

A Brazilian proposal would have indicated that it was a pur-

[12] U.N.C.I.O., III, 623. Doc. 2, G/29, May 5, 1945.
[13] *Ibid.*, 536–537. Doc. 2, G/14 (k), May 5, 1945.
[14] *Ibid.*, 404, 427. Doc. 2, G/7 (p), May 1, 1945.

pose of the United Nations "to define matters which constitute the domain of international law, i.e., those which transcend the domestic competence of the states; within the limits of such definition, to vote the secondary laws or laws pertaining to application." [15]

A Belgian proposal, after providing that the General Assembly should have "sovereign competence to interpret the provisions of the Charter" and that it could submit general conventions to States for "their approval in accordance with the appropriate constitutional procedure," continued:

(c) If the General Assembly is of the opinion that the obligations involved in any draft general convention are mere corollaries of principles it already recognizes as compulsory, or that the general observance of these obligations is necessary for the maintenance of international peace and security, it may decide that the convention in question will come into force for all States Members of the Organization and, should occasion arise, for third-party States, as soon as it has been ratified under the conditions contemplated for the coming into force of amendments to the Charter.[16]

A proposed Egyptian amendment would have declared it to be a purpose of the United Nations "(b) To determine, define, codify and develop the rules of international law and international morality." [17]

A Lebanese proposal suggested adding to the purposes of the United Nations: "To create a permanent Committee of Jurists whose function shall be the periodic codification or consolidation of existing principles of international law together with the modifications thereof which shall be deemed necessary from time to time." [18]

A Liberian proposal provided that "the General Assembly

[15] *Ibid.*, 243. Doc. 2, G/7 (e) (1), May 3, 1945.
[16] *Ibid.*, 339. Doc. 2, G/7 (k) (1), May 4, 1945.
[17] *Ibid.*, 453. Doc. 2, G/7 (q) (1), May 5, 1945.
[18] *Ibid.*, 473. Doc. 2, G/14 (c), May 2, 1945.

shall also initiate studies which should lead to the Codification of International Law"; [19] and an Australian proposal stipulated that "the General Assembly shall be responsible for initiating studies and making recommendations . . . (c) for promoting the development and revision of the rules and principles of international law." [20]

At the San Francisco Conference these proposed amendments were considered in Committee II/2. At its third meeting on 9 May 1945, the Committee adopted the joint amendment of the four sponsoring powers providing that "the General Assembly should initiate studies and make recommendations . . . for the encouragement of the development of international law." [21] The other amendments proposed by various governments were consolidated by a sub-committee into a series of questions [22] to be discussed and determined by the Committee. At its tenth meeting on 21 May 1945, Committee II/2 decided certain questions as follows:

1. Should the Assembly be empowered to initiate studies and make recommendations for the codification of international law?

An affirmative answer was given by a vote of 27 to 8.

2. Should the Assembly be empowered to initiate studies and make recommendations for promoting the revision of the rules and principles of international law?

An affirmative answer was given by a vote of 16 to 7. [23]

[19] *Ibid.*, 465. Doc. 2, G/14 (a), May 2, 1945.

[20] *Ibid.*, 545–546. Doc. 2, G/14 (1), May 5, 1945.

[21] U.N.C.I.O., IX, 21–22. Doc. 203, II/2/8, May 10, 1945, Summary Report of Third Meeting of Committee II/2.

[22] *Ibid.*, 346–348. Doc. 416, II/2/A/3, May 18, 1945, Second Report of Subcommittee A.

[23] *Ibid.*, 69–70. Doc. 507, II/2/22, May 23, 1945. Liang, *loc. cit.*, 67, citing the Verbatim Records, U.N.C.I.O. Documents, Vol. 62, lists the vote on the first question as 24 to 8; and on the second question as 16 to 8. U.N. Doc. A/122, 17 October 1946, Secretariat Memorandum on Progressive Development of International Law and Its Codification, p. 11, lists the votes as 27 to 8 and 16 to 8 respectively.

Two questions based upon the Philippines amendment, quoted above, which would have conferred legislative authority on the General Assembly, were decisively rejected:

3. Should the Assembly be authorized to enact rules of international law which should become binding upon members after such rules shall have been approved by the Security Council?

There were 1 affirmative and 26 negative votes.

4. Should it be provided that upon the failure of the Security Council to act on such rules within a period specified in the Charter, they should become effective as binding, in the same manner as if they had been approved by the Security Council?

There were no affirmative votes and 26 negative votes.[24]

After thus determining almost unanimously that the General Assembly should have no legislative power to enact binding rules of international law, the Committee devoted two meetings to the Belgian amendments which would have empowered the General Assembly to draft and submit to States general conventions for their appropriate constitutional approval and, in some cases, to bring them into force without the approval of States. During the discussion "some delegates felt that the Assembly was not the appropriate body to undertake the detailed and difficult work of drafting actual conventions," preferring that "drafting should be done by special conferences set up for the purpose." [25] The Belgian delegate, Senator Henri Rolin, "objected to the idea of calling *ad hoc* conferences to formulate conventions on the ground that the personnel of conferences was liable to be different each time, whereas a team spirit favorable to cooperation would grow up among representatives who met constantly in Assembly meetings over a period of years." [26] Other delegates were of the

24 U.N.C.I.O., IX, 70.
25 *Ibid.*, 75. Doc. 536, II/2/24, May 24, 1945. Summary Report of Eleventh Meeting of Committee II/2, held May 23, 1945.
26 *Ibid.*, 79. Doc. 571, II/2/27, May 25, 1945. Summary Report of Twelfth Meeting of Committee II/2, held May 24, 1945.

opinion that the power of initiating conventions had already been conferred on the General Assembly by amendments previously adopted, and that nothing could be gained by an additional amendment. As a result, the proposed amendment empowering the Assembly to submit general conventions to States for their approval narrowly failed to obtain the required two-thirds majority, there being only 25 affirmative votes and 13 negative.[27] The Commission then voted unanimously against the following part of the Belgian proposal:

Should the General Assembly have the power of imposing conventions when, in its opinion, these are mere corollaries of principles it already recognizes as compulsory, or when it believes that the general observance of the obligations embodied in the convention is necessary for the maintenance of international peace and security? [28]

When the drafting sub-committee of Committee II/2 disagreed as to whether the Committee had intended the words "development of international law" to cover the concept of "promoting the revision of the rules and principles of international law" (both texts having received the approval of the Committee), alternative texts were drafted for the choice of the Committee.[29] Providing that "6. The General Assembly should initiate studies and make recommendations for the purpose of promoting international cooperation . . ." the First Alternative continued:

[27] *Ibid.*, 80. At the Fourth Meeting of Commission II on June 21, 1945, the Belgian and Australian delegates stated that they had decided not to press for a review of the rejected amendment on the ground that other provisions of the Charter would permit the General Assembly to participate in the drafting of conventions. U.N.C.I.O., VIII, 206–208. Doc. 1151, II/17, June 22, 1945, Verbatim Minutes of Fourth Meeting of Commission II.

[28] U.N.C.I.O., IX, 79–80.

[29] *Ibid.*, 423–424. Doc. 795, II/2/B/11, June 5, 1945, Summary Report of Seventh Meeting of Subcommittee B of Committee II, held June 5, 1945.

and also for the codification of international law, the encouragement of its development and the promotion of its revision.

The Second Alternative read:

and also for the encouragement of the progressive development of
international law and for its codification.[30]

At its twenty-first meeting, on 7 June 1945, the Committee,
rejecting the argument that "development" meant adding to
existing rules and "revision" meant modifying them, approved
the Second Alternative by 28 votes to 8 (for the First Alternative).[31]

After this vote, the amended text of paragraph 6, Section B,
Chapter V of the Dumbarton Oaks Proposals was sent to the
Coordination Committee, from which it emerged with minor
verbal changes as Article 13, paragraph 1 (a) of the United
Nations Charter.

Analysis of the documentary materials set forth above reveals:

1. The governments participating in the formulation of the
United Nations Charter were overwhelmingly opposed to conferring legislative power on the United Nations to enact binding rules of international law.

2. As a corollary, they also rejected proposals to confer on
the General Assembly the power to impose general conventions
on States by some form of majority vote.

3. On the other hand, even before the convening of the San
Francisco Conference, there was strong support for conferring
on the General Assembly the more limited power to initiate
studies and make recommendations in the field of international
law; and, at the Conference, the required two-thirds majority
was easily found for this purpose.

4. Apparently because "codification" of international law

[30] *Ibid.*, 419–420. Doc. 792, II/2/B/10, June 5, 1945, Third Report of
Subcommittee II/2/B.

[31] *Ibid.*, 177–178. Doc. 848, II/2/46, June 7, 1945, Summary Report
of Twenty-first Meeting of Committee II/2.

was regarded by some governments as "consolidation" or "restatement" of existing law and implied "rigidity . . . without provision for modification," the terms of reference for the General Assembly's powers in this field were more generally phrased as "development and revision" of international law.

5. In the final drafting the word "revision" was dropped because it would lay too much emphasis on change and because the concepts of "progressive development" and "codification" would include some elements of revision and "establish a nice balance between stability and change." [32]

Implementation of Article 13, Paragraph 1 (a): *The First Stage* [33]

On the initiative of the United States, the question of implementing the General Assembly's obligation under Article 13, paragraph 1 (a) of the Charter to initiate studies and make recommendations for the purpose of encouraging the progressive development of international law and its codification was placed on the agenda of the 2nd Part of the 1st Session of the General Assembly.[34] At its 46th plenary meeting on 31 October 1946, the Assembly referred the question to its Sixth Committee without debate.[35] A joint proposal by the United States and China [36] and proposals by Argentina [37] and Saudi Arabia [38] suggested the appointment of a committee to consider the procedures to be recommended for the discharge of the Gen-

---

[32] *Ibid.,* 178.

[33] See also Manley O. Hudson, "Encouragement of the Development of International Law by the United Nations," 41 A.J.I.L. 104–106 (1947); Liang, *loc. cit.,* 68–69, and the citations given below, in note 45, page 15.

[34] U.N. Doc. A/98, 2 Aug. 1946.

[35] U.N. Journal, No. 20: Supplement A (A/PV.46), 272; A/163, 29 Oct. 1946.

[36] A/C.6/54, 6 Nov. 1946.   [37] A/C.6/72, 17 Nov. 1946.

[38] A/C.6/81, 21 Nov. 1946; and more detailed suggestions of a program of work in A/C.6/108, 3 Dec. 1946.

eral Assembly's responsibilities under Article 13, paragraph 1
(a). A recommendation to that effect was made in the unanimous report of a sub-committee [39] and, after some discussion [40]
of the size of the proposed committee, the Sixth Committee
adopted in substance the report and resolution of its sub-committee.

The Report of the Sixth Committee,[41] stressing the need for
a considered and comprehensive study of methods and calling
attention to "the difficulties encountered in past efforts to
promote the progressive development of international law and
its codification," envisaged the possibility of a "fresh approach"
to the problem. Pursuant to this Report, the General Assembly
at its 55th plenary meeting [42] on 11 December 1946, unanimously adopted resolution 94 (I) as follows:

The General Assembly,
Recognizes the obligation laid upon it by Article 13 paragraph
1, sub-paragraph a, of the Charter to initiate studies and make
recommendations for the purpose of encouraging the progressive
development of international law and its codification;
Realizes the need for a careful and thorough study of what has

[39] A/C.6/114, 4 Dec. 1946, Draft Report and Resolution proposed by
Sub-Committee 1: The Progressive Development of International Law
and Its Codification. The Sub-Committee was composed of representatives of Belgium, Canada, China, Cuba, Czechoslovakia, Egypt, Norway,
U.S.S.R., United States, and United Kingdom. Its Chairman was Professor Frede Castberg (Norway), its Vice-Chairman, Mr. Georges Kaeckenbeeck (Belgium), and its Rapporteur, Mr. E. R. Hopkins (Canada).

[40] For discussion in the Sixth Committee see GAOR, 1st Session, Part
II, 1946, Sixth Committee, Summary Records 165–169 (31st meeting,
6 Dec. 1946). Suggestions for the size of the proposed committee ranged
from seven to twenty-one. The Sixth Committee agreed to recommend
a membership of sixteen so that it might be "genuinely representative
of the main forms of civilization and of the principal legal systems of
the world." At the 55th plenary meeting of the General Assembly, Brazil
was added as a seventeenth member, ostensibly in recognition of the
"strong legal tradition" of Latin American States.

[41] A/222, 6 Dec. 1946, Progressive Development of International Law
and Its Codification, Report of the Sixth Committee.

[42] U.N. Journal, No. 58: Supplement A (A/PV.55), 470–473.

already been accomplished in this field as well as of the projects and activities of official and unofficial bodies engaged in efforts to promote the progressive development and formulation of public and private international law, and the need for a report on the methods whereby the General Assembly may most effectively discharge its obligations under the above-mentioned provision:

Therefore,

Resolves to establish a Committee of seventeen Members of the United Nations to be appointed by the General Assembly on the recommendation of the President, each of these Members to have one representative on the Committee;

Directs the Committee to study:

(a) The methods by which the General Assembly should encourage the progressive development of international law and its eventual codification;

(b) Methods of securing the co-operation of the several organs of the United Nations to this end;

(c) Methods of enlisting the assistance of such national or international bodies as might aid in the attainment of this objective; and to report to the General Assembly at its next regular session.

Requests the Secretary-General to provide such assistance as the Committee may require for its work.[43]

At the same plenary meeting the following States were appointed to the Committee by the General Assembly on the recommendation of the President: Argentina, Australia, Brazil, China, Colombia, Egypt, France, India, Netherlands, Panama, Poland, Sweden, Union of Soviet Socialist Republics, United Kingdom, United States of America, Venezuela, and Yugoslavia.[44]

[43] General Assembly Resolution 94 (I), Progressive Development of International Law and Its Codification. A/64/Add.1, 31 Jan. 1947. Resolutions Adopted by the General Assembly during the Second Part of Its First Session, p. 187.

[44] *Ibid.,* 188.

Implementation, Second Stage:
The Committee on the Progressive Development of International Law and Its Codification

The Committee on the Progressive Development of International Law and Its Codification held thirty meetings at Lake Success, New York, from 12 May 1947, to 17 June 1947,[45] of which twenty meetings were devoted to a consideration of its major task: "Study of the methods by which the General Assembly should encourage the progressive development of International Law and its eventual codification."[46] During this period the Committee was composed as follows: *Chairman,* Sir Dalip Singh (India); *Vice-Chairmen,* Vladimir Koretsky (U.S.S.R.) and Antonio Rocha[47] (Colombia); *Rapporteur,* J. L. Brierly (U.K.); Enrique Ferrer Vieyra (Argentina); W. A.

[45] See A/AC.10/SR. 1–30. See also Yuen-li Liang, "International Law: First Phase of the Work to Fulfill the Charter," 33 A.B.A.J. 765–768, 844–846 (1947); Liang, "The Progressive Development of International Law and Its Codification under the United Nations," 1947 *Proceedings,* American Society of International Law, 24–40; Liang, "The General Assembly and the Progressive Development and Codification of International Law," 42 A.J.I.L. 66–97 (1948); Liang, "Methods for the Encouragement of the Progressive Development of International Law and Its Codification," 2 *Year Book of World Affairs* 237–271 (1948); Liang, Le Développement et la Codification du Droit International, *Recueil des Cours,* Académie de Droit International de la Haye, Vol. 73 (1948–II), 411–527; Philip C. Jessup, "U.N. Committee on the Progressive Development of International Law and Its Codification—Report of the U.S. Representative," U.S. *Department of State Bulletin,* XVII, No. 420, July 20, 1947, pp. 121–127; Shabtai Rosenne, "The International Law Commission, 1949–59," 1960 B.Y.I.L. 104, 112–122 (1961).

[46] As phrased in Item 3(a) of the Provisional Agenda, A/AC.10/1, 5 May 1947. This item was discussed at the second to fifteenth meetings inclusive, and also at the twenty-third to twenty-eighth meetings during which the Report of the Rapporteur (A/AC. 10/40, 5 June 1947 and A/AC.10/43, 6 June 1947) was under discussion. Other matters referred to the Committee (cf., A/AC.10/1) are not discussed here.

[47] Professor Jesus M. Yepes served as Colombian representative at some of the meetings.

Wynes [48] (Australia); Gilberto Amado (Brazil); Shuhsi Hsu (China); Osman Ebeid [49] (Egypt); Henri Donnedieu de Vabres (France); J. G. de Beus (Netherlands); Roberto de la Guardia (Panama); Alexander Rudzinski [50] (Poland); Erik Sjöborg [51] (Sweden); Philip C. Jessup (U.S.); Carlos Eduardo Stolk [52] (Venezuela); Milan Bartoš (Yugoslavia); *Secretary,* Yuen-li Liang (U.N. Secretariat). Dr. Ivan Kerno, Assistant Secretary-General of the United Nations in Charge of the Legal Department, also participated actively in the work of the Committee.

The Committee had available a series of valuable studies on the development of international law and its codification prepared by the Division for the Development and Codification of International Law of the United Nations Secretariat under the direction of Dr. Yuen-li Liang, Director.[53] Although, as Dr.

[48] Replaced by A. H. Body at some of the meetings.

[49] Although Wabid Rafaat is listed for Egypt in A/AC.10/13, the summary records indicate that only Osman Ebeid participated for Egypt.

[50] Replaced by Alexander Bramson at some of the meetings.

[51] Replaced by Sture Petrén at some of the meetings.

[52] Replaced by Perez Perozo at most of the meetings, although Mr. Perez Perozo is not listed as a representative in A/AC.10/13.

[53] A/AC.10/5, 29 April 1947, *Historical Survey of Development of International Law and Its Codification by International Conferences,* 119 pp. (mimeographed).

A/AC.10/6, 2 May 1947, *Bibliography on the Codification of International Law,* 14 pp. (mimeographed).

A/AC.10/7, 6 May 1947, (with Corr. 1 and 2), Memorandum on *Methods for Encouraging the Progressive Development of International Law and Its Eventual Codification,* 8 pp. (mimeographed).

A/AC.10/8, 6 May 1947, (with Corr. 1), Outline of *The Codification of International Law in the Inter-American System with Special Reference to the Methods of Codification,* 31 pp. (mimeographed).

A/AC.10/22, 16 May 1947, (with Addenda 1–4), *Methods for Enlisting the Cooperation of Other Bodies, National and International,* concerned with International Law, 22 pp. (mimeographed).

A/AC.10/25, 16 May 1947, *Note on the Private Codification of Public International Law,* 14 pp. (mimeographed).

With the exception of A/AC.10/6 and 22, these mimeographed documents have been printed in 41 A.J.I.L., Supp. pp. 27–147 (1947).

Liang has observed,[54] most of these memoranda were designed to provide background information for the Committee, the Secretariat Memorandum on *Methods for Encouraging the Progressive Development of International Law and Its Eventual Codification* [55] was cast in a more influential role by decision of the Committee: [56] it was adopted as a basis of discussion along with a memorandum prepared by the Rapporteur, Professor Brierly,[57] and a subsequent joint proposal of the United States and Chinese delegations.[58] A number of memoranda and suggestions indicating the views of their Governments were submitted by members of the Committee. After general discussion, the Committee decided questions of principle relating to the organization, scope, functions, and methods of an International Law Commission and adopted a report [59] recommending the establishment of such a Commission and setting forth provisions designed to serve as the basis for its Statute. Since the Committee did not itself draft a Statute for the Commission, the discussions and recommendations of the Committee are summarized below under the relevant articles of the Statute of the International Law Commission.

[54] See his note in 41 A.J.I.L., Supp., p. 30 (1947).

[55] A/AC.10/7.

[56] A/AC.10/SR.7, 7th Meeting, 21 May 1947.

[57] A/AC.10/26, 16 May 1947. Referring to the twofold task of progressive development and codification of international law, Professor Brierly recommended in par. 12 of his memorandum: "In document A/AC.10/7 the Secretariat has made valuable suggestions in both these matters, and I propose that we might take this paper as the basis of our discussions."

[58] A/AC.10/33, 23 May 1947, Proposal Regarding the Organization and Procedures of the Commission of Experts on International Law (CEIL), Proposed Jointly by the Delegations of the United States and China. See also A/AC.10/SR.11, pp. 2–3.

[59] A/AC.10/51, 17 June 1947, reissued as A/331.

Implementation, Third Stage:
The Adoption of the Statute of the International Law Commission

During the 2nd Session of the General Assembly, the United States took the initiative at the 37th meeting of the Sixth Committee by submitting a draft resolution [60] calling for the establishment of an International Law Commission which should function on a part-time basis,[61] but otherwise largely following the recommendations of the Committee on the Progressive Development of International Law and Its Codification. After general debate which concluded with the statement of Mr. Kaeckenbeeck, Rapporteur, that "the majority of the [Sixth] Committee favoured the setting up of an international law commission," the Committee "adopted by a large majority, those not voting for, abstaining," a proposal to establish a sub-committee "to draft a resolution and report back to the Committee." [62] By its terms of reference, the Sub-Committee (designated Sub-Committee 2) appears to have been intended as more than a mere drafting committee.

[60] A/C.6/137, 24 Sept. 1947, reprinted in GAOR, 2nd Session, 1947, Sixth Committee, Summary Records, Annexes, 182. Amendments were proposed to the United States draft by the United Kingdom (A/C.6/138) and Canada (A/C.6/142), *ibid.*, 185. A proposal by France (A/C.6/139) called for the establishment of an International Law Commission but would "reserve to the General Assembly the initiative of the studies to be undertaken by the Commission." *Ibid.*, 184. A Soviet Proposal (A/C.6/141) would have entrusted further preparatory work and the codification of certain topics to the Committee on the Progressive Development of International Law and its Codification pending the election of an International Law Commission at the 3rd Session of the General Assembly. *Ibid.*, 186.

[61] Sixth Committee, Summary Records, 5–6 (37th meeting, 25 Sept. 1947).

[62] *Ibid.*, 15 (38th meeting, 26 Sept. 1947). Sub-Committee 2 was composed of representatives of Australia, Brazil, China, Colombia, Dominican Republic, France, Greece, Netherlands, Poland, Sweden, U.S.S.R., U.K., U.S., and Yugoslavia. *Ibid.*, 16. The Sub-Committee elected Liu Chieh (China) as Chairman and J. P. A. François (Netherlands) as Rapporteur. Cf., A/C.6/193.

At the 40th meeting of the Sixth Committee, Sub-Committee 2 presented an interim report, stating, *inter alia,* that it had "unanimously rejected the idea of a Commission whose members would have to devote their whole time to this work"; that by a vote of 13-2 the Sub-Committee had agreed that the Commission should be composed of fifteen members; and that, following a long discussion, the Sub-Committee had voted 8 to 7 in favor of electing the members of the International Law Commission at the present session of the General Assembly.[63] After brief discussion which referred mostly to postponing the election, the Chairman, Faris Bey El-Khouri, ruled that since there had been no objection to the adoption at the present session of a Statute for the Commission, he would consider the point accepted. The Committee then voted, by 33 to 14, to postpone the election of the Commission until the next session.[64]

Sub-Committee 2 held fifteen meetings—for which no official summary records appear to exist—and presented to the Sixth Committee a detailed Report of its discussions and substantive decisions and a Draft Resolution to which was annexed a draft Statute of the International Law Commission.[65] At its 58th meeting, on 20 November 1947 the Sixth Committee, without general debate, adopted the proposed Statute of the International Law Commission by a vote of 35-4-1.[66] Disappointment over the decision to postpone the election of an International Law Commission until 1948 led a majority

[63] A/C.6/150, 30 Sept. 1947, *ibid.,* Annexes, 187.

[64] *Ibid.,* 24–27 (40th meeting, 2 Oct. 1947).

[65] A/C.6/193, 18 Nov. 1947. The draft Statute has been omitted from the reproduction of A/C.6/193 in the Annexes to the Sixth Committee, *loc. cit.,* 188–204.

[66] Sixth Committee, *loc. cit.,* 147–157 (A/C.6/SR. 58). Prior to the vote the Committee rejected or modified a series of Soviet amendments (A/C.6/199, 19 Nov. 1947, Annexes, p. 205) and, on motion of the United Kingdom, deleted a provision that only nationals of Members of the United Nations were eligible for election to the Commission. Cf., below, under Article 3 of the Statute, p. 46.

of Sub-Committee 2 to favor the maintenance as an interim body of the Committee on the Progressive Development of International Law and Its Codification.[67] A resolution entrusting to this proposed interim body the preparation of a report suggesting questions which the General Assembly might refer to the International Law Commission and the preparation of a draft declaration on the rights and duties of States was rejected by the Sixth Committee by a vote of 25 to 15,[68] and a resolution was adopted instructing the Secretary-General to do the necessary work in preparation for the International Law Commission.[69]

At its 123rd plenary meeting, on 21 November 1947, the General Assembly adopted resolution 174 (II), establishing the International Law Commission and approving its annexed Statute, by a vote of 44–0–6. Prior to the vote the Soviet delegation declared that it would have to abstain because of the rejection of amendments it had proposed in the Sixth Committee.[70]

The text of the General Assembly resolution 174 (II) on the *Establishment of the International Law Commission* reads as follows:

The General Assembly,

Recognizing the need for giving effect to Article 13, paragraph 1, subparagraph a, of the Charter, stipulating that the General Assembly shall initiate studies and make recommendations for the purpose of encouraging the progressive development of international law and its codification;

Having studied the report of the Committee directed by reso-

[67] Cf. A/C.6/194, 18 Nov. 1947, Annexes, 206.
[68] Sixth Committee, *loc. cit.*, 157–162 (59th meeting, 20 Nov. 1947).
[69] *Ibid.*, 162. A/C.6/196 (France), *ibid.*, 204 as modified by A/C. 6/200 (U.S.S.R.), *ibid.*, 209. Adopted by the General Assembly as GA Res. 175 (II).
[70] A/PV.123, 21 Nov. 1947, pp. 1272–1278. Cf. A/504, 20 Nov. 1947. Report of the Sixth Committee on the Report of the Committee on the Progressive Development of International Law and Its Codification.

lution 94 (I) of the General Assembly of 11 December 1946 to study:

(a) The methods by which the General Assembly should encourage the progressive development of international law and its eventual codification;

(b) Methods of securing the co-operation of the several organs of the United Nations to this end;

(c) Methods of enlisting the assistance of such national or international bodies as might aid in the attainment of this objective.

Recognizing the desirability of establishing a commission composed of persons of recognized competence in international law and representing as a whole the chief forms of civilization and the basic legal systems of the world;

Resolves to establish an "International Law Commission," the members of which shall be elected at the third regular session of the General Assembly, and which shall be constituted and shall exercise its functions in accordance with the provisions of the annexed Statute.[71]

[71] A/519, pp. 105 ff. The text of the annexed Statute is here omitted. See Appendix, below, pp. 362–369.

PART II

THE STATUTE OF THE INTERNATIONAL LAW COMMISSION:

ITS DRAFTING AND INTERPRETATION IN PRACTICE

(A.) The Object of the International Law Commission[1]

Article 1

1. The International Law Commission shall have for its object the promotion of the progressive development of international law and its codification.

2. The Commission shall concern itself primarily with public international law, but is not precluded from entering the field of private international law.

The text of Article 1 was drafted by Sub-Committee 2[2] of the Sixth Committee of the General Assembly at its 4th Session in 1947 on the basis of the recommendations of the Committee on the Progressive Development of International Law and Its Codification. That Committee had considered whether implementation of Article 13, paragraph 1 (a) of the Charter could best be accomplished by the establishment of one Commission charged with the promotion of the progressive development of international law and its codification or whether more than

---

[1] The text of the Statute of the International Law Commission here reproduced is taken from A/CN.4/4/Rev. 1 (1962), *Statute of the International Law Commission,* which is based on the text found in GA res. 174 (II), 21 Nov. 1947, A/519, pp. 105–110. The text earlier printed in A/CN.4/4, 2 Feb. 1949, *Statute of the International Law Commission and Other Resolutions of the General Assembly relating to the International Law Commission,* was apparently based on the text found in A/504, 20 Nov. 1947, Report of the Sixth Committee, which varies in several respects (notably in Articles 3, 6, 16 and 17) from the text of GA res. 174 (II).

[2] A/C.6/193, 18 Nov. 1947, Sixth Committee, Report and Draft Resolution adopted by Sub-Committee 2 (with annexed draft Statute of the International Law Commission); reprinted GAOR, 2nd Session, 1947, Sixth Committee, Summary Records, Annexes, p. 188, without the text of the Statute.

one Commission was desirable. Although differences in method were envisaged with reference to progressive development and codification, it was considered desirable to entrust both tasks to a single Commission. Proposals to establish separate commissions for public, for private, and for penal international law were discussed but the Committee decided unanimously to recommend the establishment of a single Commission,[3] with the further recommendation that the Commission "when dealing with questions in the field of private international law should consider the appropriateness of consultation with the Netherlands Government" in relation to the work of The Hague Conferences on Private International Law.[4]

Sub-Committee 2 of the Sixth Committee accepted unanimously the recommendations of the Committee on the Progressive Development of International Law and Its Codification that a single Commission be established for promoting the progressive development of international law and its codification and that the Commission should be called "The International Law Commission" (*"La Commission du Droit International"*).[5] However, sharp divergences in Sub-Committee 2

[3] A/AC.10/51, 17 June 1947 (reissued as A/331, 18 July 1947), *Report of the Committee on the Methods for Encouraging the Progressive Development of International Law and Its Eventual Codification*, par. 3. See also the Summary Records of the Committee and supporting documents, especially A/AC.10/10; A/AC.10/26; A/AC.10/SR.4; A/AC.-10/SR.6; A/AC.10/SR.7 (for decision of the Committee).

[4] A/AC.10/51, p. 1 n.

[5] A/C.6/193, par. 2. Of alternative titles for the Commission considered by the Committee on the Progressive Development of International Law and Its Codification, its own title was considered "long and unwieldy," the title "Commission of Experts in International Law" was objectionable because United Nations practice already gave "experts a third place after delegates and advisors, and also in other countries [*sic*] the word 'experts' denoted persons of rather low rank;" and "Commission of Jurists" was also objectionable because "for English lawyers the word 'jurist' was not very acceptable." The name "International Law Commission" was suggested by Professor Brierly and unanimously accepted by the Committee. See A/AC.10/SR.15, pp. 14–15; A/AC.

on the desirability of including private international law within the competence of the International Law Commission had led to the compromise stated above in paragraph 2 of Article 1 of the Statute. Principal considerations for its adoption appeared to be the practical difficulty of securing persons of equal competence in both public and private international law, the belief that most countries would prefer the International Law Commission to be composed of experts on public international law, and the belief that the "Commission will always be able to call on experts if there are insufficient specialists in private international law among the members" of the International Law Commission.[6]

During its 1st Session in 1949, the International Law Commission reviewed twenty-five topics of international law with a view to possible codification,[7] using as a basis of discussion a memorandum of the United Nations Secretariat which stated that no attempt was made therein "to survey subjects of private international law." [8] The fourteen topics selected for codification were all in the field of public international law. It is noteworthy that during its first sixteen sessions, the Commis-

---

10/SR.18, p. 4; A/AC.10/51, par. 3. The summary records indicate that the Committee, at the suggestion of its French member, approved "Commission *de* Droit International" as the correct translation of "International Law Commission." A/AC.10/SR.18, p. 4. However, the French expression now used is "Commission *du* Droit International."

[6] A/C. 6/193, par. 16, pp. 17–18.

[7] *Yearbook of the International Law Commission, 1949. Summary Records and Documents of the First Session including the Report of the Commission to the General Assembly,* A/CN.4/Ser. A, 1949, pp. 32–59, 280–281 (cited hereafter as Yearbook, ILC, 1st Session, 1949). For more detailed examination of the selection of topics, see below under commentary on Article 18 of the Commission's Statute.

[8] A/CN.4/1, 5 November 1948, *Survey of International Law in relation to the Work of Codification of the International Law Commission —Preparatory Work within the purview of Article 18, paragraph 1, of the Statute of the International Law Commission, Memorandum submitted by the Secretary-General,* p. 19. Hereafter cited as A/CN.4/1, *Survey.*

sion has worked exclusively in the field of public international law.

The provision of paragraph 1 of Article 1 that the object of the Commission shall be "the promotion of the progressive development of international law and its codification" has not been interpreted by the Commission as preventing it from dealing with questions of international law submitted to it by the General Assembly merely because, in the Commission's view, the special project submitted did not require the application of the procedures of its Statute for codification or for progressive development. The question was debated at the 1st Session of the Commission and certain members appear to have misconceived the issue in posing it as a question whether the Commission could sometimes act "outside" the provisions of its Statute.[9] The recommendations made by the Commission to the General Assembly with regard to "special projects" submitted by the latter to the Commission are discussed below (pp. 277 ff., 308–310).

[9] Yearbook, ILC, 1st Session, 1949, pp. 175–177, 179–182.

B. The Organization of the International Law Commission

Article 2

1. The Commission shall consist of twenty-five members who shall be persons of recognized competence in international law.[1]

2. No two members of the Commission shall be nationals of the same State.

3. In case of dual nationality, a candidate shall be deemed to be a national of the State in which he ordinarily exercises civil and political rights.

The Drafting of Paragraph 1

Two questions to which the Committee on the Progressive Development of International Law and Its Codification gave close attention were the size of the proposed International Law Commission and the capacity in which its members should serve, i.e., should they perform their functions as representatives of governments or in their individual capacities as persons of recognized competence in international law? For the United States, Professor Philip C. Jessup, stressing the necessity of securing "the full-time services of the most highly skilled and competent individuals" for the development and codification of international law because "this task is no side issue but one of central importance in the whole programme of the United Nations," [2] proposed the establishment of a nine-member Commission of Experts on International Law.[3]

[1] As amended in 1961.
[2] A/AC.10/11, pp. 4, 6. See also A/AC.10/SR.2, pp. 3–4; A/AC.10/14.
[3] A/AC.10/14; A/AC.10/33.

Professor J. L. Brierly (United Kingdom), emphasizing the need for "obtaining a scientific restatement of the law by independent experts," proposed a Commission "consisting possibly of seven lawyers of international repute, selected purely on their individual capacities and in no sense as representatives of governments": the risk of "political appointments" should be avoided.[4] Mr. Erik Sjöborg (Sweden) also favored a Committee of Experts and underlined the need "to eliminate the risk of political appointments" to it.[5] Dr. J. G. de Beus (Netherlands), while supporting "a fairly small Codification Commission consisting of international lawyers of the highest standing," doubted "whether codification *exclusively* by experts would yield the best possible results." [6] For Brazil, Mr. Gilberto Amado, while endorsing the idea of a small committee of expert jurists, warned against "jurists shut up in an ivory tower" and stated that "the work of codification, like that of the development of international law, must be carried out in cooperation with the political authorities of States." Moreover, not only individual competence but geographical representation should be considered in selecting members of the Commission in order to ensure representation of the principal legal systems of the world.[7] Dr. Shuhsi Hsu (China), supporting the United States proposal, favored "equitable geographical representation, while aiming primarily at securing personal competence." [8] For Poland, Dr. Alexander Rudzinski proposed a Commission of Experts of "at least eleven in order to make it possible to have the main forms of civilization and the principal legal systems of the world represented on it." However, he

[4] A/AC.10/16, p. 3; A/AC.10/17, p. 3; A/AC.10/SR.2, p. 5.

[5] A/AC.10/24, p. 2.

[6] A/AC.10/18, pp. 2–3; A/AC.10/23. The arguments advanced by the Netherlands representative against codification exclusively by experts appear somewhat contradictory: experts out of touch with their governments "might be inclined to depart from the requirements of international law as practiced by states"; and restatement by experts is purely static and can only "freeze" international law.

[7] A/AC.10/28; A/AC.10/SR.4, p. 3.

[8] A/AC.10/31; A/AC.10/SR.3, p. 5.

wished to subordinate the Commission of Experts to "a programming and policy group of jurists representing their respective governments." [9]

The only outright advocate of an International Law Commission composed of representatives of governments was Professor Vladimir Koretsky of the Soviet Union. Since he considered the conclusion of multilateral conventions as the only proper method for both the progressive development and the codification of international law and since the United Nations "was not a super-state legislative body," [10] it followed, he suggested, that members of the Commission should not be independent experts: experts would be isolated from those who had to determine "the will of the people"; there was no need "for an olympic oracle endowed with greater powers than governments themselves had." In fact, he "felt quite proud of being a representative of his government" on the present Committee on the Progressive Development of International Law and Its Codification and proposed that it be continued instead of recommending the establishment of a new commission of experts. [11]

The documents of the Committee do not record any formal vote on whether the proposed International Law Commission should be composed of individual experts or of representatives of governments, but the rejection of the latter alternative is implicit in the provisions of the Statute of the International Law Commission which deal with election to the Commission and its composition (Articles 2–11), particularly in the provisions of Article 8 stressing the individual competence of members and the representative character of the Commission as a whole. [12] The designation of the members of the Commission as "members" and as "persons of recognized competence in international law" rather than as "experts" does not negate

[9] A/AC.10/20.
[10] A/AC.10/32, p. 2.
[11] A/AC.10/SR. 4, pp. 6–7, and Add. 1, p. 4.
[12] See commentaries to Article 8, below, pp. 62–64, and Article 11, below, pp. 75 ff.

the above conclusion, but was decided upon because of the disparaging sense in which the term "experts" was sometimes employed.[13]

With reference to the size of the Commission, the Committee, in a series of votes, rejected proposals that it be composed of fifteen, thirteen, or eleven members and provisionally adopted by a narrow majority a proposal for a Commission of nine members.[14] However, upon reconsideration, the Committee voted by a majority to recommend a Commission of fifteen members. Considerations adverted to before the Committee were the desirability of having a Commission small enough to work efficiently but large enough to represent differing legal systems and the "three main fields of international law" (i.e., public, private, and penal international law), and to provide adequate representation for smaller States.[15]

The Committee's recommendation of a Commission of fifteen members was adopted, after debate, by Sub-Committee 2 of the Sixth Committee by a vote of thirteen to two.[16] At the 58th meeting of the Sixth Committee, on 20 November 1947, a Norwegian proposal to provide for a Commission of thirteen members was rejected by 27 votes to 6; and a proposal by the Dominican Republic to increase the size of the Commission "to seventeen or even twenty-one" to permit more adequate representation was rejected by 22 votes to 9.[17] The Statute adopted by the General Assembly in 1947 thus provided in Article 2:

1. The Commission shall consist of fifteen members who shall be persons of recognized competence in international law.

[13] A/AC.10/SR.23, p. 5; and above, p. 26, n. 5.

[14] A/AC.10/SR.11, pp. 3–4; A/AC.10/51, par. 4.

[15] A/AC.10/SR. 23, pp. 10–14. Mr. Sjöborg (Sweden) "considered that the five great powers would undoubtedly each have a seat on the I.L.C. and a membership of nine would only leave four seats for all the other States. . . ." *Ibid.,* p. 11.

[16] A/C.6/193, par. 4.

[17] GAOR, 2nd Session, 1947, Sixth Committee, Summary Records, 155–156. The Dominican proposal was put only with reference to a "Commission to be composed of seventeen members."

The Enlargement of 1956

Subsequent to the breaking of the admissions deadlock in 1955 and the admission of a substantial number of new Members to the United Nations, the General Assembly was confronted with proposals to increase the size of several bodies, including the International Law Commission. The Sixth Committee debated the problem of increasing the size of the Commission, at its 482nd to 485th meetings, 23 to 28 November 1956.[18] While some representatives maintained that an increase in the membership of the United Nations did not warrant an increase in the size of the International Law Commission, the majority believed that the provision of Article 8 of the Commission's Statute requiring "in the Commission as a whole representation of the main forms of civilization and of the principal legal systems of the world" could be better assured by increasing the size of the Commission from fifteen to twenty-one.

After discussion, the Chairman noted the existence of a "gentlemen's agreement" (originally proposed by Mr. García Amador of Cuba[19]) that the six additional seats on the Commission should be allocated as follows:

three to nationals from African and Asian Members of the United Nations; one to a national from Western Europe; one to a national from Eastern Europe; and one, in alternation, to a national from Latin America and a national from the British Commonwealth countries not otherwise included in any recognized regional grouping.[20]

The Report of the Sixth Committee adds: "It was also understood that the distribution between different forms of civilization and legal systems would be maintained in respect of the existing fifteen seats." [21]

[18] GAOR, 11th Session, 1956, Sixth Committee, Summary Records, 11–25; *ibid.,* Annexes, Agenda item 59, A/3427, 5 Dec. 1956, Report of the Sixth Committee.

[19] Sixth Committee, *loc. cit.,* 15 (483rd meeting).

[20] A/3427, par. 13.

[21] *Ibid.* Mr. Pathak (India), asserting that the second part of Article

Mr. Jean Spiropoulos (Greece) pointed out that the question of increasing the membership of the Commission "should be considered not only from the political, but also from the scientific, point of view." He added:

If the sole concern of the International Law Commission was existing law, the membership of fifteen might suffice. It should not be forgotten, however, that it was also the Commission's function to lay the groundwork for the creation of international law and to promote its progressive development, adopting new rules where necessary. . . . Although the Commission's work was merely preparatory, since its conclusions had subsequently to be accepted by States in the form of conventions, it spoke for the international community in the matter of codification. Hence it was essential that the principal legal systems of the world should be duly represented on it.[22]

The Sixth Committee unanimously adopted a draft resolution increasing the size of the International Law Commission from fifteen to twenty-one members.[23] By resolution 1103 (XI), the General Assembly, at its 623rd plenary session on 18 December 1956, by a vote of 75–0–1,

---

8 of the Commission's Statute "was not at present respected," expressed the following view:

"The fifteen members of the Commission comprised five nationals of the Great Powers, four nationals of Latin American countries, three of western European countries, one from an eastern European country and two from Asian countries. Although the African and Asian countries accounted for one-third of the membership of the United Nations, Africa was not represented on the International Law Commission, and Asia, the home of several legal systems, was represented quite inadequately." *Ibid.*, Sixth Committee, Summary Records, 11 (482nd meeting, 23 Nov. 1956).

[22] *Ibid.*, 13, par. 31.

[23] *Ibid.*, 25, (485th meeting, 28 Nov. 1956). The vote was 68–0–1. The representative of Guatemala declared that he had abstained "because, as would appear from the summary records, the Committee had reached an understanding on a number of points with which his delegation was not in agreement." *Ibid.*, par. 41. Earlier, the Guatemalan representative had expressed the view that Latin America was entitled to "five permanent seats in the enlarged International Law Commission." *Ibid.*, 19.

1. *Decides* to amend as follows article 2, paragraph 1, of the Statute of the International Law Commission:

"The Commission shall consist of twenty-one members, who shall be persons of recognized competence in international law";

2. Decides, as a consequence, to amend as follows Article 9, paragraph 1, of the said Statute:

"The twenty-one candidates who obtain the greatest number of votes and not less than a majority of the votes of the members present and voting shall be elected." [24]

Immediately prior to the adoption of the resolution of amendment, Mr. K. H. Bailey (Australia), as Rapporteur of the Sixth Committee, stated for the record:

The Committee wishes me to draw the attention of the General Assembly to paragraph 13 of the report, for that paragraph places on record the existence of certain understandings reached between groups of delegations as to the manner of allocating the additional seats on the International Law Commission.[25]

The Enlargement of 1961

The significant increase in the number of African States attaining independence and membership in the United Nations in 1960 caused the United States, at the 16th Session of the General Assembly in 1961, to join with Cameroun, Colombia, India, Japan, Liberia, Nigeria, and Sweden in sponsoring a resolution proposing the enlargement of the International Law Commission by two (from twenty-one to twenty-three members). In introducing the proposal [26] at the 689th meeting of the Sixth Committee on 4 October 1961, Mr. Francis Plimpton (U.S.) pointed out that since the International Law Commission had been increased in size from fifteen to twenty-one members in 1956, twenty-one new States had become Members of the United Nations "including nineteen from the central

[24] GAOR, 11th Sess., 1956, Plenary Meetings, p. 728 (A/PV.623, Agenda item 59); A/3572, p. 53.

[25] A/PV.623, 18 Dec. 1956, p. 728, par. 82.

[26] Cf. A/4805, 20 July 1961, and A/C.6/L.481; GAOR., 16th Session, Annexes, Agenda item 77.

and southern part of the African continent," and that no person from this area was a member of the International Law Commission. While admitting that a Commission of even twenty-one members "was well in excess of the ideal size for a body whose function was the study and drafting of complex legal instruments," he urged not "a general enlargement of the Commission, but rather a specific enlargement, limited to the one geographical area not presently represented on that body." [27]

At the time this proposal was made (October 1961) the International Law Commission was composed of twenty-one members, all of whose terms expired on 31 December 1961. Although they had been elected not as representatives of governments but (in accordance with Articles 2 and 8 of the Commission's Statute) as individuals "of recognized competence in international law" and in accordance with the criterion "that in the Commission as a whole representation of the main forms of civilization and of the principal legal systems of the world should be assured," the geographical and national composition of the Commission in 1961 was as follows:

Africa	1	United Arab Republic
America, North	1	United States
America, Latin	4	Brazil, Cuba, Mexico, Uruguay
Asia	6	China, India, Iran, Iraq, Japan, Turkey
Europe, Western	6	Austria, France, Italy, Netherlands, Sweden, United Kingdom
Europe (Communist)	3	Czechoslovakia, Union of Soviet Socialist Republics, Yugoslavia
	——	
	21	

[27] A/C.6/SR.689, meeting of 4 Oct. 1961; GAOR, 16th Session, 1961, Sixth Committee, Summary Records, 7.

Mr. Platon Morozov (U.S.S.R.), observing that "the importance of the Commission's work was steadily increasing" and noting the danger that it "might become too large a body to work effectively," thought that the Sixth Committee should undertake a basic re-examination of the distribution of seats in the Commission, keeping in mind its "real optimum size" and giving African, Asian, and Communist States greater representation.[28] Mr. Dadzie (Ghana), supported eventually by the representatives of Ethiopia, Indonesia, Iran, Lebanon, Libya, Senegal, and Thailand,[29] proposed that the size of the Commission be increased by four, from twenty-one to twenty-five.[30] He further proposed that the twenty-five seats be distributed as follows:

Six should be allotted to Western Europe and North America, six to the Asian countries, four to Africa, five to Eastern Europe and four to Latin America.[31]

Since the States which are permanent members of the United Nations Security Council customarily have nationals on the International Law Commission, the proposal of Ghana would have reduced the representation of other Western European States by one—for the benefit of the Communist bloc—in addition to giving the Communist bloc one of the four new seats, the other three going to Africa. The Communist bloc attempted to justify the increase of its members on the Commission from three to four or five by invoking a number of criteria other than "the main forms of civilization" and "the principal legal systems of the world": for example, "the principle of equitable representation of political systems"; "the number and importance of countries" supporting various legal systems; the desirability of giving "the socialist and the Asian and African Powers more influence in the Commission's

---

[28] A/C.6/SR.689, meeting of 4 Oct. 1961; *loc. cit.,* 8–9.
[29] Cf. A/C.6/SR.697; *loc. cit.,* 49.
[30] A/C.6/L.481/Add. 1, Annexes, Agenda item 77, p. 2.
[31] A/C.6/SR.690; *loc. cit.,* 13, par. 14.

work"; [32] the belief that "the socialist countries whose efforts were aimed at furthering the cause of peace and peaceful co-existence" were insufficiently represented; [33] and the injustice of giving only three seats on the Commission to "the socialist legal system which was entirely new in principle, being based on the elimination of class exploitation and which had been adopted by more than 1,000 million people in countries which accounted for more than 40% of the world's production." [34]

In reply, it was pointed out that the Communist States, with less than one-tenth of the membership of the United Nations, had three seats on the International Law Commission, which was more than one-tenth of its membership,[35] and that the request for four or five Communist seats would give them "a higher proportion of seats, in relation to the total number of States, than any other region." [36] This seemed unnecessary "because their spokesmen always held identical views." [37] "No independent States had come into existence and no new legal systems had evolved in the regions of Western Europe, North America, Latin America and eastern Europe since 1956"; all the States in those regions had been parties to the Gentleman's Agreement of 1956 and the enlargement of the Commission was needed only to give representation to new States not parties to that agreement.[38]

Titillated by this diversion of attempting to redistribute seats in the International Law Commission in accordance with unabashed political criteria, members of the Sixth Committee indulged in arithmetical and geographical gymnastics. Only the wiser voices distinguished between relevant and irrelevant political considerations. Thus, Mr. van Panhuys (Netherlands) observed:

[32] A/C.6/SR.689 (Morozov); *loc. cit.*, 8–9.
[33] A/C.6/SR.690 (Pechota, Czechoslovakia); *loc. cit.*, 12.
[34] A/C.6/SR.698, 18 Oct. 1961, (Morozov); *loc. cit.*, 54.
[35] A/C.6/SR.694 (Plimpton); *loc. cit.*, 36.
[36] A/C.6/SR.690 (Evans, U.K.); *loc. cit.*, 11.
[37] A/C.6/SR.694 (Plimpton); *loc. cit.*, 36.
[38] A/C.6/SR.695 (Mustafa, Pakistan); *loc. cit.*, 41.

In his view the Commission's task was twofold: to codify existing rules of international law and to promote the progressive development of that law. In the latter respect, the Commission partook of the nature of a law-creating agency, or at least the character of an advisory body to the General Assembly, which itself possessed quasi law-making functions. It was precisely that quasi law-making element that justified governments in taking political factors into consideration when electing members of the International Law Commission. In determining the representation of the main forms of civilization and the principal legal systems of the world, therefore, it was natural that they should take into consideration the composition of the United Nations as a whole. That did not mean, of course, that members of the Commission should be elected by some purely mathematical formula or that they should be justified in regarding themselves as the representatives of Governments or, what was even worse, as the representatives of blocs. Such a conception would be entirely contrary to the Commission's Statute.[39]

Mr. Alberto Ulloa (Peru) recalled that "the Commission had been conceived from a functional and not a geographical standpoint" and added:

Article 8 of the Statute required that the main forms of civilization and the principal legal systems of the world should be represented—not "all" forms of civilization and "all" legal systems. Moreover, since international law consisted primarily of public law, it was the principal systems of public law and not of private law that were implied. And since the differences between legal systems were most apparent in private law and there was considerable uniformity in public law, only a few systems needed to be represented. The only absolute requirement concerning membership in the International Law Commission related to individuals. There was no reason why the membership of the commission should not be of the highest order, for, while political systems might vary from region to region, "civilizations" and "legal systems" were not geographical concepts.[40]

At the 695th meeting, on 13 October 1961, the United States

[39] A/C.6/SR.695; *loc. cit.,* 39.   [40] A/C.6/SR.696; *loc. cit.,* 46.

agreed to accept an amendment increasing the size of the Commission by four instead of two seats, with the understanding that the new seats were for "the Afro-Asian States exclusively," the "essential condition" being that the existing distribution based on the Gentleman's Agreement of 1956 would continue in effect for the other twenty-one seats.[41] The debate then turned on whether the 1956 Gentleman's Agreement was still binding. Mr. Morozov characterized the concession made by the sponsors of the United States proposal as an indication "that the United States and other colonial [42] Powers had failed in their attempt to keep their dominant position in the International Law Commission"; he called for a new Gentleman's Agreement because "it was inadmissible that the Western countries should continue to hold twice as many seats as the socialist countries." [43] He opposed a Uruguayan suggestion that "the question whether the 1956 agreement would be maintained had to be decided before the Committee voted on the draft resolution and amendment before it," [44] observing, in part, that

the question of redistributing the seats on the Commission could not be decided by a simple majority vote. . . . It would amount to imposing the view of one group of States on others, whereas the 1956 agreement on the redistribution of seats—although not a signed instrument—had been reached unanimously with the participation of all delegations.[45]

The redistribution of seats by majority vote would, he said, be "undemocratic." The next day Mr. Morozov repudiated the 1956 Gentleman's Agreement, stating:

With the adoption of draft resolution [A/C.6/L.481], the 1956 "Gentleman's Agreement" would cease to exist and no amount of

[41] A/C.6/SR.695; *loc. cit.*, 41–42.

[42] It will be recalled that the co-sponsors with the United States had included Cameroun, Colombia, India, Japan, Liberia, Nigeria, and Sweden.

[43] A/C.6/SR.694; *loc. cit.*, 37.

[44] A/C.6/SR.697; *loc. cit.*, 50.   [45] *Ibid.*

ingenious reasoning would serve to revive it. His delegation wished to make it quite clear that it would no longer consider itself bound by that agreement.[46]

By a vote of 87 to 0, the Sixth Committee, on 18 October 1961, adopted the amended draft resolution to increase the size of the International Law Commission from twenty-one to twenty-five.[47] Upwards of forty delegations went on record as regarding the 1956 Gentleman's Agreement as still in force, and about fifteen delegations took the opposite view.[48]

By resolution 1647 (XVI), adopted on 6 November 1961, without objection, the General Assembly amended Article 2, paragraph 1, of the Statute of the International Law Commission so as to read:

1. The Commission shall consist of twenty-five members who shall be persons of recognized competence in international law.[49]

Geographically, the composition of the Commission in 1962 was:

Africa	4	Cameroun, Dahomey, Nigeria, United Arab Republic
America, North	2	Canada, United States
America, Latin	4	Brazil, Ecuador, Mexico, Uruguay
Asia	6	Afghanistan, China, India, Iraq, Israel, Japan
Europe, Western	6	Austria, Finland, France, Italy, Spain, United Kingdom
Europe (Communist)	3	Poland, Union of Soviet Socialist Republics, Yugoslavia
	25	

[46] A/C.6/SR.698, meeting of 18 Oct. 1961; *loc. cit.*, 54.
[47] *Ibid.*, 56.
[48] In addition to the Summary Records, see GAOR, 16th Session, 1961, Annexes, Agenda item 77, A/4939, 26 Oct. 1961, Report of the Sixth Committee.
[49] A/PV.1047, p. 563; A/5100, p. 61.

It is not without interest to note that in order to obtain this geographical and national distribution of seats in the election of the Commission on 28 November 1961, the General Assembly appears to have complied literally with the 1956 Gentleman's Agreement as well as with the purpose of its own 1961 amendment to the Statute.

The basic requirement that the members of the Commission "shall be persons of recognized competence in international law" has, on occasion, been minimized in the preoccupation with political and geographical factors.[50] For further observations on this point, see the commentary on Article 8 (pp. 62–64).

Article 2, Paragraphs 2 and 3

2. No two members of the Commission shall be nationals of the same State.

3. In case of dual nationality a candidate shall be deemed to be a national of the State in which he ordinarily exercises civil and political rights.

These paragraphs were designed to incorporate the provisions and, to some extent, the phraseology of Article 3 of the Statute of the International Court of Justice.[51] Dr. Yuen-li Liang, Secretary of the Committee on the Progressive Development of International Law and Its Codification, informed the Committee that reference to Article 3 of the Statute of the Court had been made in the Report of the Rapporteur "for the reason that no two members of the same nationality should

[50] See the interesting analysis of Rosenne, "The International Law Commission, 1949–59," 36 B.Y.I.L. 125–130, with tables (1960).

[51] Article 3 of the Statute of the International Court of Justice reads as follows:

"1. The court shall consist of fifteen members, no two of whom may be nationals of the same state.

"2. A person who for the purposes of membership in the Court could be regarded as a national of more than one state shall be deemed to be a national of the one in which he ordinarily exercises civil and political rights."

be on the International Law Commission," and the Committee accepted the desirability of this conclusion without debate.[52] A proposal by the Soviet representative on the Sixth Committee of the General Assembly to delete Article 2, paragraph 2, of the draft Statute of the International Law Commission in order "to avoid difficulties arising in instances of dual nationality" was rejected by the Committee, apparently on the ground that paragraph 3 dealt with that problem.[53]

The admonitions in Article 2, as well as in certain other articles of the Statute, appear to be addressed to those taking part in the electoral process—that is, the representatives of States in the General Assembly, the States which they represent, the General Assembly itself, and, when the International Law Commission fills a casual vacancy, to the members of the Commission and to the Commission itself. By adopting the resolution containing the Statute of the International Law Commission, the General Assembly adopted regulations to govern its own conduct in the situations provided for, as well as to govern the conduct of the electors.

At its 454th meeting, on 2 June 1958, the International Law Commission received a communication from Mr. Abdullah El-Erian, a national of the United Arab Republic who had been elected to the Commission from Egypt on 18 December

[52] A/AC.10/SR.23, pp. 15–16. The Report of the Committee provided, in part, that members of the International Law Commission should be elected "following the principles laid down in Article 3 and the procedure contained in Articles 8–12 of the Statute of the International Court of Justice." A/AC.10/51, par. 5 (b).

[53] A/C.6/SR.58, pp. 2–3; Summary Records, 149–150. The problem was apparently whether, for example, the Commission might include both a Soviet member and a Ukrainian member where the latter also possessed Soviet nationality. For the comparable problem in relation to British nationality with reference to the Court, see Manley O. Hudson, "The Twenty-Fourth Year of the World Court," 40 A.J.I.L., 1, 16, (1946); Hudson, *The Permanent Court of International Justice, 1920–1942—A Treatise*, 158, 183, 264–265, 367 (1943); Walter Pollak, "The Eligibility of British Subjects as Judges of the Permanent Court of International Justice," 20 A.J.I.L., 714–725 (1926).

1956. Referring to the fact that Mr. Faris Bey El-Khouri, who had been elected to the Commission from Syria, was now a national of the United Arab Republic, and having regard to the provision of Article 2, paragraph 2, of the Commission's Statute that no two members of the Commission shall be nationals of the same State, Mr. El-Erian submitted his resignation. The Commission accepted the resignation.[54]

[54] Yearbook, ILC, 10th Session, 1958, I, 118; II, 79.

Article 3

The members of the Commission shall be elected by the General Assembly from a list of candidates nominated by the Governments of States [1] Members of the United Nations.

This text was drafted by Sub-Committee 2 of the Sixth Committee of the 1947 General Assembly.[2] The Committee on the Progressive Development of International Law and Its Codification had considered two methods for the election of members of the International Law Commission: (1) appointment by the members of the International Court of Justice (as proposed by the United Kingdom and Sweden);[3] (2) election jointly by the General Assembly and the Security Council, following the procedure prescribed in Articles 8-12 of the Statute of the International Court of Justice for the election of judges (as proposed by the United States, China, and Brazil).[4] Although the second method had been recommended by the Committee by a vote of 12-1-3,[5] the United States changed its position and, in the Sixth Committee, advocated election by the General Assembly alone.[6]

Sub-Committee 2 "considered that there was no reason to associate the Security Council with the work of codifying inter-

[1] The text of Article 3 found in A/CN.4/4, 2 Feb. 1949, omits the word "States."

[2] A/C.6/193, par. 7, and Article 3 (1), 18 Nov. 1947.

[3] A/AC.10/51; A/AC.10/16, p. 3, (U.K.); A/AC.10/24, pp. 2–3, (Sweden). The United Kingdom proposal was rejected by a vote of 3–9–6. A/AC.10/SR.12, p. 4.

[4] A/AC.10/14, par. 6, (U.S.); A/AC.10/33, p. 2, (Joint proposal by U.S. and China); A/AC.10/28, (Brazil). This method of election was also supported by the U.S.S.R. A/AC.10/SR.11, p. 5. Argentina opposed participation of the Security Council in the election of members of the International Law Commission as contrary to the legal equality of States. A/AC.10/SR.12, p. 3.

[5] A/AC.10/SR.12, p. 5; A/AC.10/51, par. 5.

[6] GAOR, 2nd Session, 1947, Sixth Committee, Summary Records, 5 (37th meeting, 25 Sept. 1947); A/C.6/137, *ibid.*, 182.

national law, which under Article 13 (1) (a) of the Charter, was entrusted to the General Assembly." Rejecting the analogy of election to the Court, the Sub-Committee unanimously recommended that members of the International Law Commission be elected by the General Assembly alone.[7]

Article 3 of the draft Statute prepared by Sub-Committee 2 contained a second paragraph, which provided: "2. Only nationals of Members of the United Nations shall be eligible for election." This provision had been adopted by the Sub-Committee by a vote of 8 to 5 on the ground that nationals of non-Member States might not be committed to the principles of the Charter and it would complicate matters to have them participating in the codification of law among Members of the United Nations.[8] In the Sixth Committee, the United Kingdom representative challenged the validity of this reasoning and moved the deletion of Article 3 (2). The Commission, he said, "would be codifying international law: all international law." The Sixth Committee adopted the motion to delete paragraph 2 by a vote of 19-15-1.[9]

No national of any non-Member of the United Nations has been elected to the International Law Commission.[10]

Article 3 restricts the eligibility of candidates to those persons inscribed on the list and contains no exception such as is found in Articles 7 and 12 (2) of the Statute of the International Court of Justice.[11] In a Memorandum prepared by the Secretariat with reference to Election of Members of the Inter-

[7] A/C.6/193, par. 7.   [8] A/C.6/193, par. 9.

[9] GAOR, 2nd Session, 1947, Sixth Committee, Summary Records, 150–151 (58th meeting, 20 Nov. 1947).

[10] Professor Georges Sauser-Hall, a national of Switzerland, and Professor Massimo Pilotti, a national of Italy, both States then being non-Members of the United Nations, were nominated by the United Kingdom in 1948. Cf. A/576/Rev. 3, 28 Oct. 1948.

[11] By Article 12 (2) of the Court's Statute, a person may be included in a list prepared by a joint conference of the General Assembly and the Security Council even though he was not included in the original list of nominations referred to in Article 7.

national Law Commission, it is stated: "Those whose names appear on the list will be the only persons eligible (articles 3 and 7)." [12]

When the Commission was considering recommendations concerning a possible revision of its Statute in 1951, it unanimously decided not to propose any change in the method of electing members.[13]

[12] A/697, 29 Oct. 1948, par. 2. Cf. A/2399, 22 June 1953, par. 9; A/3459, 14 Dec. 1956, par. 2; A/4779, 16 June 1961, par. 9.
[13] Yearbook, ILC, 3rd Session, 1951, I, 130.

Article 4

Each Member may nominate for election not more than four candidates, of whom two may be nationals of the nominating State and two nationals of other States.

This text was drafted by Sub-Committee 2. The Committee on Progressive Development of International Law and Its Codification had adopted a United States-Chinese proposal:

The Government of each State Member of the United Nations should nominate, as candidates for membership of the international law commission, not more than two of its own nationals, and not more than eight persons of other nationalities. In making their nominations, the Governments are recommended to consult their highest court of justice, their legal faculties and schools of law, their national academies and national sections of international academies devoted to the study of law and, where such exist, the national groups in the Permanent Court of Arbitration.[1]

In the Committee, Professor Vladimir Koretsky (U.S.S.R.) considered that the nomination of eight non-nationals by each State was exaggerated; he expressed a preference for two.[2] In reply, Professor Philip C. Jessup (U.S.) explained that the purpose of the proposal (assuming an International Law Commission of nine) was to permit each State to make nominations for the entire membership of the Commission, "inclusive of one alternate for its own member"; however, he suggested that the Committee might wish to follow the procedure of Article 5 (2) of the Statute of the International Court of Justice "so that nominations could also be made of one national and three non-nationals." [3] The Committee, by a vote of 8–6–3, adopted the proposal permitting the nomination of eight non-nationals.[4]

[1] A/AC.10/51 (A/331), par. 5; A/AC.10/33 (Joint U.S.-Chinese proposal).
[2] A/AC.10/SR.23, p. 14, (meeting of 10 June 1947).
[3] *Ibid.*   [4] *Ibid.*, p. 15.

Sub-Committee 2 unanimously recommended that this number be reduced from eight to two, in order to alleviate difficulties of nomination and selection.[5] There is no explanation in its Report of the omission of the second sentence (based on Article 6 of the Statute of the International Court of Justice) recommending that Governments consult certain bodies prior to making their nominations. Article 4 of the Statute of the International Law Commission was adopted without discussion and without separate vote by the Sixth Committee and the General Assembly.

Unlike Article 5 (2) of the Court's Statute, Article 4 of the Statute of the International Law Commission appears to limit the nomination of non-nationals to two.

On 5 April 1948, Lebanon nominated (*"par erreur,"* observed the Secretariat) four nationals for the International Law Commission. The Secretariat included them in its list on a provisional basis pending receipt of corrected nominations in accordance with Article 4 of the Statute.[6] Three of the four Lebanese nominations are omitted in the revised list.[7]

When considering the possible revision of its Statute in 1951, the Commission "decided by a majority of 10 to recommend the retention of the existing system" with regard to the nomination of candidates for the Commission.[8]

As is indicated below in the commentary on Articles 6 and 7, States have not complied literally with the provision of Article 4 that, of four candidates, "two may be nationals of the nominating State and two nationals of other States." For the elections of 1953, 1956, and 1961, some States nominated three or four non-nationals (see pp. 53–54).

[5] A/C.6/193, par. 6.

[6] A/576, 15 July 1948. The French text reads: *"Le Liban a présenté par erreur quatre candidats nationaux."*

[7] A/576/Rev. 1, 22 July 1948. See also, comment on Article 7 of the Statute, below, pp. 52 ff.

[8] Yearbook, ILC, 3rd Session, 1951, I, 130–131.

Article 5

The names of the candidates shall be submitted in writing by the Governments to the Secretary-General by the first of June of the year in which an election is held, provided that a Government may in exceptional circumstances substitute for a candidate whom it has nominated before the first of June another candidate whom it shall name not later than thirty days before the opening of the General Assembly.

This provision was adopted by Sub-Committee 2, by a vote of 11 to 4, with a view to giving governments sufficient time to examine lists of nominees which would be current at the opening of the General Assembly. The Sub-Committee decided against itemizing or defining "exceptional circumstances." [1]

Although the Statute of the International Law Commission contains no provision comparable to that found in Article 5 (1) of the Statute of the International Court of Justice, by which the Secretary-General is required to invite nominations, it is customary for the Secretary-General to issue such an invitation to the governments of all United Nations Members.[2]

The requirement of Article 5 that substitute candidates may be named not later than thirty days before the opening of the General Assembly has not been strictly applied. Although the 8th Session of the General Assembly opened on 15 September 1953, the Secretary-General, on 30 September 1953, informed the Members of the United Nations that the Union of Soviet Socialist Republics had decided to replace Professor F. I.

[1] A/C.6/193, par. 6.

[2] Cf. A/2399, 22 June 1953, par. 7, which states that such an invitation was issued for the 1953 election on 25 Feb. 1953. On 23 Jan. 1956, the Secretary-General transmitted such an invitation for the 1956 election. A/3155, 1 Aug. 1956, par. 7. On 10 Feb. 1961, the Secretary-General requested nominations for the 1961 election, to be submitted by 1 June 1961. A/4779, 16 June 1961, par. 1.

Kozhevnikov by Professor S. B. Krylov as its national candidate.[3] No question appears to have been raised as to the conformity of this decision with Article 5, and Judge Krylov was elected to the Commission by the General Assembly.

In 1956, a number of candidates were nominated after the deadlines set forth in Article 5. Of these late nominees, Abdullah El-Erian, Faris Bey El-Khouri, and Kisaburo Yokota were elected to the Commission.[4]

In 1961, the Secretariat apparently decided to enforce the June 1 deadline stipulated in Article 5 and to decline to receive tardy nominations.[5] However, the nomination by the Netherlands of Professor A. J. P. Tammes on 9 September 1961 was circulated by the Secretariat at the request of that Government.[6] The nomination was later withdrawn by the Netherlands prior to the election.[7]

Because the General Assembly, by resolution 1647 (XVI) of 6 November 1961, increased the size of the International Law Commission from twenty-one to twenty-five members, with a view to providing seats for nationals of new African States, the General Assembly decided, by the same resolution, to request the Secretariat, "by way of exception" to include in the list of candidates for the 1961 election to the Commission names communicated before 15 November 1961.[8] Four new candidates were presented, of which one was from an African State, two from Asian States, and one from a Latin American State.

[3] A/2399/Add. 3, 30 Sept. 1953. Cf., also A/2399/Add. 4, 22 Oct. 1953.
[4] Cf. A/3155, 1 Aug. 1956, and Add. 1, 27 Sept. 1956, Add. 3, 7 Dec. 1956, and Add. 4, 12 Dec. 1956.
[5] Cf. A/C.6/SR.699, meeting of 19 Oct. 1961, for explanation of Mr. Stavropoulos, Legal Counsel; GAOR, 16th Session, 1961, Sixth Committee Summary Records, 62, par. 40.
[6] A/4866, 13 Sept. 1961.
[7] A/4779/Add. 1, 16 Nov. 1961, par. 3.
[8] *Ibid.*, par. 1.

Article 6

The Secretary-General shall as soon as possible communicate to the Governments of States Members the names submitted, as well as any statements of qualifications of candidates that may have been submitted by the nominating Governments.

Article 7

The Secretary-General shall prepare the list referred to in article 3 above, comprising in alphabetical order the names of all the candidates duly nominated, and shall submit this list to the General Assembly for the purposes of the election.

The provisions of Article 6 and 7 were drafted by Sub-Committee 2. Based in some degree on Article 7 of the Statute of the International Court of Justice, these Articles provide for earlier communication to Governments of Members of the names submitted and are more explicit as to the statement of qualifications of candidates.

The Secretariat prepares an alphabetical list of candidates with indication of their nationality and the State or States nominating them. Multiple nominations are frequent.

The pertinent documents submitted by the Secretary-General to Member Governments and to the General Assembly, are classified below:

(1) *First Election*, 3 November 1948: A/PV.154 and 155.
  List of candidates nominated: A/576/Rev. 3, 28 October 1948.
  Curricula vitae of candidates: A/576/Rev. 1 and Adds. 2, 4, 5.

Nominations were made by 47 of the 58 States Members of the United Nations, the names of 74 candidates being presented.[1] Six States making nominations named no national candidates.

[1] Three names were withdrawn prior to the election. Cf. A/PV.154, p. 378.

(2) *Second Election,* 23 October 1953: A/PV.453 and 454.
List of candidates nominated: A/2500/Rev. 1, 21 October 1953.
Statements of Qualifications: A/2399, 22 June 1953, and Adds. 1, 2, 3, 4.

Nominations were made by 46 of the 60 States Members of the United Nations, the names of 38 candidates being presented. Eighteen States making nominations named no national candidate. Eight States appeared to disregard the provisions of Article 4 of the Statute that "Each Member may nominate for election not more than four candidates, of whom two may be nationals of the nominating State and two nationals of other States" (see p. 49). The Dominican Republic, Ecuador, and El Salvador each nominated four non-nationals, but no nationals; Colombia, Cuba, Mexico, and Yugoslavia each nominated one national and three non-nationals; and Argentina nominated three non-nationals.

(3) *Third Election,* 18 December 1956: A/PV. 623.
List of candidates nominated: A/3155/Rev. 1, 14 December 1956.
Statements of Qualifications: A/3156, 6 August 1956, and Adds. 1 and 2.

Nominations were made by 56 of the 81 States Members of the United Nations, the names of 50 candidates being presented. Sixteen States making nominations named no national candidate. In apparent disregard of Article 4 of the Statute, Colombia and Iceland each nominated four non-nationals, but no nationals; Costa Rica nominated three non-nationals; Brazil, China, Cuba, Dominican Republic, Mexico, and Panama each nominated one national and three non-nationals.

(4) *Fourth Election,* 28 November 1961: A/PV.1067.
List of candidates nominated: A/4779, 16 June 1961 and A/4779/Add. 1, 16 November 1961.
Statements of Qualifications: A/4780, 28 June 1961, and Adds. 1, 2, 3, 4.

Nominations were made by 65 of the 103 States Members of the United Nations, the names of 47 candidates being presented.[2] Twenty-five States making nominations named no national candidate. In apparent disregard of Article 4 of the Statute, Colombia nominated four non-nationals but no nationals; Guinea and Honduras each nominated three non-nationals but no nationals; Afghanistan, Brazil, El Salvador, Indonesia, Italy, Mexico, Netherlands, and United Arab Republic each nominated one national and three non-nationals.

Persons nominated for election to the International Law Commission at one or more of the elections of 1948, 1953, 1956, or 1961 are listed below, with indication of their nationality.[3] The names of members currently serving on the Commission are printed in bold type and designated by an asterisk. The names of former members of the Commission are printed in italics. Other persons listed were not elected to the Commission. The numbers in parentheses following each name indicate the first to fourth elections, as explained above, for which the person concerned was nominated.

List of Candidates, 1948–1961

Adle, Mostafa (1)..................................Iran
*Ago, Roberto [4] (3)(4)...........................Italy
Alfaro, Ricardo J.[5] (1)(2)(3)...................Panama
Alsan, Zeki Mesut (2)............................Turkey

[2] Five names were withdrawn prior to the election (cf. A/4779/Adds. 1 and 2), leaving 42 at the date of the election.

[3] Nominations withdrawn prior to the balloting are not here listed where the records contain indication of such withdrawal.

[4] Elected member of the Commission in 1956; re-elected in 1961; participated in the 9th and subsequent Sessions.

[5] Elected member of the Commission in 1948; participating in 1st to 5th Sessions, inclusive; elected by the Commission to fill a casual vacancy in 1958; participated in 10th and 11th Sessions; resigned upon election to the International Court of Justice.

*Amado, Gilberto [6] (1)(2)(3)(4)............Brazil
 Anderson, H. G. (1)..............................Iceland
 Antokoletz, Daniel (1)..........................Argentina
 Arguello Vargas, Mariano (2)(3)(4).....Nicaragua
 Aycinena Salazar, Luis (3)....................Guatemala
 Badawi, Hilmy Bahgat (1)....................Egypt
 Bailey, Kenneth H. (1).......................Australia
 Baldivieso, Enrique (1).......................Bolivia
 Balladore-Pallieri, Giorgio (3)...............Italy
 Barros Jarpa, Ernesto (1).......................Chile
*Bartoš, Milan [7] (1)(2)(3)(4) ....Yugoslavia
 Beauvoir, Vilfort (1)...........................Haiti
 Belaúnde, Victor Andrés (1)................Peru
 Bermudez, Antonio (1)..........................Honduras
 Biguria Sinibaldi, Gabriel (1)...............Guatemala
 Bilsel, Cemil (1)................................Turkey
 Bocobo, Jorge (2)..................................Philippines
 Bourquin, Maurice (2).........................Belgium
 Brierly, James L.[8] (1)...........................United Kingdom
*Briggs, Herbert W.[9] (4)......................United States
 Bystricky, Rudolf (4)..........................Czechoslovakia
 Caceres, Julian R. (1)............................Honduras
*Cadieux, Marcel [10] (4)..........................Canada
 Camey Herrera, Julio (1)...................Guatemala
 Carbajal Victorica, Juan José (1)........Uruguay
 Cardahi, Chukri (1)..............................Lebanon

[6] Elected member of the Commission in 1948; re-elected in 1953, 1956 and 1961; has participated in every Session of the Commission.

[7] Elected member of the Commission in 1956; re-elected in 1961; participated in 9th and subsequent Sessions.

[8] Elected member of the Commission in 1948; participated in 1st to 3rd Sessions, inclusive, resigning prior to 4th Session.

[9] Elected member of the Commission in 1961, participating in 14th and subsequent Sessions.

[10] Elected member of the Commission in 1961, participating in 14th and subsequent Sessions.

Castillo Arriola, Eduardo (2)................Guatemala
*Castrén, Erik [11] (4)..............................Finland
Castro, Hector David (1)........................El Salvador
Cisneros Sanchez, Manuel (4)................Peru
Concepcion, Roberto (3)........................Philippines
Córdova, Roberto [12] (1)(2)...................Mexico
Cuadra Pasos, Carlos (1)........................Nicaragua
Devrin, Sinasi (1)....................................Turkey
Diaz Cisneros, Cesar (1)........................Argentina
Dickinson, Edwin D. (1)........................United States
Dihigo, Ernesto (1)................................Cuba
Dominguez Campora, Alberto (1)........Uruguay
Edmonds, Douglas L.[13] (3)...................United States
*El-Erian, Abdullah [14] (3)(4)................Egypt (and U.A.R.)
*Elias, Tesilimi Olawole [15] (4)............Nigeria
El-Khouri, Faris [16] (1)(2)(3)...................Syria
Erim, Nihat [17] (4)....................................Turkey
Escudero, Gonzalo (3)...........................Ecuador
Fidel Duron, Jorge (2).........................Honduras
Fitzmaurice, Sir Gerald [18] (3)................United Kingdom

[11] Elected member of the Commission in 1961, participating in 14th and subsequent Sessions.

[12] Elected member of the Commission in 1948; re-elected in 1953; participated in 1st to 6th Sessions, inclusive; resigned upon election to the International Court of Justice.

[13] Elected by the Commission to fill a casual vacancy in 1954; re-elected in 1956; participated in 6th to 13th Sessions, inclusive.

[14] Elected member of the Commission in 1956; participated in 9th and part of 10th Session, resigning in 1958 in favor of Faris El-Khouri when Egypt and Syria united to form the United Arab Republic; re-elected member of the Commission in 1961, participating in 14th and subsequent Sessions.

[15] Elected member of the Commission in 1961, participating in 14th and subsequent Sessions.

[16] Elected member of the Commission in 1948; re-elected in 1953 and 1956; participated in 2nd to 11th Sessions, inclusive.

[17] Elected by the Commission to fill a casual vacancy in 1959; participated in 11th to 13th Sessions, inclusive.

[18] Elected by the Commission to fill a casual vacancy in 1955; re-

Franco y Franco, Tulio (1)..................Dominican Republic
François, J. P. A.[19] (1)(2)(3)..............Netherlands
Gamboa, Melquiades (4)......................Philippines
García Amador, Francisco V.[20] (2)(3).Cuba
García Bauer, Carlos (2)......................Guatemala
García Salazar, Arturo (1)(2)..............Peru
Gneina Bey, Mahmoud Samy (1)........Egypt
Gros, André[21] (4)...................................France
Guachalla, Luis Fernando (1)..............Bolivia
Gunewardene, R. S. S. (4)...................Ceylon
Herrera Mendoza, Lorenzo (1)............Venezuela
Hsu, Shuhsi[22] (1)(2)(3)......................China
Hudson, Manley O.[23] (1)......................United States
Iberico Rodriguez, Mariano (3)............Peru
Jessup, Philip C. (1)............................. United States
Jiménez, Roberto (1)...........................Panama
*Jiménez de Aréchaga, Eduardo [24] (4).Uruguay
*Kanga, Victor [25] (4)..............................Cameroun
Kernisan, Clovis (1)..............................Haiti
Kerno, Ivan S. (2)................................Czechoslovakia
Khan, Chaudhri N. A. (3)...................Pakistan

---

elected in 1956; participated in 7th to 12th Sessions, inclusive; resigned upon election to the International Court of Justice.

[19] Elected member of the Commission in 1948; re-elected in 1953 and 1956; participated in 1st to 13th Sessions, inclusive.

[20] Elected member of the Commission in 1953; re-elected in 1956; participated in 6th to 13th Sessions, inclusive.

[21] Elected by the Commission to fill a casual vacancy in 1961; re-elected in 1961; participated in 13th, 14th, and 15th Sessions; resigned upon election to the International Court of Justice.

[22] Elected member of the Commission in 1948; re-elected in 1953 and 1956; participated in 1st to 13th Sessions, inclusive.

[23] Elected member of the Commission in 1948; participated in 1st to 4th Sessions, inclusive.

[24] Elected by the Commission to fill a casual vacancy in 1960; re-elected in 1961; participated in 12th and subsequent Sessions.

[25] Elected member of the Commission in 1961; has not participated in the work of the Commission.

Khoman, Thanat [26] (2)(3)......................Thailand
Koretsky, Vladimir M.[27] (1)................Union of Soviet Socialist Republics
Kozhevnikov, Feodor I.[28] (1)..................Ukrainian S.S.R.
Krylov, Sergei B.[29] (2).............................Union of Soviet Socialist Republics
*Lachs, Manfred [30] (4) ....Poland
Lauterpacht, Hersch [31] (2)......................United Kingdom
Lavalle, Juan Bautista de (2)(4)............Peru
*Liu Chieh [32] (4)...................................China
Lopez Pineda, Julian (3)........................Honduras
*Luna García, Antonio de [33] (4).............Spain
Manzanares, Gustavo (2)....................... Nicaragua
Martinez Moreno, Raul S. (1)............Argentina
Matine-Daftary, Ahmed [34] (1)(2)(3)(4)....Iran
Maung, E. (1)...Burma
Mora, Alfonso Maria (4)........................Ecuador
Morales, Carlos (1)...............................Venezuela
Munir, Muhammed (4).......................Pakistan

[26] Elected member of the Commission in 1956; resigned in 1960; participated in 9th and 11th Sessions.

[27] Elected member of the Commission in 1948; resigned in 1952; participated only in 1st Session; withdrew at the first meeting of the 2nd Session.

[28] Elected by the Commission to fill a casual vacancy in 1952; participated in 4th and 5th Sessions.

[29] Elected member of the Commission in 1953; participated in 7th and 8th Sessions.

[30] Elected member of the Commission in 1961, participating in 14th and subsequent Sessions.

[31] Elected by the Commission to fill a casual vacancy in 1952; re-elected in 1953; participated in 4th to 6th Sessions, inclusive; resigned upon election to the International Court of Justice.

[32] Elected member of the Commission in 1961, participating in 14th and subsequent Sessions.

[33] Elected member of the Commission in 1961, participating in 14th and subsequent Sessions.

[34] Elected member of the Commission in 1956; participated in 9th to 13th Sessions, inclusive.

Myint Thein, T. M. T. S. (2)(3)............Burma
Munez, Ernesto A. (3)............................El Salvador
Ocampo, Luis D. C. (3)........................Chile
Padilla Nervo, Luis [35] (3)(4)...............Mexico
*Pal, Radhabinod [36] (2)(3)(4)...............India
*Paredes, Angel Modesto [37] (1)(4)........Ecuador
Paredes, Quintin (1)............................Philippines
Parker, John J.[38] (2)............................United States
Paysse Reyes, Hector (4)....................Uruguay
Pena Lopez, Rolando (1)....................Chile
Perera, A. B. (3)................................Ceylon
*Pessou, Obed [39] (4)...............................Dahomey
Pilotti, Massimo (1)............................Italy
Planas Suarez, Simon (1)....................Venezuela
Poliansky, Nicolai N. (1)....................Byelorussian S.S.R.
Pratt de Maria, Gilberto (3)...............Uruguay
Radovanovic, Ljubomir (1)...............Yugoslavia
Ramirez Boettner, Luis (3)..................Paraguay
Rau, Sir Benegal N.[40] (1)..................India
*Reuter, Paul [41]......................................France
Rivera Hernandez, Alejandro (2)........Honduras
Rolz Bennet, José (3)............................Guatemala

[35] Elected by the Commission to fill a casual vacancy in 1955; re-elected in 1956 and 1961; participated in 8th to 15th Sessions, inclusive; resigned upon election to the International Court of Justice.

[36] Elected by the Commission to fill a casual vacancy in 1952; re-elected in 1953, 1956, and 1961; participated in 5th, 6th, 8th, and subsequent Sessions.

[37] Elected member of the Commission in 1961, participating in 14th and subsequent Sessions.

[38] Elected member of the Commission in 1953; he resigned without ever attending a meeting of the Commission.

[39] Elected member of the Commission in 1961, participating in 14th and subsequent Sessions.

[40] Elected member of the Commission in 1948; resigned in 1952; participated only in 1st Session.

[41] Elected by the Commission to fill a casual vacancy in 1964.

*Rosenne, Shabtai [42] (4)........................Israel
*Ruda, José Maria [43]..........................Argentina
Ruiz Moreno, Isidoro (3).....................Argentina
Salamanca Figueroa, Carlos [44] (2)(3).... Bolivia
Sandström, A. E. F. [45] (1)(2)(3)............Sweden
Sangoudhai, Yut (2)(3)........................Thailand
Sapena Pastor, Raúl (3)........................Paraguay
Sauser-Hall, Georges (1).......................Switzerland
Sayre, Francis B. (1)(2)(3)........................United States
Scelle, Georges [46] (1)(2)(3).....................France
Sinco, Vicente G. (1).............................Philippines
Sologuren, Santiago (2).......................Bolivia
Soueidi, Tewfik (1)..............................Iraq
Spiropoulos, Jean [47] (1)(2)(3)................Greece
Suphamongkhon, Konthi (4)................Thailand
*Tabibi, Abdul Hakim [48] (4)................Afghanistan
Taborda Ferreira, Vasco (3)................Portugal
Tajibnapis, S. H. (4)............................Indonesia
Taner, Tahir (1)(2)................................Turkey
Trias de Besgiro, José M. (3)................Spain
Trujillo, José V. (3)...............................Ecuador
Truong Cang (3)(4)...............................Cambodia
*Tsuruoka, Senjin [49] (4)........................Japan

[42] Elected member of the Commission in 1961, participating in 14th and subsequent Sessions.

[43] Elected by the Commission to fill a casual vacancy in 1964.

[44] Elected member of the Commission in 1953; participated in the 6th to 8th Sessions, inclusive.

[45] Elected member of the Commission in 1948; re-elected in 1953 and 1956; participated in 1st to 13th Sessions, inclusive.

[46] Elected member of the Commission in 1948; re-elected in 1953 and 1956; deceased 1961; participated in 1st to 12th Sessions, inclusive.

[47] Elected member of the Commission in 1948; re-elected in 1953 and 1956; resigned upon election to the International Court of Justice; participated in 1st to 9th Sessions, inclusive.

[48] Elected member of the Commission in 1961, participating in 14th and subsequent Sessions.

[49] Elected by the Commission to fill a casual vacancy in 1961; re-elected in 1961; participated in 13th and subsequent sessions.

*Tunkin, Grigory I. [50] (3)(4)................Union of Soviet
                                             Socialist Republics
Ulloa Sotomayor, Alberto (1)(3)............Peru
Urquia, Miguel R. (3)(4)......................El Salvador
Ursua, Francisco A. (1)......................Mexico
Vacha, Phya Srivisar (1)......................Thailand
Valle Candia, Modesto (3)(4)...............Nicaragua
Varela Acevedo, José Pedro (1)............Uruguay
Vega Bolanos, Andrés (1)...................Nicaragua
*Verdross, Alfred [51] (3)(4)......................Austria
Verosta, Stephan (3)(4)..........................Austria
Waithayakon, H.R.H. Prince Wan (1)... Thailand
*Waldock, Sir Humphrey [52] (4)............United Kingdom
*Yasseen, Mustafa Kamil [53] (4)............Iraq
Ycaza, Gabriel Pino (1)......................Ecuador
Yepes, Jesus Maria [54] (1)(2)...................Colombia
Ylagan, Pedro (2)................................Philippines
Yokota, Kisaburo [55] (3)......................Japan
Zourek, Jaroslav [56] (1)(2)(3)...............Czechoslovakia

[50] Elected member of the Commission in 1956; re-elected in 1961;
participated in 9th and subsequent Sessions.
[51] Elected member of the Commission in 1956; re-elected in 1961;
participated in 9th and subsequent Sessions.
[52] Elected by the Commission to fill a casual vacancy in 1961; re-
elected in 1961; participated in 13th and subsequent Sessions.
[53] Elected by the Commission in 1960 to fill a casual vacancy; re-
elected in 1961; participated in 12th and subsequent Sessions.
[54] Elected member of the Commission in 1948; participated in 1st to
5th Sessions, inclusive.
[55] Elected member of the Commission in 1956; resigned in 1961; participated in 9th to 12th Sessions, inclusive.
[56] Elected member of the Commission in 1948; re-elected in 1953 and
1956; did not attend the first three Sessions, but participated in the 4th
to 13th Sessions, inclusive.

Article 8

At the election the electors shall bear in mind that the persons to be elected to the Commission should individually possess the qualifications required and that in the Commission as a whole representation of the main forms of civilization and of the principal legal systems of the world should be assured.

The text of Article 8 is based closely on Article 9 of the Statute of the International Court of Justice.[1] The Committee on the Progressive Development of International Law and Its Codification recommended "that special emphasis be laid on the provisions of Article 9 of the [Court's] Statute" in the election of members of the International Law Commission.[2]

The third preambular paragraph of General Assembly resolution 174 (II) of 21 November 1947, to which the Statute of the International Law Commission is attached, recognizes the desirability of a Commission "composed of persons of recognized competence in international law and representing as a whole the chief forms of civilization and the basic legal systems of the world." In adopting this text, the Sixth Committee modified a Soviet proposal which, in the view of the United States, placed "too much emphasis on representation of the chief forms of civilization." [3]

[1] Article 9 of the Statute of the International Court of Justice reads:
"At every election, the electors shall bear in mind not only that the persons to be elected should individually possess the qualifications required, but also that in the body as a whole the representation of the main forms of civilization and of the principal legal systems of the world should be assured."

[2] A/AC.10/51, par. 5 (b).

[3] Cf. GAOR, 2nd Session, 1947, Sixth Committee, Summary Records, 147 (58th meeting, 20 Nov. 1947) and A/C.6/199, 19 Nov. 1947.

The admonition to electors "that the persons to be elected to the Commission should individually possess the qualifications required" is an obvious reference to the requirements of Article 2 of the Statute that members of the Commission "shall be persons of recognized competence in international law."

It is common knowledge, both within the Commission and in the confraternity of international law, that this basic requirement has not always been met. On the other hand, the Commission has always included in its membership persons of outstanding competence who are in the grand tradition of international law. Few of the Commission's members had no recognized competence in international law prior to their election. Moreover, with a few notable exceptions, the most competent persons nominated have been elected to the Commission. Where persons lacking competence in international law are the sole nominees of their governments, the play of political and geographical factors has, on occasion, ensured their election despite the more basic requirement of competence. Where the political formulae governing allocation of seats in the Commission practically guarantee certain seats to certain States or regions, embarrassment to the electors can be obviated by the exercise of more care by governments in nominating their candidates.[4]

The requirement of Article 8 that representation of the main forms of civilization and of the principal legal systems of the world should be assured in the Commission as a whole is a clear indication of the General Assembly's decision that the members of the International Law Commission, like the judges of the International Court of Justice, should not be regarded as representatives of States. Although the historic formula— which made possible the establishment of a Permanent Court of International Justice—is lacking in precision, the criteria of "main forms of civilization" and "principal legal systems of

[4] Cf. Rosenne, *loc. cit.*, 130.

the world" have served to temper a crude preoccupation with purely political, ideological,[5] or geographical considerations.[6]

[5] For the argument advanced by Professor Koretsky at the 39th meeting of the International Law Commission in 1950 that Professor Shuhsi Hsu, because of the Communist take-over of China, "had clearly ceased to represent the Chinese legal system," see commentary on Article 11, below (pp. 78 ff.).

[6] Cf. the commentary on Article 2, above (pp. 33 ff.).

Article 9

1. The twenty-five candidates who obtain the greatest number of votes and not less than a majority of the votes of the Members present and voting shall be elected.

2. In the event of more than one national of the same State obtaining a sufficient number of votes for election the one who obtains the greatest number of votes shall be elected and if the votes are equally divided the elder or eldest candidate shall be elected.

Except for the replacement of "fifteen candidates" with "twenty-one candidates" in 1956 and with "twenty-five candidates" in 1961, this text is identical with that prepared by Sub-Committee 2 of the Sixth Committee in 1947,[1] and contained in Article 9 of the Statute from 1949 to 1956. The increases in the size of the Commission in 1956 and 1961 are discussed elsewhere.[2]

Prior to each election, the Secretary-General transmits to all Member States a memorandum outlining the method of voting and calling to the attention of electors the requirements set forth in Articles 2 and 8 of the Statute.[3]

Two ballots were required to elect the Commission in 1948,[4] three ballots in 1953,[5] and one ballot each in 1956 [6] and in 1961.[7] No occasion to apply the second paragraph of Article 9 has yet arisen.

[1] A/C.6/193.
[2] See commentary on Article 2, above (pp. 33 ff.).
[3] Cf. A/697; A/2399; A/3459; A/4779.
[4] A/PV.154 and 155.
[5] A/PV.453 and 454.
[6] A/PV.623.
[7] A/PV.1067.

Article 10

The members of the Commission shall be elected for five years. They shall be eligible for re-election.

Until amended in 1955 to provide for a five-year term, Article 10 of the Statute provided that members of the Commission should be elected for three years, with the possibility of re-election.

The Committee on the Progressive Development of International Law and Its Codification considered the question of the length of the term of office of members of the Commission in connection with two other question: (1) whether the International Law Commission should be established as a permanent organ of the United Nations and (2) whether it should function on a full-time or part-time basis.

At the second meeting of that Committee, Professor Philip C. Jessup, stressing the need to create "an effective instrument" for the progressive development of international law and its codification, proposed, on behalf of the United States, the establishment of a full-time international law commission for a provisional period of three years, after which the situation could be re-examined with a view to continuing the Commission on a permanent basis or considering some new form of organization.[1]

At its 7th meeting, the Committee unanimously decided to recommend the establishment of a single commission for carrying out the progressive development of international law and its codification, and the Chairman (Sir Dalip Singh, India) then raised the question discussed in the following excerpt from the Summary Records:

Should the Committee to be established be permanent or tempo-

[1] Cf. A/AC.10/SR.2, 13 May 1947; A/AC.10/11, pp. 5–6 and A/AC. 10/14, 12 May 1947 (Suggestions by the United States).

rary, or temporary with a view to permanence, and if so, what would be the initial period of its appointment.

Professor BRIERLY (Rapporteur) suggested that the Committee be temporary with a view to permanence and that the initial period should be three years.

On a question asked by Prof. KORETSKY (Union of Soviet Socialist Republics) whether permanence in this connection referred to permanence of the Committee or to permanent appointment of its members, Prof. BRIERLY observed that he had in view the permanence of the Committee, not the permanent appointment of its members.

The CHAIRMAN stated that there was general agreement on this point.[2]

In reply to the question, "How long individual members of the Commission, as distinct from the Commission as such, should hold office?" the Summary Records of the 11th meeting state:

The Committee *agreed* unanimously (the Delegates of Yugoslavia and the Union of Soviet Socialist Republics abstaining) that members of the Commission should be appointed for three years.[3]

The Report of the Committee to the General Assembly therefore contains the following recommendation:

6. The Committee hopes that the ILC may be a permanent body, but they also feel that it might be desirable, in the first instance, to establish it on a provisional basis. They recommend therefore that its members be elected for a term of three years, but that they be eligible for re-election if the Commission is continued in being after this experimental period.[4]

Sub-Committee 2 of the General Assembly's Sixth Committee unanimously favored "the establishment of an 'International Law Commission' . . . as recommended by the Committee on the Progressive Development of International Law

[2] A/AC.10/SR.7, meeting of 21 May 1947, p. 2.
[3] A/AC.10/SR.11, meeting of 26 May 1947, p. 6.
[4] A/AC.10/51, 17 June 1947, par. 6.

and Its Codification" and also unanimously agreed that the terms of office of members of the Commission should be three years, "in accordance with the proposal contained in the Report," including eligibility for re-election.[5]

The Sixth Committee and the General Assembly therefore adopted as the text of Article 10: "The members of the Commission shall be elected for three years. They shall be eligible for re-election."

At its 2nd Session in 1950, the International Law Commission experienced some embarrassment in accepting new assignments from the Economic and Social Council (nationality of married women) and the General Assembly (territorial waters), in appointing Rapporteurs, and in planning its future program because the term of office of its members was due to expire in 1951.[6]

In the Sixth Committee of the General Assembly in October 1950, the United Kingdom representative, Sir Frank Soskice, called attention to these circumstances.[7] In the general debate which followed (as summarized in the Report of the Sixth Committee):

A majority of the delegations were in favour of extending the term of office of the present members of the Commission from three to five years. In support of this view, it was pointed out that the Commission would not be able to finish some of its most important tasks during the current period of office and that work in progress on these tasks should not be interrupted by a change in membership. In particular, it would be highly detrimental to the efficiency of the Commission if new rapporteurs had to take over subjects on which a considerable volume of work had already been done.[8]

Although it was argued that the problem might arise even at the end of the extended period, the Sixth Committee, by a

[5] A/C.6/193, 18 Nov. 1947, pars. 2, 5, and 10.
[6] Cf. Yearbook, ILC, 2nd Session, 1950, I, 247–255 (71st meeting, 19 July 1950).
[7] GAOR, 5th Session, 1950, Sixth Committee, Summary Records 91 (226th meeting, 23 Oct. 1950).
[8] A/1639, 8 Dec. 1950, par. 14.

vote of 37–8–2, approved the extension of the term of office of members elected in 1948 from three years to five.[9] The General Assembly adopted the resolution by a vote of 45–2–5.[10] The text of the resolution provided, in part, that "the term of office of the present members of the Commission shall be extended by two years, making a total period of five years from their election in 1948."

The members had been elected at the 154th and 155th plenary meetings of the General Assembly, both held on 3 November 1948, but the International Law Commission did not convene for its 1st Session until 12 April 1949 and there is no indication in the records whether the term of office of members of the Commission was regarded as commencing from the date of election or from the 1st of January following that election. At its 189th meeting, on 9 June 1953, the International Law Commission confirmed its decision, taken at a private meeting the previous day, "that in accordance with the practice in United Nations organs, the present term of office of its members should expire on 31 December 1953." [11]

During its 7th Session in 1955, the International Law Commission decided to recommend to the General Assembly an amendment to Article 10 of its Statute providing that members should be elected for five-year terms, commencing with those elected to take office 1 January 1957. The Commission considered that a change of the term of office from three to five years would be beneficial to the continuity of its work. The Commission drafted the text of the proposed amended Article 10 as follows:

The members of the Commission shall be elected for *five* years. They shall be eligible for re-election.[12]

[9] Sixth Committee, *loc. cit.*, 117 (229th meeting, 28 Oct. 1950).

[10] A/PV.320, 12 Dec. 1950; A/1775, p. 77, GA res. 486 (V), 12 Dec. 1950.

[11] Yearbook, ILC, 5th Session, 1953, II, 231 (Report, par. 172) and *ibid.*, I, 27.

[12] A/2934, Report, International Law Commission, Seventh Session, pars. 27–28; Yearbook, ILC, 7th Session, 1955, II, 41–42.

The proposal was the subject of a lively debate in the Sixth Committee of the General Assembly. Advocates of a five-year term stressed the lessons of experience and the importance of continuity in the work of the Commission, whose main function was to promote the gradual development and codification of international law. Opponents of the proposed amendment (who included many Latin American States) denied that continuity of the Commission's work depended on continuity of membership and feared that the longer term would prejudice the election of new members to the Commission and, thereby, the principle of geographical representation.

At its 446th meeting, the Sixth Committee approved the amendment drafted by the Commission by a vote of 33–11–8.[13] By resolution 985 (X), 3 December 1955, the General Assembly, by a vote of 46–4–4, amended Article 10 of the Commission's Statute in the terms recommended by the Commission.[14]

Full-Time or Part-Time Commission?

The question whether members of the International Law Commission should function on a full-time or a part-time basis was thoroughly debated in the Committee on the Progressive Development of International Law and Its Codification. At the second meeting of that Committee, Professor Philip C. Jessup, as stated above, proposed, on behalf of the United States, the establishment of a full-time international law commission for a provisional period of three years.[15]

At the 11th meeting of that Committee, Mr. Jessup "insisted that work in the Commission should be whole-time." Dr. Ivan Kerno, Assistant Secretary-General for Legal Affairs, referred

13 Cf. GAOR, 10th Session, 1955, Sixth Committee, Summary Records, 5–23 (442nd to 446th meetings, October 1955) and *ibid.*, Annexes, Agenda item 50, A/3028, 17 Nov. 1955, Report of the Sixth Committee, pars. 15–20.

14 A/PV.550, 3 Dec. 1955, par. 123 (Draft Res. II, based on A/C.6/L.351).

15 A/AC.10/SR.2, 13 May 1947; A/AC.10/11, pp. 5–6; and A/AC.10/14.

to the considerable expenditure which would be required if legal experts of the highest standing were to devote their whole time to the work of the Commission and the difficulty in obtaining persons of outstanding reputation, whose services might be needed by their own governments or who might hesitate to accept a full-time appointment which would prevent them from doing other work, such as teaching. On the question of deleting the words "full-time service" from a U.S.–Chinese proposal that the salary of members should be "proportionate to the dignity and importance of the position as a full-time service," the Committee vote was 2–10 (against deletion)–3. The U.S.–Chinese proposal was then adopted by a vote of 9–0–6.[16] A Soviet proposal at the 24th meeting to reverse this decision for full-time service was rejected by a vote of 10–5–1.[17]

The Report of the Committee therefore provided in paragraph 5 (d):

(d) All the members of the Committee were agreed that the members of the International Law Commission should receive a salary proportionate to the dignity and importance of their office, but there was some difference of opinion on the question whether they should be required to render full-time service. By a majority of nine votes to five [sic] the Committee thought that this would be both desirable and necessary. . . .[18]

Sub-Committee 2 of the 1947 Sixth Committee rejected both proposals (salary[19] and full-time service.) On the latter point, its Report observes:

The first question was whether the ILC should consist of members who would devote the whole of their time to this work, as the

[16] A/AC.10/SR.11, meeting of 26 May 1947, pp. 6–7, and A/AC.10/SR.11/Corr. 1, 12 June 1947. For the U.S.–Chinese proposal, see A/AC.10/33, 23 May 1947.

[17] A/AC.10/SR.24, meeting of 11 June 1947, pp. 2 ff.

[18] A/AC.10/51, 17 June 1947. The vote recorded in the summary records was 10–5–1. Cf. A/AC.10/SR.24, p. 2.

[19] This will be discussed in the commentary on Article 13 of the Statute.

Committee on the Progressive Development of International Law and Its Codification had decided by nine votes to five [sic]. Whilst recognizing that such a composition of the Commission would have its advantages, the Sub-Committee was of the unanimous opinion that, in view of the imperative necessity for the greatest possible reduction in the United Nations budget, this proposal could not be accepted. Moreover, the Sub-Committee considered that such a composition would make the acceptance of membership more difficult for the outstanding jurists who would be needed for the work of codification of International Law.[20]

It may be regarded as unfortunate that considerations of economy have played so preponderant a role in decisions about the International Law Commission.[21]

At the 226th meeting of the Sixth Committee on 23 October 1950, Sir Frank Soskice (U.K.) "suggested that to appoint some of the members of the International Law Commission on a full-time basis would greatly speed up its work." [22] At the 227th meeting, Mr. Fitzmaurice (U.K.) stated that although the United Kingdom had earlier opposed the appointment of members of the Commission on a full-time basis, it had changed its attitude in the light of two year's experience and "was now prepared to consider the appointment of some full-time members as a possible solution." [23] The suggestion was opposed by Mr. Morozov (U.S.S.R.): persons participating in the Commission's work on a permanent basis would "become United Nations staff members" and the proposal might deprive the Commission of the services of most eminent jurists.[24]

[20] A/C.6/193, 18 Nov. 1947, par. 4. Cf. A/C.6/150, 30 Sept. 1947, p. 2.

[21] Cf. GAOR, 2nd Session, 1947, Sixth Committee, Summary Records, 4–15 (37th and 38th meetings) and commentary on Articles 12 and 13 of the Statute, below. At the 58th meeting of the Sixth Committee, on 20 Nov. 1947, Mr. Georges Kaeckenbeeck (Rapporteur) observed: "In the Sub-Committee it had been decided, for reasons of economy, that the commission would work on a part-time basis: accordingly the members would not be given a salary. . . ." Ibid., 156.

[22] GAOR, 5th Session, 1950, Sixth Committee, Summary Records, 91 (226th meeting, 23 Oct. 1950).

[23] Ibid., 101, (227th meeting) par. 48.

[24] Ibid., par. 8.

The Sixth Committee decided to request the advice of the International Law Commission [25] and the General Assembly adopted on 12 December 1950 the following resolution:

The General Assembly

Considering that it is of the greatest importance that the work of the International Law Commission should be carried on in the conditions most likely to enable the Commission to achieve rapid and positive results,

Having regard to certain doubts which have been expressed whether such conditions exist at the present time,

Requests the International Law Commission to review its Statute with the object of making recommendations to the General Assembly at its sixth session concerning revisions of the Statute which may appear desirable, in the light of experience, for the promotion of the Commission's work.[26]

At its 3rd Session in 1951, the International Law Commission devoted several meetings to a review of its Statute.[27] After consideration of alternatives, the Commission recommended that the work of the International Law Commission should be placed on a full-time basis with a view to expediting its work.

This recommendation of the Commission was discussed by the General Assembly's Sixth Committee at its 295th to 297th meetings on 22 to 24 January 1952.[28] While some delegations favored the recommendation that the International Law Commission should be established on a full-time basis, most delegations believed that it was premature to make so fundamental a change in the Commission: they believed that "the prevailing political situation was unpropitious to rapid progress in inter-

[25] *Ibid.*, 113, 117 (229th meeting, 28 Oct. 1950).
[26] Resolution 484 (V), adopted at the 320th plenary meeting, 12 Dec. 1950. A/1775, p. 76.
[27] See Report of the International Law Commission covering the Work of its Third Session, 16 May–27 July 1951, Yearbook, ILC, 1951, II, 137–139; and Summary Records of 83rd, 96th, 97th, 112th, and 129th meetings, *ibid.*, I.
[28] GAOR, 6th Session, 1951–1952, Summary Records, Sixth Committee 261–273. See also A/2088, 29 Jan. 1952. Report of the Sixth Committee, *ibid.*, Annexes, Agenda item 49 (c).

national law"; that a larger increase in the Commission's output would impose an excessive burden on the General Assembly and on governments asked to comment on draft texts; that it would be difficult to find suitable candidates who would accept full-time appointment to the Commission; that expense was a serious consideration. The Sixth Committee therefore adopted a resolution deciding "for the time being not to take any action in respect of the revision of the said Statute until it has acquired further experience of the functioning of the Commission," and the General Assembly, at its 368th plenary meeting, on 31 January 1952, adopted the resolution without change.[29]

Perhaps the issue has not been finally settled. Criticisms—such as those sometimes heard in the General Assembly's Sixth Committee—of the productivity of the International Law Commission are misplaced in view of the General Assembly's policy of treating the codification and development of international law as a limited and part-time function, on which too much money should not be spent. In time, the work may come to be regarded as too important to leave on a part-time basis.

[29] GA res. 600 (VI), 31 Jan. 1952, A/2119, p. 85.

Article 11

In the case of a casual vacancy, the Commission itself shall fill the vacancy having due regard to the provisions contained in articles 2 and 8 of this Statute.

This method of filling casual vacancies in the Commission was the choice of Sub-Committee 2 of the Sixth Committee after consideration of eight possible methods.[1]

The special importance of the problem arises from the fact that the International Law Commission meets in the spring and the General Assembly in the fall; and if vacancies on the Commission were to be filled by the normal method of nomination and election, the work of the Commission would be hampered by less than full participation. In fact, casual vacancies have existed in the Commission just prior to eight of the sixteen sessions of the Commission.

A suggestion by Professor Koretsky (U.S.S.R.) that "the State to which the member belonged would provide a substitute" or an alternate did not find favor with the Committee on the Progressive Development of International Law and Its Codification, probably because, as Professor Brierly (U.K., Rapporteur) observed, "such nomination by a single State would conflict with the principle" of having the members of the Committee elected by the United Nations.[2] That Committee therefore recommended that casual vacancies be filled by the Security Council from a list of persons selected by the International Law Commission from the panel of previous nominees to the Commission and that the person so chosen should hold office only until the next General Assembly elected a member by its regular procedures.[3]

Sub-Committee 2 rejected this proposal, as well as a proposal

[1] A/C.6/193, par. 8.
[2] A/AC.10/SR.12, meeting of 27 May 1947, pp. 5–6.
[3] A/AC.10/51, par. 5 (c).

75

to have casual vacancies filled by the International Court of Justice, as being incompatible with the fact that the codification and progressive development of international law were functions of the General Assembly. Proposals that the vacancy be filled by the candidate receiving the largest vote in the preceding election or from a limited number of elected alternates were rejected as failing to ensure equitable representation of various legal systems on the Commission. A proposal that a substitute member be elected for each member who was elected was rejected, in part, because substitute members could not be expected to be available or at the Commission's disposal at all times.

The Report of the Sub-Committee therefore records that in "view of the disadvantages inherent in all the above methods, the Sub-Committee finally adopted, by ten votes with three abstentions," the method set forth in Article 11 of the Commission's Statute, by which the Commission itself fills casual vacancies.[4]

The Sixth Committee, on 20 November 1947, rejected, by a vote of 26 to 3, a proposed Soviet amendment to place the filling of casual vacancies in the President of the previous session of the General Assembly, rather than in the Security Council, in a manner otherwise like the proposal made by the Committee on Progressive Development of International Law and Its Codification.[5]

In adopting Article 11, Sub-Committee 2 rejected a suggestion that the International Law Commission should confine its choice to a previous nominee included in the list referred to in Article 7 of the Commission's Statute.[6]

Article 11 therefore provides wide discretionary power for

[4] A/C.6/193, par. 8.
[5] GAOR, 2nd Session, 1947, Sixth Committee, Summary Records, 151 (58th meeting) and A/C.6/199, 19 Nov. 1947 (Soviet amendments), Annex 1i, p. 205.
[6] Sixth Committee, *loc. cit.,* 151, Statement of Mr. W. E. Beckett (U.K.).

the Commission to fill casual vacancies, although the Commission is admonished by that Article to name only "persons of recognized competence in international law" (Art. 2, par. 1); not to elect two nationals of the same State (Art. 2, par. 2); and, while stressing individual qualifications, to bear in mind the criterion of a Commission representing as a whole "the main forms of civilization" and the "principal legal systems of the world" (Art. 8).

Suggested Amendment of Article 11

At the 10th Session of the General Assembly in 1955, the United States representative in the Sixth Committee raised the question whether Article 11 of the Statute of the International Law Commission should not be amended so as to confer on the General Assembly the power to fill casual vacancies in view of the extension of the term of office of members from three to five years.[7] By resolution 986 (X), 3 December 1955, the General Assembly referred the question to the International Law Commission for its opinion.[8] The Commission discussed the question at its 333rd and 336th meetings, on 25 and 30 April 1956. The view expressed by certain members that the General Assembly was better qualified than the Commission to fill casual vacancies because it could take more effective account of the political factors was decisively rejected by the Commission by a vote of 8–2–3.[9] In its Report to the General Assembly covering the work of the International Law Commission during its 8th Session, the Commission observed:

The Commission decided not to adopt that proposal, for the reason, *inter alia,* that, as the General Assembly meets shortly after the session of the Commission, the filling of such vacancies by the General Assembly would be delayed with the result that the Com-

[7] GAOR, 10th Session, 1955, Sixth Committee, Summary Records, 47 (452nd meeting, 2 Nov. 1955). Cf. A/3028, 17 Nov. 1955, Report of the Sixth Committee, pp. 6–7, 12, *ibid.,* Annexes, Agenda item 50.

[8] A/3116, p. 45.

[9] Yearbook, ILC, 8th Session, 1956, I, pp. 2–3, 16–17.

mission would have to work for at least one session with the vacancy unfilled.[10]

At the 11th Session of the General Assembly, the proposal to amend Article 11 of the International Law Commission was abandoned.[11]

The Soviet Attempt to Interpret Article 11 as Authorizing the International Law Commission to Create a Casual Vacancy by Excluding the Chinese Member

At the opening meeting of the 2nd Session of the International Law Commission—the 39th, on 5 June 1950—Professor Koretsky of the U.S.S.R., with the threat that he would take no further part in the work of the Commission if his proposal were not accepted, demanded that the Commission "stop Mr. Shuhsi Hsu from taking part in its work and, in accordance with article 11 of its Statute, . . . elect a representative of the legal system of the Chinese People's Republic." Mr. Hsu, said Professor Koretsky, "had been elected following nomination by the former Kuomintang Government which he thus represented, and hence he had clearly ceased to represent the Chinese legal system."

Judge Manley O. Hudson, as Chairman of the Commission, stated that he had carefully studied the question and the precedents and ruled the proposal out of order, reading the following decision:

The members of the Commission were elected in 1948 to serve for three years. They do not represent states or governments; instead, they serve in a personal capacity as persons of "recognized competence in International Law" (article 2 of the Statute). Being a creation of the General Assembly, the Commission is not competent to challenge the latter's application of article 8 of the Statute. Nor can it declare a "casual vacancy" under article 11 in these

[10] *Ibid.*, II, p. 301, par. 38.
[11] GAOR, 11th Session, 1956, Summary Records, Sixth Committee, 9–10 (481st meeting, 21 Nov. 1956).

circumstances. Mr. Koretsky's proposal is therefore out of order. This decision follows a precedent established by the Advisory Committee on Administrative and Budgetary Questions.[12]

The Commission sustained the Chairman's ruling by a vote of 10 to 1 and Professor Koretsky refused to attend any further meetings of the Commission, but did not submit his resignation as a member until 22 May 1952.[13]

A similar motion, made by Professor F. I. Kozhevnikov, who had been elected by the Commission to replace Professor Koretsky, was ruled out of order on the same grounds by Professor J. P. A. François, Chairman, at the 184th meeting of the Commission on 1 June 1953, and the ruling of the Chairman was sustained by a vote of 7 to 2.[14]

Although the proposal that the Commission declare a casual vacancy in pretended conformity with Article 11 of the Statute has not again been made, at the beginning of the 7th Session, Professor S. B. Krylov of the U.S.S.R., supported by Professor Jaroslav Zourek of Czechoslovakia, protested the presence of Mr. Hsu "who in no sense could be said to represent China." The Chairman, Mr. A. E. F. Sandström, observing that members of the Commission "did not represent their countries, but served as individuals in their personal capacity," ruled, without challenge, that "the Commission was unable to take note of such a statement."[15] At the beginning of the 9th and 10th Sessions of the Commission, Professor Grigory I. Tunkin of the U.S.S.R. expressed regret that the "legal system" of the People's Republic of China "was not represented" on the Commission, and the Chairmen of the respective sessions, Professor Zourek at the 9th, and Judge Radhabinod Pal at the 10th, stated "that the Commission took note of Mr. Tunkin's statement."[16]

[12] Yearbook, ILC, 2nd Session, 1950, I, 1–2; II, 364–365.
[13] *Ibid.*, 4th Session, 1952, I, 2.
[14] *Ibid.*, 5th Session, 1953, I, 1–2.
[15] *Ibid.*, 7th Session, 1955, I, 1 (282nd meeting, 2 May 1955).
[16] *Ibid.*, 9th Session, 1957, I, 2 (383rd meeting, 24 April 1957) and *ibid.*, 10th Session, 1958, I, 5 (432nd meeting, 29 April 1958).

At the beginning of the 11th Session in 1959, Professor Tunkin objected to the nomination of Mr. Hsu as First Vice-Chairman of the Commission, observing, in part, that it was

regrettable that the legal system of the great Chinese people was not represented in the Commission. When he had raised that matter at the previous session, he had been told that the members of the Commission were elected in their personal capacity; he had pointed out, however, that they were nominated by Governments.

In reply, the Chairman of the Commission, Sir Gerald Fitzmaurice, ruled, without challenge, that

the Commission had to respect the terms of its Statute. All members were elected in their personal capacity, whatever might be the method of nomination, and any member was eligible for any office.

Mr. Hsu was thereupon elected First Vice-Chairman of the Session by a vote of 11–1–2.[17]

*Practice of the International Law Commission
in Filling Casual Vacancies*

The question of filling casual vacancies on the International Law Commission first appeared as an agenda item at the 4th Session of the Commission in 1952. On motion of Judge Manley O. Hudson, the Commission decided that the filling of casual vacancies should first be discussed at a private meeting of members of the Commission.[18] This practice has been consistently followed as to later vacancies and only the results of some of the decisions made at private meetings appear on the record since the proceedings in private meetings are not published. Nevertheless, some information about the practice of the Commission in applying Article 11 of its Statute may be

[17] *Ibid.,* 11th Session, 1959, I, 1 (479th meeting, 20 April 1959). See also *ibid.,* 13th Session, 1961, I, 194–195 (612th meeting, 16 June 1961) and *ibid.,* 14th Session, 1962, I, 1 (628th meeting, 24 April 1962).
[18] Yearbook, ILC, 4th Session, 1952, I, 2 (135th meeting, 4 June 1952).

garnered from the published Summary Records of the Commission.

At the 136th meeting on 5 June 1952, Judge Hudson proposed that, in view of the resignation of Professor James L. Brierly, of the United Kingdom, "the Commission should declare the existence of a casual vacancy and proceed to fill it, in accordance with Article 11 of its Statute." The proposal was adopted and the Chairman called for "nominations for a successor to Mr. Brierly." Mr. Hudson proposed the election of Professor H. Lauterpacht of the United Kingdom and the minutes record that he was unanimously elected.[19] There is no record of other nominations for this vacancy and no indication in the record of the views of the United Kingdom Government.

The Commission then declared that a casual vacancy existed as a result of the resignation of Professor Vladimir M. Koretsky of the U.S.S.R. The Assistant Secretary-General of the United Nations for Legal Affairs, Mr. Ivan S. Kerno, had informed the Commission that, in submitting his resignation, Professor Koretsky had recommended that the Commission should elect in his place, Professor F. I. Kozhevnikov of the U.S.S.R. Mr. Kerno also stated that the Soviet Minister to Switzerland had forwarded a list of the principal publications in the field of international law of Professor Kozhevnikov.[20]

Professor Kozhevnikov was nominated by a member of the Commission and unanimously elected.

At the same 4th Session, the International Law Commission filled the casual vacancy caused by the resignation of Sir Benegal Rau of India by electing Mr. Radhabinod Pal of India whose candidature had been proposed in a communication from the Indian *chargé d'affaires* in Switzerland.[21]

At its 6th Session in 1954, the Commission was confronted with filling the casual vacancy created by the resignation of Judge John J. Parker of the United States, who had been elected by the General Assembly in 1953 but who had resigned

[19] *Ibid.,* 3.   [20] *Ibid.,* 2–3.   [21] *Ibid.,* 245, 251.

without participating in any session of the Commission. The Summary Record for 28 June 1954 laconically states that at a private meeting "the members of the Commission *had decided* to elect Judge Douglas L. Edmonds" of the United States.[22] No motion to elect him is found in the Summary Records and the French text states that "les membres de la Commission *ont élu*" Judge Edmonds at a private meeting.[23] The record is devoid of any hint of the preoccupations of the Commission between 3 June and 28 June 1954, when the decision was finally made to elect the officially designated United States candidate.

During its 7th Session the Commission filled two more casual vacancies. The Summary Record of the 287th meeting on 9 May 1955, states "that the Commission *had decided* at a private meeting to elect Sir Gerald Fitzmaurice" (U.K.) in place of Sir Hersch Lauterpacht, who had been elected to the International Court of Justice. The French text states more accurately that "la Commission, au cours d'une séance privée, *a élu* Sir Gerald Fitzmaurice." [24]

The Summary Record of the 292nd meeting, states, in part:

1. After a short discussion, it was decided by 9 votes to 1, with 2 abstentions, to hold a private meeting on the question of filling the casual vacancy caused by Mr. Córdova's [Mexico] resignation.

2. On the resumption, the CHAIRMAN announced that Mr. Luis Padilla Nervo [Mexico] *had been elected*.[25]

The Summary Records of the 10th Session of the Commission record (433rd meeting, 30 April 1958) "that the Commission had elected Mr. Ricardo J. Alfaro of Panama, by a majority of votes at a private meeting, to fill the casual va-

[22] Yearbook, ILC, 6th Session, 1954, I, 72. Italics added.

[23] A/CN.4/SR. 256.

[24] A/CN.4/SR.287, 9 May 1955, par. 16. Cf. Yearbook, ILC, 7th Session, 1955, I, 25. Italics added.

[25] A/CN.4/SR.292, 16 May 1955, pars. 1, 2; Yearbook, ILC, 7th Session, 1955, I, 51. Italics added.

cancy caused by the resignation of Mr. Jean Spiropoulos [Greece] consequent upon his election to the International Court of Justice." [26]

At its 11th Session in 1959, the Chairman announced at its 486th meeting, 1 May 1959, that, at a private meeting, the Commission had elected Mr. Nihat Erim (Turkey) to fill the casual vacancy created by the resignation of Mr. Abdullah El-Erian (United Arab Republic).[27] The latter had been elected member from Egypt, and when Egypt and Syria combined to form the United Arab Republic, Mr. El-Erian submitted his resignation, having regard to the provision of Article 2, paragraph 2, of the Commission's Statute that no two members of the Commission shall be nationals of the same State and to the fact that Mr. Faris Bey El-Khouri, elected from Syria, was a national of the United Arab Republic.[28]

At the 12th Session of the Commission, the Chairman announced at the 540th meeting, on 16 May 1960, that "the members of the Commission, meeting in private, had elected two persons to fill the vacancies" caused by the election of Mr. Ricardo J. Alfaro (Panama) to the International Court of Justice and by the resignation of Mr. Thanat Khoman (Thailand). The new members elected were Mr. Eduardo Jiménez de Aréchaga (Uruguay) and Mr. Mustafa Kamil Yasseen (Iraq).[29]

At the beginning of the 13th Session of the Commission in 1961, three vacancies existed. The Chairman announced, at the 581st meeting on 2 May 1961, that "the Commission, meeting in private, had elected" Sir Humphrey Waldock (U.K.) to fill the vacancy caused by the election of Sir Gerald Fitzmaurice (U.K.) to the International Court of Justice, Mr. André Gros (France) to fill the vacancy caused by the death of Professor Georges Scelle (France) and Mr. Senjin Tsuruoka (Japan) to

[26] Yearbook, ILC, 10th Session, 1958, I, 5.
[27] Yearbook, ILC, 11th Session, 1959, I, 34.
[28] Yearbook, ILC, 10th Session, 1958, II, 79.
[29] Yearbook, ILC, 12th Session, 1960, I, 81.

fill the vacancy caused by the resignation of Mr. Kisaburo Yokota (Japan).[30]

Several interesting conclusions emerge from this pattern. Of the fifteen casual vacancies filled by the Commission, the first three were filled by election in public meetings of the Commission, after consideration of nominees in private meetings. The other twelve vacancies—i.e., all those commencing with the 6th Session in 1954—have been filled by election in private meetings. Although Article 11 of the Statute provides that "the Commission itself shall fill the vacancy," the Summary Records have, on occasion, stated that "the members of the Commission" had elected or "decided to elect" a particular nominee.

In filling the first six vacancies, the Commission elected persons of the same nationality as the previous incumbent. Commencing, however, with the 10th Session in 1958, the Commission elected a person of Panamanian nationality, who had been a previous member of the Commission, to replace a Greek national; a Turkish national to replace an Egyptian (U.A.R.); a Uruguayan to replace a Panamanian; and a national of Iraq to replace a national of Thailand. For filling the three vacancies at its 13th Session in 1961, the Commission elected, in each case, a person of the same nationality as the previous incumbent. At its 16th Session in 1964, the Commission elected a French national, Mr. Paul Reuter, to succeed a French national and an Argentine national, Mr. José Maria Ruda, to succeed a Mexican.

Prior to its 16th Session, the number of nominations received or considered by the Commission in filling casual vacancies was not public knowledge. It appears that in filling some of its casual vacancies, the Commission has felt free to go beyond candidates officially nominated and to seek other candidates from the same region or from unrepresented geographical regions, although on one occasion the Commission

---

[30] A/CN.4/SR. 581, par. 12 (provisional summary record); the words quoted do not appear in Yearbook, ILC, 13th Session, 1961, I, 2.

did not feel free to disregard an "official" nominee on the ground that he was not a person of recognized competence in international law.

At its 16th Session in 1964, a Commission document—A/CN.4/168/Add. 1, 9 May 1964—was issued informing members of the Commission that the Governments of Panama, France, Iran, and Argentina had each nominated a national for the vacancies caused by the resignations of Mr. André Gros (France) and Mr. Luis Padilla Nervo (Mexico) upon their election to the International Court of Justice. In addition to *curricula vitae* of the candidates, the document referred to includes portions of the notes or letters submitted to the United Nations on behalf of the candidates.

It may be concluded that the International Law Commission has exercised its right under Article 11 with a sense of responsibility, with full regard to the provisions of Article 8 of its Statute and, except on one occasion, with regard to Article 2.

Article 12

The Commission shall sit at the European Office of the United Nations at Geneva. The Commission shall, however, have the right to hold meetings at other places after consultation with the Secretary-General.

Until amended by General Assembly resolution 984 (X), 3 December 1955, the first sentence of Article 12 provided that "the Commission shall sit at the headquarters of the United Nations."

The Summary Records of the Committee on the Progressive Development of International Law and Its Codification reveal some hesitation as to the seat of the proposed International Law Commission. Dr. Yuen-li Liang, Secretary of the Committee, suggested that "it would be for the Commission itself to decide where its seat would be." Professor Vladimir Koretsky (U.S.S.R.), after expressing the hope "that the Commission's seat would not be at the headquarters of the United Nations," proposed (when the Committee voted for a full-time International Law Commission) "that the Commission, which received its authority from the General Assembly, should be situated at the headquarters of the United Nations, but might hold meetings elsewhere." The Chairman ruled the proposal adopted.[1] A subsequent proposal to leave to the Commission the decision "where it would exercise its activities" was rejected by the Committee after Professor J. L. Brierly (Rapporteur) had observed that such a proposal would have been more acceptable if it had been decided to require of the Commission part-time, rather than full-time, service.[2] The Committee therefore recommended in its Report:

It was agreed that the Commission should have its headquarters

[1] A/AC.10/SR.11, meeting of 26 May 1947, pp. 6–8.
[2] A/AC.10/SR.24, meeting of 11 June 1947, pp. 4–6.

at the seat of the United Nations, though it might decide from time to time to hold its sessions at other places; and that the Secretary-General should be requested to make available to it the services of the Division for the Development and Codification of International Law of the Secretariat.[3]

Sub-Committee 2 of the Sixth Committee of the General Assembly modified this proposal in its Report of 18 November 1947, by recommending that the "seat" of the Commission should be established at the United Nations Headquarters and that the "right to meet" elsewhere should be "after consultation with the Secretary-General." [4] The Sixth Committee and the General Assembly adopted, without debate, the Sub-Committee's draft Article 12, as follows:

The Commission shall sit at the headquarters of the United Nations. The Commission shall, however, have the right to hold meetings at other places after consultation with the Secretary-General.

The variation in the French version, providing that

La Commission a son siège au siège de l'Organisation des Nations Unies

appears to have passed unnoticed at the time.[5]

At the 104th meeting of the International Law Commission, Mr. Ivan Kerno, Assistant Secretary-General in charge of the Legal Department, observed of the requirement of prior consultation by the Commission of the Secretary-General:

[3] A/AC.10/51, par. 5 (d).   [4] A/C.6/193, par. 10.

[5] Cf. A/CN.4/4, 2 Feb. 1949, Statute of the International Law Commission, Art. 12. See also GAOR, 10th Session, 1955, Sixth Committee, Summary Records, 7, where Mr. Stavropoulos (Legal Counsel) pointed out to the Sixth Committee at its 442nd meeting on 11 Oct. 1955, that the variation was a "drafting error dating back to the original formulation of the International Law Commission's Statute." He added:

"The original text, prepared in English, had stated: 'The Commission shall sit at . . .' The French translation had wrongly read: '*La Commission a son siège* . . .' It was wrong to speak of the Commission's seat (*siège*). The point to determine was where it should meet."

88   INTERNATIONAL LAW COMMISSION

That requirement had been included in the Statute for the reason that the large number of meetings held each year compelled the Secretary-General to prepare a very tight calendar.[6]

Application of Article 12

The application of Article 12 proved to be a source of considerable annoyance to the International Law Commission. After holding its 1st Session in New York in 1949, the Commission has annually availed itself of its right under the second sentence of Article 12 to hold meetings at other places after consultation with the Secretary-General. Except for the 6th Session in 1954 which, for lack of space in the European Headquarters of the United Nations in Geneva,[7] had to be transferred to UNESCO Headquarters in Paris, the Commission has since 1949 regularly met in Geneva.

Opposition to the decisions of the International Law Commission to hold its sessions in Geneva developed at an early stage in the Advisory Committee on Administrative and Budgetary Questions, in the Secretariat, and in the General Assembly's Fifth Committee. As early as 8 August 1949, the Advisory Committee complained that it had been unable to find any evidence that the Statute of the International Law Commission had been referred to the Fifth Committee for consideration of its financial implications, in accordance with rule 142 of the rules of procedure of the General Assembly.[8] In repeating this complaint to the 208th meeting of the Fifth Committee, on 26 October 1949, Mr. Thanassis Aghnides, Chairman of the Advisory Committee, added that neither the Advisory Committee

[6] A/CN.4/SR.104, meeting of 15 June 1951, par. 17. This paragraph is among those omitted in reproducing A/CN.4/SR.104 in the Yearbook of the ILC, 1951, I, 186.

[7] GAOR, 10th Session, 1955, Sixth Committee, Summary Records, 7 (442nd meeting, par. 43) where Mr. Spiropoulos, Chairman of the International Law Commission, informed the Sixth Committee that it was because of the Geneva Conference on Indo-China.

[8] A/934, par. 39, 2nd Report of 1949 of the Advisory Committee to the General Assembly.

nor the Fifth Committee had been informed of the Statute of the International Law Commission before it was adopted. He made the curious observation "that the position might have been more satisfactory if the matter had gone through the usual channels." [9]

This complaint, which certainly became irrelevant after the Commission's first year, was nevertheless repeated in 1952 when the Advisory Committee, quoting Article 12 of the International Law Commission's Statute, complained that "sessions away from Headquarters, have constituted the rule rather than the exception." [10] When this report (A/2251) was discussed in the Fifth Committee, Mr. Brennan (Australia) thought that by accepting Article 12 of the Commission's Statute, the General Assembly "had largely compromised its budgetary powers to determine where a subsidiary organ should meet." Mr. Aghnides asserted that Article 12 of the International Law Commission's Statute "raised an important constitutional issue. It was a dangerous precedent; since the principle of the separation of powers had been adopted [*sic*], such an organ should not have the power to decide as it pleased where to meet." [11] At the 391st meeting of the Fifth Committee, on 15 October 1953, Mr. Liveran (Israel) observed that "if the Fifth Committee considered itself bound, and rightly so, to secure the maximum use of a Headquarters designed to meet the needs of all United Nations bodies, it should . . . decide where meetings should take place." [12]

Secretariat opposition to having the Commission meet in Geneva crystallized in 1953. While pointing to financial and administrative difficulties,[13] main reliance was placed by the

[9] A/C.5/SR.208, 26 Oct. 1949, par. 14; GAOR, 4th Session, 1949, Fifth Committee, Summary Records, 141.

[10] A/2251, 8 Nov. 1952, 10th Report, Advisory Committee to 7th Session, General Assembly, par. 4.

[11] A/C.5/SR.365, 17 Nov. 1952, pars. 35–37; GAOR, 7th Session, 1952, Fifth Committee, Summary Records, 152.

[12] A/C.5/SR.391, 15 Oct. 1953, par. 7; *ibid.*, 8th Session, 79.

[13] Cf. A/CN.4/SR.112, meeting of 27 June 1951, pars. 1 ff., remarks of

Secretariat on General Assembly resolution 694 (VII) of 20 December 1952. By this resolution, the General Assembly, in order to fix "a long-term pattern of conferences to allow for the rational and economic distribution of meetings between Headquarters and Geneva and to permit the proper utilization of staff and conference facilities at both places," decided to establish a four-year program of conferences, commencing 1 January 1954, under which sessions for all Headquarters-based bodies should be held in New York and sessions of Geneva-based bodies should be held in Geneva, with certain exceptions. Exceptions (a) and (c) provided:

(a) The regular summer session of the Economic and Social Council would be held each year in Geneva during which period no other meetings of United Nations bodies would be held in Geneva; . . .

(c) The International Law Commission would meet in Geneva only when its session could be held there without overlapping with the summer session of the Economic and Social Council. . . .[14]

In communicating the text of this resolution to the International Law Commission, the Secretariat pointed out that "the International Law Commission could, if it decided to meet in Geneva, hold a yearly session there lasting eight weeks beginning with the third week in August." [15]

The International Law Commission dutifully scheduled its next session in accordance with the Secretariat's suggestion [16] and let the Secretariat discover for itself that a session of the

---

Ivan Kerno, Assistant Secretary-General, to the International Law Commission. These paragraphs have been omitted from the Yearbook, ILC, 1951, I, 257 but see *ibid.*, 221–222, 262 ff.; Yearbook, ILC, 1952, I, 41 (par. 66), 59 (par. 1), 77 (par. 90); Yearbook, ILC, 1953, I, 285–290.

[14] A/2361, p. 69. Reaffirmed for a further period of five years ending in 1962 by resolution 1202 (XII), 13 Dec. 1951, A/3805, p. 39.

[15] A/CN.4/74, 20 May 1953, Note by Secretariat on Date and Place of Sixth Session, International Law Commission. Cf. Yearbook, ILC, 5th Session, 1953, I, 285 ff.

[16] Yearbook, ILC, 5th Session, 1953, I, 27.

Commission commencing the third week of August would be most undesirable because it would overlap with the General Assembly's annual session, would postpone by a year consideration of the Commission's annual Report by the Assembly, would prevent members of the Commission from serving in the Sixth Committee of the Assembly, and would create staff difficulties.

In a message to the Commission pointing out these difficulties, the Secretariat stated that the 1954 budget estimates provided funds for a meeting of the Commission at Headquarters and stressed economy, the "wording of Article 12 of the ILC Statute" and the difficulty of "obtaining supplemental appropriations as in previous years." [17]

In discussing this message, members of the Commission questioned the Secretariat's estimate of the additional expense of holding a meeting in Geneva instead of New York [18] but, as the Chairman, Professor François, pointed out, this was irrevelant:

> The General Assembly had agreed that the necessary expenditure could be incurred, since the only proviso which it had made about holding the Commission's sessions in Geneva was that they should not overlap the summer sessions of the Economic and Social Council.[19]

The problem of the Commission then became when to hold its sessions so that they would not overlap with the Economic and Social Council. After a thorough discussion,[20] the Commission summarized the problems involved in scheduling its sessions in paragraphs 173 to 176 of its Report covering its 5th Session (1953), as follows: [21]

> 173. The Commission decided, after consulting the Secretary-General in accordance with the terms of Article 12 of its Statute

---

17 *Ibid.,* 285 ff. Communication from Messrs. Lall and Stavropoulos.
18 The Secretariat estimate of $25,000.
19 Yearbook, ILC, 5th Session, 1953, I, 285 (226th meeting, par. 65).
20 *Ibid.,* 285–290 (226th and 227th meetings).
21 *Ibid.,* II, 232.

and receiving the views of the latter, to hold its next session in Geneva, Switzerland, for a period of ten weeks, beginning on 17 May 1954. The Commission is unanimously in favour of Geneva as a meeting-place in preference to New York, as general conditions in Geneva are more conducive to the efficiency in the kind of work the members of the Commission have to perform. In particular, the library facilities in the European Office with material gathered and organized since the days of the League of Nations, have proved to be unsurpassed in the field of international law.[22]

174. The Commission is aware that General Assembly Resolution 694 (VII) adopted on 20 December 1952, provides that the International Law Commission would meet in Geneva only when its session could be held there without overlapping with the summer session of the Economic and Social Council. Such overlapping as there might be if the Commission met in Geneva beginning on 17 May 1954 is, in the opinion of the Commission, hardly avoidable under present circumstances. There are grave objections to holding the session after the session of the Economic and Social Council. The session would then overlap with the session of the General Assembly with the result that the report by the Commission could not be considered by the General Assembly until its following session, that the Secretariat would have difficulties in assigning adequate staff to serve the Commission, and that certain members who are also members of delegations to the General Assembly might not be able to attend the sessions of the Commission.

175. On the other hand, a ten weeks' session to be held in its entirety before the summer session of the Economic and Social Council would also be open to objection. It would have to begin towards the end of April 1954, and those members of the Commission who are university professors would not be able to attend meetings before 1 June at the earliest. The Commission would therefore be deprived of their co-operation for more than a month.[23] Under these circumstances, the opening date of 17 May

[22] See further, Alfaro Memorandum, *ibid.,* I, 286–287.

[23] See Professor Lauterpacht's forceful statements at the 227th meeting of the Commission on 30 July 1953, *ibid.,* 288–290, and the 240th meeting on 14 Aug. 1953, where he placed on record a statement reading, in part, as follows:

"The decision to convene the Commission for 17 May 1954 was dic-

was accepted in order to reduce to a minimum both the overlapping with the Council session and the period during which the Commission would have to be without the presence of some of its members.

176. As regards the length of the session a period of ten weeks is considered as a minimum. Because of lack of time the Commission has been forced to postpone the consideration of . . . important subjects. . . . It is therefore imperative for the fulfillment of the task entrusted to the Commission that it shall be able to devote sufficient time to its work.

The problem arose again at the 6th and 7th Sessions of the International Law Commission. When the Commission provisionally decided on 28 June 1954 [24] to hold its 7th Session in Geneva in 1955, the reply was received from Headquarters that "the Secretary-General, for budgetary and other reasons, favoured the Commission's seventh session being held in New York for a period of eight, and not ten, weeks, as suggested by the Commission." [25]

When the Fifth Committee discussed budget estimates for 1955, the right of the International Law Commission to decide, after consultation with the Secretary-General, to meet in Geneva was again questioned. With complete disregard for Article 12 of the Commission's Statute, the United States and

---

tated by the desire to meet the wishes of the General Assembly with a view to effecting economies. The probable result of that decision is that the Commission may have to meet with one-quarter or more of its members absent. The value of the deliberations and decisions of a Commission so constituted is bound to suffer in consequence of the absence of a considerable number of members. Moreover, such deliberations and decisions are likely to be re-opened when the Commission is complete. The result must be a waste of time and money.

"The necessity for the decision taken by the Commission is also regrettable inasmuch as, for reasons of small and doubtful economies, it prevents some members from associating themselves with the work of the Commission at all its stages." *Ibid.,* 387.

24 Yearbook, ILC, 6th Session, 1954, I, 72 (256th meeting, 28 June 1954).

25 *Ibid.,* 163 (274th meeting, 23 July 1954).

Danish representatives asserted that it was for the General Assembly to decide where the Commission should meet. Mr. Aghnides saw the question as an unconstitutional usurpation by the International Law Commission of the General Assembly's "administrative and budgetary powers." On the other hand, the Netherlands representative deprecated the fact that at each session the General Assembly had to decide where the International Law Commission should meet. He proposed that the Assembly should recognize the tradition established and authorize the expenditure of the additional $6,950 required for a Geneva meeting which provided better working conditions for the Commission. The funds were voted.[26] The debate appears to have been primed by a report of the Advisory Committee on Administrative and Budgetary Questions which marshaled budgetary, administrative, and policy reasons why the International Law Commission should not be allowed to hold its sessions in Geneva.[27]

A comparable decision of the International Law Commission at its 7th Session to hold its 8th Session in Geneva evoked a telegram from Headquarters that "for budgetary reasons and for reasons of principle" the Secretary-General favored a New York session.[28] This evoked the comment from one member of the Commission that "the telegram from Headquarters simply meant that the Secretariat was unwilling to assume responsibility for endorsing the Commission's preliminary decision because it involved financial considerations." [29]

At both Sessions, the International Law Commission maintained its preliminary decision to meet for ten weeks in Geneva. As Professor Scelle had earlier observed, although the Commission had a duty to consult the Secretary-General on the place

[26] A/C.5/SR.450, 4 Nov. 1954, pars. 23, 28, 42, 18, and 51; GAOR, 9th Session, 1954, Fifth Committee, Summary Records, 120–123.

[27] A/2766, 25 Oct. 1954, 10th Report to 9th Session, General Assembly.

[28] Yearbook, ILC, 7th Session, 1955, I, 168 (311th meeting, 14 June 1955, par. 16).

[29] *Ibid.*, par. 19.

of its sessions, it was for the Commission itself to decide.[30] In its Report covering its 7th Session, the Commission emphasized "that ten weeks is the indispensable minimum period it would require to carry out the work entrusted to it." [31]

Despite the success of the Commission in securing acceptance of its view that it should hold an annual session of not less than ten weeks in Geneva, its yearly struggle with the Secretariat and the Advisory Committee was an annoyance. At its 7th Session in 1955, the Commission therefore adopted unanimously a proposal by Mr. García Amador to request the General Assembly to amend Article 12 of the Commission's Statute so as to provide that "the Commission shall sit at the European Office of the United Nations at Geneva" instead of "at the headquarters of the United Nations." [32] Mr. García Amador thought such an amendment should eliminate difficulties in the future.

In the Report covering its 7th Session, the Commission commented:

26. In support of this proposal, the members affirmed that the European Office affords the best conditions for their work; that the atmosphere of Geneva is more favourable than that of New York for the studies of a body of technical experts called upon to solve legal problems, setting aside the political contingencies of the moment as far as possible; that Geneva has an exceptionally well planned law library which is more complete than that at United Nations Headquarters and contains, *inter alia,* a remarkable collection of legal works in European languages. The members also stressed that, in their view, the transfer of the Commission' seat [*sic*] from New York to Geneva was calculated to simplify arrangements for its sessions by the United Nations Secretariat.[33]

The proposal met a favorable reception in the Assembly's Sixth Committee. There was wide acceptance of the reasons

[30] Yearbook, ILC, 5th Session, 1953, I, 287.
[31] Yearbook, ILC, 7th Session, 1955, II, 42, par. 30.
[32] *Ibid.*, I, 167 (311th meeting).   [33] *Ibid.*, II, 41.

advanced by the Commission. The proposed amendment was regarded as merely confirming established practice and not necessarily implying the establishment of a permanent seat for the Commission in Geneva. Several members stressed the need for favorable working conditions over budgetary considerations. On 12 October 1955, the Sixth Committee adopted the resolution to amend Article 12 in the language proposed by the International Law Commission by a vote of 49–0–3.[34]

The Secretariat and the Advisory Committee, however, had not had their last word. In the First Report of the Advisory Committee on Administrative and Budgetary Questions to the 10th Session of the General Assembly, 21 July 1955, that budgetary committee had not only recommended deletion from the 1956 Budget Estimate of the Secretary-General of the additional amount required to permit the International Law Commission to meet in Geneva, but had presumed to set forth policy arguments as to why, in its judgment, the International Law Commission should not meet in Geneva.[35] In addition to the argument drawn from Article 12 that the "Commission shall sit at the Headquarters of the United Nations," the Advisory Committee pointed out that for the seven years 1950 to 1956 the additional cost of holding sessions of the Commission will have exceeded $100,000; that the character of the Commission as a Headquarters-based body was being transformed, "a fact which appears to have prompted the Commission's decision of 14 June 1955 to recommend an amendment" to Article 12 of its Statute to provide that the Commission shall sit at Geneva; and that the purpose of the restrictive clause in Article 12 requiring the Commission to consult the Secretary-General before holding meetings away from Headquarters was being

[34] GAOR, 10th Session, 1955, Sixth Committee, Summary Records, 10 (443rd meeting) and *ibid.* Annexes, Agenda item 50, A/3028, 17 Nov. 1955, Report of the Sixth Committee, pars. 6–12, and draft resolution I (A/C.6/L.349).

[35] GAOR, 10th Session, 1955, Supplement No. 7 (A/2921), pars. 33 ff. See also A/2766, 25 Oct. 1954, in which the Advisory Committee detailed its reasons for opposing the holding of the 1955 session of the International Law Commission in Geneva.

frustrated: "only an exceptional and compelling reason can justify a disregard of representations made by the chief administrative officer of the United Nations."

After the Sixth Committee had disagreed with these arguments by recommending the amendment to Article 12 by which the Commission should sit in Geneva, the Advisory Committee on Administrative and Budgetary Questions returned to the attack in a Report on the financial implications of the resolutions of the Sixth Committee.[36] Reiterating its arguments on the administrative and financial advantages of holding sessions of the Commission in New York, the Advisory Committee even ventured the opinions that if the Geneva Library of the United Nations was better than the Headquarters Library, there were other good libraries in New York which "would appear largely to offset this disadvantage"; and there was "the additional but fundamental consideration that it is principally at Headquarters—in the Assembly, the Councils and the Commissions—that the United Nations is building up a jurisprudence and contributing through that process to the development of international law." The Advisory Committee therefore condemned the proposed amendment to Article 12 of the Commission's Statute as "an avoidable expenditure of United Nations funds" and refused to recommend its adoption.

In the presence of Mr. Jean Spiropoulos, President of the International Law Commission, and Mr. Thanassis Aghnides, Chairman of the Advisory Committee on Administrative and Budgetary Questions, the arguments were gone over again in the General Assembly's Fifth Committee. It took no stand on the proposed amendment, but merely informed the General Assembly of the appropriation needed for the International Law Commission to hold its 1956 session in Geneva.[37]

On 3 December 1955, the General Assembly at its 550th

[36] A/3037, 21 Nov. 1955, 21st Report, Advisory Committee, GAOR, 10th Session, Annexes, Agenda item 50, p. 17.
[37] A/C.5/SR. 514, 23 Nov. 1955, pars. 47 ff., Summary Records, 150 ff.; A/3052, 1 Dec. 1955, Report of the Fifth Committee, pars. 1–6, Agenda item 50, p. 19.

plenary session adopted, by a vote of 55–0–2, resolution 984 (X) amending Article 12 of the Statute of the International Law Commission in the language proposed by the Commission.[38]

The amendment of Article 12 of the Commission's Statute to provide that the Commission shall sit at the European Office of the United Nations at Geneva eliminated the annual wrangle with the Advisory Committee on Administrative and Budgetary Questions but failed to solve the problem of fixing a time for sessions of the Commission which (1) would not overlap with the summer session of the Economic and Social Council, (2) would permit a full attendance of academic members, and (3) would be of adequate length.

Efforts of the Commission to reach an accommodation with the Economic and Social Council by which the latter would postpone to a later date the opening of its summer session were unavailing because the Council's rules of procedure require its summer session to end at least six weeks before the regular session of the General Assembly, so that its documentation may be prepared for the Assembly.[39] When considering the financial implications of the amendment to Article 12 which is discussed above, the Secretary-General noted that to avoid additional expense incidental to overlapping of meetings, "it is the Secretary-General's understanding that pending review of resolution 694 (VII) the Assembly's injunction that there should be no overlap between sessions of the International Law Commission and the Economic and Social Council would continue to be observed." [40]

The problem arose every year [41] and was fully discussed at the 12th Session of the Commission in 1960, when Sir Gerald

[38] A/PV.550, p. 398; A/3116, p. 45.

[39] Cf. Yearbook, ILC, 5th Session, 1953, I, 294; *ibid.*, 1960, 12th Session, I, 295.

[40] A/C.5/640, 11 Nov. 1955, par. 10; Annexes, 10th Session, 1955, Agenda item 50, p. 13.

[41] Yearbook, ILC, 8th Session, 1956, II, 302; *ibid.*, 9th Session, 1957, II, 145; *ibid.*, 10th Session 1958, I, 180; *ibid.*, 11th Session, 1959, I, 94.

Fitzmaurice observed that he "did not object to the principle but only to the rigid manner in which it had been applied." [42]

In view of the importance of the work of the International Law Commission and the desirability of facilitating full attendance, the obvious solution was for the General Assembly to rescind its rule preventing the Commission from sitting at the same time as the summer session of the Economic and Social Council. During the 14th Session of the Commission, the question was raised in the presence of Mr. Constantin Stavropoulos, Legal Counsel and representative of the Secretary-General, at a private meeting of the Commission on 1 June 1962. With his approval, the Commission decided on the first Monday of May as the most convenient opening date for its regular annual sessions.[43] At the 17th Session of the General Assembly in 1962, the Secretary-General,[44] the Advisory Committee on Administrative and Budgetary Questions,[45] the Fifth Committee,[46] and the Sixth Committee [47] recommended the elimination of the restrictive clause preventing the sessions of the International Law Commission from overlapping those of the Economic and Social Council. By resolution 1851 (XVII), 19 December 1962, the General Assembly removed the restriction.[48]

[42] *Ibid.*, 12th Session, 1960, I, 294–296, 307.

[43] *Ibid.*, 14th Session, 1962, II, 193, Report, par. 83.

[44] A/5317, 1 Dec. 1962, par. 12 and Annex I, GAOR, 17th Session, 1962, Annexes, Agenda item 65.

[45] *Ibid.*, par. 14.

[46] A/5376, 18 Dec. 1962, Report of Fifth Committee, *ibid.*, p. 7, pars. 3 and 6.

[47] A/5287, 14 Nov. 1962, Report of Sixth Committee, par. 56, *ibid.*, Agenda item 76, p. 18.

[48] A/5217, p. 53.

Article 13

Members of the Commission shall be paid travel expenses, and shall also receive a special allowance, the amount of which shall be determined by the General Assembly.

Until amended by General Assembly resolution 485 (V), 12 December 1950, the text of Article 13 had read: "Members of the Commission shall be paid travel expenses and shall also receive a *per diem* allowance at the same rate as the allowance paid to members of commissions of experts of the Economic and Social Council." [1] This original text of Article 13 had been drafted by Sub-Committee 2 of the 1947 Sixth Committee of the General Assembly.[2] The Committee on the Progressive Development of International Law and Its Codification had unanimously recommended "that the members of the International Law Commission should receive a salary proportionate to the dignity and importance of their office" although "there was some difference of opinion whether they should be required to render full-time service." [3] Sub-Committee 2 explained its draft of Article 13 of the proposed Statute in the following terms:

11. The Sub-Committee supported the proposal that the members of the ILC should have the right to be paid their travelling expenses. The Sub-Committee also agreed that the members of the ILC should receive a *per diem* allowance at the same rate as the allowance paid to members of commissions of experts serving the Economic and Social Council. Opinions at first differed as to the amount of that allowance. Several members of the Sub-Committee considered that eminent jurists, who would have to be absent for considerable periods from their important occupations in order to devote their time to the work of the ILC, should receive a larger *per diem* allowance than that granted to members or experts of

[1] A/CN.4/4, 2 Feb. 1949.   [2] A/C.6/193, 18 Nov. 1947, p. 20.
[3] A/AC.10/51, 17 June 1947, par. 5 (d).

other commissions. Since it appeared difficult to fix a definite amount at the present time, it was proposed that the amount be fixed by the competent authorities, taking into consideration the dignity and importance of the office. This suggestion was not, however, adopted because it would involve too many practical difficulties. The idea that members should receive an allowance proportionate to the services rendered to the United Nations was abandoned, and the *per diem* allowance was fixed at the amount paid to experts of United Nations bodies.[4]

At the 58th meeting of the Sixth Committee, Mr. Georges Kaeckenbeeck (Rapporteur) observed, in part:

In the Sub-Committee it had been decided for reasons of economy, that the commission would work on a part-time basis; accordingly the member would not be given a salary and [French text: *ou*] an allowance which would be difficult to estimate. Travel expenses at least, should be reimbursed, and a *per diem* should also be granted, the maximum which the United Nations could pay, so that the world's most eminent jurists might consider it worth while to leave their lucrative employment and give their time for the sake of the commission.[5]

The Secretary-General fixed the *per diem* at $20.

The Report of the International Law Commission to the General Assembly on the work of its 1st Session (1949) contains the following paragraph under the rubric "Emoluments for Members of the Commission":

42. In the view of the majority of the Commission, experience had shown that the *per diem* allowance provided for under article 13 of the Statute of the Commission, is hardly sufficient to meet the living expenses of members. Assuming that the Commission will be in session for at least two months each year, its work will entail for each of the members the sacrifice of a substantial part of his income; for those members who are asked to serve as rap-

[4] A/C.6/193, par. 11.
[5] GAOR, 2nd Session, 1947, Sixth Committee, Summary Records, 156 (58th meeting, 20 Nov. 1947).

porteurs and as such to do extensive work in the interim between sessions of the Commission, it would involve an even greater sacrifice. Since, in fact, most members are dependent on their current earnings, it would be in the interest of the work of the Commission, in order to enable the time of its members to be enlisted in this work, that methods should be explored by which service in the Commission may be made less onerous financially. To this end, the General Assembly may wish to reconsider the terms of article 13 of the Statute of the Commission.[6]

The Sixth Committee discussed this suggestion at its 167th and 168th meetings.[7] In presenting the request to the Sixth Committee, Judge Manley O. Hudson, Chairman of the International Law Commission, observed that it was illogical to put members of the Commission on the same footing as members of the commissions of experts of the Economic and Social Council which met for short periods; he had himself devoted half his time to the work of the Commission since its establishment. In view of "the importance and scope of the International Law Commission's work, it was not sufficient to give its members a *per diem* allowance during the period when they were attending sessions," particularly an allowance that barely enabled them to meet their needs.[8] On 18 October 1949, the Sixth Committee adopted, by a vote of 40–1–7, a resolution approving the views expressed in paragraph 42 of the Report of the International Law Commission and requested the Fifth Committee to study them with a view to the amendment of Article 13 of the Commission's Statute, "bearing in mind the importance of the work of the Commission, the high qualifications of its members and the manner of their election." [9]

Commenting on this request, a Secretariat Report dated 21 October 1949 observed in part:

[6] Yearbook, ILC, 1st Session, 1949, 284–285.

[7] GAOR, 4th Session, 1949, Sixth Committee, Summary Records, 159 ff. (18 Oct. 1949).

[8] *Ibid.*, 159, pars. 30 ff.

[9] *Ibid.*, 165; also A/C.5/320, 18 Oct. 1949, Fifth Committee, Annex, I, 71.

As to the remuneration of members of the Commission, the following alternatives are possible:

(1) To increase payments for members of the Commission, thus establishing an exception for this group as compared with such other groups as expert commissions of the Economic and Social Council. The Secretary-General would hesitate to take such action because it might establish a precedent for other commissions.

(2) As suggested by the Chairman of the International Law Commission in his statement to the Sixth Committee, to compare for purposes of remuneration and subsistence, the members of this Commission to *ad hoc* judges of the International Court of Justice . . . [then calculated at a *per diem* fee of $30, plus subsistence allowance of $20, for a total *per diem* of $50].[10]

When Judge Hudson appeared before the 208th meeting of the Fifth Committee on 26 October 1949, he again questioned the propriety of placing the International Law Commission in the same category as sub-commissions of the Economic and Social Council and suggested the possibility of treating members of the International Law Commission on the same basis as *ad hoc* judges of the International Court of Justice who received allowances in the order of $50 a day.[11] However, the Fifth Committee had received a report from the Advisory Committee on Administrative and Budgetary Questions which had declined to recommend an increase in the *per diem* allowance of members of the International Law Commission beyond the $20 fixed by the Secretary-General,[12] and the Fifth Committee decided to ask the Secretary-General, in consultation with the Advisory Committee, to submit a report setting forth, *inter alia,* any distinguishing factors which would make the International Law Commission different from other United Nations commissions.

This Secretariat and Advisory Committee Report of 9 No-

[10] A/C.5/325, Fifth Committee, Annex, I, 75.
[11] A/C.5/SR.208, 26 Oct. 1949; GAOR, 4th Session, 1949, Fifth Committee, Summary Records, 141.
[12] A/1051, 25 Oct. 1949, Eleventh Report of 1949; *ibid.,* Annex, I, 107.

vember 1949 made a superficial comparison of the International Law Commission with five sub-commissions (such as the Sub-Commission on Statistical Sampling) of the Economic and Social Council, the International Civil Service Advisory Board, the Committees on Contributions and on Investments, and the Advisory Committee on Administrative and Budgetary Questions as to such matters as composition, length of sessions, and method of election or appointment, but completely underestimated the distinctive character of the work of the International Law Commission, the exceptional qualifications required for the performance of that work, and the fact that the International Law Commission was the only organ of those with which it was compared which was endowed with a formal Statute.[13]

The Report proceeded to answer in the negative the questions:

(a) Whether exceptions should be made in the amount of the subsistence allowances paid to the members of expert bodies;

(b) Whether fees of some nature should be paid to the members of the International Law Commission, during the meetings of the Commission, because of any special characteristics of that Commission or its members as compared with other commissions for which subsistence allowances are paid.

The basis was thus firmly laid for treating the International Law Commission as just another sub-commission, and the Fifth Committee declined to recommend any increase in the *per diem* of the International Law Commission.[14] Members of the Sixth Committee expressed their dissatisfaction, but took no action.[15]

[13] A/C.5/347, 9 Nov. 1949, *ibid.*, Annex, I, 90.

[14] A/C.5/SR.222, 11 Nov. 1949, Fifth Committee, Summary Records, 205.

[15] GAOR, 4th Session, 1949, Sixth Committee, Summary Records, 432 ff. (206th meeting, 25 Nov. 1949, pars. 14–51). Cf. also A/1196, 3 Dec. 1949, Report of the Sixth Committee, 4th Session, pars. 30–35, Agenda item 49.

Perhaps the difficulties with which the International Law Commission has been confronted as to the time and place of its meetings, as well as in the matter of its appropriate emoluments, may be traced to the down grading which the Commission is given in this Secretariat-Advisory Committee Report of 9 November 1949. A contrary view of the Commission was expressed in the Sixth Committee by Sir Hartley Shawcross (U.K.):

. . . his Government had regarded the establishment of the International Law Commission, under Article 13 of the Charter, as a step of the greatest importance, both for international law and for the comity of nations. . . . Although the Commission had been established by the General Assembly, it should not be put on the same footing as the other subsidiary organs of the Assembly. . . . His Government regarded the International Law Commission as an organ whose authority and independence in international law were second only to the International Court of Justice.[16]

At its 2nd Session in 1950, members of the International Law Commission criticized their characterization by the Fifth Committee as "experts": they were legal advisers, and, unlike commissions of experts, the International Law Commission was endowed with a formal Statute.[17] In the Report covering its 2nd Session, the Commission again suggested that the General Assembly might wish to reconsider the terms of Article 13 of the Commission's Statute in order to make service on the Commission less onerous financially.[18]

The Assembly's Sixth Committee considered the question

[16] *Ibid.,* 105 (159th meeting, 12 Oct. 1949). See also the remarks of Maurtua (Peru), *ibid.,* 5th Session, 1950, p. 106 (228th meeting, 26 Oct. 1950, pars. 34–36); and Fitzmaurice (U.K.) that "the International Law Commission in its eight years of existence, had established for itself in the legal world a reputation second only to that of the International Court of Justice," *ibid.,* 11th Session, 1956, p. 16 (483rd meeting, 26 Nov. 1956, par. 13).

[17] Yearbook, ILC, 2nd Session, 1950, I, 255–256 (71st meeting, 19 July 1950).

[18] *Ibid.,* II, 367, par. 21.

at its 226th to 229th meetings from 23 to 28 October 1950.[19]
Against the view that members of the International Law Commission should not receive subsistence allowances larger than
those granted other experts, the great majority of delegations
favored a revision of Article 13 of the Commission's Statute.
By a vote of 37–1–6, the Sixth Committee adopted a resolution
which, noting the inadequacy of the emoluments paid to the
members of the International Law Commission, the importance, nature, and scope of their work, the eminence of its
members, and their method of election and the length of sessions, proposed amendment of Article 13 as follows:

Members of the Commission shall be paid travel expenses and
shall also receive a special allowance, the amount of which shall
be determined by the General Assembly.

By an accompanying *voeu,* also adopted on 28 October 1950,
the Sixth Committee recommended that the special allowance
referred to in its resolution should be $35 per day. This *voeu*
was adopted by a vote of 31–8–5, after the power of the Sixth
Committee to fix the amount by resolution had been questioned.[20]

The Fifth Committee debated at its 258th and 259th meetings, on 31 October and 3 November 1950, the question of
subsistence allowances for experts. Having decided that this
allowance should be $25 a day for meetings at Headquarters
and $20 elsewhere, the Committee "on administrative grounds"
refused to recommend special treatment for members of the
International Law Commission, and rejected the *voeu* of the
Sixth Committee.[21]

At the 320th plenary meeting of the General Assembly on

[19] GAOR, 5th Session, 1950, Sixth Committee, Summary Records, 91–
117.

[20] *Ibid.,* 114–117 (229th meeting, 28 Oct. 1950). See also, *ibid.,* Annexes, Agenda item 52, A/1639, 8 Dec. 1950, Report of Sixth Committee,
pars. 6–16.

[21] A/C.5/SR.258, 31 Oct. 1950, and 259, 3 Nov. 1950, pp. 133–141.
See also, A/1648, 9 Dec. 1950, Report of the Fifth Committee on financial

12 December 1950, an amendment was submitted by fifteen States to the Sixth Committee's resolution B (for amendment of Article 13 of the International Law Commission's Statute) providing:

The General Assembly . . .

2. *Fixes* the special allowance for members of the International Law Commission at $35 per day.[22]

This amendment was adopted by a vote of 41–4–12 and the amended resolution amending Article 13 of the Statute of the International Law Commission was then adopted by a vote of 43–2–10.[23] The General Assembly thus exercised its right to increase the emoluments of members of the Commission despite the opposition of the Secretary-General and the Assembly's Fifth Committee.

On 6 August 1954, the Secretary-General, pursuant to General Assembly resolution 775 (VIII) of 27 November 1953, submitted to the Fifth Committee a Report on the System of Allowances to Members of Commissions, etc.[24] Noting the desirability for uniformity in subsistence fees, the Report called attention to the exceptional position of members of the International Law Commission in relation to "the cardinal principle" established by the General Assembly "that there is no element of fee for services rendered in the subsistence allowance." In commenting on this Report, the Advisory Committee on Administrative and Budgetary Questions recommended that no exceptions should be authorized, such as the special allowance for members of the International Law Commission.[25]

The Fifth Committee considered these reports insofar as they

---

implications of resolution B proposed by the Sixth Committee, Annexes, Agenda item 52, p. 14.

[22] A/1640, 8 Dec. 1950, *ibid.*, p. 14.

[23] Res. 485 (V), A/PV.320, 12 Dec. 1950.   [24] A/2687, 6 Aug. 1954.

[25] A/2688, Second Report to the 9th Session, General Assembly, Supplement No. 7, pars. 259–263.

related to the allowance for members of the International Law Commission at its 433rd and 434th meetings on 5 and 6 October 1954. After deciding unanimously that subsistence allowances should, in principle, be uniform, the Committee, by a vote of 21–15–9, decided that the special allowance granted to members of the International Law Commission should be continued during the current term of office of members of the Commission.[26] As adopted by the General Assembly at its 504th plenary meeting, 4 December 1954, paragraph 4 of resolution 875 A (IX) read:

The General Assembly . . .

4. *Decides* that the special allowance of $35 authorized for members of the International Law Commission by resolution 485 (V) of 12 December 1950 should be continued until 31 December 1956, pending consideration by the General Assembly at its eleventh session of the application of a uniform system to all eligible bodies.[27]

The Secretariat returned to the attack in a Report of the Secretary-General on the system of allowances to members of commissions, dated 7 June 1956. Erroneously stating (par. 9) that the special subsistence allowance of members of the International Law Commission was "the only rate of subsistence allowance which varies from the uniform rates laid down in resolution 459 (V)," the Report raises the question whether that special allowance should not be terminated as of 1 January 1957, thus reducing the subsistence allowance of members of the International Law Commission from $35 to $20 *per diem*.[28] The Advisory Committee on Administrative and Budgetary Questions on 3 August 1956 reiterated its position that no exceptions should be permitted to the uniform system and that the "one exception" remaining was the special allowance

[26] A/C.5/SR.434, 6 Oct. 1954.

[27] A/2890, p. 36. The vote in the General Assembly on paragraph 4 was 41–9–3. A/PV.504, p. 360.

[28] A/3130, 7 June 1956, pars. 5–10; GAOR, 11th Session, 1956, Annexes, Agenda item 52.

of the International Law Commission.²⁹ The Fifth Committee at its 534th meeting, on 20 November 1956, adopted the recommendation of the Advisory Committee by a vote of 56–0–12.³⁰ By resolution 1075 (XI) and Annex, unanimously adopted on 7 December 1956,³¹ the General Assembly established a uniform rate of "subsistence" allowances for all eligible bodies and reiterated the principle that a subsistence allowance "shall not include any element of fee or remuneration for services rendered." ³²

Although the International Law Commission was not referred to in this resolution, the Report of the Fifth Committee to the General Assembly expressed the opinion that the resolution applied to the International Law Commission and would discontinue the special allowance of members of that Commission.³³

Members of the Sixth Committee took a different view: the "special" allowance authorized by Article 13 of the International Law Commission's Statute was not identical with the "subsistence" allowance for which uniformity had been established.³⁴ The Sixth Committee therefore adopted, by a vote of 38–0–16, on 18 December 1956, a resolution noting that the reasons which had justified granting a "special" allowance to members of the International Law Commission were still valid, pointing out that resolution 1075 (XI), which dealt only with subsistence allowances, "does not affect Article 13 of the Statute of the International Law Commission," and confirming that "a

²⁹ A/3161, 3 Aug. 1956, pars. 3–4, Third Report to 11th Session General Assembly; *ibid.*, p. 7.

³⁰ A/C.5/SR.534, pars. 27–37. Agenda item 52. Cf. also Report of Fifth Committee to 11th Session, General Assembly, A/3426, 5 Dec. 1956, pars. 3–8, *ibid.*, p. 8.

³¹ A/PV.612, 7 Dec. 1956.

³² A/3572, pp. 39–40.

³³ A/3426, pars. 3–8. Cf. A/3520, 6 Feb. 1957, Report of Sixth Committee, par. 101, Annexes, 11th Session, Agenda item 53.

³⁴ GAOR, 11th Session, 1956, Sixth Committee, Summary Records, 117 (501st meeting, 18 Dec. 1956).

special allowance of $15 per day continues to be payable to members of the Commission, in addition to subsistence allowance at the normal uniform rate." [35]

This resolution was referred back to the Fifth Committee which requested a report from the Advisory Committee on Administrative and Budgetary Questions. The Advisory Committee suggested to the Fifth Committee that the Sixth Committee was interfering with the Fifth Committee's "exclusive competence to initiate and submit proposals of a *purely administrative nature"*; that the special allowance "hitherto" paid to members of the International Law Commission "was invariably regarded as a subsistence allowance which did not carry with it any element of remuneration or fee"; and that it could not concur with the Sixth Committee's proposal "which appears to conflict with the intent of the Assembly that a uniform rate of *subsistence* allowance should be applied without exception." [36]

The Fifth Committee, with some irritation at the Sixth Committee, indulged in a thorough debate of the special allowance of $35 a day granted to members of the International Law Commission.[37] Although Mr. Aghnides, Chairman of the Advisory Committee, insisted that the allowance of $35 was "a subsistence allowance pure and simple, and contained no other elements," [38] and was strongly of the opinion that the International Law Commission should conform to the uniform system, the Fifth Committee backed down to the extent of agreeing that a special allowance of $15 a day, as suggested by the Sixth Committee's resolution, should be continued to members of the Commission for one year (the 1957 session), while the Secretary-General studied "the matter of paying special allowances or honoraria to members of expert bodies of the

35 *Ibid.,* Annexes, Agenda item 53, p. 91.
36 *Ibid.,* 89, A/3497, 14 Jan. 1957. 38th Report, Advisory Committee, etc. Italics added.
37 A/C.5/SR.568, 17 Jan. 1957 and SR.569, 21 Jan. 1957, pp. 207–213.
38 A/C.5/SR.569, par. 17.

United Nations," the report to be submitted to the 12th Session of the General Assembly with the comments of the Advisory Committee thereon.[39]

At its 658th plenary meeting on 21 February 1957, the General Assembly adopted, by a vote of 56-0-12, the Sixth Committee's resolution without the modifications suggested by the Fifth Committee; i.e., General Assembly resolution 1106 (XI) confirms that "a special allowance of $15 per day continues to be payable to the members of the Commission, in addition to subsistence allowance at the normal uniform rate." [40]

In its Report covering the work of its 9th Session (1957), the International Law Commission included three paragraphs dealing with emoluments of members of the Commission. It drew attention to paragraph 42 of its report for 1949, pointed out that the considerations which had led the General Assembly to establish a special allowance for members of the Commission were still operative, and expressed the opinion that the case of each technical commission should be decided on its merits. So far as its own position was concerned the work of the Commission made heavy demands on its members, involving loss of time and money from normal activities for as much as one fourth of a year.[41] Members of the General Assembly's Sixth Committee expressed themselves in favor of maintaining emoluments at existing levels for the International Law Commission.[42]

At its 613th and 615th meetings, in October 1957, the Fifth Committee [43] examined the system of honoraria and special

[39] A/3539, 14 Feb. 1957, Report of the Fifth Committee on financial implications of draft resolution II proposed by Sixth Committee.

[40] A/3572, resolutions adopted by General Assembly, 11th Session, 1956–1957, pp. 54–55.

[41] Yearbook, ILC, 1957, II, 145, pars. 30–32.

[42] Cf. GAOR, 12th Session, 1957, Annexes, Agenda item 53, A/3768, 6 Dec. 1957, Report of the Sixth Committee, par. 13. Cf. A/C.6/SR.510, 30 Sept. 1957, par. 21, p. 10.

[43] A/C.5/SR.613 and 615, 25 and 29 Oct. 1957; GAOR, 12th Session, 1957, Fifth Committee, Summary Records, 67–68, 73–76.

allowances to members of United Nations commissions on the basis of reports from the Secrtary-General [44] and the Advisory Committee on Administrative and Budgetary Questions.[45] In an Annex to the Secretary-General's report, the historical development of special allowances to members of the International Law Commission and others is traced in detail. Despite previous assertions by the Secretary-General [46] and by the Advisory Committee [47] that the "special" allowance of $35 *per diem* granted to members of the International Law Commission was the only exception to the uniform system of "subsistence" allowances, the Secretary-General's Report admitted that the Chairman of the Advisory Committee, Mr. Thanassis Aghnides, had been receiving "a special allowance of $50 per day (inclusive of subsistence allowance at the uniform rate)" during sessions of the Advisory Committee since 1948.[48]

Since Mr. Aghnides had insistently opposed the special allowance for members of the International Law Commission, the information that he himself was receiving one may have simplified the problem of the International Law Commission. The Report of the Advisory Committee submitted to the Fifth Committee on 18 October 1957, while not mentioning Mr. Aghnides' special allowance,[49] suggested that the policy choice lay between (*a*) continuing currently authorized exceptional payments and (*b*) abolishing "altogether these payments, thus treating members of all expert bodies in an identical manner." The Advisory Committee indicated its preference for continu-

---

[44] A/C.5/713, 20 Sept. 1957; *ibid.*, Annexes, Agenda item 41, p. 23.
[45] A/3705, 18 Oct. 1957, 10th Report, *ibid.*, p. 5.
[46] A/3130, 7 June 1956, par. 9.
[47] A/3161, 3 Aug. 1956, par. 4.
[48] A/C.5/713, par. 5 (iv), and Annex, pars. 24–27.
[49] In fact, the report may be in error in stating that, except for the President and members of the Permanent Central Opium Board and the Drug Supervisory Body and the Chairman, Special Rapporteurs and members of the International Law Commission, "the general principle against payment of honoraria to members of United Nations bodies has been maintained." A/3705, pars. 6 and 7.

ing present exceptional payments, but urged that all payments over and above the uniform subsistence allowance should be regarded as honoraria and should be paid in a lump sum.[50]

The Fifth Committee recommended to the General Assembly that there be only two types of payments to members of "expert" bodies: (1) a uniform subsistence allowance; and (2) payments additional to this allowance. The Committee recommended, by a vote of 39–6–10, "that the currently authorized exceptional payments should be continued"; and by other votes, that all exceptional payments should be regarded as honoraria and shall be fixed in terms of an appropriate annual lump sum "calculated on the basis of the normal duration of the meetings of the body concerned" for members in attendance.

On this basis, the Fifth Committee recommended that an annual honorarium of $5,000 should be paid to the Chairman of the Advisory Committee on Administrative and Budgetary Questions and an annual honorarium of $1,000 each to members of the International Law Commission, with a maximum of $2,500 to the Chairman and Special Rapporteurs who prepare specific reports or studies between sessions. The amount of $1,000 for members of the Commission was calculated on the basis of a "special allowance" of $15 *per diem* for a ten-week session.[51]

At its 729th plenary meeting on 13 December 1957, the General Assembly adopted the above-mentioned recommendations of the Fifth Committee by a vote of 48–0–7.[52]

[50] *Ibid.*, pars. 8–10.

[51] A/3766, 5 Dec. 1957, Report of the Fifth Committee to the 12th Session of the General Assembly, pars. 5–6, Annexes, 12th Session, Agenda item 41, p. 60; A/C.5/SR.613 and 615. This "special allowance" is in addition to the standard "subsistence allowance," which, by res. 1588 (XV), 20 Dec. 1960, was increased to $23 *per diem* for meetings held in Geneva and $30 for meetings held in New York, A/4684, p. 56.

[52] GAOR, 12th Session, 1957, Plenary Meetings, p. 592 (Agenda item 41, Report of the Fifth Committee, A/3766), A/PV.729, pars. 4–5.

The financial disadvantage for members of the International Law Commission of calculating their approved special allowance in terms of a fixed annual honorarium based on a ten-week session became apparent in January 1963 when members of the Commission serving on the "sub"-committees on State Responsibility and on Succession of State and Governments in Geneva received no special allowance.[53] If, in response to demands that the Commission should expedite its heavy work schedule, the Commission should meet regularly more than once a year, the question of its emoluments should be examined in less restrictive terms.

By stating in paragraph 4 of its Report of 18 October 1957, that

> 4. The General Assembly has never dissented from the decision of the Fifth Committee that intangible factors, such as importance of the work assigned to an expert body, or the eminence of its membership, cannot appropriately determine the proper level of a *subsistence* allowance,

the Advisory Committee appears to recognize that these factors may appropriately be considered in determining an honorarium.[54]

It may be doubted whether an annual honorarium of $1,000 takes adequate account of such factors for members of the International Law Commission. Experience has demonstrated

---

[53] See A/C.5/939, 29 Oct. 1962, Note of the Secretary-General, estimating "subsistence at the authorized rate of $23 per day for the duration of the meetings"; GAOR, 17th Session, 1962, Annexes, Agenda item 76; A/5278, 5 Nov. 1962, Report of Advisory Committee.

[54] A/3705, 18 Oct. 1957. Italics added. However, in its Report of 25 July 1961, the Advisory Committee again expressed its opposition "to the payment to members of expert bodies of any addition, by way of honorarium, to the normal subsistence allowance." A/4813, par. 3, GAOR, 16th Session, 1961, Annexes, Agenda item 54, pp. 8 ff., with comprehensive review of the question of honoraria, Memorandum by the Secretary-General. See also A/5005, 1 Dec. 1961, Report of Fifth Committee, *ibid.*, p. 14, par. 10, and approval by General Assembly at its 1082nd plenary meeting, 18 Dec. 1961.

that the earlier characterization of the Commission in the category of sub-commissions was misplaced. It would be more in accordance with the dignity and the importance of the Commission's work to provide emoluments for its members in the order of emoluments paid to *ad hoc* judges of the International Court of Justice.

The Statute of the International Law Commission makes no provision for a separate budget for the Commission. The legal, language, and secretarial staff assigned to the Commission in conformity with Article 14 of its Statute is, of course, an expense of the Secretariat. The United Nations Budget Estimates for the Financial Year 1964,[55] under the item "Sessions of the General Assembly, . . . Commissions," contains a line, under the rubric "Travel and other expenses of members" of the International Law Commission, listing *expenses* for 1962 as $84,835; *appropriations* for 1963 as $111,100; and *estimates* for 1964 as $91,500.

Honoraria for Special Rapporteurs

The Annex to the Report of 20 September 1957 of the Secretary-General on the system of honoraria and special allowances of members of commissions sets forth the historical development of the practice of granting honoraria to Special Rapporteurs of the Commission.[56]

Pointing in its 1949 Report to the inadequacy of the *per diem* allowance granted, the International Law Commission stated that its members who served as Special Rapporteurs and did extensive work between sessions had to make an even greater sacrifice of their time and income.[57] In October 1949, the General Assembly's Sixth Committee, approving the views expressed by the Commission, asked the Fifth Committee to study the subject, "bearing in mind the importance of the

[55] GAOR, 18th Session, 1963, Supplement No. 5 (A/5505), p. 10.
[56] A/C.5/713, 20 Sept. 1957, Annexes, Agenda item 41, Annex, pars. 2–8.
[57] Yearbook, ILC, 1949, p. 284, Report, par. 42.

work of the Commission, the high qualifications of its members and the manner of their election." [58]

Although the Fifth Committee, on advice of the Advisory Committee on Administrative and Budgetary Questions and of the Secretary-General, rejected the payment of a special allowance to members of the International Law Commission, it agreed that an honorarium not exceeding $1,500 in any one case would be appropriate for Special Rapporteurs in respect of work performed by them between sessions of the Commission.[59] The General Assembly approved such honoraria for Special Rapporteurs of the International Law Commission.

The Annex to the Secretary-General's Report of 20 September 1957, above mentioned, observes that the recommendation of honoraria for Special Rapporteurs of the International Law Commission "marked an important departure," since

until that time, it had been the accepted practice of the United Nations to entrust technical research projects either to the Secretariat or, where that was not feasible, to outside experts appointed by the Secretary-General for a stipulated fee. Members of commissions or committees had not previously undertaken such projects, and it was the specific provision in the Statute of the International Law Commission concerning the appointment of rapporteurs on selected topics that led the Fifth Committee exceptionally to recommend the payment of research project grants, in the form of honoraria, to the rapporteurs of the International Law Commission.[60]

In a report by the Advisory Committee on Administrative

[58] GAOR, 4th Session, 1949, Sixth Committee, Summary Records, 165 (168th meeting, 18 Oct. 1949, par. 61); A/C.5/320, 19 Oct. 1949.

[59] A/C.6/L.79, Letter dated 14 Nov. 1949, communicating the reply of the Chairman of the Fifth Committee, *ibid.*, Annexes, Agenda item 49, p. 11. See also, A/C.5/SR.208, 26 Oct. 1949 and A/C.5/SR.222, 11 Nov. 1949, GAOR, 4th Session, 1949, Fifth Committee, Summary Records, 140 ff., 205 ff. The Secretary-General had assumed an annual fee of $2,000 for Rapporteurs. See A/C.5/325, 21 Oct. 1949, 5th Committee, Annex, I, 75.

[60] A/C.5/713, Annex, par. 5.

and Budgetary Question to the Fifth Committee on 20 November 1952, that committee submitted a draft resolution—which was later adopted without change by the General Assembly as resolution 677 (VII)—providing:

The General Assembly . . .

Recognizing that the appointment of a person as rapporteur of a United Nations body confers honour upon his country and distinction upon himself,

1. *Considers* that no such appointment should carry remuneration;

2. *Requests* all organs of the United Nations to bear in mind in future the views of the General Assembly as expressed in the present resolution.[61]

The occasion for submitting this resolution was a proposal in the Economic and Social Council to appoint a Rapporteur to make a special study. The General Assembly, despite the adoption of the resolution, made provision for the continued payment during 1953 of honoraria to Special Rapporteurs of the International Law Commission.[62]

In 1953, in its 1st Report to the 8th Session of the General Assembly, the Advisory Committee returned to the attack and suggested that the decision taken in 1949 to pay honoraria to Special Rapporteurs of the International Law Commission should now be reviewed in the light of the General Assembly's resolution 677 (VII) according to which Rapporteurs should not be remunerated.[63] The General Assembly paid no attention to this suggestion.

[61] A/2264, 20 Nov. 1952, 16th Report, on payment of honoraria to Rapporteurs of the United Nations bodies, Agenda item 42, 7th Session, General Assembly, Annexes, p. 62. The Fifth Committee approved the Advisory Committee's draft resolution at its 366th meeting, 21 Nov. 1952, by a vote of 46–0–2, although some representatives regarded it as too rigid. A/C.5/SR.366, pars. 81–87, O.R. pp. 163–164; A/2352, 20 Dec. 1952, Report of Fifth Committee, pars. 27–29, *ibid.*, Annexes, p. 78. The General Assembly unanimously adopted resolution 677 (VII), at its 410th plenary meeting, 21 Dec. 1952, A/2361, p. 52.

[62] A/C.5/713, Annex, par. 7.   [63] A/2403, 30 June 1953, par. 57.

In his report of 6 August 1954 on the system of allowances, the Secretary-General questioned the "absolute terms in which the General Assembly expressed its opinion on the remuneration of rapporteurs" in resolution 677 (VII), and suggested that it might be desirable to amend it so as to conform to the actual practice of paying honoraria "to special rapporteurs for work between sessions as illustrated in the annual appropriations for the International Law Commission." [64] In its 2nd Report of 1954 to the 9th Session of the General Assembly, the Advisory Committee declined to support the proposals of the Secretary-General as regards the International Law Commission and the opium boards because "there is no satisfactory alternative to the position taken by the General Assembly in resolution 677 (VII)" [65]—a resolution which, it will be remembered, the Advisory Committee had itself drafted.

At its 433rd and 434th meetings on 5 and 6 October 1954, the Fifth Committee considered these reports. By a vote of 44–1–2, it accepted the recommendations of the Secretary-General and the Advisory Committee that honoraria should not be paid to Rapporteurs or members of United Nations bodies for work performed during the sessions of those bodies. It then decided by a vote of 26–13–8, that an honorarium should be paid for specific reports prepared between sessions by the Chairman and Rapporteurs of the International Law Commission.[66]

By resolution 875B (IX), adopted at its 504th plenary meeting on 4 December 1954,

The General Assembly

1. *Reaffirms* the provisions of resolution 677 (VII) of 21 December 1952 under which the Assembly considered that no appointment of a rapporteur should carry remuneration;

2. *Decides*, however, that special circumstances exist in the case

[64] A/2687, 6 Aug. 1954, par. 24 B.   [65] A/2688, pars. 264–269.
[66] A/C.5/SR.433, 5 Oct. 1954; A/C.5/SR.434, 6 Oct. 1954, O.R., 9th Session, Fifth Committee, pp. 15–23; A/2814, 30 Nov. 1954, Report of Fifth Committee to 9th Session, General Assembly, pars. 10–17.

of the International Law Commission justifying the payment of honoraria for specific reports prepared by its Chairman or special rapporteurs between sessions of the Commission.[67]

When in 1957 the General Assembly, on recommendation of the Fifth Committee, fixed the honoraria of the Chairman and Rapporteurs of the International Law Commission at $2,500 annually, subject to the preparation of specific reports between sessions, the additional $1,500 above the $1,000 honorarium for members of the Commission was for the preparation of specific reports between sessions.[68] In practice, therefore, the Chairman of the International Law Commission receives no extra allowance unless he is also a Special Rapporteur. The heavy burden placed on a Special Rapporteur of the International Law Commission involves a sacrifice of time and income for which an annual sum of $1,500 appears grossly inadequate.

[67] A/2890, Resolutions adopted by General Assembly, 9th Session, p. 36.

[68] A/PV.729, 13 Dec. 1957, pars. 4–5; A/3766, 5 Dec. 1957, Report of Fifth Committee to 12th Session, General Assembly, par. 6.

Article 14

The Secretary-General shall, so far as he is able, make available staff and facilities required by the Commission to fulfil its task.

The availability of the expert services of the United Nations Secretariat for the International Law Commission was envisaged by paragraph 5 (d) of the Report of the Committee on the Progressive Development of International Law and Its Codification.[1] The actual drafting of Article 14 was by Sub-Committee 2 of the General Assembly's 1947 Sixth Committee.

The Report of Sub-Committee 2 envisaged the relation of the Secretariat to the International Law Commission as not only that of "an administrative body" but also "a center of scientific research." The rejection by the Sub-Committee of a full-time International Law Commission implied, for some members of the Sub-Committee, that the Secretariat should be entrusted with preparatory work for the Commission, even if certain experts were temporarily engaged for this purpose.[2]

The Sub-Committee did not exclude the possibility that the International Law Commission might wish to consult experts outside the Secretariat; but some members of the Sub-Committee feared that specialists, whether or not temporarily attached to the Secretariat, "would be recruited chiefly from near the seat of the Secretariat, [and] the Commission might be given too one-sided advice." By a vote of 10 to 4 the Sub-Committee rejected a proposal that the Commission would consult "only experts recommended by an international scientific institution." [3]

At every session of the International Law Commission, Dr. Yuen-li Liang, Director of the Codification Division of the

[1] A/AC.10/51, 17 June 1947. Cf. also A/AC.10/14, 12 May 1947, Suggestions by the United States, par. 10.
[2] A/C.6/193, 18 Nov. 1947, par. 12.   [3] *Ibid.*, par. 13.

Office of Legal Affairs of the United Nations Secretariat, has·
served as Secretary of the Commission with the assistance of
members of the staff of that division. Dr. Liang, a distinguished
and able international lawyer, has effectively participated in
the work of the Commission, although without a vote. At the
earlier sessions of the Commission, Dr. Ivan S. Kerno, Assistant Secretary-General for Legal Affairs, "represented" the Secretary-General at its meetings. Since 1953, Dr. Liang has also
performed this function. Communications with the Secretary-
General and arrangements for staff and facilities have been
made through Dr. Liang.

As is stated in the commentary on Article 12 of the Commission's Statute, the International Law Commission has held all
of its sessions in Geneva except for its 1st Session which was
held in New York in 1949 and its 6th Session, which was held
in 1954 at UNESCO Headquarters in Paris because of the lack
of available facilities in Geneva. Sessions in Geneva have usually
been held in the Palais des Nations, the European Headquarters
of the United Nations, although, on occasion, the Commission
has met at the International Labor Office.[4]

When the International Law Commission, at its 1954 session, requested the Secretary-General to arrange, as from 1955,
for simultaneous Spanish translations,[5] the Advisory Committee on Administrative and Budgetary Questions opposed it
on grounds of economy: "This service is not available at the
European Office, and Spanish interpreters will have to be assigned from Headquarters." The Advisory Committee, as an
additional argument against Geneva sessions of the International Law Commission, pointed out that, also for reasons of
economy, only three of the ten substantive officers of the Division for the Development and Codification of International

---

[4] In 1961, the Commission, because of the requirements of other
United Nations conferences, was unceremoniously moved during its
session from the Council Chamber to another room in the Palais des
Nations and finally to the International Labor Office.

[5] Yearbook, ILC, 6th Session, 1954, II, 162.

Law are assigned to sessions away from Headquarters.[6] The Secretary-General has quite properly declined to regard economic considerations as the decisive criterion for providing facilities and staff necessary for the Commission to fulfill its task.

General Assembly resolution 175 (II), adopted at its 123rd plenary meeting on 21 November 1947, instructed the Secretary-General "to do the necessary preparatory work for the beginning of the activity of the International Law Commission, particularly with regard to the questions referred to it by the second session of the General Assembly, such as the draft declaration on the rights and duties of States." [7] Pursuant to this resolution, the legal staff of the Secretariat, sometimes with the assistance of international lawyers temporarily engaged for that purpose, prepared a number of noteworthy studies for consideration by the International Law Commission. These studies include:

Survey of International Law in Relation to the Work of Codification of the International Law Commission.[8]

Preparatory Study Concerning a Draft Declaration on the Rights and Duties of States.[9]

The Charter and Judgment of the Nürnberg Tribunal— History and Analysis.[10]

Ways and Means of Making the Evidence of Customary International Law More Readily Available.[11]

Historical Survey of the Question of International Criminal Jurisdiction.[12]

Among memoranda on substantive legal questions which

[6] A/2766, 25 Oct. 1954, 10th Report to the 9th Session of the General Assembly, par. 6.

[7] A/CN.4/4, 2 Feb. 1949, p. 8.

[8] A/CN.4/1, 5 Nov. 1948 and A/CN.4/1/Rev. 1, 10 Feb. 1949. Professor H. Lauterpacht prepared this *Survey.* Cf. Yearbook, ILC, 12th Session, 1960, I, 52, par. 33.

[9] A/CN.4/2, 15 Dec. 1948, and Add. 1, 22 April 1949.

[10] A/CN.4/5, 3 March 1949.   [11] A/CN.4/6, 7 March 1949.

[12] A/CN.4/7, 27 May 1949 (mimeographed), and A/CN.4/7/Rev. 1, 27 May 1949 (printed).

have been prepared for the International Law Commission by
or for the Secretariat, the following may be mentioned:

*Comments on Judge Hudson's Working Paper on Article 24
of the Statute of the International Law Commission.*[13]

*Memorandum présenté par le Secrétariat sur le régime de la
haute mer.*[14]

Memorandum on Arbitral Procedure.[15]

*Memorandum concerning a Draft Code of Offences Against
the Peace and Security of Mankind.*[16]

Survey of the Problem of Multiple Nationality.[17]

*Commentary on the Draft Convention on Arbitral Pro-
cedure adopted by the International Law Commission at its
Fifth Session.*[18]

Diplomatic Intercourse and Immunities.[19]

*Practice of the United Nations in relation to certain ques-
tions raised in connection with the articles on the Law of
Treaties.*[20]

*Juridical Regime of Historic Waters, Including Historic
Bays.*[21]

*Future Work in the Field of the Codification and Progressive
Development of International Law.*[22]

*The Succession of States in Relation to Membership in the
United Nations.*[23]

[13] A/CN.4/27, 6 June 1950; Yearbook, ILC, 1950, II, 33.

[14] A/CN.4/32, 14 July 1950; Yearbook, ILC, 1950, II, 67. Prepared
by Professor Gilbert Gidel.

[15] A/CN.4/35, 21 Nov. 1950; Yearbook, ILC, 1950, II, 157.

[16] A/CN.4/39, 24 Nov. 1950; Yearbook, ILC, 1950, II, 278. This memorandum was prepared by Professor Vespasien V. Pella at the request
of the Secretariat.

[17] A/CN.4/84, 14 May 1954; Yearbook, ILC, 1954, II, 52.

[18] A/CN.4/92, April 1955; later issued as a printed document, 1955.
V. 1.

[19] A/CN.4/98, 21 Feb. 1956; Yearbook, ILC, 1956, II, 129.

[20] A/CN.4/121, 23 June 1959; Yearbook, ILC, 1959, II, 82.

[21] A/CN.4/143, 9 March 1962; Yearbook, ILC, 1962, II, 1.

[22] A/CN.4/145, 22 March 1962; Yearbook, ILC, 1962, II, 84.

[23] A/CN.4/149, 3 Dec. 1962, and Add. 1, 21 June 1963; Yearbook,
ILC, 1962, II, 101.

Succession of States in Relation to General Multilateral Treaties of which the Secretary-General is the Depositary.[24]

Digest of Decisions of International Tribunals Relating to State Succession.[25]

Resolutions of the General Assembly Concerning the Law of Treaties.[26]

Special Missions.[27]

Digest of Decisions of National Courts Relating to the Succession of States and Governments.[28]

State Responsibility—Summary of the discussions in various United Nations organs and the resulting decisions.[29]

Digest of the Decisions of International Tribunals Relating to State Responsibility.[30]

The Secretariat, sometimes with the assistance of international lawyers temporarily engaged for the purpose, has also published for the assistance of the International Law Commission the following volumes in the *United Nations Legislative Series*:

Laws and Regulations on the Regime of the High Seas:

Vol. I, (1) Continental Shelf; (2) Contiguous Zones; (3) Supervision of Foreign Vessels on the High Seas. ST/LEG/SER.B/1, 11 January 1951.

Vol. II, Laws relating to Jurisdiction over Crimes Committed Abroad or on the High Seas. ST/LEG/SER.B/2, 14 December 1951.

Laws and Practices concerning the Conclusion of Treaties. ST/LEG/SER.B/3, December 1952.

Laws Concerning Nationality. ST/LEG/SER.B/4, July 1954.

Laws concerning the Nationality of Ships. ST/LEG/SER.B/5, November 1955.

---

[24] A/CN.4/150, 10 Dec. 1962; Yearbook, ILC, 1962, II, 106.
[25] A/CN.4/151, 3 Dec. 1962; Yearbook, ILC, 1962, II, 131.
[26] A/CN.4/154, 14 Feb. 1963; Yearbook, ILC, 1963, II.
[27] A/CN.4/155, 11 March 1963; Yearbook, ILC, 1963, II.
[28] A/CN.4/157, 18 April 1963; Yearbook, ILC, 1963, II.
[29] A/CN.4/165, 7 February 1964.   [30] A/CN.4/169, 16 April 1964.

Laws and Regulations on the Regime of the Territorial Sea.
    ST/LEG/SER.B/6, December 1956.

*Laws and Regulations regarding Diplomatic and Consular
    Privileges and Immunities.* ST/LEG/SER.B/7, 1958.

*Supplement to Laws and Regulations on the Regime of the
    High Seas (Volumes I and II) and Laws concerning the
    Nationality of Ships.* ST/LEG/SER.B/8, 1959.

*Supplement to the Volume on Laws concerning Nationality,
    1954.* ST/LEG/SER.B/9, 1959.

*Legislative Texts and Treaty Provisions Concerning the
    Legal Status, Privileges and Immunities of International
    Organizations.* ST/LEG/SER.B/10, 1959.

(Same), Vol. II, ST/LEG/SER.B/11, 1961.

The reports of the Special Rapporteurs of the International
Law Commission on the substantive topics they have under
study appear to be their own work, with little or no assistance
from the Secretariat. Although this probably reflects the choice
of Special Rapporteurs rather than any unwillingness on the
part of the Secretariat, Mr. Shuhsi Hsu observed at the 83rd
meeting of the International Law Commission on 17 May
1951:

If the Commission could ask the Secretariat to take over a larger
part of its tasks, it would be spared the necessity of considering
whether there was any occasion for some of its members to serve on
a full-time basis, and the rapporteurs too might possibly be de-
lighted to see their burden lightened. The Legal Department was
the branch of the Secretariat with the smallest staff. If such a task
were assigned it, its staff would have to be increased and the Department would benefit. Since the proposal that all the members
of the Commission be appointed on a full-time basis had been
rejected, the Commission could meet the demands made upon it by
means of more extensive collaboration on the part of the Secretariat.[31]

[31] Yearbook, ILC, 1951, I, 5, par. 22 Cf. Mr. Georges Scelle: "Would
it not be possible to provide the Secretariat with sufficient resources to
enable the rapporteurs to apply to it regularly for the study of certain
points of detail?" *Ibid.,* 9 par. 63. See also below, p. 241.

Publication of the Commission's Records

At the 322nd meeting of the International Law Commission on 29 June 1955, Professor Serge Krylov took the initiative in suggesting the publication of a Yearbook of the International Law Commission.[32] The limited availability and impermanent mimeographed form of authoritative studies and the summary records of the Commission had been a matter of concern to international lawyers both within and outside the United Nations for some years. Supporting the proposal, the Chairman of the Commission, Mr. Spiropoulos, found it "most extraordinary that the deliberations and conclusions of a private body like the Institute of International Law should be given great weight whereas a public body established by the United Nations and with great responsibilities should not publish any of its documents." [33] The Krylov proposal was unanimously adopted by the Commission [34] in terms which requested the General Assembly to consider the possibility of publishing the Commission's documents and summary records in a United Nations Juridical Yearbook.[35]

By resolution 987 (X), 3 December 1955, adopted on the Report of its Sixth Committee,[36] the General Assembly:

1. *Requests* the Secretary-General to arrange as soon as possible for the printing of the following documents relating to the first seven sessions of the International Law Commission:

(a) The studies, special reports, principal draft resolutions and amendments presented to the Commission, in their original languages;

[32] Yearbook, ILC, 7th Session, 1955, I, 238–240.
[33] *Ibid.,* par. 15.
[34] *Ibid.,* 246 (323rd meeting), pars. 63–64.
[35] Cf. *ibid.,* II, 42 (par. 35 of the Commission's Report) for the text of A/CN.4/L. 62/Rev. 1.
[36] GAOR, 10th Session, 1955, Annexes, Agenda item 50, containing, *inter alia*, A/3028, 17 Nov. 1955, Report of the Sixth Committee; A/3052, 1 Dec. 1955, Report of the Fifth Committee on financial implications of A/3028; and the text of the resolution. See also *ibid.,* Sixth Committee, Summary Records, 17–47 (A/C.6/SR.445–452).

(b) The summary records of the Commission, initially in English;

2. *Requests* the Secretary-General also to arrange for the printing each year, in English, French and Spanish, of the documents mentioned in the preceding paragraph relating to future sessions of the Commission;

3. *Invites* the International Law Commission to express its views for the guidance of the Secretary-General with respect to the selection and editing of the documents to be printed. . . .

The International Law Commission discussed the publication of its documentation at its 8th Session in 1956,[37] and in paragraphs 39 to 45 of its Report recommended that the annual publication should be entitled "Yearbook of the International Law Commission"; and that it should consist of three parts: documents issued in preparation of a session; summary records, including working documents issued during a session; and the report on the work of the session. The Commission (par. 42) considered it "indispensable that the report on each session be included in the Yearbook, and also that the latter be provided with an index." [38]

The first volumes of the *Yearbook of the International Law Commission* to appear in print were Volume I for 1956 and a single-volume *Yearbook* for 1949, both of which were published in 1956. By 1963 the series was complete through the 1961 session of the Commission but there has been considerable delay in publishing subsequent volumes. Despite the expression of the Commission's view that it was "indispensable" that the *Yearbook* be provided with an index, no Volume II, containing documents, is indexed; and the *Yearbooks* since 1956 (which has a most inadequate index and no table of contents) have no index whatever. Although not all documents

[37] Yearbook, ILC, 8th Session, 1956, I, 3–4, 14–16 (333rd and 336th meetings).

[38] *Ibid.*, II, 301. See also A/CN.4/L.67, 26 April 1956, Note by the Secretariat on Publication of the Documents of the International Law Commission, *ibid.*, 234.

are printed in the *Yearbooks,* the editing is otherwise commendable except for the difficulties caused by the failure to provide an index for each volume.

The long-delayed publication of the records of the International Law Commission should aid it by encouraging more knowledgeable and constructive criticism of its work.

C. The Codification and Progressive Development of International Law

Article 15

In the following articles the expression "progressive development of international law" is used for convenience as meaning the preparation of draft conventions on subjects which have not yet been regulated by international law or in regard to which the law has not yet been sufficiently developed in the practice of States. Similarly, the expression "codification of international law" is used for convenience as meaning the more precise formulation and systematization of rules of international law in fields where there already has been extensive State practice, precedent and doctrine.

Although this text was drafted by Sub-Committee 2 of the Sixth Committee of the 1947 General Assembly,[1] it follows closely the ideas and phraseology of paragraph 7 of the Report of the Committee on the Progressive Development of International Law and Its Codification.[2]

Stemming from Article 13 (1) (a) of the United Nations Charter, which provides, in part, that "The General Assembly shall initiate studies and make recommendations for the purpose of: (a) . . . encouraging the progressive development of international law and its codification"; and from General Assembly resolution 94 (I) of 11 December 1946, by which the Committee on the Progressive Development of International

[1] A/C.6/193, 18 Nov. 1947.
[2] A/AC.10/51, 17 June 1947; see below, p. 137.

Law and Its Codification was directed "to study (a) the methods by which the General Assembly should encourage the progressive development of international law and its eventual codification," [3] Article 15 of the Commission's Statute attempts to provide a criterion for distinguishing the progressive development of international law from its codification and to lay the foundation for the differing methods deemed applicable to each in the succeeding articles of the Statute.

The desirability of adopting different working methods for codification and for the development of international law was the subject of prolonged controversy in the Committee. In submitting to the Committee a United States proposal on 13 May 1947, Professor Philip C. Jessup observed, in part:

The task of this Commission thus embraces the dual function of planning for the ascertainment and reflection of the existing customary law, and of devising the most appropriate procedures for the development of new law to meet the world's needs.

The methods and procedures, he continued, would vary depending upon whether the task was codification or the development of international law.[4]

The United Nations Secretariat had prepared for the Committee a *Memorandum on Methods for Encouraging the Progressive Development of International Law and Its Eventual Codification* [5] in which codification by international conventions and by scientific restatements had been distinguished. It is there stated:

The convention method . . . has many drawbacks when it is considered as a method for securing international agreement on general rules and principles of international law. The diverse interests of governments makes it difficult for international agreement to be secured concerning the rules of conduct which are to be bind-

[3] A/64/Add. 1, p. 187.
[4] A/AC.10/11, 13 May 1947, p. 5. Cf. also A/AC.10/SR.10 and A/AC. 10/33.
[5] A/AC.10/7, 6 May 1947.

ing upon states in the indefinite future, and covering situ
which cannot be foreseen. Also, the failure of governments t
agreement, for political reasons, in a conference convened tc
rules of international law, would seem to cast doubt upon certain
rules of international law whose validity had been admitted for a
very long time and which had hitherto generally been assumed to
be part of customary international law. The disappointing results
of the first Codification Conference at The Hague in 1930 may, to
a considerable extent, be attributed to the difficulties inherent in
attempting to codify international law by the convention method.[6]

On the other hand, the preparation of scientific restatements
of international law by a committee of jurists functioning
under the United Nations might have utility for judges and
statesmen:

Though lacking the imperative authority of legislative enact-
ments or treaty stipulations, such restatements would commend
themselves by their own intrinsic value, and exercise a persuasive
influence. . . . Their authority will be increased if they are
adopted by resolutions of the General Assembly. . . . [and] the
preparation of such restatements might be considered as a useful
preliminary step which would prepare the ground for the eventual
codification of international law by international agreement.[7]

In the view of the United Kingdom Government, expressed
by Professor J. L. Brierly, the convention method was quite
inappropriate for codification:

. . . codification is, or should be a scientific task, and the disadvantage of attempting to codify the law in conventions is that
the problem then ceases to be scientific and inevitably becomes
predominately [sic] political. . . . Codification is primarily a task
of ascertaining and declaring the law which already exists, and
which is binding on states whether they approve its content in

[6] A/AC.10/7, p. 7.
[7] Ibid., p. 8. Cf. the statements of the representative of the Netherlands in which it was urged that methods of codification by scientific restatement and by international convention could be combined in one
system. A/AC.10/18, 14 May 1947 and A/AC.10/23, 16 May 1947.

every detail or not. It is true that it must necessarily involve the correction of minor inconsistencies in the existing rules of the law and the filling of lacunae for which these rules do not provide, and the distinction between legislation and codification can, therefore, not be a strictly scientific one. None the less the distinction is broadly true; the main purpose of codification is not to find rules which are acceptable to the parties, which is inevitably the first consideration in a convention, but to state what the rules already are.[8]

The representative of Sweden, Mr. Erik Sjöborg, opposed the codification of existing international law by international conferences by quoting from a letter of the Swedish Government to the League of Nations, 6 July 1931:

The Swedish Government considers that it is not to a codification conference that one should assign the task of defining the scope and effect of existing customary law. This task, in its opinion belongs rather to the international courts and writers on doctrine. A codification conference should adopt such principles as it deems necessary and valuable without deciding whether their adoption constitutes a consecration or a revision of existing customary law.[9]

He also quoted with approval from the letter of 21 August 1931, of the Swiss Government to the League of Nations:

It is not the task of a codification conference to register existing international law, but to lay down rules which it would appear desirable to introduce into international relations in regard to the subjects dealt with. Their work should, therefore, mark an advance on the present state of international law. In certain cases, indeed, it would be extremely difficult to say what the existing law really is, as it is not clearly known or is a matter of controversy. It would be most unfortunate if the attempt to discover an adequate solution of an important problem were abandoned on the ground that no such solution is to be found in the existing positive law. One of the fundamental tasks of codification conferences should be to choose between disputed rules and, within the limits of their

[8] A/AC.10/16, 12 May 1947, pp. 2–3.
[9] A/AC.10/24, 16 May 1947, p. 4.

agenda, to fill up the gaps in a law whose deficiencies and obscurities are obvious.)

Attempts to restate the existing law, continued the Swiss letter, would run into the difficulty that agreement might be unattainable without mutual concessions; and the law emerging from such bargains would be a retrograde compromise, not a reflection of the law in force.[10]

The Swedish Government was prepared to support the method of scientific restatement of existing law by an impartial group of jurists, but opposed the submission of the results of their studies to the General Assembly for approval. The Swedish proposal then seems to confuse the issue by suggesting that the scientific restatements of the jurists should be submitted to an *ad hoc* international conference whose function would be "not to reach any conclusions on the content of the experts' statements, but to draw up conventions instituting rules which the contracting parties consider necessary or expedient and with which they undertake to comply without specifying, however, whether such rules are part of existing customary law or not." [11] Essentially, the Swedish position set forth appeared to express a preference for progressive development over the codification of international law.

At the 4th meeting of the Committee, on 15 May 1947, Professor Vladimir Koretsky (U.S.S.R.) questioned whether it was necessary to make such a marked distinction between development and codification of international law as his colleagues had done: [12]

In his opinion codification was not only registering what exists

[10] *Ibid.,* pp. 4–5, and A/AC.10/5, pp. 86–87.

[11] *Ibid.,* p. 3 and A/AC.10/SR.3, 14 May 1947. Cf. the later statement of Mr. Sjöborg at the 10th meeting on 23 May 1947: "After the failure of the 1930 Codification Conference no one in the League of Nations had any doubt that the method of conventions was the only one that could be used." A/AC. 10/SR.10, p. 5, and below, p. 137, n. 20.

[12] A/AC.10/SR.4, 15 May 1947, p. 5 and Add. 1, 28 May 1947.

but more, the noting of what had [not] [13] been done, the cleansing of existing law of its errors and the proceeding to the laying down of new rules. Codification should reflect the ideals of peace, justice, freedom, equality, etc., the principles upheld by every true democracy. This aim would be achieved by giving the existing law new forms and adapting it to new systems.

Professor Koretsky concluded that the same method should be applied to both codification and the progressive development of international law: "In order to arrive at obligatory norms it would be necessary to conclude international conventions." [14]

In reply, Professor Brierly pointed out at the 6th meeting on 20 May 1947, that the "development of international law" was a broader concept than that of codification. The development of international law included, as the Secretariat Memorandum A/AC.10/7 had suggested, the preparation of uniform treaty clauses, encouragement of ratifications and accessions, encouraging the development of customary international law through the judicial process as well as its extension by international legislation, i.e., by the conclusion of international conventions to regulate fields of activity on which no agreed rules exist.

Only one of these methods of developing international law, namely, international legislation, had any relation to codification. The question, therefore, was whether sufficient distinction existed between legislation and codification to justify devising different procedures in relation to them. He restated the problem as follows:

The distinction ordinarily made is that codification is the process of declaring the existing law, legislation is its extension into new

[13] Note the French translation: *"Selon lui, codifier n'est pas seulement enregistrer ce qui existe, c'est surtout indiquer ce qui n'a pas été fait, épurer le droit existant,"* etc.

[14] *Ibid.*, p. 6. Cf. also later statement by Professor Koretsky on 22 May 1947, A/AC.10/32, 23 May 1947, and A/AC.10/SR.9, 22 May 1947, pp. 12–15.

fields. Now some members of the Committee have very properly pointed out that codification cannot be absolutely limited to declaring the existing law. As soon as you set out to do this, you discover that the existing law is often uncertain, that for one reason or another there are gaps in it which are not covered. If you were to disregard these uncertainties and these gaps and simply include in your code, rules of existing law which are absolutely certain and clear, the work would have little value. Hence, the codifier, if he is competent for his work, will make suggestions of his own; where the rule is uncertain, he will suggest which is the better view; where a gap exists, he will suggest how it can best be filled. If he makes it clear what he is doing, tabulates the existing authorities, fairly examines the arguments pro and con, he will be doing his work properly. But it is true that in this aspect of his work he will be suggesting legislation—he will be working on the *lex ferenda,* not on the *lex lata*—he will be extending the law and not merely stating the law that already exists.

But it does not follow from this fact that codification necessarily involves a certain measure of developing the law by legislation, that, therefore, legislation and codification are merely two names for the same process. The difference may be one of degree only, but it is important all the same, . . . and I submit . . . that in codification, which is primarily though not exclusively concerned with stating the *existing* law, one method is the most useful, and that in legislation, where the question what is the existing law is unimportant and the aim is to create law in the future as it ought to be, another method of working is to be preferred.[15]

After further debate, the Committee failed to adopt the report of a sub-committee which appeared to embody the Soviet thesis in the following form: [16]

[15] A/AC.10/30, 20 May 1947, pp. 2–3, and A/AC.10/SR.6, pp. 3–4. Cf. also the views expressed by Professor Brierly at the 10th meeting on 23 May 1947, A/AC.10/35, 28 May 1947, and A/AC.10/SR.10.

[16] A/AC.10/SR.12, p. 1 (meeting of 27 May 1947). Although the record states on p. 1, that the text was "adopted unanimously by the Sub-Committee," on p. 7 it is stated that the members of the Sub-Committee were divided on whether "the same procedures should be followed for the codification of international law as for its progressive development."

That the Commission in carrying out its activities concerning the codification of international law shall present its recommendations to the General Assembly if it finds that codification of the subject is desirable or necessary, in the form of drafts of multipartite conventions.

Instead of putting this proposal to a vote, the Chairman asked the Committee to vote on a Soviet motion to delete the words in parentheses in the introductory part of the joint proposal by the United States and China defining the progressive development of international law as follows:

I. For Progressive Development (which contemplates the extension of law to new areas not yet regulated by law or in which the law has not yet been highly developed or formulated in the practice of states).[17]

The Soviet motion to delete was lost by a vote of 4 (for)-8 (against)-3 (abstentions), and the Chairman declared "the whole of the introductory part" adopted.[18]

The corresponding definition of codification of international law was adopted at the 14th meeting on 29 May 1947, by a vote of 11–0–4, as follows:

For codification (which, as regards the methods referred to below, contemplates the more precise formulation and the more systematic arrangement of the law in areas where there has been extensive state practice, precedent and doctrine).[19]

After thus establishing the distinction between the progres-

In any case, the Chairman stated "that it was too early to take any decision on the report submitted by the Sub-Committee" (p. 3) and "that this report had not yet been adopted by the plenary Committee" (p. 7). Professor Koretsky's later assertion, on 29 May 1947, that the Committee had adopted on 27 May the Sub-Committee's Report proposing "that all recommendations to the General Assembly should be worked out in the form of a multipartite convention" was denied by the Chairman on the basis of the record. A/AC.10/SR.15, pp. 11–12. Cf. also *ibid.*, pp. 1–2.

[17] A/AC.10/33, 23 May 1947, p. 3.   [18] A/AC.10/SR.12, p. 7.
[19] A/AC.10/SR. 14, pp. 5–8.

sive development of international law and codification, the Committee proceeded to debate and adopt the differing procedures considered suitable for each.

As regards its recommendation which was embodied in Article 15 of the Statute of the International Law Commission, the Committee's Report read as follows:

7. The Committee recognized that the tasks entrusted by the General Assembly to the ILC might vary in their nature. Some of the tasks might involve the drafting of a convention on a subject which has not yet been regulated by international law or in regard to which the law has not yet been highly developed or formulated in the practice of states. Other tasks might on the other hand involve the more precise formulation and systematization of the law in areas where there has been extensive state practice, precedent and doctrine. For convenience of reference, the Committee has referred to the first type of task as "progressive development" and to the second type of task as "codification," and it suggests the following procedures which it considers would be appropriate respectively in each of these cases. The Committee recognizes that the terms employed are not mutually exclusive, as, for example, in cases where formulation and systematization of the existing law may lead to the conclusion that some new rule should be suggested for adoption by states. . . .[20]

10. For the codification of international law, the Committee recognized that no clear-cut distinction between the formulation of the law as it is and the law as it ought to be could be rigidly maintained in practice. It was pointed out that in any work of codification, the codifier inevitably has to fill in gaps and amend

[20] A/AC.10/51, 17 June 1947, par. 7. The representative of Sweden dissented, in his statement annexed to the Summary Record of 11 June 1947, A/AC.10/SR.24, pp. 14–15, from the view that codification might take place through scientific restatements. In his view, the General Assembly would be infringing both the sovereignty of States and the competence of the International Court of Justice to state existing law if the Assembly were to adopt by resolution a report of the International Law Commission "tending to establish the content of existing international law." He believed the convention method alone satisfactory for codification as well as for progressive development.

the law in the light of new developments. The Committee, by a majority vote, however, agreed that for the purposes of procedures adopted below, the definition given in paragraph 7 above would be applicable.[21]

Sub-Committee 2 of the 1947 Sixth Committee of the General Assembly "adopted" by a vote of 14 to 1 (Sweden) paragraph 7 of the Report of the Committee on the Progressive Development of International Law and Its Codification and proceeded to draft Article 15 of the International Law Commission's Statute.[22]

The Sixth Committee considered at its 58th meeting on 20 November 1947, a Soviet amendment (no. 4) the purpose of which was to require that the convention method be used by the International Law Commission for the codification of international law as well as for its progressive development. The amendment was rejected by a vote of 25 to 9,[23] although several representatives had questioned the utility, or even the possibility, of maintaining a rigid distinction between codification and progressive development of international law.[24]

During its 3rd session in 1951, the International Law Commission in the course of reviewing its Statute pursuant to General Assembly resolution 484 (V),[25] considered the question of the distinction between the codification and the progressive development of international law.[26] Judge Hudson observed:

The Commission's Statute established a very sharp distinction between the development of international law and its codification. But in practice, there could be no codification without development. He would be in favour of minimizing the distinction by adopting the same procedure for both.[27]

21 A/AC.10/51, par. 10.   22 A/C.6/193, 18 Nov. 1947, par. 15.
23 GAOR, 2nd Session, 1947, Sixth Committee, Summary Records, 151. The text of the proposed Soviet amendment is in A/C.6/199, 19 Nov. 1947, par. 4. *Ibid.*, 205.
24 *Ibid.*, 4 ff. (37th and 38th meetings, 25 and 26 Sept. 1947).
25 Text in Yearbook, ILC, 3rd Session, 1951, II, 137.
26 *Ibid.*, I, 123, 132–135, 260.   27 *Ibid.*, 123, par. 120.

That would avoid, he added, "the Commission's having to decide in each case whether the subject dealt with was progressive development or codification."[28] The suggestion commanded wide support in the Commission.[29]

However, Dr. Ivan Kerno, Assistant Secretary-General, while agreeing that the procedures could be made more flexible, stated that the "fundamental difference between progressive development and codification was that, in the case of the former the initiative lay with the General Assembly alone, while in regard to the latter it was shared with the Commission."[30] Dr. Yuen-li Liang, Secretary of the Commission, admitting that the distinction "was hardly defensible scientifically," explained that at the time the Statute was being drafted the main preoccupation had been to avoid enshrining the method of codification by international convention as the sole method for codification. Article 23 was "the keystone of the Statute," and it recognized the possibility of codification by scientific restatements.[31] As for the distinction in the Statute between codification and progressive development, "it had been adopted after two and a half months of reflection, and its adoption had been the only means of obtaining Mr. Koretsky's support." Advocating the method of international conventions in all cases, Mr. Koretsky's views had been met in the Statute as to progressive development but he had been induced to agree to scientific restatements among other methods, for codification.[32]

Mr. Spiropoulos defended the distinction between codification and development and denied that it had hampered the Commission's work, although it was too rigid.[33] Professor Brierly agreed that "the distinction should be maintained, but that the Statute should be improved by making the procedure laid down for the two cases more flexible."[34]

[28] *Ibid.*, 132, par. 133.
[29] *Ibid.*, 133, par. 149.
[30] *Ibid.*, 132, par. 135.
[31] *Ibid.*, 132–133.
[32] *Ibid.*, 134, par. 156.
[33] *Ibid.*, 133, par. 151.
[34] *Ibid.*, 134, par. 159.

On reconsideration, the Commission decided to state in its Report to the General Assembly that

on the whole the Commission is unable to say that either lack of clarity in the statutory provisions, or inflexibility of the procedures prescribed, has interfered with its achievement of "rapid and positive results." [35]

The tactical reason for not pressing for greater flexibility in the procedures for progressive development and for codification probably lay in the fact that the Commission was recommending in the same Report that it be put on a full-time basis and preferred to await a decision on that question before suggesting other amendments to its Statute.

Two years later, in its 1953 Report, the Commission, pointing out that its *Draft Convention on Arbitral Procedure* fell within the category both of the progressive development and the codification of international law, added:

It is probable that the same cumulation of functions must apply, in varying proportions, to other aspects of the work of the Commission. Thus, the position is similar with respect to the questions of the continental shelf and of statelessness covered by chapters III and IV of the report.[36]

By the time of its 1956 Report, the Commission had come to the conclusion that in "preparing its rules on the law of the sea, the Commission has become convinced that, in this domain at any rate, the distinction established in the Statute between these two activities [codification and development] can hardly be maintained." [37]

The considerations, based on its experience, which led the International Law Commission to conclude that the distinctions established in its Statute between codification and progressive development of international law are unsuitable for

[35] *Ibid.,* II, 139, par. 71 of the Report.
[36] Yearbook, ILC, 5th Session, 1953, II, 208, par. 54.
[37] Yearbook, ILC, 8th Session, 1956, II, 255, par. 26. Cf. below pp. 299 ff.

practical application are discussed below in more detail in Chapter 3 (pp. 276 ff.) on "Recommendations of the International Law Commission to the General Assembly." It was foreseen from the outset that the distinction was basically and practically unsound, but political considerations had dictated its incorporation in the Statute. The lessons of experience suggest that Articles 15 to 23 of the Commission's Statute might advantageously be redrafted to provide more flexibility in the procedural methods for codification and progressive development of international law.

Progressive Development
of International Law

Article 16

When the General Assembly refers to the Commission a proposal for the progressive development of international law, the Commission shall follow in general a procedure on the following lines:

(*a*) It shall appoint one of its members to be Rapporteur;

(*b*) It shall formulate a plan of work;

(*c*) It shall circulate a questionnaire to the Governments, and shall invite them to supply within a fixed period of time data and information relevant to items included in the plan of work;

(*d*) It may appoint some of its members to work with the Rapporteur on the preparation of drafts pending receipt of replies to this questionnaire;

(*e*) It may consult with scientific institutions and individual experts; these experts need not necessarily be nationals of Members of the United Nations. The Secretary-General will provide, when necessary and within the limits of the budget, for the expenses of these consultations of experts;

(*f*) It shall consider the drafts proposed by the Rapporteur;

(*g*) When the Commission considers a draft to be satisfactory, it shall request the Secretary-General to issue it as a Commission document. The Secretariat shall give all necessary publicity to this document which shall be accompanied by such explanations and supporting material as the Commission considers appropriate. The publication shall include any information supplied to the Commission in reply to the questionnaire referred to in sub-paragraph (*c*) above;

(*h*) The Commission shall invite the Governments to submit their comments on this document within a reasonable time;

(*i*) The Rapporteur and the members appointed for that

purpose shall reconsider the draft taking into consideration these comments and shall prepare a final draft and explanatory report which they shall submit for consideration and adoption by the Commission;

(*j*) The Commission shall submit the draft so adopted with its recommendations through the Secretary-General to the General Assembly.

The texts of Articles 16 and 17 of the Commission's Statute were drafted by Sub-Committee 2 of the 1947 Sixth Committee and followed generally the proposals of the Committee on the Progressive Development of International Law and Its Codification with certain changes indicated below.

The principal point at issue was whether the General Assembly or the International Law Commission should decide what questions should be examined by the Commission in its function of developing international law. The Soviet view, – repeatedly expressed by Professor Koretsky before the Committee on the Progressive Development of International Law and Its Codification, was that the General Assembly should determine the topics both for progressive development and for codification.[1] In opposing a joint United States–Chinese proposal that the International Law Commission might include in its program for the progressive development of international law (A) projects referred by the General Assembly, (B) projects recommended through the Secretary-General by governments, by United Nations organs other than the General Assembly, by specialized agencies, or by certain other international organizations, and (C) topics initiated by the International Law Commission itself,[2] Professor Koretsky observed that it would be for the General Assembly "to issue instructions" to the International Law Commission "and to choose the topics where rules of international law were needed"; "every draft must first

[1] A/AC.10/SR.4, p. 7; A/AC.10/SR.6, p. 9; A/AC.10/SR. 11, p. 9; A/AC.10/SR.13, pp. 13–15; A/AC.10/SR.14, p. 10.
[2] Cf. A/AC.10/33, 23 May 1947, pp. 3–5.

be considered from the political aspect"; "every draft or subject should first be examined by the political body." [3] The initiative should be in the General Assembly and not left to the Commission.[4]

Since the Committee had adopted [5] point (B) of the United States–Chinese proposal (which was later embodied in Article 17 of the Commission's Statute), Professor Jessup suggested the omission of point (C) for the practical reason that the Commission, which was to be set up for an initial period of three years, would have enough work assigned to it: "He definitely did not wish to be understood as having dropped the principle that the Commission should take the initiative in its work." [6] When Professor Koretsky later suggested that the same practical reasons adverted to by Professor Jessup applied equally to the Commission's initiative with regard to topics for codification, and proposed the deletion of this "right of initiative," Professor Jessup stated that his sacrifice of the initiative of the Commission with regard to the development of international law "was made with an eye to the Commission's work in the field of codification." [7]

Professor Koretsky did not press for a vote on his proposal and opposed a United States proposal, adopted by the Committee by a vote of 13 to 3, which recommended that the General Assembly adopt a resolution instructing the Commission "to survey the whole field of customary International Law with a view to selecting topics for codification." [8]

The Statute of the Commission has been interpreted as giving the Commission the right to initiate projects for the codification but not for the progressive development of international law.[9] Proposals for the progressive development of international law come, by Article 16 of the Statute, from the Assembly or, by Article 17, are transmitted to the Commission by

[3] A/AC.10/SR.13, pp. 13, 15.   [4] A/AC.10/SR.14, p. 10.
[5] Cf. A/AC.10/SR.13, and below, p. 154.   [6] A/AC.10/SR.14, p. 4.
[7] *Ibid.*, p. 5.   [8] *Ibid.*, p. 6.
[9] See above, p. 139 and below, pp. 168, 171.

the Secretary-General of the United Nations on the submission of Members of the United Nations, the principal organs of the United Nations other than the General Assembly, specialized agencies or certain official bodies established by inter-governmental agreement. Neither article explicitly recognizes a right of initiative in the Commission, but, while Article 16 appears to require the Commission to proceed with the topic proposed by the General Assembly, Article 17 gives the Commission the discretion to decide whether it deems it appropriate to proceed with the study of proposals submitted to it.

At the 96th and 97th meetings of the International Law Commission on 5 and 6 June 1951, when it was considering possible recommendations for the revision of its Statute, Mr. El-Khouri, "in order to render the work of the Commission more fruitful," proposed that Article 1 of the Commission's Statute be amended by adding: "The Commission may discuss and submit to the General Assembly proposals of a legislative character." No action was taken on the proposal which was intended to confer on the Commission an initiative in proposing projects for the progressive development of international law.[10]

Fears expressed by members of the Committee on the Progressive Development of International Law and its Codification that, without close contact with the views of governments, the International Law Commission might become a body of "jurists shut up in an ivory tower," [11] "might be inclined to depart from the requirements of international law as practiced by states," [12] or might become "an olympic oracle endowed with greater powers than governments themselves had," [13] influ-

[10] Yearbook, ILC, 3rd Session, 1951, I, 122, 133.
[11] Mr. Amado (Brazil), A/AC.10/28, 19 May 1947, p. 2.
[12] Mr. de Beus (Netherlands), A/AC.10/23, 16 May 1947, p. 4.
[13] Mr. Koretsky (U.S.S.R.), A/AC.10/SR.4, 16 May 1947, p. 7 Cf. also A/AC.10/SR.15, 30 May 1947, pp. 4 ff., and similar views that the jurists on the Commission should not lose contact with political realities expressed in the Sixth Committee of the General Assembly. GAOR, 2nd Session, 1947, Sixth Committee, Summary Records, 6, 10.

enced the fourfold relationship established by Article 16 between the work of the Commission and the views of governments with reference to the development of international law:

1. Governments seek the support of the General Assembly for reference of a particular proposal to the International Law Commission.

2. Governments have the opportunity of providing the Commission with data and information reflecting the national view as to relevant questions of international law by replying to the questionnaires provided for by Article 16 (*c*).

3. Governments have the opportunity under Article 16 (*h*), of submitting their observations on the drafts prepared by the International Law Commission, and the Commission is required by Article 16 (*i*) to take into consideration these comments.

4. Governments participate in the formulation of the decisions of the General Assembly with regard to the final reports of the Commission on a particular subject.

This mutually beneficial relationship between governments and the Commission, is complemented by the freedom of action of the Commission to formulate and carry out a plan of work, to exercise its expert judgment in the preparation of drafts, and, in its discretion, to consult with scientific institutions and individual experts.

In the Committee on the Progressive Development of International Law and Its Codification, Professor Koretsky had strongly opposed [14] the United States–Chinese proposal that the Rapporteur appointed by the Commission need not be a member of the Commission.[15] The Committee nevertheless rejected a Yugoslav motion to delete this provision by a vote of 4(to delete)–11–0,[16] and later confirmed this decision by a vote

[14] A/AC.10/SR.11, p. 8.

[15] A/AC.10/33, p. 3, (A.1.) Professor Jessup had expressed the opinion that each Rapporteur should be an expert in his subject and, therefore, not necessarily a member of the Commission. A/AC.10/SR.12, p. 8.

[16] A/AC.10/SR.12, meeting of 27 May 1947, p. 8.

of 7(to limit Rapporteurs to members of the Commission)–8 (against)–1(abstention).[17] Sub-Committee 2 of the 1947 Sixth Committee rejected the recommendation of the Committee and drafted Article 16 (*a*) to read: "The Commission shall appoint one of its members to be Rapporteur." They preferred not to "depart from the practice generally followed by international commissions as well as by other organs of the United Nations" and thought it unlikely that "amongst the eminent jurists composing the Commission, no one can be found capable of acting as Rapporteur." [18]

For the same reasons, Sub-Committee 2, in drafting Article 16 (*d*), rejected the Committee's recommendation that membership on sub-committees appointed to work with the Rapporteur need not be limited to members of the Commission.[19]

On the other hand, Sub-Committee 2 sustained the Committee on the Progressive Deveolpment of International Law and Its Codification in its decision that the Commission should have wide freedom to consult scientific institutions and individual experts. This freedom had been opposed by Professor Koretsky in the Committee.[20] The question had been reopened in Sub-Committee 2 and its Report contains the following observations:

Some members of the Sub-Committee were doubtful about consulting specialists, whether these were attached temporarily to the Secretariat, or the Commission applied to them directly. They were afraid that by consulting specialists, who would inevitably be very few in number, and who, if only for reasons of economy, would be recruited chiefly from near the seat of the Secretariat, the Commission might be given too one-sided advice. For this reason it was suggested that it be made a rule that the Commission

[17] A/AC.10/SR.24, meeting of 11 June 1947, pp. 8–9. Cf. Report, A/AC.10/51, par. 8 (a).

[18] A/C.6/193, p. 10.

[19] *Ibid.* Cf. Report, A/AC.10/51, par. 8 (d); and A/AC.10/SR, 13. pp. 2–3; and A/AC.10/SR.24, pp. 10–11, for the views of Professor Koretsky.

[20] A/AC.10/SR.13, pp. 3–5.

may apply for advice only to international scientific institutions. The idea that only experts recommended by an international scientific institution may be consulted by the Commission, was rejected by ten votes to four. The majority considered that the Commission should not be denied the right to choose for itself the experts whom it thought the best qualified. . . .[21]

Sub-Committee 2 therefore drafted Article 16 (e) to establish this freedom of consultation. A Soviet proposal to delete the second sentence of Article 16 (e) was rejected by the Sixth Committee at its 58th meeting on 20 November 1947, by a vote of 26 to 6.[22]

The Commission has not regarded the right of consultation given to it by Article 16 (e) and, by implication, by Article 21 of its Statute, as conferring on any individual the right to be heard by the Commission. At its 9th meeting, on 25 April 1949, the Commission was confronted with a request from Mr. Victor A. Belaúnde, Chairman of the Peruvian delegation to the General Assembly, to be heard by the Commission on the subject of the *Draft Declaration on Rights and Duties of States,* a subject on which he had been Rapporteur at the 9th International Conference of American States at Bogotá in 1948. Members of the Commission thought it should be careful not to establish a precedent granting persons or organizations the right to be heard when the Statute granted no such right. It was decided that Mr. Belaúnde should be invited to meet informally with members of the Commission prior to the opening of the next meeting.[23] The minutes of the 10th meeting of the Commission, on 26 April 1949, record that "before the meeting was called to order," Mr. Belaúnde was invited to respond to a series of questions put to him by the Chairman of the Commission, Judge Hudson, and then he withdrew.[24]

At the 283rd meeting of the Commission, on 3 May 1955, a

[21] A/C.6/193, p. 8 (par. 13).
[22] GAOR, 2nd Session, 1947, Sixth Committee, Summary Records 152 (Soviet amendment 5).
[23] Yearbook, ILC, 1st Session, 1949, pp. 69–70.   [24] *Ibid.,* 76.

proposal by Mr. Krylov to allow Mr. J. Balicki, "the observer for Poland at the Commission's seventh session," to address the Commission, presumably on the Polish charge of piracy in the China seas, was rejected by the Commission, by a vote of 6–3–1, on the ground expressed by the Chairman (Mr. Sandström):

> The methods of communication between governments and the Commission had been set forth in the Commission's Statutes and it was quite clear that they contained no provision for oral communications. It would therefore, be contrary to the Statutes to accede to Mr. Krylov's request.[25]

At the invitation of the Chairman of the Commission, Mr. Manuel S. Canyes, Observer for the Pan American Union, was invited to address the 357th meeting of the Commission on 31 May 1956,[26] and it has now become customary practice for the Commission or its chairman to invite observers from Inter-American organs or from the Asian African Legal Consultative Committee to make a statement to the Commission.[27] Professors Milton Katz, Louis B. Sohn and R. R. Baxter of the Harvard Law School were invited by the Commission to comment on the draft on Responsibility of States being prepared under the auspices of the Harvard Law School at the invitation of Dr. Yuen-li Liang, Secretary of the Commission.[28]

Consultation of experts has taken place pursuant to decisions of the Commission or on the initiative of its individual members. As Special Rapporteur on the topic, *Nationality, including Statelessness,* Judge Manley O. Hudson reported to the Commission that he had

[25] Yearbook, ILC, 7th Session, 1955, I, 6–7. Cf. also *ibid.,* 25–26.

[26] Yearbook, ILC, 8th Session, 1956, I, 130.

[27] See, e.g., Yearbook, ILC, 12th Session, 1960, I, 264–266, statement of Dr. Antonio Gomez Robledo, Observer for the Inter-American Juridical Committee; *ibid.,* 13th Session, 1961, I, 97, statement of Dr. José J. Caicedo Castilla, Observer for the Inter-American Juridical Committee; *ibid.,* 15th Session, 1963, I, 202, statement of Justice Thambiah, Observer for the Asian African Legal Consultative Committee.

[28] Yearbook, ILC, 8th Session, 1956, I, 248–249; *ibid.,* 11th Session, 1959, I, 147–148, 152–154; *ibid.,* 12th Session, 1960, I, 266–268.

promptly placed himself in contact with the United Nations High Commissioner for Refugees, to avail himself of the High Commissioner's generous offer of assistance to the Commission. The High Commissioner was good enough to request Dr. Paul Weis to render assistance to the special rapporteur. Dr. Weis arrived in Cambridge, Massachusetts, on 6 October 1951, and devoted seven weeks to working with the special rapporteur.[29]

At the 173rd meeting of the Commission, on 28 July 1952, the Chairman announced "that, as the outcome of an informal meeting of the Commission," Judge Hudson had submitted the following proposal:

In reliance on article 16 (*e*) and article 21 (1) of its Statute, the Commission decides to invite Dr. Ivan Kerno to serve, after his separation from the Secretariat, as an individual expert of the Commission charged with work on the elimination or reduction of statelessness, under the general direction of the Chairman of the Commission.

It also decides to report the above decision to the Secretary-General.

Mr. Kozhevnikov opposed the principle of appointing an Assistant Rapporteur who was not a member of the Commission. By a vote of 11 to 2 the Commission decided that it "could appoint individuals to serve as experts on the Commission, in reliance on article 16 (*e*) and 21 [par. 1] of its Statute." By a similar vote of 11 to 2 the Commission rejected a motion by Mr. Kozhevnikov that it should appoint one of its members as Assistant Rapporteur on *Statelessness*. The Commission then decided by a vote of 11–0–2 to adopt the proposal of Judge Hudson.[30]

Four days earlier, at its 171st meeting, on 24 July 1952, the

[29] A/CN.4/50, 21 Feb. 1950, par. 5; Yearbook, ILC, 4th Session, 1952, II, 4, and I, 100 (155th meeting).

[30] Yearbook, ILC, 4th Session, 1952, I, 190–191, 252; II, 68, par. 32. Despite the confusion in some of the passages quoted, it appears from par. 32 of Commission's Report that Mr. Kerno served as an expert "of," not "on," the Commission.

Commission decided, by a vote of 8–2–1, that the Rapporteur on the *Regime of the Territorial Sea,* Professor J. P. A. François, should consult "experts in order to seek clarification of certain technical aspects of the problem, and that the Secretary-General should be requested to provide the necessary expenses for any such consultation." [31] Dr. Liang, Secretary of the Commission, quoted Article 16 (*e*) of the Commission's Statute as authorizing such consultation. The problem was one of delimiting the territorial sea of two adjacent States and some members of the Commission doubted whether experts would be of much assistance in the absence of proof that a rule of international law existed on the subject. To the Rapporteur, "it appeared to be necessary to convene a joint conference of jurists and scientific experts to solve the technical question at issue." The Commission rejected these views and suggested that the Rapporteur should present it with a proposal after he had consulted experts.[32] This procedure was followed and the Report of the Committee of Experts on Technical Questions concerning the Territorial Sea is found in the Annex to A/CN.4/61/Add.1, 18 May 1953, Addendum to Second François Report on the Territorial Sea.[33]

With reference to Article 16 (*g*), there was unanimous agreement in the Committee on the Progressive Development of International Law and Its Codification that the Commission's drafts, with the replies of governments, should be published and given wide circulation. Professor Koretsky preferred "publication in book form which would be available to the public and all organizations and would enable the drafts to be laid before the public opinion and published in law magizines." [34]

Apparently no questionnaire pursuant to Article 16 (*c*), has ever been circulated by the International Law Commission.

Pursuant to paragraph (*h*) of Article 16, the Commission de-

[31] *Ibid.,* I, 185. The quotation is from the Report of the Commission, *ibid.,* II, 68, par. 39.

[32] *Ibid.,* I, 182–185.   [33] *Ibid.,* 1953, II, 77.

[34] A/AC.10/SR.13, p. 7.

cided to invite comments by governments on its *Draft Articles on the Continental Shelf and Related Subjects* in 1951.[35] Due to its policy of not identifying which articles of a draft were codification of existing law and which were in the nature of progressive development of international law, the Commission referred both to Article 16 (*h*) and to Article 21 (2) when it made requests for observations of governments on its drafts on *Statelessness* (1953),[36] *Diplomatic Intercourse and Immunities* (1957),[37] *Consular Intercourse and Immunities* (1960),[38] *Conclusion of Treaties* (1962),[39] *Invalidity and Termination of Treaties* (1963),[40] and *Application, Effects, Modification and Interpretation of Treaties* (1964).[41]

[35] Yearbook, ILC, 3rd Session, 1951, II, 139–140.
[36] Yearbook, ILC, 5th Session, 1953, II, 221, Report, par. 120.
[37] Yearbook, ILC, 9th Session, 1957, II, 132, Report, par. 12.
[38] Yearbook, ILC, 12th Session, 1960, II, 145, Report, par. 18.
[39] A/5209, Report, ILC, 14th Session, 1962, par. 19.
[40] A/5509, Report, ILC, 15th Session, 1963, par. 13.
[41] A/5809, Report, ILC, 16th Session, 1964, par. 16.

Article 17

1. The Commission shall also consider proposals and draft multilateral conventions submitted by Members of the United Nations, the principal organs of the United Nations other than the General Assembly, specialized agencies, or official bodies established by inter-governmental agreement to encourage the progressive development of international law and its codification, and transmitted to it for that purpose by the Secretary-General.

2. If in such cases the Commission deems it appropriate to proceed with the study of such proposals or drafts, it shall follow in general a procedure on the following lines:

(a) The Commission shall formulate a plan of work, and study such proposals or drafts, and compare them with any other proposals and drafts on the same subjects;

(b) The Commission shall circulate a questionnaire to all Members of the United Nations and to the organs, specialized agencies and official bodies mentioned above which are concerned with the question, and shall invite them to transmit their comments within a reasonable time;

(c) The Commission shall submit a report and its recommendations to the General Assembly. Before doing so, it may also, if it deems it desirable, make an interim report to the organ or agency which has submitted the proposal or draft;

(d) If the General Assembly should invite the Commission to proceed with its work in accordance with a suggested plan, the procedure outlined in article 16 above shall apply. The questionnaire referred to in paragraph (c) of that article may not, however, be necessary.

As stated in the commentary to Article 16 of the Statute (p. 144), the provisions of Article 17 of the Commission's Statute originated in Part I-B of the joint United States–Chinese proposals of 23 May 1947 providing that the initiative for suggesting topics for the progressive development of international law should not be the exclusive prerogative of the General Assembly. Specifically, the joint proposal authorized the Commission to consider (1) projects, (2) draft conventions already formulated but not signed by plenipotentiaries, and (3) draft conventions already signed by plenipotentiaries and transmitted to the Commission by the Secretary-General on the submission of governments, United Nations organs other than the General Assembly, specialized agencies, and certain other categories of international organizations.[1]

The representatives of the Union of Soviet Socialist Republics, Yugoslavia, and Poland opposed the proposal in the Committee on the Progressive Development of International Law and Its Codification on the grounds, first, that under the United Nations Charter, the General Assembly had the sole initiative in determining what topics or projects should be submitted to the International Law Commission—either for progressive development or for codification—and second, that otherwise the Commission might be overburdened with projects submitted by an increasing number of international organizations.[2] Despite these and other arguments, the Committee, by a vote of 12–3–2, adopted the provisions contained in I–B of the United States–Chinese proposal.[3]

The arguments were raised again in Sub-Committee 2. By a vote of 10 to 4, the Sub-Committee retained the proposal, but deleted provision (3) relating to draft conventions already signed by plenipotentiaries because it "has certain political aspects which make it inadvisable for a legal commission to initiate action."[4]

[1] A/AC.10/33, I-B, pp. 4–5.
[2] A/AC.10/SR.13, pp. 13–16; A/AC.10/SR.14, pp. 2–4; A/AC.10/SR. 25, pp. 5–8; A/AC.10/SR.26, pp. 1–6; A/AC.10/37, 2 June 1947 (Polish Memorandum).
[3] A/AC.10/SR.13, p. 15 (meeting of 28 May 1947).
[4] A/C.6/193, p. 11 (*re* par. 9 of the Committee's Report).

At the 58th meeting of the Sixth Committee on 20 November 1947, a Soviet motion to delete Article 17 was rejected by a vote of 28 to 8.[5]

The application of Article 17 of its Statute has given the International Law Commission concern in two respects: the fear that the Commission might be overburdened with projects submitted pursuant to Article 17; and the cumbersome nature of the procedures it appears to call for.

During its 2nd Session, in 1950, the International Law Commission received from the Secretary-General a letter transmitting a resolution of the Economic and Social Council which, noting that the Commission had selected the topic of *Nationality* for codification, proposed to the International Law Commission "that it undertake as soon as possible the drafting of a convention to embody" certain specified principles on the nationality of married women which had been recommended by the Commission on the Status of Women (E/1712, par. 37). The Commission was requested to "determine at its present session whether it deems it appropriate to proceed with this proposal," and, if so, when.[6]

At its 71st meeting, on 19 July 1950, the Commission engaged in a debate as to the appropriate application of Article 17 of its Statute to this request.[7] Judge Hudson noted the "complicated" procedure provided for by Article 17, paragraph 2: sub-paragraph (*b*) called for the circulation of a questionnaire; under sub-paragraphs (*c*) and (*d*) the Commission would have to submit a report to the General Assembly and "would apparently have to wait for the Assembly to invite it to proceed in accordance with article 16." The procedure provided by Article 17 "had to be followed" but he regarded it as "ill-suited to the case in hand." What the Commission was invited

---

[5] GAOR, 2nd Session, 1947, Sixth Committee, Summary Records, 152 (Soviet amendment 6).

[6] A/CN.4/33, 18 July 1950, Yearbook, ILC, 2nd Session, 1950, II, 363, 366.

[7] Yearbook, ILC, 2nd Session, 1950, I, 247–255.

to do in this particular case was merely to perform a drafting function; but the stipulated recommendations it was requested to embody in the draft would not bind the Commission.[8]

Other members questioned the advisability of regarding the International Law Commission as a body which could be called upon to draft principles with the merits of which it might not agree. Mr. Hsu thought it important to decide "whether the Commission's task was to develop international law and, where necessary, to draft conventions, or whether the Commission had been set up for the purpose of drafting conventions for other bodies" on the basis of principles designated by the latter.[9]

Mr. Sandström and Mr. Kerno suggested that the resolution of the Economic and Social Council could be interpreted as not confining the Commission to a mere task of drafting but as a request to give some priority to aspects of the question of nationality which had been selected by the Commission itself for codification.[10] Other members of the Commission thought that no organ except the General Assembly was entitled to tell the Commission which topics should be given priority.[11] The debate was affected by the heavy agenda of the Commission and the fact that the terms of its members were due to expire after one more annual session. Mr. Kerno "agreed with Mr. Hudson that articles 16 and 17 were clumsy and complicated, but thought article 17 could be made more flexible" and adapted to each individual case. As for the argument based on the fact that members of the Commission had been elected for three-year terms, Mr. Kerno pointed out that "the Commission was a permanent body" and could plan a program of work on that basis.[12]

Although the Commission, in a series of 6 to 6 votes, declined to set a date, it adopted the following "decision":

The International Law Commission
Deems it appropriate to entertain the proposal of the Economic

[8] *Ibid.,* 248.   [9] *Ibid.*   [10] *Ibid.,* 248–249.   [11] *Ibid.,* 253.
[12] *Ibid.,* 249.

and Social Council in connexion with its contemplated work on the subject of "nationality, including statelessness,"

Proposes to initiate that work as soon as possible.[13]

After the vote, Mr. Kerno, Assistant Secretary-General, "drew attention to the fact that the Commission had applied article 17 of its Statute for the first time. . . . The various organs referred to in article 17, paragraph 1, could submit proposals and drafts. . . . Under article 17, paragraph 2, however, it was for the Commission to decide . . . as to the utility of the proposed study." [14]

A year later, Professor Scelle observed of the request of the Economic and Social Council that the Commission "had left it on the table," adding that "if the Commission were obliged to conform to all the provisions of article 17 of its Statute it would be impossible for it to carry out its work." [15] He regarded Article 17 "as one of the most baneful" and hoped the Commission would state in its Report: "The Commission has found, in particular that the provisions of article 17 were such as to hamper and delay its work." [16] Despite proposals to recommend the amendment of Article 17 in order to give the Commission more discretionary powers as to the circulation of questionnaires and more flexibility in its application,[17] the Commission decided not to make any specific recommendations to the General Assembly for revision of its Statute pending a decision by the Assembly on the Commission's recommendation that it be made a full-time body.[18]

At the 124th meeting of the Commission, on 13 July 1951, Judge Hudson suggested the appointment of a Rapporteur to deal with the subject of statelessness. The question had been submitted by the Economic and Social Council under resolution 319 B III(XI) of 11 August 1950, which requested the International Law Commission to prepare a draft convention or

---

[13] *Ibid.*, 249–255; *ibid.*, II, 367, par. 20.   [14] *Ibid.*, I, 252.

[15] Yearbook, ILC, 3rd Session, 1951, I, 261, 112th meeting, 27 June 1951.

[16] *Ibid.*, 265.   [17] *Ibid.*, 8–10, 134–135, 355–358.

[18] *Ibid.*, II, 139, par. 71.

conventions for the elimination of statelessness.[19] Dr. Yuen-li Liang, Secretary of the Commission, questioned whether a Rapporteur should be appointed until Article 17, paragraph 2 (d) had been complied with and the General Assembly had invited the Commission to proceed with the topic of statelessness. In the debate which followed, views were expressed for and against the necessity of literal compliance with the various procedural stages envisaged in Article 17. The Commission resolved the difficulty by deciding to study "the question of nationality, including statelessness." Since the topic of nationality was already on the Commission's agenda, the Commission decided that it could appoint a Rapporteur without obtaining the consent of the General Assembly, under Article 17, paragraph 2 (d), to proceed with the study of statelessness.[20] The Report of the International Law Commission covering the work of its 3rd Session, 1951, states that the *"Commission decided to initiate work on the topic of 'nationality, including statelessness' which it had selected for codification at its first session"* and that the elimination of statelessness "lies within the framework of the topic." [21]

At the 4th Session of the Commission in 1952, Judge Hudson, as Special Rapporteur on *Nationality, including Statelessness,* presented a report, Annex II to which consisted of a working paper with attached *Draft Convention on Nationality of Married Persons.*[22] In introducing his report and draft convention at the 155th meeting of the Commission on 2 July 1952, Judge Hudson observed that since the International Law Commission "had merely been asked to draft a text" on certain principles recommended by the Commission on the Status of

19 *Ibid.,* 121–122. A/CN.4/47, 31 May 1951, Secretariat Note on Elimination of Statelessness.

20 Yearbook, ILC, 1951, I, 354–358.

21 *Ibid.,* II, 140, par. 85. Italics added. If the topic really called for codification rather than the progressive development of international law, Article 17 was not applicable.

22 A/CN.4/50, 21 Feb. 1952, Yearbook, ILC, 4th Session, 1952, II, 3, 12–13.

Women, "it would be unnecessary for the Commission to express any views on the principles upon which the draft convention was to be based, or to analyse the consequences of their application." Professor Lauterpacht thought "that it would be a deplorable development if the Commission were to prepare for submission to the General Assembly texts, the underlying principles of which it had not itself approved." Other speakers pointed out that the Commission had decided at its 71st meeting to consider the question of nationality of married women only in connection with the general subject of nationality, and objected to consideration of the Rapporteur's draft convention without opportunity for more thorough preparation. At the suggestion of Judge Hudson, the following proposal was put to a vote:

> The Commission decides, complying with the proposal of the Economic and Social Council, to draft a convention embodying the principles recommended by the Commission on the Status of Women.
> In doing so, it does not express any approval of those principles.

The proposal was rejected by a vote of 8–3–1.[23]

The Commission has thus clearly established the principle that it is not merely a body to draft proposals which it has not itself approved.

The fear that the International Law Commission might be overburdened with projects submitted pursuant to Article 17 of the Statute has not materialized. The only projects submitted under that Article have been the two requests of the Economic and Social Council with reference to the nationality of married women and the elimination or reduction of statelessness.

It is the General Assembly which has crowded the agenda of

[23] Yearbook, ILC, 4th Session, 1952, I, 100–103; II, 67. The Commission decided to communicate the draft prepared by Judge Hudson along with the Summary Records of its 155th meeting to the Economic and Social Council. *Ibid.*, I, 106.

the Commission with special projects (see below, pp. 320 ff.). Although some members of the Commission have tended to regard such assignments as an interference with the normal work of codification,[24] Professor Spiropoulos took a different view. It was undeniable that the submission of projects such as the definition of aggression slowed up the Commission's progress on codification. However:

It was quite right that the General Assembly should consult the Commission. It needed the advice of an independent body with recognized juridical competence. Otherwise, it could either apply to the International Court of Justice and ask for advisory opinions, or set up an *ad hoc* committee, whose members being appointed by their respective governments could not of course inspire the same confidence. Thus the part played by the Commission in that direction was an essential one.[25]

Article 17 remains a potential source of concern because a very small number of projects submitted thereunder would tie up the Commission's sessions.

[24] See commentary on Article 18, below and pp. 177, 320.
[25] Yearbook, ILC, 3rd Session, 1951, I, 7, par. 33.

Codification of International Law

Article 18

1. The Commission shall survey the whole field of international law with a view to selecting topics for codification, having in mind existing drafts, whether governmental or not.

2. When the Commission considers that the codification of a particular topic is necessary or desirable, it shall submit its recommendations to the General Assembly.

3. The Commission shall give priority to requests of the General Assembly to deal with any question.

The text of Article 18 was drafted by Sub-Committee 2 of the 1947 Sixth Committee on the basis of paragraph 11 of the Report of the Committee on the Progressive Development of International Law and Its Codification.

At the second meeting of that Committee on 13 May 1947, the United States offered a plan in accordance with which the International Law Commission would prepare drafts upon topics submitted to it by the General Assembly or on such subjects as the Commission itself might determine.[1] At its 14th meeting, on 29 May 1947, the Committee considered a modified United States–Chinese proposal, the first part of which read as follows:

The Committee recommends to the General Assembly that it adopt a resolution instructing CEIL [2] to survey the whole field of customary International Law with a view to selecting topics for codification, having in mind previous governmental and non-governmental projects.[3]

In introducing this proposal, Professor Jessup observed that

[1] A/AC.10/14, 12 May 1947, pars. 7–8.
[2] "Commission of Experts on International Law," a designation employed prior to adoption of the name "International Law Commission."
[3] A/AC.10/SR.14, p. 6.

"what they had in mind was that the General Assembly should not have to instruct the Commission of Experts to consider a specific topic but should indicate, in general lines, what areas the Commission was to cover." [4]

Professor Koretsky (U.S.S.R.) immediately expressed the view that the Commission "should have no right of initiative in matters of codification." Since "codification involved the systematization of custom, of the practices of States . . . only governments themselves could take the initiative in such matters." He proposed that the right of initiative accorded by the proposal to the Commission be deleted, as had been done with reference to the Commission's freedom to initiate projects for the progressive development of international law.[5] When Professor Jessup explained that he had abandoned the initiative for the Commission with reference to development of international law "with an eye to the Commission's work in the field of codification," Professor Koretsky did not press for a vote on his proposal. Instead, by a vote of 13 to 3, the Committee adopted the United States–Chinese proposal quoted above.

The Committee then adopted, by a vote of 14–0–2, the second part of the United States–Chinese proposal, as follows:

The resolution might further provide that if the General Assembly requests CEIL to prepare a draft convention on any subject or to explore the necessity or desirability of preparing a draft convention on any subject, CEIL shall give precedence to complying with such requests.[6]

After a discussion regarding drafting, during which Professor Jessup stated that the purpose was to indicate "(1) that the General Assembly instruct the ILC to select topics, and (2) that the General Assembly itself submit topics to the ILC," [7] the Committee agreed that the following paragraph should be inserted in its Report:

---

[4] *Ibid.,* p. 5.   [5] *Ibid.* See above, under Article 16 (pp. 143–144).
[6] *Ibid.,* p. 6.   [7] A/AC.10/SR.26, p. 11 (meeting of 12 June 1947).

11. The Committee by a majority decided to recommend to the General Assembly that it adopt a resolution instructing ILC to survey the whole field of customary international law, together with any relevant treaties, with a view to selecting topics for codification, having in mind previous governmental and non-governmental projects; that if the ILC finds that codification of a particular topic is desirable or necessary, it should present its recommendations to the General Assembly in the form of draft articles of multipartite conventions; and that, if the General Assembly should request the ILC to prepare a draft convention on any subject, or to explore the necessity or desirability of preparing such a draft convention, ILC should give precedence to complying with such request.[8]

In Sub-Committee 2 of the Sixth Committee, the provision by which the Commission would survey the whole field of international law was again questioned by certain delegations: "in their opinion the activity of the ILC should be confined solely to questions referred to it by the General Assembly; they were against giving the ILC any right of initiative." [9] A proposal to delete paragraph 11 of the Report of the Committee on the Progressive Development of International Law and Its Codification obtained 7 votes *for* and 7 votes *against*. "After a lengthy discussion," states the Report of Sub-Committee 2, the Sub-Committee voted 10 to 5 to give the initiative in selecting topics for codification to the International Law Commission by adopting the phraseology which now appears in Article 18 of the Commission's Statute.[10]

At the 58th meeting of the Sixth Committee, on 20 November 1947, Soviet motions to delete Article 18, paragraphs 1 and 3, of the Statute of the International Law Commission were rejected by votes of 28 to 8 (par. 1) and 28 to 3 (par. 3).[11]

[8] A/AC.10/51, par. 11.
[9] A/C.6/193, Report of Sub-Committee 2, pp. 12–13.
[10] *Ibid.*, p. 13,
[11] GAOR, 2nd Session, 1947, Sixth Committee, Summary Records, 152–153.

The Right of the Commission to Initiate Codification Projects:
The Commission's Interpretation of Article 18, paragraph 2

During its 1st Session in 1949, the International Law Commission was confronted with several problems involving the interpretation of Article 18 of its Statute. The attempt in Sub-Committee 2 to deprive the Commission of the right to initiate topics for codification had been defeated and the Sub-Committee report specifically states: "It should be noted that a proposal to give the right of initiative to the ILC had been adopted by ten votes to five." [12] However, in adopting the proposal contained in paragraph 11 of the Report of the Committee on the Progressive Development of International Law and Its Codification that "if the ILC finds that codification of a particular topic is desirable or necessary, it should present its recommendations to the General Assembly *in the form of draft articles of multipartite conventions,*" Sub-Committee 2 omitted [13] the words here italicized which, in the context, had clearly indicated that such recommendations necessarily followed, instead of preceded, the actual codification of a topic by the Commission.

Looking only at the words of Article 18, paragraph 2, that "When the Commission considers that the codification of a particular topic is necessary or desirable, it shall submit its recommendations to the General Assembly," Professor Koretsky interpreted them to mean that the Commission must obtain the approval of the General Assembly for any topic selected by the Commission for codification *prior* to undertaking the actual work of codification; otherwise, he said, the word "recommendations" in Article 18 (2) would mean merely that "the Commission need simply notify the General Assembly of its decisions." The question, he thought, was political as well as technical: the Commission was an organ of the General As-

[12] A/C.6/193, p. 13, *re* par. 11.
[13] In fact, the words "in the form of draft articles" were transferred to Article 20 of the Commission's Statute as an obligation to "prepare its drafts in the form of articles."

sembly and should not presume to codify topics which might not command the political support of the States composing the General Assembly.[14]

In the opinion of Professor Brierly, the recommendation of the Commission under Article 18 (2) "could only be made after a thorough study of the subject, which would involve the application of articles 19 and the following and would inevitably lead to the recommendation referred to in article 22. Article 18 therefore could only refer to the same final recommendation." [15]

Reference to the inadequate Summary Records of Sub-Committee 2 failed to throw light on the meaning of Article 18 (2) [16] and the Commission decided that it had the responsibility and the right to interpret its own Statute.[17] After three days of debate, the Commission, by a vote of 10 to 3, replied in the affirmative to the question propounded by its Chairman, Judge Hudson, as follows:

Has the Commission competence to proceed with its work according to the procedure provided in articles 19 to 23, without awaiting the General Assembly's decision on the recommendations submitted by the Commission under article 18, paragraph 2? [18]

A contrary decision would largely have nullified the authority granted to the Commission by its Statute in the field of codification.

In paragraphs 9 to 12 of its Report to the General Assembly covering the work of its 1st Session, the International Law Commission informed the General Assembly of the interpretation placed by the Commission on Article 18 (2) of its Statute,[19] and at the 158th meeting of the Sixth Committee of the General Assembly, Judge Hudson, as Chairman of the Commission, called attention to this interpretation.[20] In the debate

[14] Yearbook, ILC, 1st Session, 1949, pp. 15, 20–21, 26–27.
[15] Ibid., 19.   [16] Ibid., 16, n. 1, and 23–26.
[17] Ibid., 28, and preceding debate.
[18] Ibid., 32 (4th meeting, 18 April 1949).   [19] Ibid., 279–280.
[20] GAOR, 4th Session, 1949, Sixth Committee, Summary Records, 101, par. 51, Cf. also remarks of other members of the Commission before the

which followed, representatives of eleven States criticized the Commission's interpretation of Article 18 (2) of its Statute, and twenty supported the Commission's interpretation or its right to make such an interpretation.[21] Although many members wished the Sixth Committee to endorse the phraseology of the question propounded in the Commission by Judge Hudson and answered by it in the affirmative, Professor Koretsky insisted upon a vote on a proposal drafted by him which, he asserted, stressed the need for approval of the General Assembly, as follows:

Is it necessary that the General Assembly should approve the topics recommended by the International Law Commission for the codification of International Law so that the Commission could pursue its work in the field of selected topics in accordance with articles 18 to 22 of its Statute?

The Sixth Committee answered the question in the negative by a vote of 21–9–16.[22] The Committee then voted to "take note" of Chapter II of the Report of the International Law Commission, Professor Bartoš (Yugoslavia) observing that his delegation "considered that, in so voting, it had given a dispensation to the Commission, which his delegation thought had exceeded its powers." [23] A Philippines amendment stating that the General Assembly "*authorizes* the codification of the three topics recommended by the International Law Commission, namely: (1) Law of treaties, (2) Arbitral procedure, (3) Regime of the high seas," [24] was opposed by several members on the ground that "no authorization of the codification of the

---

Sixth Committee: Mr. Amado, *ibid.*, 104, 111; Mr. Spiropoulos, *ibid.*, 115–116. Mr. Hsu regretted the decision of the Commission on its competence, *ibid.*, 133.

[21] *Ibid.*, 101–145 (158th to 164th meetings, 11–15 October 1949). The Commission's interpretation was criticized by representatives of the Philippines, U.S.S.R., Yugoslavia, Argentina, Ukrainian S.S.R., Poland, Norway, Venezuela, Czechoslovakia, Peru, and China.

[22] *Ibid.*, 141, 143 (vote on A/C.6/L.39).   [23] *Ibid.*, 143.
[24] *Ibid.*, 135 (A/C.6/L.35).

topics selected by the International Law Commission was necessary," and was rejected by a vote of 27–10–10.[25] The Sixth Committee then adopted by a vote of 36–0–7 the following draft resolution (A/C.6/331/Rev. 1):

The General Assembly,

Noting from part I of the report of the International Law Commission covering its first session that the Commission has dealt, *within its competence,* with the studies entrusted to it by the General Assembly *in relation to the codification and progressive development of international law,*

   1. *Congratulates* the Commission on the work it has undertaken and on the work still in progress;

   2. *Approves* part I of the report of the International Law Commission.[26]

The words here italicized—*"within its competence . . . in relation to the codification and progressive development of international law"*—were intended by the sponsor of the resolution, Mr. Chaumont (France), to make clear General Assembly approval of the particular exercise of competence by the Commission which had been challenged, and were approved by a separate vote of 27–3–16.[27]

[25] *Ibid.*, 144–145. The words quoted are from the remarks of Mr. G. G. Fitzmaurice, *ibid.*, 144.

[26] *Ibid.*, 145. Adopted as resolution 373 (IV) by the General Assembly, at its 270th plenary meeting, of 6 Dec. 1949, A/1251, p. 66. At this meeting, Mr. Mattar (Lebanon) pointed out that by adopting this resolution "the General Assembly would be giving its sanction to the interpretation which the International Law Commission and the Sixth Committee had placed on the International Law Commission's competence under articles 18 to 23 of its statute." GAOR, 4th Session, 1949, plenary, 538 (A/PV.270).

[27] GAOR, 4th Session, 1949, Sixth Committee, Summary Records, 145. Cf. Mr. Chaumont's observations, *ibid.*, 107, 122, 127. The Report of the Sixth Committee states that it was the sense of the Sixth Committee that it did not consider the authorization of the General Assembly necessary in order that the Commission might continue to work on codification of the topics selected by the Commission. A/1196, 3 Dec. 1949, par. 40. *Ibid.*, Annexes to plenary meetings, Agenda item 49, p. 194. Cf. below, pp. 319–320.

Despite the expression of a strongly held minority view to the contrary, the General Assembly has thus unequivocally recognized the competence of the International Law Commission to interpret its Statute and approved the particular interpretation made by the Commission that Article 18, paragraph 2, did not require the Commission to obtain the prior consent of the General Assembly before engaging upon the codification of topics selected by the Commission.

Selection of Topics for Codification by the Commission

The second problem relating to Article 18 which confronted the International Law Commission during its 1st Session was the selection of topics for codification. Over the opposition of Professor Koretsky, Article 18, paragraph 1, had been adopted in terms which granted the International Law Commission the right to "survey the whole field of international law with a view to selecting topics for codification." In the application of this provision, three issues were raised in the Commission: (1) By whom should the selection be made? (2) Should selection be on the basis of a comprehensive plan or on an *ad hoc* basis? (3) What were the criteria for selection?

In opening the first meeting of the International Law Commission, Dr. Ivan Kerno, Assistant Secretary-General of the United Nations, observed that the Commission's Statute

offered a compromise between the codification of international law through official conventions, as had been tried under the auspices of the League of Nations, and codification through the unofficial scientific restatement of positive law as very well exemplified in the words [*sc.*: works] of the "Harvard Research."

4. With regard to codification, the Statute left the members of the Commission quite free to plan their real work and carry it out. He hoped that the Commission would give serious consideration to the suggestion contained in the *Survey of International Law* (A/CN.4/1/Rev.1) that codification should be looked upon as forming part of a comprehensive, long-range plan for the eventual codification of international law as a whole.[28]

28 Yearbook, ILC, 1st Session, 1949, p. 9.

By resolution 175 (II), adopted 21 November 1947, the General Assembly had instructed the Secretary-General "to do the necessary preparatory work for the beginning of the activity of the International Law Commission" [29] and the Secretariat had invited Professor Hersch Lauterpacht to collaborate with it the preparation of a *Survey of International Law in Relation to the Work of Codification of the International Law Commission,* the subtitle of which is "Preparatory work within the purview of Article 18, paragraph 1, of the Statute of the International Law Commission." [30]

In this *Survey,* attention is called to the distinction made "for convenience" in Article 15 of the Commission's Statute between the codification and the progressive development of international law and to the recognition by the drafting committees that "the terms employed are not mutually exclusive" and that "no clear-cut distinction between the formulation of the law as it is and the law as it ought to be could be rigidly maintained in practice." [31] From this premise, the conclusion is reached that the task of the Commission in the matter of codification is "not confined to a mere restatement of the existing law." [32] It followed, continued the *Survey,* that the measure of agreement on any particular topic, as ascertained by uniform governmental practice, judicial precedent and doctrine, "cannot be regarded as an adequate criterion for the selection of topics for codification." [33] What were the criteria for determining whether, in the words of Article 18, paragraph 2, "the codification of a particular topic is necessary or desirable?" In the words of the *Survey:*

---

[29] A/CN.4/1, 5 Nov. 1948, p. 1.

[30] *Ibid.,* and Rev. 1. See also the views expressed by Professor Lauterpacht after the experience of serving as a member of the International Law Commission. Lauterpacht, "Codification and Development of International Law," 49 A.J.I.L. 16–43 (1955). Cf. Julius Stone, "On the Vocation of the International Law Commission," 57 Columbia Law Review 16–51 (1957).

[31] Cf. A/AC.10/51, pars. 7, 10; A/C.6/193, pp. 9, 12.

[32] *Survey,* p. 4.

[33] *Ibid.,* 7, 11.

There is room for the view that a topic is ripe for codification in this sense if the importance of the subject-matter—from the point of view of the necessities of international intercourse, of the wider needs of the international community, and of the authority of international law—requires that, notwithstanding any existing disagreements, an attempt should be made to reduce it to the form of a systematized and precise branch of international law. . . .

The experience of codification under the League of Nations . . . shows that the decisive criterion must not be the ease with which the task of codifying any particular branch of international law can be accomplished, but the need for codifying it.[34]

Since the function of the Commission in codifying international law is not "determined by the necessity of producing such drafts only as are intended to materialize as conventions to be adopted by a considerable number of States," [35] the Commission—undertaking "the regulation of urgent and *novel* questions requiring a legislative effort" under its procedures for the progressive development of international law—could fit its codification activities into a comprehensive, long-range plan eventually covering the entire field of international law.[36] The "independent creative function" of the Commission would thus permit selection of topics for codification precisely because of "existing divergencies and uncertainties" or even because an undisputed legal rule requires re-examination in the light of modern developments and the interests of justice and of international social progress.[37] The *Survey* devoted Part II, covering 40 pages, to an examination of possible topics which might be selected for codification by the Commission.[38]

At the 1st meeting of the Commission, on 12 April 1949, Professor Koretsky questioned the utility of the *Survey of International Law* and suggested that the Secretariat should be instructed to prepare a program of work for the Commission "including the list of topics to be codified." [39] After the Chair-

[34] *Ibid.*, 11, 13.   [35] *Ibid.*, 15.   [36] *Ibid.*, 14.
[37] *Ibid.*, 15, 65–66.   [38] *Ibid.*, 19–58.
[39] Yearbook, ILC, 1st Session, 1949, p. 11.

man, Judge Hudson, had stated that it was not for the Secretariat, but for the Commission, to select topics for codification,[40] Professor Koretsky modified his proposal to suggest that the choice of topics for codification be postponed until a Rapporteur, aided by members of the Commission and officials of the Secretariat, had made a provisional selection which might even be submitted to governments for an expression of their "views and preferences." [41] The argument of Professor Koretsky that this method would "enable the Commission to save much time" did not impress the Commission. It proceeded to examine and select topics largely on the basis of the *Survey of International Law.*[42]

The significance of the rejection by the Commission of Professor Koretsky's suggestion lies in the interpretation thus placed on Article 18, paragraph 1, of its Statute that the selection of topics for codification is a prerogative of the Commission; and, in view of the interpretation previously placed by the Commission on paragraph 2 of Article 18, this prerogative is not shared with the General Assembly. This is not to say that preferences expressed by the General Assembly would not weigh heavily with the Commission, even in the absence of a priority request under paragraph 3 of Article 18.

The Choice of Topics

The proposal found in the *Survey of International Law,* that the selection of topics for codification by the Commission should be on the basis of a comprehensive plan found some support in the Commission but, in view of the difficulties and delays envisaged for such an approach, was dropped in favor of an *ad hoc* selection.[43] As summarized in the Commission's 1st Report to the General Assembly, paragraph 14:

The Commission discussed the question whether a general plan of codification, embracing the entirety of international law, should

40 *Ibid.,* par. 24.   41 *Ibid.,* 29.   42 *Ibid.,* 32–59.
43 *Ibid.,* 16 ff., 29 ff., 32 ff., 53 ff.

be drawn up. Those who favoured this course had in view the preparation at the outset of a plan of a complete code of public international law, into the framework of which topics would be inserted as they were codified. The sense of the Commission was that, while the codification of the whole of international law was the ultimate objective, it was desirable for the present to begin work on the codification of a few of the topics, rather than to discuss a general systematic plan which might be left to later elaboration.[44]

As for the actual criteria which should govern the selection of topics, there were also wide differences of opinion. Professor Koretsky wanted the Commission to be certain that States were interested in having a particular topic codified.[45] Judge Hudson, referring to Article 23 of the Commission's Statute, emphasized the great latitude left to the Commission since not all topics need be codified with a view to the adoption of an international convention.[46] Mr. Amado, observing that the Commission's "choice of topics must not depend on the prospects of their codification being accepted," added that

there was no need for the Commission to restrict itself to the formulation of universally accepted traditional rules. Its main duty was to fill the many gaps in existing law, to settle dubious interpretations . . . and even to amend existing law in the light of new developments. . . . The Commission must choose . . . topics offering difficulties to be solved and gaps prejudicial to the very prestige of international law.[47]

To Professor François, the choice of topics was a practical problem. On what topics did there seem a real possibility of international agreement? It "would be better to obtain positive results on one or two less important questions" than to formulate an impracticable general systematic plan.[48]

The Commission declined to accept suggestions that the choice of topics for codification be submitted to a sub-com-

[44] *Ibid.*, 280.   [45] *Ibid.*, 21, 29.   [46] *Ibid.*, 15.   [47] *Ibid.*, 18.
[48] *Ibid.*, 17.

mittee for recommendations and at its 4th, 5th, and 6th meetings proceeded, on the basis of Part II of the *Survey of International Law,* to make its own selection. No votes were taken;
but, after opportunity for comments, the Chairman ruled in
each case that the topic should or should not be placed on the
provisional list. Professor Koretsky made no substantive comments for or against the inclusion of any topic except that of
the *Law of War,* which he opposed as a topic for codification.
The Summary Records are not particularly enlightening as to
the criteria applied in selecting or rejecting a topic. After the
provisional list was drawn up, Professor Koretsky observed that
"selection had been guided by intuition, scientific considerations and the personal experience of its members rather than
by objective realities." [49]

Topics which the Commission discussed but did not include
in its provisional list were:

1. Subjects of International Law
2. Sources of International Law
3. Obligations of International Law in relation to the Law of the State
4. Fundamental Rights and Duties of States
5. Domestic Jurisdiction
6. Recognition of Acts of Foreign States.
7. Obligations of Territorial Jurisdiction
8. The Territorial Domain of States
9. Pacific Settlement of International Disputes
10. Extradition
11. The Law of War
12. The Law of Neutrality

Judging from the few comments made, some of the topics
were not included because they grouped unrelated questions
together (e.g., *Obligations of Territorial Jurisdiction, The
Territorial Domain of States*), were broadly phrased *(Recognition of Acts of Foreign States)* or of no practical interest

[49] *Ibid.*, 55.

(Sources of International Law). The Rights and Duties of States was on the agenda as a special topic. *Domestic Jurisdiction,* it was thought, could be examined in relation to other topics. By failing to include this topic, the Commission may perhaps be charged with a lack of imagination. On other topics, the opinion prevailed that it was "not advisable" to list them at present. The reasons for not including the *Law of War* at "the very beginning" of the Commission's work are set forth in a special paragraph of the Commission's 1st Report.[50]

The topics selected by the Commission for its provisional list were: [51]

1. Recognition of States
2. Succession of States and Governments
3. Jurisdictional Immunities of States and their Property
4. Jurisdiction with regard to Crime Committed outside National Territory
5. Regime of the High Seas
6. Regime of Territorial Waters
7. Nationality
8. Treatment of Aliens
9. Right of Asylum
10. Law of Treaties
11. Diplomatic Intercourse and Immunities
12. Consular Intercourse and Immunities
13. State Responsibility
14. Arbitral Procedure

The list is declared in paragraph 17 of the Commission's Report to the General Assembly to be "provisional" and it is stated "that additions or deletions might be made after further study by the Commission or in compliance with the wishes of the General Assembly." [52]

The current practical importance of these topics, supported in most cases by the availability of materials, may have been the determining factors in their selection.

The Summary Records are only slightly more explicit as to the reasons why the Commission voted to give priority to cer-

[50] *Ibid.,* 281, par. 18.   [51] *Ibid.,* 53.   [52] *Ibid.,* 281.

tain topics. Judge Hudson proposed that the Commission study two questions: (1) the *Law relating to Treaties,* "on which there was ample documentation"; and (2) *Arbitral Procedure* "which was directly linked to the application of Article 33 of the United Nations Charter." [53] Mr. Brierly agreed that these two questions were "of paramount importance" and it would create a most favorable impression if the Commission could conclude its work on them "within a relatively short time." Professor Scelle agreed with regard to the *Law of Treaties,* although it was "a classic question which would produce much less impression on public opinion than the questions of nationality and statelessness." As for *Arbitral Procedure,* he said, that "could be left in the background without much inconvenience for the arbitration system, which had worked smoothly for a hundred years or so, would not suffer thereby." [54] Mr. Yepes wished priority to be given to the *Right of Political Asylum,* which, he thought, could be dealt with by a committee "in a matter of a few days." Professor Koretsky favored giving priority to the (1) *Regime of the High Seas,* which was "not a controversial question"; (2) *Statelessness,* "which had considerable political significance"; and (3) *Consular Intercourse and Immunities,* "which often led to great friction between States." [55]

In a series of preferential votes the Commission voted, at its 7th meeting on 21 April 1949, as follows:

Law of Treaties	12 votes
Arbitral Procedure	9 votes
Regime of the High Seas	5 votes
Nationality	5 votes
Right of Political Asylum	3 votes
Consular Immunities	3 votes

The Chairman ruled that the *Law of Treaties* and *Arbitral Procedure* "would head the list of topics selected for codification"; and, by an additional vote, it was decided to add the

[53] *Ibid.,* 57.   [54] *Ibid.,* 57.   [55] *Ibid.,* 56.

Regime of the High Seas, in preference to *Nationality,* as a third topic.[56]

The actual choice of topics by the Commission received wide approval in the debate of the Sixth Committee during its 4th Session in 1949 and was endorsed by General Assembly resolution 373 (IV) of 6 December 1949, quoted above (see p. 167).

The adoption by the International Law Commission in 1949 of a list of topics for codification was explicitly—and obviously —provisional. By the conclusion of its 13th Session in 1961, the Commission had completed drafts on five topics[57] included in its provisional list and had undertaken work or placed on its agenda aspects of five other topics[58] from the list. The question of preparing a new list of topics for codification by the Commission and of assigning priorities was discussed at length in 1960 and 1961 in the Sixth Committee of the General Assembly and in 1962 in the Commission itself and is discussed below in Chapter 4 on "The International Law Commission and the Sixth Committee of the General Assembly (pp. 326 ff.).

Priority to Requests by the General Assembly

The provision of the 3rd paragraph of Article 18 that the "Commission shall give priority to requests of the General Assembly to deal with any question" had its origin, as stated above (see pp. 161 ff.), in the Committee on the Progressive Development of International Law and Its Codification. At its 1st Session in 1949, the International Law Commission adopted an agenda which, after listing the planning by the Commission of its codification program pursuant to Article 18, paragraph 1, included four topics which the General Assembly requested the

[56] *Ibid.,* 58–59.

[57] *Regime of the High Seas; Regime of Territorial Waters; Diplomatic Intercourse and Immunities; Consular Intercourse and Immunities; Arbitral Procedure.*

[58] *Nationality, including Statelessness; Treatment of Aliens; Right of Asylum; Law of Treaties; State Responsibility.*

Commission to consider: 2 *Draft Declaration on the Rights and Duties of States;* 3(a) *Formulation of the Nürnberg Principles;* 3(b) *Draft Code of Offences Against the Peace and Security of Mankind;* and 4 *Desirability and Possibility of Establishing International Criminal Jurisdiction.*[59]

The Commission was eager to get started on the work of codification and experienced jurists on the Commission viewed without enthusiasm some of the tasks presented to it by the diplomats and politicians of the General Assembly's Sixth Committee. Professor Scelle, referring to the 3rd paragraph of Article 18,

considered that it need not necessarily be interpreted as giving priority to every request of the General Assembly. That priority must not slow up the main work of the Commission and should therefore only apply in cases concerning the codification of international law.[60]

"Too narrow an interpretation of the priority mentioned in Article 18," he added, "would place the Commission entirely at the disposal of the General Assembly"; the main work of the Commission was the codification of international law.[61] Judge Hudson observed that:

From the fact that article 16 was placed in the section on the progressive development of international law and that paragraph 3 of article 18 was placed in the section on the codification of international law, he concluded that the priority referred to in that paragraph applied only to questions being examined with a view to codification.

Unless the General Assembly itself specified whether its proposal was submitted under Article 16 for progressive development or called for the application of Article 18, paragraph 3, "it would be for the Commission to determine, as each case arose, in which category the Assembly's proposal or request should be classified." [62]

59 A/CN.4/3; Yearbook, ILC, 1st Session, 1949, p. vi.
60 Yearbook, 1949, p. 12.   61 *Ibid.,* 14.   62 *Ibid.,* 14–15.

Mr. Spiropoulos agreed that the main task of the Commission was to codify international law but warned that even without invoking Article 18, "the Commission could not ignore the categorical requests made to it by the supreme body of the United Nations." [63]

Judge Hudson agreed that "regardless of the interpretation placed upon article 18, paragraph 3 of the Statute, the Commission could not, in the course of the current session, fail to consider items 2, 3, and 4 of the agenda relating to the special questions referred to it by the General Assembly." [64]

The Commission gave no explicit interpretation to Article 18, paragraph 3, at its 1st Session. It gave priority, in fact, to the items submitted by the General Assembly, after the Commission had planned its program of codification. Since, however, at its 2nd and 3rd Sessions, the Commission regarded these items as special projects not falling within the Statute's provisions relating to codification (or development) of international law, there may be some doubt whether Article 18, paragraph 3, was regarded as applicable to these particular requests of the General Assembly.[65]

General Assembly requests to the International Law Commission to undertake projects or to give priority to the codification of certain topics are discussed below in Chapter 4 on "The International Law Commission and the Sixth Committee of the General Assembly" (pp. 320 ff.).

[63] *Ibid.*, 12.   [64] *Ibid.*, 13.
[65] See commentary on Article 23, below, pp. 198 ff., and Chapter 3, Recommendations made by the International Law Commission to the General Assembly, below, pp. 276 ff.

Article 19

1. The Commission shall adopt a plan of work appropriate to each case.

2. The Commission shall, through the Secretary-General, address to Governments a detailed request to furnish the texts of laws, decrees, judicial decisions, treaties, diplomatic correspondence and other documents relevant to the topic being studied and which the Commission deems necessary.

Article 19 was drafted by Sub-Committee 2 of the 1947 Sixth Committee on the basis of paragraph 12 (c) of the Report of the Committee on the Progressive Development of International Law and Its Codification,[1] which, in turn, stemmed from proposal II-D of the joint United States—Chinese proposals before that Committee.[2] The only issue discussed in the Committee was whether governments should be permitted to make comments on the Commission's drafts on codification before they were submitted to the General Assembly. This point is discussed in connection with Article 21, below (p. 191).

Sub-Committee 2 deleted detailed procedures regarding rapporteurs, interim drafts, etc., in sub-paragraphs (a), (b) and (d) of paragraph 12 of the Committee's Report. The view prevailed in the Sub-Committee that the Commission should be permitted to work out its own plan of work and procedures. The text of Article 19 of the Statute was adopted by the Sub-Committee by a vote of 10–2–3,[3] and aroused no comment in the Sixth Committee.

After the Commission had decided at its 1st Session to undertake the codification of the *Law of Treaties, Arbitral Procedure,* and the *Regime of the High Seas,* it decided at its 33rd meeting, on 3 June 1949, to request governments to furnish the information mentioned in Article 19, paragraph 2, of its

---

[1] A/AC.10/51, p. 8.   [2] A/AC.10/33, p. 5.   [3] A/C.6/193, p. 13.

Statute and to instruct the Rapporteurs to decide, together with the Chairman of the Commission and the Secretary-General, what documents they would require. Professor Koretsky objected that it would be a violation of the Statute to request the information from governments before the General Assembly had approved the Commission's choice of topics for codification or to delegate the Commission's powers to request documents. By a vote of 12 to 1, the Commission decided that it was entitled to follow the procedure proposed and, by a vote of 9–1–3, it voted to make the request.[4]

Without designating the article of the Statute on which it was basing its request, the International Law Commission decided at the same time to request the views of governments as to the offences to be included in a *Draft Code of Offences against the Peace and Security of Mankind*. At its 4th Session in 1952, the Commission decided to request governments for information on their practice regarding the delimitation of the territorial sea of two adjacent States. In 1950 and 1951, information on the *Problem of Statelessness* was requested of governments for the benefit of the Commission, not by the Commission itself, but by the Economic and Social Council which had referred the topic to the Commission.

Information on these requests and compliance by Governments, is set forth below, with citations.[5]

Requests for Information

1. *Law of Treaties.* 1949. Decision to request information: Yearbook, ILC, 1st Session, 1949, pp. 238–239, 281. Replies were received from eleven governments: Canada, Costa Rica, Denmark, France, Israel, Netherlands, Philippines, Poland,

---

[4] Yearbook, ILC, 1st Session, 1949, pp. 238–239, 281.

[5] For more detailed analysis, see Herbert W. Briggs, "Official Interest in the Work of the International Law Commission: Replies of Governments to Requests for Information or Comment," 48 A.J.I.L. 603–612 (1954). On requests for comments by governments on drafts of the Commission, see below, pp. 193 ff., commentary on Article 21.

South Africa, United Kingdom, United States. Several replies contained no information. No replies were made by forty-eight governments. *Texts of replies*: A/CN.4/19, 23 March 1950, Yearbook, ILC, 2nd Session, 1950, II, 196–221.

2. *Arbitral Procedure*. 1949. Decision to request information: as above under *Law of Treaties*. Replies were received from the same eleven governments. *Texts: loc. cit.*, 151–156.

3. *Regime of the High Seas*. 1949. Decision to request information: as above under *Law of Treaties*. Replies were received from ten governments—those listed above, except the Netherlands. *Texts: loc. cit.*, 52–65.

4. *Offences against the Peace and Security of Mankind*. 1949. Decision to request views of governments: Yearbook, ILC, 1st Session, 1949, pp. 216–219, 283. Replies were received from seven governments: France, Netherlands, Pakistan, Poland, South Africa, United Kingdom, United States. *Texts*: Yearbook, ILC, 2nd Session, 1950, II, 249–253.

5. *The Problem of Statelessness*. 1950, 1951. Information was requested of governments by the Economic and Social Council pursuant to resolutions 319 B III (XI), 11 and 16 August 1950, and 352 (XII), 13 March 1951. Replies were received from the governments of twenty-nine Members of the United Nations: Argentina, Australia, Belgium, Burma, Canada, Chile, China, Czechoslovakia, Denmark, Ecuador, Egypt, France, Greece, India, Iran, Israel, Luxembourg, New Zealand, Norway, Pakistan, Poland, Sweden, Syria, Turkey, South Africa, United Kingdom, United States, Uruguay, Yugoslavia. Of 60 Members of the United Nations, 31 made no reply. Replies were received from the governments of seven States not Members of the United Nations: Austria, Ceylon, Finland, Ireland, Japan (GHQ, SCAP), Jordan, Switzerland. *Texts* (mimeographed): E/1869 and 19 addenda (1950–1951), and E/2164 and 24 addenda (1952–1954). For analysis, see E/2230 (A/CN.4/56), 26 May 1952.

6. *Delimitation of the Territorial Sea of Two Adjacent States*. 1952. Decision to request information on practice of

States: Yearbook, ILC, 4th Session, 1952, I, 186; II, 68, Report, par. 39. Replies were received from twelve governments: Belgium, Burma, Denmark, Dominican Republic, El Salvador, France, Netherlands, Norway, Sweden, United Kingdom, United States, Yugoslavia. *Texts*: A/CN.4/71, 12 May 1953, and 2 addenda; Yearbook, ILC, 5th Session, 1953, II, 79–89.

Article 20

The Commission shall prepare its drafts in the form of articles and shall submit them to the General Assembly together with a commentary containing:

(*a*) Adequate presentation of precedents and other relevant data, including treaties, judicial decisions and doctrine;

(*b*) Conclusions relevant to:

(i) The extent of agreement on each point in the practice of States and in doctrine;

(ii) Divergencies and disagreements which exist, as well as arguments invoked in favour of one or another solution.

The drafting of this Article follows closely proposal II-F of the joint United States–Chinese proposals [1] as embodied in paragraph 13 (a) and (b) of the Report of the Committee on the Progressive Development of International Law and Its Codification.[2]

Sub-Committee 2 of the 1947 Sixth Committee inserted the words "and shall submit them to the General Assembly" in the opening paragraph. The Report of the Sub-Committee contains the statement: "Draft conventions presented by a minority of the International Law Commission will also be submitted to the General Assembly," [3] but no such provision is to be found in the Statute of the Commission.

During the consideration of the draft on *Arbitral Procedure,* at the 4th Session of the Commission in 1952, Professor Lauterpacht stressed the importance of preparing a full commentary on the draft in accordance with Article 20. Such a commentary, he said, "would be a scientific work of the highest

[1] A/AC.10/33, pp. 5–6.　　[2] A/AC.10/51, pp. 8–9.
[3] A/C.6/193, pp. 13–14.

value, and would, perhaps, in some respects be more important than the draft itself." It "touched on a most important aspect of the Commission's work" because of "its influence on public opinion and governments." In his opinion, the Commission would not be doing justice either to itself or to the subject "if it confined itself to short commentaries such as had been appended to the draft articles on the regime of the continental shelf." [4] Dr. Liang, Secretary of the Commission, agreed that "mere legal texts, without a full commentary, lacked persuasive value." [5] The Chairman, Mr. Alfaro, noted that a majority of the Commission appeared to agree that a commentary as prescribed in Article 20 was indispensable but it would be a time-consuming task. He asked the Commission to decide whether, pending the completion of such a full commentary, it wished to submit its draft on a provisional basis, with a briefer commentary, to the forthcoming session of the General Assembly. [6]

Mr. Kerno, Assistant Secretary-General, observed that the relation between Article 20 and Articles 21 and 22 of the Statute was "far from clear." Both Articles 20 and 22 called for the submission to the General Assembly of the Commission's drafts, Article 20 with a full commentary, the nature of which was specified, and Article 22 with an explanatory report to be submitted with the recommendations of the Commission. Mr. Kerno rejected the possible interpretation that the Statute required the Commission to submit its drafts to the General Assembly both before and after requesting the Secretary-General, pursuant to Article 21, to submit them to governments for comment. In his view, the Commission had to submit a draft to the General Assembly only once and the submission of a draft with full commentary to the General

---

[4] Yearbook, ILC, 4th Session, 1952, I, 94, 98 (154th meeting, 1 July 1952).

[5] *Ibid.*, 98.

[6] *Ibid.*, 99 (155th meeting, 2 July 1952).

Assembly followed, instead of preceded, the submission of a draft to governments for their comments.[7]

After further discussion, the Commission decided, at its 156th meeting on 3 July 1952, to have its draft on *Arbitral Procedure,* with brief explanatory comments on each article, issued as a Commission document and submitted to governments for their observations, pursuant to Article 21. It was also decided that the Special Rapporteur "be invited to prepare and to present to the Commission at its next session a full commentary on the draft on arbitral procedure, with a view to the submission of the final draft and commentary to the General Assembly in 1953." In reaching this decision, the Commission rejected a motion by Professor Kozhevnikov calling, *inter alia,* for the preparation of the "detailed commentary before transmitting it to governments." [8]

In paragraph 15 of its Report the Commission states:

15. It was also decided that the final draft should be accompanied by a detailed commentary, as envisaged in Article 20 of the Statute, giving an account and an analysis of the relevant practice, including arbitration treaties and compromissory clauses, arbitral decisions and the literature of the subject. That commentary, *to be prepared by the Secretariat* under the direction of and in consultation with the Special Rapporteur, should be available to the Commission at the next session.[9]

The *Commentary on the Draft on Arbitral Procedure* [10] prepared by the Secretariat was submitted to the International

[7] *Ibid.,* 99. He added that "the procedure laid down in Article 21 came before that proposed in Article 20, chronologically speaking." *Ibid.,* 104.

[8] *Ibid.,* 103–105; *ibid.,* II, 58, Report, par. 14.

[9] *Ibid.,* II, 58–59. Italics added. The designation of the Secretariat to prepare the commentary first appears in an alternative text submitted by Professor Lauterpacht, as Rapporteur (A/CN.4/L.36, 4 Aug. 1952), par. 5. The proposal was adopted by the Commission, without discussion, at its 180th meeting on 5 Aug. 1952. *Ibid.,* I, 237.

[10] A/CN.4/L.40, 5 May 1953. Revised edition issued as A/CN.4/92 (1955. V. 1).

Law Commission at its 5th Session in 1953, and the question arose whether this *Commentary*, for which the Secretariat assumed entire responsibility, could be approved by the Commission as the commentary envisaged by Article 20 of the Statute. Professor Lauterpacht, who had been urging a full commentary on the subject, was apparently not satisfied with the Secretariat *Commentary* and stated that Article 22 of the Commission's Statute which called for an "explanatory report" was now applicable. He was not certain that the Commission need submit the full commentary called for by Article 20. Mr. Kozhevnikov, who also disliked parts of the Secretariat *Commentary*, thought "that it was Articles 16 and 22 of the Statute that were applicable in the present instance." He questioned whether the Commission could "on its own behalf submit commentaries prepared by the Secretariat." Moreover, he questioned the objectivity of the Secretariat *Commentary* which he regarded as "concealing" minority views and divergencies in the Commission.[11]

In later discussion, Professor Lauterpacht reached the conclusion that the Commission's current Report, along with the Secretariat *Commentary*, revised and supplemented, "did constitute a commentary conforming with the provisions of Article 20 of the Statute." [12] Mr. Kozhevnikov concurred that "by the terms of Article 20 of its Statute, the Commission was required to submit its comments with any final texts it might present to the General Assembly" but questioned whether the Secretariat's *Commentary* should be considered as an official product of the Commission.[13] Dr. Liang, Secretary of the Commission, observed "that the Secretariat did not expect that the commentary should be identified with the Commission in the sense that the Commission would be understood as having approved its substance." However, the Commission had asked

[11] Yearbook, ILC, 5th Session, 1953, I, 64–65 (194th meeting, 15 June 1953).
[12] *Ibid.*, 284 (226th meeting, 29 July 1953).
[13] *Ibid.*, 292 (227th meeting, 30 July 1953).

the Secretariat to prepare it. An analogy was the Secretariat *Study of Statelessness* (E/1112), which had been prepared and published at the request of the Economic and Social Council, although that Council "could not be held responsible for its content." [14] Mr. Zourek thought that the Commission was being "invited to pronounce on the value of a document which it had not discussed." Instead of "being drafted in support of the controversial majority view of the nature of arbitral procedure," he said, "the commentary would have presented the case in better perspective had it explained first the classical doctrine of arbitral procedure, then that the majority of the Commission thought that that doctrine did not meet present needs, and, finally, that some members had disagreed." [15] Mr. Sandström supported the inclusion in the Commission's Report to the General Assembly of certain additional comments suggested by Mr. Zourek on the ground, *inter alia,* that Article 20 of the Commission's Statute "obliged it to refer to 'divergencies and disagreements which exist, as well as arguments invoked in favour of one or another solution.' " [16]

By a vote of 7–3–2, the Commission adopted at its 227th meeting,[17] the following paragraph of its Report to the General Assembly:

13. The Commission was greatly aided in its work during the fifth session by the detailed commentary prepared by the Secretariat in accordance with a decision taken at the fourth session by reference to article 20 of the Statute. In the opinion of the Commission that commentary, which contains an account and analysis of the existing practice in the matter of arbitral procedure and of available jurisprudence and doctrine, constitutes a valuable contribution to the study and the application of the law of arbitral procedure. It is also the view of the Commission that, after being revised and supplemented by the Secretariat in the light of the

[14] *Ibid.,* 292, par. 54.
[15] *Ibid.,* 292–293.
[16] *Ibid.,* 323 (232nd meeting, 5 Aug. 1953).
[17] *Ibid.,* 293.

decisions taken by the Commission at its fifth session the commentary should be published.[18]

The last sentence, as proposed by Mr. Yepes, had originally ended with the words "the commentary should be published *as a Commission document and sent to the General Assembly with the final draft on arbitral procedure.*" The italicized words were deleted by the Commission in order to "make it clear that the Commission had no responsibility for the substance of the commentary." [19]

The conclusions to be drawn from the practice of the Commission in this instance appear to be:

1. that the Commission has interpreted Article 20 of its Statute in the sense suggested by Dr. Kerno, i.e., as not requiring submission of a draft with comment to the General Assembly both prior and subsequent to applying Article 21 by submitting a draft with comment to governments for their observations;

2. that the full commentary as specified in Article 20 is for submission to the General Assembly with the final draft, explanatory report and recommendations called for in Article 22;

3. that the provisional draft submitted to governments pursuant to Article 21 should be accompanied by an explanatory comment, pending the completion of the full commentary envisaged in Article 20.

This practice seems a workmanlike and justifiable interpretation of the ambiguous provisions of the Statute.

During the 13th Session of the Commission, at its 591st meeting, on 17 May 1961, Professor Verdross "pointed out that, in accordance with the Commission's practice, the commentary was deemed to constitute an integral part of the draft" and that it would be logical to insert a paragraph of the commentary on *Consular Intercourse and Immunities* in Article 15 of the draft itself. Mr. Amado could not agree: "commentaries were not on the same footing as the articles themselves."

[18] *Ibid.,* II, 201.   [19] *Ibid.,* I, 291–293.

Mr. Yasseen observed that the "commentaries adopted by the Commission were deemed to constitute, for the members of the Commission, the true interpretation of the article to which they were appended." The Chairman, Professor Tunkin, speaking as a member of the Commission, "said that the adoption of a commentary by the Commission did not mean that the members were ready to include its contents in the text of the articles. The commentaries constituted an interpretation, while the articles set forth the rules of law." Moreover, because of the pressure of time, commentaries received less thorough consideration than the texts of articles.[20]

Without overlooking the distinctions referred to by Mr. Amado and Mr. Tunkin, it appears that Mr. Yasseen was correct in calling attention to the fact that the commentaries, as well as the black-letter texts, set forth the Commission's views. In fact, the commentaries not only interpret, but sometimes qualify the text of articles to which they are appended; and both text and commentary are adopted by the Commission prior to their reference to the General Assembly.

[20] Yearbook, ILC, 13th Session, 1961, I, 58–59.

Article 21

1. When the Commission considers a draft to be satisfactory, it shall request the Secretary-General to issue it as a Commission document. The Secretariat shall give all necessary publicity to the document including such explanations and supporting material as the Commission may consider appropriate. The publication shall include any information supplied to the Commission by Governments in accordance with article 19. The Commission shall decide whether the opinions of any scientific institution or individual experts consulted by the Commission shall be included in the publication.

2. The Commission shall request Governments to submit comments on this document within a reasonable time.

Article 21 was drafted by Sub-Committee 2 of the 1947 Sixth Committee on the basis of sub-paragraphs (e) and (c) of paragraph 13 of the Report of the Committee on the Progressive Development of International Law and Its Codification.[1] The joint United States–Chinese proposals before that Committee, distinguishing procedures for the progressive development of international law from procedures for the codification or restatement of existing law, made no provision for the submission of codification drafts to governments for their comments prior to the submission of the Commission's final drafts to the General Assembly.[2] Professor Koretsky (U.S.S.R.), supported by the representatives of Sweden, Yugoslavia, Poland, and Brazil, thought the Commission should consult governments

[1] A/AC.10/51, p. 9. Cf. A/C.6/193, p. 14.
[2] Cf. A/AC.10/33, pp. 4 and 6.

in time to reflect their views in the Commission's final drafts, and moved that the drafts should be published and presented to governments with a request for comments prior to the submission of a final draft to the General Assembly. The motion prevailed by a vote of 7–6–3.[3]

At the 27th meeting on 13 June 1947, a motion to require that governments be requested to comment on a project before the Commission had actually prepared a draft, i.e., at the time the Commission requested governments to submit pertinent data and documents relevant to a topic under consideration, was rejected by a vote of 8 to 6.[4] The Committee, by a vote of 6–7–2, declined to delete its previously adopted provision that governments should be asked to comment on drafts which the Commission had provisionally adopted, despite the view expressed by Professor Jessup that "the work of codification was primarily legal and scientific, and not political" and "the intervention of the Governments in the scientific work of codification should not be stressed."[5]

According to Article 21, observed Dr. Liang, Secretary of the Commission, the Commission transmitted "drafts," not "preliminary drafts," to governments for comment.[6]

Compliance by States with Requests for Information or Comment

From 1947 to 1963 governments have been requested to provide information for the International Law Commission on six topics;[7] and, on a dozen drafts prepared by the Commission, governments have been asked to submit comments for its consideration. All requests have been made officially through the Secretary-General of the United Nations, although the Statute of the Commission requires this procedure explicitly only with reference to requests made pursuant to Article 19 (2). Not all

[3] A/AC.10/SR.15, meeting of 29 May 1947, pp. 3–7.
[4] A/AC.10/SR.27, pp. 1–8.   [5] *Ibid.*, pp. 2, 4, 8.
[6] Yearbook, ILC, 4th Session, 1952, I, 237.
[7] See above, pp. 180 ff., commentary on Article 19.

requests for information or comment have been initiated by the International Law Commission, some of them having been made pursuant to resolutions of the General Assembly or of the Economic and Social Council, in one case [8] prior to the establishment of the Commission.

Analysis of the behavior of governments on the basis of the materials cited below and under Article 16 (*h*) reveals that no government has replied to all requests for information or comment. While a few governments have complied with most requests, many governments have made no replies; and others have shown interest in only a limited number of topics. Rosenne suggests that political caution rather than a lack of interest may account for the paucity of government replies.[9] In some cases, foreign offices appear to be inadequately staffed with trained personnel to permit careful juridical analysis of the Commission's proposals and they are submerged in the daily pressures of a busy legal adviser's office. Since the time limits set by the United Nations Secretariat for receiving replies from governments, although occasioned by working schedules, were often too short, the International Law Commission has decided to rearrange its working schedule so as to permit a normal two-year period for receipt of observations of governments.[10]

Although the number of replies of governments and the quality of many of these replies leave much to be desired, some of them have been prepared with admirable professional skill and provide new evidence and perceptive analyses of the practice of States. Carefully prepared documents are of more utility to the International Law Commission than the often casual or personal oral comments in the General Assembly's Sixth Committee.

[8] The Panama Draft Declaration on the Rights and Duties of States.

[9] Rosenne, "The International Law Commission, 1949–59," 36 B.Y.I.L. 146 (1960).

[10] Cf. Yearbook, ILC, 10th Session, 1958, II, 107–108. The practice has been continued for the Commission's drafts on the *Law of Treaties*. Cf. Report of the Commission, 16th Session, 1964, A/5809, pars. 16, 40.

Requests Initiated by the Commission for Comments on its Drafts

1. *Draft Articles on the Continental Shelf and Related Subjects.* 1951. Decision to request comments of governments, pursuant to Article 16 (*h*) of the Statute: Yearbook, ILC, 3rd Session, 1951, I, 419; II, 139–140, Report, par. 78. Replies were received from twenty-one governments: Afghanistan, Belgium, Brazil, Burma, Chile, Denmark, Ecuador, Egypt, France, Iceland, Israel, Luxembourg, Netherlands, Norway, Philippines, Sweden, Syria, South Africa, United Kingdom, United States, Yugoslavia. The replies of Afghanistan, Burma, and Luxembourg contained no substantive comments. *Texts*: A/CN.4/55, 16 May 1952, and six addenda; A/CN.4/70, 7 May 1953; A/CN.4/86, 13 May 1954; Yearbook, ILC, 5th Session, 1953, II, 241–269 and *ibid.*, 6th Session, 1954, II, 18–20.

2. *Draft on Arbitral Procedure.* 1952. Decision to request comments pursuant to Article 21 (2) of Statute: Yearbook, ILC, 4th Session, 1952, II, 58, Report, par. 14. Replies were received from thirteen governments: Argentina, Belgium, Brazil, Chile, Denmark, India, Luxembourg, Netherlands, Norway, Sweden, United Kingdom, United States, Uruguay. The replies of Denmark and Luxembourg contained no substantive comments. *Texts*: A/CN.4/68, 1 May 1953, and 2 addenda; Yearbook, ILC, 5th Session, 1953, II, 232–241.

3. *Draft Conventions on The Elimination of Future Statelessness and on The Reduction of Future Statelessness.* 1953. Decision to request comments of governments, in accordance with Article 16 (*h*) and Article 21 (2) of the Statute: Yearbook, ILC, 5th Session, 1953, I, 329 ff.; II, 221, Report, par. 120. Replies were received from fifteen governments: Australia, Belgium, Canada, Costa Rica, Denmark, Egypt, Honduras, India, Lebanon, Netherlands, Norway, Philippines, Sweden, United Kingdom, United States. *Texts*: A/CN.4/82, 29 March 1954 and 8 addenda; Yearbook, ILC, 6th Session, 1954, II, 163–173.

4. *Provisional Articles concerning the Regime of the Territorial Sea.* 1954. Decision "in conformity with the provisions of its Statute" to request comments: Yearbook, ILC, 6th Session, 1954, I, 162–163; II, 153, Report, par. 67. Replies were received from eighteen governments: Australia, Belgium, Brazil, Egypt, El Salvador, Haiti, Iceland, India, Mexico, Netherlands, Norway, Philippines, Sweden, Thailand, South Africa, United Kingdom, United States, Yugoslavia. *Texts*: A/CN.4/90, 29 March 1955 and 6 addenda; Yearbook, ILC, 7th Session, 1955, II, 43–62.

5. *Provisional Articles on the Regime of the High Seas and revised Draft Articles on the Regime of the Territorial Sea.* 1955. Decision to request comments: Yearbook, ILC, 7th Session, 1955, II, 20, 34, Report, pars. 15, 23. Replies were received from twenty-five governments: Austria, Belgium, Brazil, Cambodia, Canada, Chile, China, Denmark, Dominican Republic, Iceland, India, Ireland, Israel, Italy, Lebanon, Nepal, Netherlands, Norway, Philippines, Sweden, Turkey, South Africa, United Kingdom, United States, Yugoslavia. *Texts*: A/CN.4/99, 12 March 1956 and 9 addenda; Yearbook, ILC, 8th Session, 1956, II, 37–101.

6. *Diplomatic Intercourse and Immunities.* 1957. Decision: "In accordance with articles 16 and 21 of its statute, the Commission decided to transmit the draft through the Secretary-General, to Governments for their observations." Yearbook, ILC, 9th Session, 1957, II, 132, Report, par. 12. Replies were received from twenty-four governments: Argentina, Australia, Austria, Belgium, Cambodia, Chile, China, Czechoslovakia, Denmark, Finland, Ghana, India, Italy, Japan, Jordan, Luxembourg, Netherlands, Pakistan, Sweden, Switzerland, Union of Soviet Socialist Republics, United Kingdom, United States, Yugoslavia. One reply was from a non-member of the United Nations (Switzerland); and the replies of Austria, Ghana, and India contained no substantive comments. *Texts:* A/CN.4/114, 17 March 1958 and 6 addenda; Yearbook, ILC, 10th Session, 1958, II, 111–139.

7. *Consular Intercourse and Immunities.* 1960. Decision: submitted in accordance with Articles 16 and 21 of the Statute to governments for comment. Yearbook, ILC, 12th Session, 1960, II, 145, Report, par. 18. Replies were received from twenty-one governments: Belgium, Chad, Chile, China, Czechoslovakia, Denmark, Finland, Guatemala, Indonesia, Japan, Netherlands, Niger, Norway, Philippines, Poland, Spain, Sweden, Switzerland, Union of Soviet Socialist Republics, United States, Yugoslavia. One reply was from a non-member of the United Nations (Switzerland); and the replies of Chad and Niger contained no substantive comments. *Texts:* A/CN.4/136, 3 April 1961 and 11 addenda; Yearbook, ILC, 13th Session, 1961, II, 129–170.

8. *Conclusion of Treaties.* 1962. Decision: submitted in accordance with Articles 16 and 21 of the Statute to governments for comment. A/5209, Report of the International Law Commission, 14th Session, 1962, par. 19.

9. *Invalidity and Termination of Treaties.* 1963. Decision: submitted in accordance with Articles 16 and 21 of the Statute to governments for their comments. A/5509, Report of the International Law Commission, 15th Session, 1963, par. 13.

10. *Application, Effects, Modification and Interpretation of Treaties.* 1964. Decision: submitted in accordance with Articles 16 and 21 of the Statute to Governments for their comments. A/5809, Report of the International Law Commission, 16th Session, 1964, par. 16.

Requests Initiated by the General Assembly

1. *Panama Draft Declaration on the Rights and Duties of States.* 1947, 1948. Pursuant to General Assembly resolutions 38 (I) and 178 (II), governments were requested to comment on the Panama Draft Declaration. Replies received from seventeen governments were reproduced in A/CN.4/2, 15 December 1948, pp. 162–214, for the use of the International Law Commission.

2. *Formulation of the Nürnberg Principles.* 1951. Pursuant

to General Assembly resolution 488 (V), 12 December 1950, observations of governments were requested on the *Formulation of the Nürnberg Principles* prepared by the International Law Commission at its 2nd Session in 1950. Yearbook, ILC, 2nd Session, 1950, II, 374–378. Replies of seven governments are found in A/CN.4/45, 19 April 1951 and 2 addenda, Yearbook, ILC, 3rd Session, 1951, II, 104–109, and were referred to the Commission for consideration in relation to its preparation of a *Draft Code of Offences against the Peace and Security of Mankind.*

3. *Draft Code of Offences against the Peace and Security of Mankind and the Question of Defining Aggression.* 1951. Pursuant to General Assembly resolution 599 (VI), 31 January 1952, comments of governments were requested on the International Law Commission's *Draft Code* and its report on the *Question of Defining Aggression* contained in its 3rd Report, Yearbook, ILC, 3rd Session, 1951, II, 131–137. Replies received from fifteen governments are reproduced in A/2162, 27 August 1952, and 2 addenda, and in GAOR, 7th Session, 1952, Annexes, Agenda item 54. They were analyzed by Jean Spiropoulos, Special Rapporteur, for the benefit of the International Law Commission's reconsideration of the *Draft Code* in 1954 in A/CN.4/85, 30 April 1954, Yearbook, ILC, 6th Session, 1954, II, 112–122.

4. *Draft Convention on Arbitral Procedure.* 1953. Pursuant to General Assembly resolution 797 (VIII), 7 December 1953, governments were again (see above p. 193) requested to comment on the International Law Commission's 1952 *Draft on Arbitral Procedure* for the benefit of the General Assembly. Replies were received from fourteen governments: Argentina, Belgium, Brazil, Canada, Chile, Costa Rica, Denmark, Greece, Honduras, India, Netherlands, Sweden, United Kingdom, Yugoslavia. *Texts:* A/2899, 2 May 1955, and 2 addenda; GAOR, 10th Session, Annexes, Agenda item 52. By resolution 989 (X), 14 December 1955, the General Assembly invited the

International Law Commission to re-examine its *Draft Convention on Arbitral Procedure* in the light of these comments and of discussions in the Sixth Committee.

Article 22

Taking such comments into consideration, the Commission shall prepare a final draft and explanatory report which it shall submit with its recommendations through the Secretary-General to the General Assembly.

Article 22 was drafted by Sub-Committee 2 on the basis of paragraph 14 of the Report of the Committee on the Progressive Development of International Law and Its Codification. It was accepted without discussion.[1]

Faithful compliance with the provisions of Article 22 has been the rule. A notable exception occurred when the Special Rapporteur on *Consular Intercourse and Immunities* was charged with ignoring comments submitted by the Chinese Government and was defended by the President of the Commission, who later observed that he had been speaking as a member of the Commission.[2]

For further comment on Article 22, see commentary on Article 20, above (pp. 184 ff.).

[1] A/AC.10/51, p. 9; A/AC.10/SR.27, p. 10; A/C.6/193, p. 14.
[2] Yearbook, ILC, 1961, I, 194–195 (612th meeting, 16 June 1961).

Article 23

1. The Commission may recommend to the General Assembly:

(*a*) To take no action, the report having already been published;

(*b*) To take note of or adopt the report by resolution;

(*c*) To recommend the draft to Members with a view to the conclusion of a convention;

(*d*) To convoke a conference to conclude a convention.

2. Whenever it deems it desirable, the General Assembly may refer drafts back to the Commission for reconsideration or redrafting.

The text of Article 23 was drafted by Sub-Committee 2 of the 1947 Sixth Committee [1] on the basis of paragraph 15 of the Report of the Committee on the Progressive Development of International Law and Its Codification.[2]

Article 23 must be understood in the light of the fact that the provision in Article 20 of the Statute that the Commission shall prepare its drafts "in the form of articles" does not mean that the Commission is obligated to recommend codification by multilateral convention where it regards the persuasive force of a scientific restatement of international law as a preferable method. The differentiation of procedures set forth in the Statute for the progressive development of international and for the codification of international law was based upon the prevailing view that the conclusion of an international convention was not always the desideratum in undertaking projects for codification of the law.[3]

The minority view, urged strongly by Professor Koretsky

[1] A/C.6/193, pp. 14–15.
[2] A/AC.10/51, p. 10.
[3] For a summary of the debate on this point, see the commentary to Article 15, above (pp. 129 ff.).

(U.S.S.R.), was that every project of the Commission, whether dealing with the development of international law or with its codification, should culminate in a multilateral convention: "academic codes" failed to "establish compulsory standards." [4]

The extreme opposite view, advanced by Professor Brierly (U.K.), was that the Commission's completed restatements should depend, for their persuasive authority on governments or courts, exclusively on their scientific merits. In time, however, governments might wish to proceed further and secure official endorsement of the restatement by General Assembly resolution or by international convention. [5]

On the other hand, the United States proposed at the 2nd meeting of the Committee on 13 May 1947, that the recommended action by the General Assembly might include mere publication of the Commission's report, or approval by General Assembly resolution, or the conclusion of an international convention. [6] The joint United States–Chinese proposals recommended on this point the same possibilities of publication and adoption by General Assembly resolution, and suggested that the conclusion of an international convention might be either through "approval of a draft convention by the General Assembly and its proposal to states for accession" or the convocation of an *ad hoc* international conference. [7]

These four possibilities survived debate in the Committee [8] and appeared in paragraph 15 of its Report as follows:

15. These recommendations might be either:
(a) that no further action be taken in view of the fact that the report has already been published, or
(b) that the General Assembly should adopt all or part of the report by resolution, [9] or

[4] A/AC.10/SR.4/Add. 1, pp. 3–4; A/AC.10/32, pp. 2 ff.
[5] A/AC.10/16, pp. 4–5.
[6] A/AC.10/14, par. 8(f). Cf. A/AC.10/11, p. 7.
[7] A/AC.10/33, proposal II. L., p. 6.
[8] A/AC.10/SR.15, pp. 8–14; A/AC.10/SR.27, p. 10.
[9] Footnote in original: "This sub-paragraph was adopted by a majority

(c) that the General Assembly should recommend the draft to States for the conclusion of a convention, or

(d) that the General Assembly should convoke a special conference to consider the conclusion of a convention.

The Committee appreciates the fact that the General Assembly might in any of these cases think fit to refer the drafts back to ILC for reconsideration and redrafting.[10]

The Report of Sub-Committee 2 contains the following:

Sub-paragraph (b) of paragraph 15 has evoked certain objections. The question has been put what would be the legal effect of the *adoption*, by the General Assembly, of the ILC report. There seemed to be no ground for believing that the text "adopted" by the General Assembly would be binding on Members in the same way as if they had ratified it in the form of a convention. Nor was there any support for the view that it would amount to a declaration in which the General Assembly expressed its opinion on the rule of law. It was felt that this power of the General Assembly to adopt or reject ILC texts would introduce into the work of codification that very political element which it was hoped to remove. Such a provision, in any case, might give rise to doubts or uncertainties which should be avoided.[11]

By a vote of 12 to 2, the Sub-Committee amended the text of sub-paragraph (b) to read as follows: "That the General Assembly should *take note of* the report by resolution," thus omitting the word "adopt." The Sub-Committee declined to delete sub-paragraph (a), as unnecessary, "on the ground that in certain cases the method provided in sub-paragraph (a) might be preferred to that envisaged in sub-paragraph (b)."

At the 58th meeting of the Sixth Committee, on 20 November 1947, the Soviet Government moved the deletion of sub-paragraph (b) and the United States moved the reinsertion of

---

of the Committee." This refers to the vote of 11–4–1 by which the Committee adopted this provision over the objection of the Soviet and other representatives. Cf. A/AC.10/SR.15, p. 13.

[10] A/AC.10/51, p. 10.   [11] A/C.6/193, pp. 14–15.

the words "or adopt" in this sub-paragraph.[12] The Soviet amendment (number 8) was rejected by a vote of 24 to 10.

Mr. Guerreiro (Brazil), speaking with reference to the United States amendment, denied that the adoption of reports of the International Law Commission by the General Assembly would transform the Assembly into an international legislative body: its recommendations "had no binding force and could not be law in the sense in which a convention was law." On the other hand, a General Assembly resolution "supported by two-thirds of the States Members of the United Nations would have great moral force and would be of greater value than a convention ratified by only a few states." [13] For the United States, Mr. John Maktos pointed out:

> There was a need for finding a new and improved way of encouraging the codification of international law. The idea was to put the additional weight of the General Assembly behind the action of the commission. Little had been accomplished by conventions. Restatements would be helpful because they would indicate what international law was in the opinion of the commission. Afterwards the General Assembly would support these findings by resolutions.[14]

Mr. Durdenevsky (U.S.S.R.) disagreed. The General Assembly should not "give its authority to the opinion of fifteen experts"; international law should be codified by conventions which were binding.

By a vote of 23 to 10, the Sixth Committee decided to insert the words "or adopt," so that sub-paragraph (*b*) would read: "To take note of or adopt the report by resolution." [15]

In explaining why Poland would have to abstain on the resolution adopting the Statute of the International Law Commission, Mr. Bramson, criticizing sub-paragraph 1 (*b*) of Article 23, wanted to know "what would be the position of the

---

[12] GAOR, 2nd Session, 1947, Sixth Committee, Summary Records, 153–155.

[13] *Ibid.*, 153.   [14] *Ibid.*, 154.   [15] *Ibid.*, 155.

International Court of Justice as to whether or not it should apply such an adopted report to States which had voted against it." [16]

In the course of the discussion of fisheries conservation by the International Law Commission at its 69th meeting on 17 July 1950, Mr. Spiropoulos warned the Commission not to confuse its two tasks—codification and development of international law. Codification, he thought, "must always relate to the law in force"; the "protection of humanity's major interests" could not be ensured by codification. Mr. Hsu reminded Mr. Spiropoulos of Article 23 of the Commission's Statute:

He asked why that article had been included if the purpose had not been to enable the Commission to fill in gaps in existing international law, to develop international law and to see whether and to what extent such development was acceptable. Article 23 had been given its present wording precisely because the Commission had a task of a very varied nature.[17]

For the application of Article 23 by the Commission, see Chapter 3 on Recommendations of the International Law Commission to the General Assembly (below pp. 276 ff.).

[16] *Ibid.*, 157.

[17] Yearbook, ILC, 2nd Session, 1950, I, 238–239. Cf. Yearbook, ILC, 3rd Session, 1951, I, 133, 135, where Mr. Hsu agreed with Dr. Liang that Article 23 "was the keystone of the Statute."

D. Promoting Availability of Customary International Law

Article 24

The Commission shall consider ways and means for making the evidence of customary international law more readily available, such as the collection and publication of documents concerning State practice and of the decisions of national and international courts on questions of international law, and shall make a report [French: *elle fait rapport*] to the General Assembly on this matter.

The text of Article 24 was drafted by Sub-Committee 2 of the 1947 Sixth Committee [1] on the basis of paragraph 18 of the Report of the Committee on the Progressive Development of International Law and Its Codification.[2]

In presenting the United States plan to the Committee on 13 May 1947, Professor Jessup observed that

it is impossible to ignore the fact that the practice of states over a very long period of years has created a body of customary international law which has frequently been applied by both national and international tribunals and which has governed the conduct of states in their mutual relations. Like all customary law, this body of legal principles cannot always be easily stated with precision. The record of the precedents and practices which are the stuff of which it is made, are scattered in numerous state papers and governmental documents and in the words of jurists who have devoted their lives to their examination and analysis. It is a painstaking and exacting task requiring the efforts of the most skillful and impartial scholars to reflect accurately this customary

[1] A/C.6/193, pp. 15–16.
[2] A/AC.10/51, p. 11.

practice of states. The United Nations can here be of assistance in stimulating the publication by governments and by private initiative, of digests or other compilations revealing such practice." [3]

A Secretariat *Memorandum on Methods for Encouraging the Progressive Development of International Law and Its Eventual Codification* suggested in section I. B. that the actual compilation of digests of international law reflecting State practice should be done on the initiation of governments and that the function of the General Assembly might be to consider the methods by which such efforts could be promoted and the materials reflecting State practice made more readily available.[4] This point of view prevailed in the Committee's discussions [5] and in paragraph 18 of its Report the Committee recommended that the International Law Commission "consider ways and means for making the evidences of customary international law more readily available by the compilation of digests of State practice, and by the collection and publication of the decisions of national and international courts on international law questions." [6] The redrafting by Sub-Committee 2 eliminated the ambiguity and made clear that the compilation, collection, and publication was not the task of the Commission itself.

At its 31st and 32nd meetings on 1 and 2 June 1949, the International Law Commission discussed [7] its duties in relation to Article 24 of its Statute on the basis of a useful Secretariat Memorandum on *Ways and Means of Making the Evidence of Customary International Law More Readily Available— (Preparatory work within the purview of article 24 of the*

---

[3] A/AC.10/11, p. 4.   [4] A/AC.10/7, 6 May 1947, pp. 5–6.

[5] A/AC.10/SR.9, pp. 11–12, is not clear on this point but see A/AC.-10/SR.7, pp. 8–11 and A/AC.10/SR.8, pp. 1–2, where comparable compilations were regarded as the task of the Secretariat, not of the International Law Commission.

[6] A/AC.10/51, p. 11.

[7] Cf. Yearbook, ILC, 1st Session, 1949, pp. 228–235.

Statute of the International Law Commission)[8] and a Secretariat Working Paper on *Possible Methods of Procuring the Publication of More Complete Collections of Evidence of Customary International Law.*[9] The Commission decided not to appoint a Rapporteur on the question but to request Judge Hudson to prepare a working paper on the subject.[10]

At its 2nd Session, the Commission devoted the 40th meeting, 6 June 1950, to a discussion of Judge Hudson's *Working Paper on Article 24 of the Statute of the International Law Commission,*[11] and Secretariat comments thereon,[12] and adopted certain recommendations [13] which are set forth in paragraphs 90 to 94 of its Report covering the work of its 2nd Session.[14] The Commission recommended, *inter alia,* the widest possible distribution of publications relating to international law issued by organs of the United Nations (par. 90); General Assembly authorization for the Secretariat to prepare and issue (par. 91) a series of United Nations publications, such as (*a*) a Juridical Yearbook, (*b*) a "Legislative Series containing the texts of current national legislation on matters of international interest," (*c*) constitutions of all States, various indices to United Nations publications, (*g*) a *répertoire* of United Nations practice regarding questions of international law, and (*h*) additional series of *Reports of International Arbitral Awards*; and that the General Assembly "call to the attention of Governments the desirability of their publishing digests of their diplomatic correspondence and other materials relating to international law" (par. 93).

These recommendations were considered by the Sixth Com-

8 A/CN.4/6, 7 March 1949, 114 pp.

9 A/CN.4/W.9, 20 May 1949, reproduced in Yearbook, ILC, 1st Session, 1949, pp. 228–229, n. 10.

10 *Loc. cit.* 235.

11 A/CN.4/16, 3 March 1950; reprinted in Yearbook, ILC, 2nd Session, 1950, II, 24.

12 A/CN.4/27, 6 June 1950; reprinted in *ibid.,* 33.

13 Yearbook, ILC, 2nd Session, 1950, I, 4–8.

14 *Ibid.,* II, 367–374, (A/1316).

mittee of the General Assembly at its 230th and 231st meetings on 30 October and 2 November 1950,[15] some members noting "that part of this vast programme of work was already being carried out by the Secretariat and that other parts of the programme entailed financial and administrative implications which required further study." [16] By a vote of 41–0–2, the Committee, on 2 November 1950, adopted a draft resolution which, as approved by the General Assembly,

Invites the Secretary-General, in preparing his future programme of work in this field, to consider and report to the General Assembly upon the recommendations contained in paragraphs 90, 91 and 93 of part II of the report of the International Law Commission, in the light of the discussion held and the suggestions made thereon in the Sixth Committee.[17]

The inclusion of the provisions of Article 24 in the Commission's Statute has proved useful. Even though some of the periodical publications such as the *Reports* and *Pleadings* of the International Court of Justice and the *United Nations Treaty Series* would have been published anyway, the United Nations has been encouraged to make more readily available the materials contained in the *Reports of International Arbitral Awards,* the *United Nations Legislative Series,* the *United Nations Juridical Yearbook,* and the *répertoires* of United Nations practice. As the French version of Article 24 indicates, the International Law Commission is not limited to making a single report in this field.

[15] GAOR, 5th Session, 1950, Sixth Committee, Summary Records, 119–131. Cf. also *ibid.,* Annexes, Agenda item 52, A/1639, 8 Dec. 1950, Report of the Sixth Committee, pars. 17–20 and res. D.
[16] A/1639, par. 19.
[17] GA res. 487 (V), 12 Dec. 1950, A/1775, p. 77.

E. Cooperation with Other Bodies

Article 25

1. The Commission may consult, if it considers necessary, with any of the organs of the United Nations on any subject which is within the competence of that organ.

2. All documents of the Commission which are circulated to Governments by the Secretary-General shall also be circulated to such organs of the United Nations as are concerned. Such organs may furnish any information or make any suggestions to the Commission.

The text of Article 25 was drafted by Sub-Committee 2 of the 1947 Sixth Committee on the basis of paragraph 19 of the Report of the Committee on the Progressive Development of International Law and Its Codification. By resolution 94 (I) of 11 December 1946, the General Assembly had directed that Committee to study "(b) Methods of securing the cooperation of the several organs of the United Nations to this end." [1] The content and drafting of the provisions of Article 25 raised little difficulty in the Committee [2] or in Sub-Committee 2 of the Sixth Committee,[3] although the Sub-Committee deleted a paragraph which had been adopted by a majority in the Committee and which specifically authorized the International Law Commission to make interim reports to competent organs of the United Nations which had submitted projects.[4] Since the deletion of this paragraph left the Commission free to do so anyway, the Soviet representative on the Sixth Committee made

[1] Cf. A/CN.4/4, p. 1.
[2] A/AC.10/SR.15, pp. 15–16; A/AC.10/SR.16, pp. 1–2; A/AC.10/SR.17, pp. 1–5; A/AC.10/SR.28, pp. 2–3.
[3] A/C.6/193, p. 16.
[4] A/AC.10/51, par. 19 (b).

an ineffectual motion to delete paragraph 2 of Article 25 of the draft Statute. The motion was rejected by a vote of 30 to 7,[5] and in view of the provisions of Article 25, paragraph 1, and Article 17 would have been ineffectual to accomplish the purpose sought even if it had not been rejected.

[5] GAOR, 2nd Session, 1947, Sixth Committee, Summary Records, 155 (amendment 9).

Article 26

1. The Commission may consult with any international or national organizations, official or non-official, on any subject entrusted to it if it believes that such a procedure might aid it in the performance of its functions.

2. For the purpose of distribution of documents of the Commission, the Secretary-General, after consultation with the Commission, shall draw up a list of national and international organizations concerned with questions of international law. The Secretary-General shall endeavour to include in this list at least one national organization of each Member of the United Nations.

3. In the application of the provisions of this article, the Commission and the Secretary-General shall comply with the resolutions of the General Assembly and the other principal organs of the United Nations concerning relations with Franco Spain and shall exclude both from consultations and from the list, organizations which have collaborated with the nazis and fascists.

4. The advisability of consultation by the Commission with inter-governmental organizations whose task is the codification of international law, such as those of the Pan American Union, is recognized.

This Article was drafted by Sub-Committee 2 on the basis of paragraph 20 of the Report of the Committee on the Progressive Development of International Law and Its Codification. By resolution 94 (I) of 11 December 1946, the General Assembly had directed that Committee to study "(c) Methods of enlisting the assistance of such national or international bodies as might aid in the attainment of this objective." [1] In further-

[1] Cf. A/CN.4/4, p. 1.

ance of this resolution, the United Nations Secretariat submitted to the Committee a tentative list of such national and international organizations.[2]

Proposals presented to the Committee by the United States, at its 2nd meeting on 13 May 1947, provided in paragraph 8 (b) and (c) for:

(b) Co-operation with such other expert groups, whether governmental or non-governmental, as might be found appropriate in each instance with a view to enlisting universal support and assistance in the development of each project.

(c) The elaboration of a draft text prepared by the Commission in the light of such suggestions as might be received through the co-operation indicated in the preceding paragraph.[3]

The joint United States–Chinese proposals of 23 May 1947, called, in proposal II. G., for "Consultation as desired with other experts, etc." [4]

For the Soviet Union, Professor Koretsky questioned whether national and international organizations should have the right to initiate questions or submit their own drafts to the International Law Commission. The United Nations was an intergovernmental organization; unofficial organizations should not be directly consulted by the Commission, but only through their governments. In his view, consultation by the Commission of national organizations was more important than consultation of international organizations.[5] Moreover, the voice of new States should be heard even prior to consulting organizations of the Great Powers "which had already developed *their* international law." [6] In order to control the national and inter-

[2] A/AC.10/22, 16 May 1947, with Annexes and addenda.

[3] A/AC.10/14, 12 May 1947, p. 2.   [4] A/AC.10/33, p. 6.

[5] Professor Koretsky opposed a French suggestion to place international organizations ahead of national organizations. He "did not wish to belittle the importance of international organizations, but wanted to emphasize the national conceptions of international law." A/AC.10/SR.17, p. 11.

[6] A/AC.10/SR.16, pp. 8–11. Italics added.

national organizations which might be consulted by the Commission, Professor Koretsky moved that they be limited to those appearing in the list prepared by the Secretary-General, after consultation with the Commission, for purposes of distribution of the Commission's documents. The motion was rejected by a vote of 11–4–1.[7]

By majority vote, the Committee therefore recommended the broad view

(a) That the ILC should be authorized to consult any national or international organization, official or non-official, if and when it believes that such a procedure might aid it in the attainment of its objectives. . . .[8]

The list of organizations drawn up pursuant to Article 26, paragraph 2, is merely for purposes of distribution of the Commission's documents. A motion to delete this paragraph was defeated in Sub-Committee 2 by a vote of 10 to 4.[9]

At the 74th meeting of the International Law Commission on 24 July 1950, Dr. Kerno, Assistant Secretary-General, observed that: "In regard to the co-operation mentioned in article 17 of the Statute . . . the initiative rested with the Members of the United Nations and others, whereas for the consultations referred to in articles 25 and 26, the initiative rested with the International Law Commission." [10]

The 3rd paragraph of Article 26 aroused no outspoken opposition despite its doubtful value. When the International Law Commission was considering the revision of its Statute in 1951, Judge Hudson observed that paragraph 3 of Article 26 no longer had any justification now that the General Assembly's resolutions concerning Franco Spain had been withdrawn.[11] It may be questioned whether it ever had any justification.

[7] A/AC.10/SR.17 (meeting of 3 June 1947), pp. 12–15.
[8] A/AC.10/51, par. 20 (a).   [9] A/C.6/193, p. 16.
[10] Yearbook, ILC, 2nd Session, 1950, I, 274.
[11] Yearbook, ILC, 1951, I, 135, par. 185.

The desirability of including paragraph 4, which was drafted as a formula to permit special reference in the Statute to the Pan American Union, was the subject of a prolonged debate.[12]

Introduced by Mr. Vieyra (Argentina) and strongly supported by other Latin American representatives, the proposal was opposed as establishing an invidious distinction between States and as an infringement of their equality. By a recorded vote of 10–4–2 the Committee decided that special reference be made to the importance of consulting the Pan American Union.[13]

The debate was reopened in Sub-Committee 2, which adopted the present text of Article 26, paragraph 4, by a vote of 13 to 2.[14] In the Sixth Committee, a Soviet motion to delete the paragraph was rejected by a vote of 31 to 6.[15]

Application of Article 26 by the Commission

The topic "Co-operation with other bodies" has appeared on the agenda of most sessions of the International Law Commission. At its 1st Session in 1949, Professor Koretsky again attempted to establish distribution of documents under paragraph 2 of Article 26 as a control on the right of the Commission to consult organizations under paragraph 1. By a vote of 10–1 the Commission decided at its 34th meeting, on 6 June 1949, "that those two paragraphs were independent of each other and that they dealt with two different questions: consultation with organizations on the one hand, and distribution of documents on the other." The Chairman, Judge Hudson, pointed out that the distinction was made quite clear in paragraph 3 of Article 26, which specifically excluded Nazi and

---

[12] A/AC.10/SR.16, pp. 3, 6–15; A/AC.10/SR.17, pp. 16–19; A/AC.10/SR.18, pp. 1–4; A/AC.10/SR.28, pp. 5–7.

[13] A/AC.10/SR.18, pp. 2–3. Cf. par. 20 (d) of the Committee's Report, A/AC.10/51, p. 13.

[14] A/C.6/193, pp. 16–17.

[15] GAOR, 2nd Session, 1947, Sixth Committee, Summary Records, 155 (amendment 10).

Fascist collaborators "both from consultations and from the list." [16] The Chairman suggested that members of the Commission should notify the Secretary-General directly of any additions or deletions which should be made in the list prepared by the Secretariat (A/CN.4/8).

During its earlier years, cooperation by the Commission with other organizations interested in the codification of international law appears to have been limited to encouraging the exchange of documents, to personal contacts and occasional personal participation by members of the Commission or its secretariat in meetings of unofficial organizations. [17] On the basis of resolutions sponsored by Mr. F. V. García Amador and adopted by the Commission at its 6th and 7th Sessions in 1954 and 1955, the Commission, pursuant to paragraph 4 of Article 26 of the Statute, established closer cooperation with the Inter-American Council of Jurists. [18] Dr. Yuen-li Liang, Secretary of the Commission, participated, at the request of the Commission, as Observer in the 3rd and 4th sessions of the Inter-American Council of Jurists held in Mexico City in 1956 and Santiago, Chile, in 1959, [19] and reported to the Commission thereon. [20] In presenting his report on the Mexico session to the Commission at its 357th meeting on 31 May 1956, Dr. Liang stated that in a plenary meeting of the Inter-American Council of Jurists "he had expressed the view that while the work of the Council was similar in character to that of the Commission, there was little scope for co-ordination and that it would be preferable for both bodies to proceed on parallel lines as before since there could be no question of duplication." [21] Dr. Manuel

[16] Yearbook, ILC, 1st Session, 1949, pp. 247, 284.

[17] Yearbook, ILC, 3rd Session, 1951, I, 358, 362; II, 141.

[18] Yearbook, ILC, 6th Session, 1954, I, 193–194; II, 162–163; Yearbook, ILC, 7th Session, 1955, I, 237–238; II, 42.

[19] *Ibid.* and Yearbook, ILC, 8th Session, 1956, II, 302.

[20] A/CN.4/102, 12 April 1956, Yearbook, ILC, 8th Session, 1956, II, 236–252; A/CN.4/124, 5 Feb. 1960, *ibid.*, 12th Session, 1960, II, 120.

[21] Yearbook, ILC, 8th Session, 1956, I, 130.

S. Canyes attended some meetings of the 8th Session of the International Law Commission as an Observer representing the Pan American Union,[22] and Dr. Antonio Gómez Robledo attended some meetings of the 12th Session of the Commission as Observer of the Inter-American Juridical Committee,[23] and was invited to address the Commission on the topic of "State Responsibility." [24] Dr. José J. Caicedo Castillo attended some meetings of the 13th and 15th Sessions as Observer for the Inter-American Juridical Committee [25] and Mr. Hugo Juan Gobbi was their Observer for the 14th Session.[26] Mr. Hafez Sabek attended parts of the 13th and 16th Sessions as Observer for the Asian African Legal Consultative Committee [27] and Justice H. W. Thambiah part of the 15th Session for the same Committee.[28]

At the 571st meeting of the Commission, on 24 June 1960, Mr. F. V. García Amador was appointed as the Commission's Observer at the 4th Session of the Asian African Legal Consultative Committee, pursuant to repeated invitations by that Committee to the Commission [29] and Mr. Eduardo Jiménez de Aréchaga attended the Cairo session of that Committee in 1964.[30]

Consultation by the Commission of individual experts and scientific institutions is discussed under Article 16 (*e*), above (pp. 147 ff.).

[22] *Ibid.*, 82, 130 and II, 302.
[23] Yearbook, ILC, 12th Session, 1960, I, 28.
[24] *Ibid.*, 264 ff., 566th meeting, 20 June 1960.
[25] Yearbook, ILC, 13th Session, 1961, I, 97; II, 129; A/5509, p. 38, par. 68.
[26] Yearbook, ILC, 14th Session, 1962, I, 176.
[27] Yearbook, ILC, 13th Session, 1961, I, 146; II, 129.
[28] A/5509, p. 38, par. 68.
[29] Yearbook, ILC, 12th Session, 1960, I, 222, 296–298.
[30] A/5509, p. 38, par. 69; A/CN.4/172.

PART III

THE COMMISSION
IN ACTION

CHAPTER 1

The Procedures and Methods of the International Law Commission

Rules of Procedure

NEITHER the Statute of the International Law Commission nor the drafting debates in the Committee on the Progressive Development of International Law and Its Codification or in Sub-Committee 2 of the Sixth Committee of the 1947 General Assembly contain any reference to rules of procedure for the Commission. At the first meeting of the Commission on 12 April 1949, Judge Manley O. Hudson, Chairman, stated in part

that the International Law Commission was a subsidiary organ of the General Assembly; as such it was governed by the provisions of rule 150 [now rule 162] [1] of the rules of procedure of the General Assembly. According to rule 150 [162], "the rules relating to the procedure of committees of the General Assembly, as well as rules 38 [45] and 55 [62], shall apply to any subsidiary organ unless the General Assembly or the subsidiary organ decides otherwise." Consequently, the International Law Commission was free to adopt the rules referred to or to draw up its own rules of procedure, either for the whole of its work or for specific items. Since it was an organ of a rather special kind, the International Law Commission could approach its work without complying too strictly with the provisions of the rules of procedure; experience would show whether it was preferable to abide by the provisions of rule 150 or to draw up special rules for the Commission.

[1] Cf. A/4700, United Nations, Rules of Procedure of the General Assembly (embodying amendments and additions adopted by the General Assembly up to 31 Dec. 1960), N.Y., Feb. 1961, p. 29. Rule 45 provides that the Secretary-General shall act in that capacity or designate a substitute at meetings, and rule 62 provides for public meetings, unless exceptionally decided otherwise by the body concerned.

He therefore proposed that the provisions of the rules of procedure referred to "in rule 150 [162], namely rules 88 to 122 [now rules 98 to 134] and rules 38 [45] and 55 [62] would be provisionally applicable to the Commission; if need arose, the Commission would draft its own rules of procedure." The Summary Record of the meeting adds: *"It was so decided."* [2]

The rules of procedure relating to committees of the General Assembly which appear to be applicable to the International Law Commission include the following: [3]

Rule 104: Each committee may set up sub-committees, which shall elect their own officers.

Rule 105: Each committee shall elect its own Chairman, Vice-Chairman and Rapporteur. These officers shall be elected on the basis of equitable geographical distribution, experience and personal competence. These elections shall be held by secret ballot.

Rule 107: If the Chairman finds it necessary to be absent during a meeting or any part thereof, the Vice-Chairman shall take his place. A Vice-Chairman acting as Chairman shall have the same powers and duties as the Chairman. If any officer of the committee is unable to perform his functions, a new officer shall be elected for the unexpired term.

Rule 108: The Chairman shall declare the opening and closing of each meeting of the committee, shall direct its discussions, ensure observance of these rules, accord the right to speak, put questions and announce decisions. He shall rule on points of order and, subject to these rules, shall have complete control of the proceedings of the committee and over the maintenance of order at its meetings. The Chairman may, in the course of the discussion of an item, propose to the committee the limitation of the time to be allowed to speakers, the limitation of the number of times each representative may speak

[2] Yearbook, ILC, 1st Session, 1949, pp. 10–11.
[3] A/4700, pp. 19–24.

on any question, the closure of the list of speeches or the closure of the debate. He may also propose the suspension or the adjournment of the meeting or the adjournment of the debate on the item under discussion.

Rule 109: The Chairman, in the exercise of his functions, remains under the authority of the committee.

Rule 110: One-third of the members of a committee shall constitute a quorum. The presence of a majority of the members of the committee is, however, required for a question to be put to the vote.

Rule 111: No representative may address the committee without having previously obtained the permission of the Chairman. The Chairman shall call upon speakers in the order in which they signify their desire to speak. The Chairman may call a speaker to order if his remarks are not relevant to the subject under discussion.

Rule 112: The Chairman and the Rapporteur of a committee or sub-committee may be accorded precedence for the purpose of explaining the conclusion arrived at by their committee or sub-committee.

Rule 113: The Secretary-General, or a member of the Secretariat designated by him as his representative, may, at any time, make oral or written statements to any committee or sub-committee concerning any question under consideration by it.

Rule 114: During the discussion of any matter, a representative may rise to a point of order, and the point of order shall be immediately decided by the Chairman in accordance with the rules of procedure. A representative may appeal against the ruling of the Chairman. The appeal shall be immediately put to the vote and the Chairman's ruling shall stand unless overruled by a majority of the members present and voting. A representative rising to a point of order may not speak on the substance of the matter under discussion.

Rule 115: The committee may limit the time to be allowed to each speaker and the number of times each representative may speak on any question. When the debate is limited and a representative has spoken his allotted time, the Chairman shall call him to order without delay.

Rule 116: During the course of a debate the Chairman may announce the list of speakers and, with the consent of the committee, declare the list closed. He may, however, accord the right of reply to any member if a speech delivered after he has declared the list closed makes this desirable.

Rule 117: During the discussion of any matter, a representative may move the adjournment of the debate on the item under discussion. In addition to the proposer of the motion, two representatives may speak in favour of, and two against, the motion, after which the motion shall be immediately put to the vote. The Chairman may limit the time to be allowed to speakers under this rule.

Rule 118: A representative may at any time move the closure of the debate on the item under discussion, whether or not any other representative has signified his wish to speak. Permission to speak on the closure of the debate shall be accorded only to two speakers opposing the closure, after which the motion shall be immediately put to the vote. If the committee is in favour of the closure, the Chairman shall declare the closure of the debate. The Chairman may limit the time to be allowed to speakers under this rule.

Rule 119: During the discussion of any matter, a representative may move the suspension or adjournment of the meeting. Such motions shall not be debated, but shall be immediately put to the vote. The Chairman may limit the time to be allowed to the speaker moving the suspension or adjournment of the meeting.

Rule 120: Subject to rule 114, the following motions shall have precedence in the following order over all other proposals or motions before the meeting:
  (a) To suspend the meeting;
  (b) To adjourn the meeting;
  (c) To adjourn the debate on the item under discussion;

(d) For closure of the debate on the item under discussion;

Rule 121: Proposals and amendments shall normally be introduced in writing and handed to the Secretary-General, who shall circulate copies to the delegations. As a general rule, no proposal shall be discussed or put to the vote at any meeting of the committee unless copies of it have been circulated to all delegations not later than the day preceding the meeting. The Chairman may, however, permit the discussion and consideration of amendments, or of motions as to procedure, even though these amendments and motions have not been circulated or have only been circulated the same day.

Rule 122: Subject to rule 120, any motion calling for a decision on the competence of the General Assembly or the committee to adopt a proposal submitted to it shall be put to the vote before a vote is taken on the proposal in question.

Rule 123: A motion may be withdrawn by its proposer at any time before voting on it has commenced, provided that the motion has not been amended. A motion which has thus been withdrawn may be reintroduced by any member.

Rule 124: When a proposal has been adopted or rejected it may not be reconsidered at the same session unless the committee, by a two-thirds majority of the members present and voting, so decides. Permission to speak on a motion to reconsider shall be accorded only to two speakers opposing the motion, after which it shall be immediately put to the vote.

Rule 125: Each member of the Committee shall have one vote.

Rule 126: Decisions in the committees of the General Assembly shall be made by a majority of the members present and voting.

Rule 127: For the purpose of these rules, the phrase "members present and voting" means members casting an affirmative or negative vote. Members who abstain from voting are considered as not voting.

Rule 128: The committee shall normally vote by a show of hands or by standing, but any representative may request a roll-call. . . .

Rule 129: After the Chairman has announced the beginning of the voting, no representative shall interrupt the voting except on a point of order in connexion with the actual conduct of the voting. The Chairman may permit members to explain their votes, either before or after the voting, except when the vote is taken by secret ballot. The Chairman may limit the time to be allowed for such explanations. The Chairman shall not permit the proposer of a proposal or of an amendment to explain his vote on his own proposal or amendment.

Rule 130: A representative may move that parts of a proposal or of an amendment shall be voted on separately. If objection is made to the request for division, the motion for division shall be voted upon. Permission to speak on the motion for division shall be given only to two speakers in favour and two speakers against. If the motion for division is carried, those parts of the proposal or of the amendment which are subsequently approved shall be put to the vote as a whole. If all operative parts of the proposal or of the amendment have been rejected, the proposal or the amendment shall be considered to have been rejected as a whole.

Rule 131: When an amendmennt is moved to a proposal, the amendment shall be voted on first. When two or more amendments are moved to a proposal, the committee shall first vote on the amendment furthest removed in substance from the original proposal and then on the amendment next furthest removed therefrom, and so on, until all the amendments have been put to the vote. Where, however, the adoption of one amendment necessarily implies the rejection of another amendment, the latter amendment shall not be put to the vote. If one or more amendments are adopted, the amended proposal shall then be voted upon. A motion is considered an amendment to a proposal if it merely adds to, deletes from or revises part of that proposal.

Rule 132: If two or more proposals relate to the same question, a committee shall, unless it decides otherwise, vote on the proposals in the order in which they have been submitted. A committee may, after each vote on a proposal, decide whether to vote on the next proposal.

Rule 134: If a vote is equally divided on matters other than elections, the proposal shall be regarded as rejected.

There are few references to rules of procedure in the Summary Records of the International Law Commission. Although the Commission may at times have approached its work without too strict attention to rules of procedure, the rules set forth above fairly describe the procedures actually followed in the Commission.

As in other United Nations bodies, the interventions of members are expressed more often in formalized statements than in the give and take of informal debate characteristic of some national legislative organs. While at times this gives the impression that speakers make prepared statements with little relation to the observations of preceding speakers, a review of the Summary Records reveals a comprehensive coverage of pros and cons and a more integrated debate than might have been expected.

After general debate on a topic, the Commission considers draft articles presented by a Rapporteur. A first reading concentrates on the principles involved and the best way of expressing them and is followed by reference to the drafting committee. The articles as modified by the drafting committee are then given a painstaking second reading. The consideration, paragraph by paragraph, of the draft Report of the Commission on the work of the session permits, in effect, a third reading of a particular draft.

A provisional draft which has been submitted to governments for their observation or which has been the subject of debate in the General Assembly's Sixth Committee is given three similar readings in the session of the Commission following the receipt of such comments. Under the guidance of the Special Rapporteur, the Commission gives careful consideration to the expression of governmental views on a pending draft.[4]

The Bureau

The officers of the Commission—known collectively as the Bureau—are elected for each session. The Commission regularly elects a Chairman, First and Second Vice-Chairmen and a (General) Rapporteur. Individual abilities and experience and geographical and political considerations play a part in their selection. The appended table gives some indication of how this selection works. While its duties are not fixed, the Bureau is consulted by the Chairman on planning the work of the Commission and on certain decisions such as the selection of Special Rapporteurs.

Length of Sessions and the Productivity of the Commission

The International Law Commission holds one annual session in the spring and experience has shown that a session of less than ten weeks provides insufficient time for the Commission to make substantial progress with its program. Even an annual ten-week session is a severely limiting factor in the long-range program of the codification and progressive development of international law. During the five-year period for which members are now elected, the Commission is in session about fifty weeks, or less than one calendar year.

Short of establishing the International Law Commission on a full-time basis—a proposal made by the Commission itself in

[4] A regrettable exception occurred during the 13th Session of the Commission when the Special Rapporteur, Professor Zourek of Czechoslovakia, neglected to refer to the observations of the Government of China, A/CN.-4/136, Add. 1, and, on being criticized by Mr. Hsu and other members, attempted to justify this arbitrary action by raising the question of which government was authorized to represent China in the United Nations. Cf. Yearbook, ILC, 13th Session, 1961, I, 194–195, pars. 61–77 (meeting of 16 June 1961).

LENGTH OF SESSIONS

Session		Date	Weeks in Session	Number of Public Meetings	Meetings
1st	1949	12 April–9 June	8	38	1st–38th
2nd	1950	5 June–29 July	8	43	39th–81st
3rd	1951	16 May–27 July	10	53	82nd–134th
4th	1952	4 June–8 August	9	49	135th–183rd
5th	1953	1 June–14 August	10	57	184th–240th
6th	1954	3 June–28 July	8	41	241st–281st
7th	1955	2 May–8 July	10	49	282nd–330th
8th	1956	23 April–4 July	10	51	331st–381st
9th	1957	23 April–28 June	10	49	382nd–430th
10th	1958	28 April–4 July	10	48	431st–478th
11th	1959	20 April–20 June	10	47	479th–525th
12th	1960	25 April–1 July	10	54	526th–579th
13th	1961	1 May–7 July	10	48	580th–627th
14th	1962	24 April–29 June	10	45	628th–672nd
15th	1963	6 May–12 July	10	49	673rd–721st
16th	1964	11 May–24 July	11	53	722nd–774th

1951 but which the General Assembly found unacceptable [5]—
various methods of speeding up the work of the Commission
have been considered.

[5] Cf. Yearbook, ILC, 3rd Session, 1951, II, 137–139 (Report, pars. 60–71); *ibid.*, I, 5–11 (83rd meeting), 122–135 (96th and 97th meetings), 262 (112th meeting); and above, comment under Article 10, Statute (see pp. 73–74).

Officers of the International Law Commission

Session	Chairman	1st Vice-Chairman	2nd Vice-Chairman	Rapporteur
1st 1949	Manley O. Hudson (U.S.)	Vladimir M. Koretsky (U.S.S.R.)	Sir Benegal N. Rau (India)	Gilberto Amado (Brazil)
2nd 1950	Georges Scelle (France)	A. E. F. Sandström (Sweden)	Faris Bey El-Khouri (Syria)	Ricardo J. Alfaro (Panama)
3rd 1951	James L. Brierly (U.K.)	Shuhsi Hsu (China)	Jesus M. Yepes (Colombia)	Roberto Córdova (Mexico)
4th 1952	Ricardo J. Alfaro (Panama)	J. P. A. François (Netherlands)	Gilberto Amado (Brazil)	Jean Spiropoulos (Greece)
5th 1953	J. P. A. François (Netherlands)	Gilberto Amado (Brazil)	F. I. Kozhevnikov (U.S.S.R.)	H. Lauterpacht (U.K.)
6th 1954	A. E. F. Sandström (Sweden)	Roberto Córdova (Mexico)	Radhabinod Pal (India)	J. P. A. François (Netherlands)
7th 1955	Jean Spiropoulos (Greece)	S. B. Krylov (U.S.S.R.)	F. V. García Amador (Cuba)	J. P. A. François (Netherlands)
8th 1956	F. V. García Amador (Cuba)	Jaroslav Zourek (Czechoslovakia)	Douglas L. Edmonds (U.S.)	J. P. A. François (Netherlands)
9th 1957	Jaroslav Zourek (Czechoslovakia)	Radhabinod Pal (India)	Luis Padilla Nervo (Mexico)	Sir Gerald Fitzmaurice (U.K.)
10th 1958	Radhabinod Pal (India)	Gilberto Amado (Brazil)	Grigory I. Tunkin (U.S.S.R.)	Sir Gerald Fitzmaurice (U.K.)
11th 1959	Sir Gerald Fitzmaurice (U.K.)	Shuhsi Hsu (China)	Ricardo J. Alfaro (Panama)	J. P. A. François (Netherlands)

Session	Chairman	1st Vice-Chairman	2nd Vice-Chairman	Rapporteur
12th 1960	Luis Padilla Nervo (Mexico)	Kisaburo Yokota (Japan)	Milan Bartoš (Yugoslavia)	Sir Gerald Fitzmaurice (U.K.)
13th 1961	Grigory I. Tunkin (U.S.S.R.)	Roberto Ago (Italy)	Eduardo Jiménez de Aréchaga (Uruguay)	Ahmed Matine-Daftary (Iran)
14th 1962	Radhabinod Pal (India)	André Gros (France)	Gilberto Amado (Brazil)	Manfred Lachs (Poland)
15th 1963	Eduardo Jiménez de Aréchaga (Uruguay)	Milan Bartoš (Yugoslavia)	Senjin Tsuruoka (Japan)	Sir Humphrey Waldock (U.K.)
16th 1964	Roberto Ago (Italy)	Herbert W. Briggs (U.S.)	Grigory I. Tunkin (U.S.S.R.)	Mustafa Kemal Yasseen (Iraq)

1. *Longer sessions or two sessions a year.* Proposals [6] that the Commission increase the length of its annual sessions to twelve weeks or hold two sessions a year run up against the hard fact that members of the Commission already make a substantial sacrifice of time and money and cannot afford to be absent from the professional activities by which they gain their livelihood more than the period of almost three months in which they are away from home. As the Commission observed in its 1951 report:

The members of the Commission elected in 1948 are, without exception, men engaged in professional activities. Some of them, indeed a majority, have responsibilities as permanent officials of their governments; some of them are professors of international law in universities; some of them are engaged in the private practice of law. . . . The Statute does not limit the number of sessions to be held each year. Yet more frequent sessions would necessitate a larger budget and some members of the Commission would have difficulty in absenting themselves from the performance of other duties.[7]

It was the logic of this situation and the important work remaining to be done in the field of codification and progressive development which led the Commission in 1951 to make its recommendation that it be placed on a full-time basis beginning in 1953.

During its 15th Session, the Commission, in view of its heavy agenda, re-examined the question of increasing its productivity at private meetings held on 5 and 8 July 1963. Finding that the difficulties of longer absence of members from their professional activities and the problem of a larger budget still existed, the Commission nevertheless decided to experiment with the possibility of holding two regular sessions of the Commission each year. The Commission therefore decided to hold

[6] Cf. Yearbook, ILC, 10th Session, 1958, II, 107–110; Zourek Report on Planning of Future Work of the Commission, A/CN.4/L. 76, 21 May 1958, *ibid.*, 74–76; and consideration thereof, *ibid.*, I, 174–180 (464th meeting).

[7] Yearbook, ILC, 3rd Session, 1951, II, 138, pars. 63, 64.

a three-week winter session in Geneva from 6 to 24 January 1964 and suggested to the General Assembly "that measures should be taken now to arrange for a winter session in January 1965." [8] The fact that the General Assembly did not comply with this request (see below, p. 307) may not be its final view.

2. *Two meetings a day.* Normally, the Commission holds only one three-hour session a day—Monday afternoons from 3 to 6 P.M. and Tuesday to Friday mornings from 10 A.M. to 1 P.M. In its 1957 Report the Commission stated

that there were solid reasons for the Commission's practice of holding only one plenary meeting a day. The nature of the work and the particular task entrusted to the Commission made it essential to leave enough time between meetings for personal preparation, reflexion and research, not only on the basic drafts and reports, but on the new points that were constantly coming up in the course of the discussions, and which required careful attention. For this necessary private and individual work of the members, it would be impossible to find adequate time on the basis of two plenary meetings a day. In addition, it would be impossible on that basis for the special rapporteur for the subject in hand, the general rapporteur and the drafting committee to keep pace with the Commission's work. The latter, indeed, would be compelled to meet mostly at night, since its meetings are usually of more than three hours duration, and the presence of its members at plenary meetings of the Commission is considered essential. . . .

Having regard to this position, the Commission felt that, within the confines of a ten-week's session, no serious increase in the speed or quantity of the work could be achieved except by the adoption of methods that would be detrimental to its quality—and the Commission believes that the quality of its work is, and must always remain, the primary consideration, both from the Commission's own point of view and that of the Assembly.[9]

3. *Dividing the Commission into Sub-Commissions.* A third

[8] Cf. A/5509, Report of the International Law Commission covering the work of its 15th Session, 1963, pars. 72, 74. The Report of the Commission covering the work of its 16th Session, 1964, states "that it is essential to hold a four-week winter session in 1966." A/5809, par. 38.

[9] Yearbook, ILC, 9th Session, 1957, II, 144–145.

suggestion for increasing the output of the Commission is that the Commission should be divided into at least two representative groups, which after general discussion in the full Commission, would deal simultaneously with separate topics. This suggestion, which originated in the General Assembly's Sixth Committee at its 11th and 12th Sessions, was examined by the International Law Commission at its 464th meeting in 1958 on the basis of a *Report on Planning of Future Work of the Commission* by Professor Jaroslav Zourek, one of its members.[10] Neither the Sixth Committee nor the International Law Commission took a formal decision on the question. Professor Zourek, in supporting the proposal despite its admitted disadvantages, "felt that the Commission should keep the initiative in its own hands and maintain its own prerogatives and rights where the organization of its work was concerned." [11] The specific proposal made by Professor Zourek was that, after general discussion, a draft would be referred to a sub-commission of not more than ten members so constituted as to include "representatives of all the world's principal legal systems"; that the meetings of the sub-commission would be conducted like plenary meetings with simultaneous translation and summary records; and that the sub-commission drafts would be submitted to the full commission for "possible discussion and adoption." [12] Members of the Commission thought the proposal might either injure the unity and *esprit de corps* of the Commission and the weight of its recommendations or involve it in repetitious arguments after drafts were reported back by the sub-commission to the full Commission.[13]

In fact, the Commission had made the experiment of assigning the topic of *Arbitral Procedure* to a committee for examination at its 9th Session, and the experiment had been abandoned. At the 404th meeting of the Commission, on 24

10 A/CN.4/L.76, *ibid.*, 10th Session, 1958, II, 74–76.
11 Yearbook, ILC, 10th Session, 1958, I, 179.
12 A/CN.4/L.76, par. 26, *ibid.*, II, 76.
13 *Ibid.*, I, 174–180, and Report of Commission, *ibid.*, II, 107–110.

May 1957, Mr. Zourek, as Chairman, proposed on behalf of "the officers of the Commission" the appointment of a committee "to consider the situation and report back to the Commission." The vagueness of the terms of reference—which were apparently intended to include a recommendation as to the form to be given the Commission's draft on *Arbitral Procedure* which had been referred back to the Commission by the General Assembly for reconsideration—were not adequately compensated for by the attempt to appoint a representative committee "to reflect in its composition the various views that had been expressed in the Commission and at the General Assembly, and bearing in mind also the fact that some members of the Commission were fully occupied with their work in the Drafting Committee." The record states that the "officers' proposals were adopted" and the Committee was composed of Messrs. Ago, Amado, El-Erian, Khoman, Padilla Nervo, Scelle, Spiropoulos, Verdross, and Zourek.[14] At its 418th meeting, on 17 June 1957, the Commission, without waiting for the conclusions of the committee it had appointed, decided to review the draft on *Arbitral Procedure* itself.[15] Possibly because of the vague terms of reference, several members of the committee believed that the Commission must itself reach certain basic decisions before the committee could operate.[16] Professor Scelle believed that because the membership of the International Law

[14] Yearbook, ILC, 9th Session, 1957, I, 104.

[15] *Ibid.,* 179. Cf. Report of the Commission, 1957, pars. 18 and 19, *ibid.,* II, 143–144. See also the observations of Dr. Yuen-li Liang, Secretary of the Commission:

"One-half the members of the Commission had participated in the committee, and the work of that body had given rise to such long discussions in the plenary Commission that the work had been retarded rather than advanced. Moreover, it was difficult to select ten members of the Commission representing different legal systems as envisaged in Mr. Zourek's plan . . . and to distinguish questions of principle from questions of detail to be referred to the sub-committee." Yearbook, ILC, 11th Session 1959, I, 162, par. 12.

[16] Cf. debate at 417th and 418th meetings, *ibid.,* 9th Session, 1957, I, 172–181.

Commission had changed since the draft on *Arbitral Procedure* had been approved, "all the articles should be discussed, in turn, by the full Commission; even if some of the work was done by the Committee, its decisions would have to be reviewed by the full Commission." He questioned "whether the Committee was genuinely representative of the Commission and whether its decisions would be accepted by the Commission as a whole." [17] While some members still believed that reference to a committee might be a useful procedure, the Commission refused, in 1958, to adopt the Zourek proposal, and contented itself with the observation that although there might be occasions "in the initial stages of drawing up a draft on a difficult or complex subject" when resort to the method of sub-commissions might be desirable, this should be done on an *ad hoc* basis.[18]

At its 14th Session in 1962, the Commission appointed what it termed "sub-committees" on *State Responsibility* and *Succession of States and Governments*.[19] The lengthy debate [20] preceding the decision to appoint these committees involved consideration of the desirability of splitting up the Commission into smaller and less representative working groups, but the issue was somewhat obscured in other policy clashes: whether to modify the Commission's traditional practice of proceeding to the appointment of Special Rapporteurs; the degree to which Special Rapporteurs should be instructed to deal with certain topics; the scope of the topics; whether the committees should be sufficiently small to act as "collective rapporteurs"; whether they should be standing consultative committees to assist the Rapporteur; whether they should meet

[17] *Ibid.*, 177–179.

[18] Yearbook, ILC, 10th Session, 1958, I, 174–180, and *ibid.*, II, 107–108, par. 62.

[19] A/5209, Report of the International Law Commission covering the work of its 14th Session, 1962, pars. 32, 54, 67–74, Yearbook, 1962, II, 188, 189, 191–192.

[20] A/CN.4/SR. 629–637, 25 April to 7 May 1962, Yearbook, ILC, 14th Session, 1962, I, 2–45.

between sessions of the Commission. The compromise reached by the Commission was to delay the appointment of Special Rapporteurs a year until the two ten-member committees had reported to the next session of the Commission on the scope and approach of the future studies to be made by the Special Rapporteurs, when appointed. The sub-committees held meetings both during the regular session of the Commission and at special ten-day sessions in Geneva in January 1963.[21] At the 686th (24 May 1963) and 702nd (18 June 1963) meetings of the Commission, during its 15th Session, the Commission approved the sub-committee reports as "an outline of a programme of work" that "would serve as a guide to the Special Rapporteur" without binding him in detail, and proceeded to the appointment of Special Rapporteurs, Mr. Ago for *State Responsibility* and Mr. Lachs for *Succession of States and Governments.*[22]

The Drafting Committee

From the beginning, the International Law Commission has found it indispensable to appoint a drafting committee to prepare final texts. At its 1st Session the Commission appears to have appointed two committees, one to deal with the drafting of *Declaration on the Rights and Duties of States*[23] and another "whose task it would be to draw up, during the present session, a working document containing a formulation of the Nürnberg principles." [24] The former is later referred to as "the

---

[21] Cf. A/CN.4/152, 16 Jan. 1963, Report by Mr. Roberto Ago, Chairman of the Sub-Committee on State Responsibility; A/CN.4/160, 7 June 1963, Report by Mr. Manfred Lachs, Chairman of the Sub-Committee on Succession of States and Governments. Each report was approved by the respective sub-committee and has annexes containing working papers and summary records of the debates. The Reports alone are reprinted as Annexes I and II to the Report of the International Law Commission covering the work of its 15th Session, 1963 (A/5509, pp. 39–42).

[22] A/CN.4/SR.686 and 702, Yearbook, ILC, 15th Session, 1963, I, 79–86, 189–194. See also A/5509, cited, pars. 51–61.

[23] Yearbook, ILC, 1st Session, 1949, p. 129.   [24] *Ibid.,* 134.

drafting committee" and the latter as "the sub-committee" in the Summary Records. At its 4th Session, in 1952, the Commission set up what the Chairman referred to as a "Standing Drafting Committee," although the committee membership was limited to that Session.[25] Commencing with the 7th Session in 1955, the chairman of the drafting committee has always been the First Vice-Chairman of the particular Session. Other members, also designated on the proposal of the Chairman of the Commission, are selected so as to take account of special knowledge of French, English, and Spanish as well as the individual qualifications of members. The General Rapporteur of a Session is always designated a member and the Special Rapporteurs participate during the discussion of their drafts. At the 11th Session of the Commission, the Commission decided "that if a member of the Drafting Committee could not attend a particular meeting, he should be replaced by an alternate of the same language or from the same geographical region." [26]

In recent years the trend has increased of referring to the drafting committee, questions not strictly of a drafting nature. In his *Report on Planning of Future Work of the Commission*,[27] Professor Zourek suggested that

the idea of referring details to smaller, but sufficiently representative, working parties for discussion should be adopted. Since it first began its work, the International Law Commission has made use of a drafting committee. In recent years, that body has often been given tasks beyond the competence of a mere drafting committee. After a discussion in plenary meeting, it has been asked to seek solutions and prepare texts for the full Commission. This procedure has proved extremely useful and has greatly helped to speed up the work. Consideration should be given to the possibility of generalizing and extending it, with a view to making it

25 Yearbook, ILC, 4th Session, 1952, I, 41.
26 Yearbook, ILC, 11th Session, 1959, I, 52.
27 A/CN.4/L.76, 21 May 1958, pars. 24 and 25; Yearbook, ILC, 10th Session, 1958, II, 76.

one of the International Law Commission's normal methods of work.

Discounting the argument that extending such a method might merely promote repetitive debate, he noted:

At its ninth session, the Commission referred a number of articles to the drafting committee after discussion in plenary meeting, without voting on them, and the drafting committee's proposals were approved by the full Commission without difficulty.

When the Commission discussed the Zourek proposals at its 464th meeting, on 16 June 1958, the fact that the drafting committees of the International Law Commission made decisions on substantive questions in addition to drafting points was noted without criticism by several speakers. Debate turned on the desirability of providing the drafting committee with technical services for simultaneous translation and summary records, some members believing that the advantages of informal committee discussion would be lost if the meetings of the drafting committee were formalized. Mr. Zourek concluded that there seemed "to be general agreement that the Drafting Committee could and should deal with questions of substance, but there was no unanimity on the question whether it should have full services or not." On the suggestion of the Chairman, Mr. Pal, the Commission decided not to take a formal decision but to include an account of the discussion in its Report.[28]

It is, therefore, surprising to read the following statement in the Report for 1958:

65. It was also decided that, in future, the Commission's Drafting Committee should be formally constituted as what it had long been in fact, namely, a committee to which could be referred not merely pure drafting points, but also points of substance which the full Commission has been unable to resolve or which seemed likely to give rise to unduly protracted discussion. It was to such a committee that the method of work to be adopted next year in

[28] *Ibid.*, I, 174–180.

respect of consular intercourse and immunities would relate. This decision would not entail any alteration in the present arrangements for the Drafting Committee. If, however, the Commission at any time decided to make greater use of the sub-commissions on points of substance, this might necessitate recourse to simultaneous interpretation and possibly summary records, thereby involving an administrative and budgetary problem calling for study by the Secretariat and an eventual decision by the Assembly.[29]

This reference to a "decision" of which no record appears in the Summary Records first appeared in paragraph 9 of Chapter V of the draft Report of the International Law Commission Covering the Work of its Tenth Session.[30] At its 477th meeting, on 3 July 1958, the Commission approved Chapter V without questioning the existence of such a decision,[31] after Sir Gerald Fitzmaurice, General Rapporteur, had observed: "So far as the Drafting Committee was concerned, he thought its status and functions were sufficiently indicated in paragraph 9 of the draft report. . . ."

Voting or Consensus?

During the 12th Session of the Commission, at its 547th meeting, on 25 May 1960, Mr. Douglas L. Edmonds

expressed concern at the procedure followed by the Commission at the present and at the eleventh sessions. Before the eleventh session, the Commission had always taken a vote on the principle embodied in each article and had then referred the text to the Drafting Committee with directions simply to review the language. In 1959 the Commission had departed from that procedure and had begun to refer all articles to the Drafting Committee without taking a decision on the substance. At the present session only one vote had been taken on a matter of principle, with the result that a number of articles on which sharp divergences of opinion subsisted had been referred to the Drafting Committee, which must therefore take decisions on matters of principle not settled by the

[29] *Ibid.,* II, 108.   [30] A/CN.4/L.78, Add. 4, 27 June 1958, par. 9.
[31] Yearbook, ILC, 10th Session, 1958, I, 252–255.

Commission itself. . . . The Commission would very likely be confronted in the closing weeks of the session with draft articles on which opinions would still be sharply divided. That being the situation, either the Commission would have no time to consider them again thoroughly or else its members would vote, in a spirit of conciliation, in favour of the Commission's report. Such a report would not constitute a report based upon the considered opinions of a majority of the members.

The Chairman, Mr. Padilla Nervo, replied that he was always willing to submit a matter to vote, if requested; however, he thought it would be unfortunate "if every matter was put to the vote at the initial discussion and a final draft emerged accompanied by a large number of minority opinions." [32]

During its 11th Session, the Commission had engaged in a very interesting debate over its methods of work, in particular over the issue of whether to avoid votes in the hope of obtaining a consensus.[33] Professor J. P. A. François, at the 515th meeting, on 15 June 1959

expressed some anxiety with regard to the method of the Commission's work, which had changed in recent years. At its earlier sessions, not every member of the Commission had stated his opinion on every point at length; after a few members had spoken on the particular subject, the discussion was closed and a vote taken. That practice had been abandoned, however, and now all members made statements on each point. Repetition was therefore inevitable. Votes were no longer taken, as the discussion had already disclosed the opinion of the majority. The procedure had some advantages in that interesting statements were made, but the Commission's work was being excessively delayed by that method. . . . He suggested that the Commission should consider returning to its original system.[34]

Professor Zourek shared these views and suggested that the Commission should carry out the decision taken at its 10th

[32] Yearbook, ILC, 12th Session, 1960, I, 137, pars. 56, 57.
[33] Yearbook, ILC, 11th Session, 1959, I, 161–164.
[34] Ibid., par. 6.

Session to refer questions to the drafting committee.[35] Mr. Radhabinod Pal said

that if Mr. Zourek's system involved a general discussion followed by referral to the sub-committee, that was in effect what the Commission had been doing. If on the other hand, it was intended that questions would be debated first in the sub-committee, then he was sure that such a system would be more repetitious than the current method.[36]

Professor G. I. Tunkin, while believing it possible to avoid repetitive argument, thought it wise to have full discussion on each point since "very often such discussion led to mutual understanding, which was much more important than the saving of a few hours." [37] He "did not agree that voting was a good way to frame rules of international law. . . . Although reaching agreement through discussion would require more time than voting, the resulting texts would probably find greater support among Governments." [38]

Sir Gerald Fitzmaurice agreed:

He did not think that members came to the sessions of the Commission merely in order to register their votes. One of the great merits of the Commission was that it was an international forum in which it was possible to persuade members to change their points of view, since they were not bound by instructions from Governments.[39]

With the Secretary of the Commission, Dr. Liang, and several members [40] even questioning whether the Commission had changed its methods of work as much as Professor François asserted, the Commission wisely refrained from taking a rigid decision as to its methods of work.

Examined more closely, the issue is not really between voting and not voting. The final drafts of the Commission and its annual Report to the General Assembly are submitted to vote;

[35] *Ibid.*, par. 8.   [36] *Ibid.*, par. 24.   [37] *Ibid.*, par. 7.
[38] *Ibid.*, par. 27.   [39] *Ibid.*, par. 33.
[40] Cf. *ibid.*, pars. 11, 22, 33.

and every article of a draft and every paragraph of the accompanying Commentary and of the Report is either voted on by the Commission or is subject to vote on the request of any member. The real issue refers more to the Commission's method of work and the desirability of reaching agreement within the Commission than to voting as such.

It is true that the drafting committee should not become a substitute for the Commission itself. Reference to the drafting committee is preceded by a searching debate in the full Commission. Even in the absence of a vote in the Commission, the drafting committee is usually able to discover the consensus, at least a majority opinion. At times, reference to the drafting committee appears to have been used as a device to cut off a protracted and repetitious debate in the Commission. Where the consensus is clear, no great harm is done and the Commission gets on with its work. Where reference to the drafting committee is premature and merely conceals a deep-seated divergence, the debate is resumed on the proposals of the drafting committee. It frequently happens, however, that positions are less strongly entrenched in considering the consensus—or proposal—of the drafting committee, one reason being that its proposals are presented late in the session. In any case, the proposals of the drafting committee are themselves subject to vote.

The issue thus narrows down to whether the method of reaching a consensus by debate, though time-consuming, is preferable to entrenching positions in recorded votes prior to the final votes on the adoption of particular articles of the draft. The issue turns, it should be repeated, not on the adoption of a draft but on the method of creating an agreed draft. It is more important to have a skillful Chairman guiding the Commission toward a free consensus than a slavish concern with methods of work.[41]

[41] Cf. Mr. Padilla Nervo: "With regard to the Commission's method of work, he felt that the best method was to work and not to discuss

The Rapporteur

Article 16 (a) of the Commission's Statute, dealing with the progressive development of international law, provides that the Commission "shall appoint one of its members to be Rapporteur." Although there is no comparable stipulation in the provisions relating to the codification of international law, the Commission has always appointed a Special Rapporteur [42] for its projects, whether of codification or of progressive development of international law, and the Rapporteur has always been a member of the Commission.

The selection of a Special Rapporteur is made by the Commission. The Summary Records are not explicit as to the reasons for the selection but it is obvious that the qualifications and experience of a member, as well as his willingness to serve, are primary considerations.[43] Not all Rapporteurs have had such obvious qualifications for their tasks as Professor J. P. A. François, whose service as Rapporteur on the question of the *Territorial Sea* at The Hague Codification Conference of 1930 made him the choice for Rapporteur on the *Law of the Sea*. However, broad knowledge and technical training as an international lawyer have qualified other members of the Commission to serve as Rapporteurs on topics with which they had not previously been closely identified. A successful Rapporteur needs not only the mastery of his topic but sound judgment, drafting skills, and persuasive ability. On occasion the U.N.

---

the method of work. In his experience in United Nations bodies he had found that discussion of ways to save time nearly invariably wasted time." Yearbook, ILC, 11th Session, 1959, I, 163, par. 32.

[42] The Rapporteur on a substantive topic is customarily referred to in the Commission as the Special Rapporteur in order to distinguish him from the Commission's General Rapporteur, elected each session to prepare the Report on the work of the session.

[43] Several members repudiated the suggestion made at the 183rd meeting of the Commission, on 8 Aug. 1952, that a person was suitable for selection as Rapporteur because he "held the majority view" on the subject. Yearbook, ILC, 4th Session, 1952, I, 251–252.

Secretariat has been able to remedy some deficiencies in the preparatory work of a Rapporteur but the relationship between a Rapporteur and the Secretariat has varied widely; some Rapporteurs are prepared to welcome assistance more than others.

At the 327th meeting of the Commission, on 5 July 1955, when the appointment of a Special Rapporteur for the topic of *Consular Intercourse and Immunities* was under consideration, the following colloquy occurred:

58. Mr. SANDSTRÖM [said that] . . . judging from his own experience, the special rapporteur would probably have to rely very considerably upon the help that could be given by the Secretariat. . . .

59. Mr. SALAMANCA asked what kind of assistance the Secretariat would be able to provide. . . .

62. Mr. LIANG (Secretary of the Commission) said that the nature of the co-operation between the Secretariat and special rapporteurs was a matter which was difficult to formalize.

63. The pattern of such co-operation had been set more or less from the outset of the Commission's work. It had always been the practice for the Secretariat to supply a survey of a topic to the special rapporteur on a particular subject if the rapporteur expressed a desire for Secretariat help. In appropriate cases of necessity, the Secretariat invited experts outside its staff to prepare such surveys.

64. Another form of assistance which the Secretariat gave was to prepare a compilation of the relevant national legislative texts. . . .

66. The preparation of a volume of that type by the Secretariat took not months, but years. . . .

77. The Secretariat gave every possible help to special rapporteurs in the task of gathering material for their work.[44]

It is perhaps ironic that it was on the topic of *Consular Intercourse and Immunities* that the Special Rapporteur declined Secretariat help.

Rapporteurs have varied in their drafting skills and it ap-

[44] Yearbook, ILC, 7th Session, 1955, I, 271.

pears that members have sometimes been too hesitant in submitting alternative draft articles for those drafted by a Rapporteur. While a multiplicity of texts can lead to confusion, members should be more willing, on occasion, to submit carefully drafted alternative texts rather than seeking minor amendments to a text submitted by the Rapporteur.[45]

The question of the extent to which the Commission should give instructions to a Special Rapporteur has been dealt with by the Commission on an *ad hoc* basis, and almost casually. At the 1st Session in 1949, several members suggested that the Commission should formulate a plan of work for each topic and determine what directives should be given to the Rapporteurs. After a cursory discussion by several members, Judge Hudson, Chairman, observed:

> No useful purpose would be served by giving limitative instructions to the Rapporteurs, who would themselves draw up the list of subjects to be studied under the items entrusted to them.

The record then states, *inter alia,* that Mr. Brierly was appointed Rapporteur "for the question of treaties," Mr. François "for the question of the regime of the high seas," Mr. Scelle "for the question of arbitral procedure," without further elaboration or instructions.[46]

When Professor H. Lauterpacht was elected Special Rappor-

[45] Par. 64 of the Commission's Report for 1958 records the Commission's decision "to ask all the members who might wish to propose amendments to the existing draft presented by the special rapporteur to come to the next session prepared to put their principal amendments in writing within a week, or at most ten days, of the opening of the session." Yearbook, ILC, 10th Session, 1958, II, 108. Apparently, only two members of the Commission availed themselves of this opportunity. Cf. A/CN.4/L.79 and 82, Yearbook, ILC, 11th Session, 1959, II, 84–86. An alternative draft formulation of the Nürnberg principles prepared by Professor Georges Scelle at the 1st Session of the Commission was discussed and rejected by the Commission at its 28th and 29th meetings. Yearbook, ILC, 1st Session, 1949, pp. 206–214.

[46] Yearbook, ILC, 1st Session, 1949, pp. 235–238 (32nd and 33rd meetings).

teur on the *Law of Treaties* in 1952, to succeed Professor Brierly, resigned, the selection was preceded by a debate as to whether the new Rapporteur should be instructed to complete Professor Brierly's work, to limit his initial work to certain aspects of the law of treaties, or to divide the work on the law of treaties with several other rapporteurs. Professor Lauterpacht effectively answered these questions by stating that, if elected, he would naturally take account of the materials prepared by Professor Brierly but could not be bound by them and that he wished to treat the entire subject of the law of treaties. The Commission thereupon elected Mr. Lauterpacht "special rapporteur on the law of treaties to succeed Mr. Brierly." [47]

The proposal that Sir Gerald Fitzmaurice, "in view of his special qualifications in the matter of the law of treaties," be appointed Rapporteur in place of Mr. Lauterpacht, resigned, was agreed to without discussion or instructions to him at the Commission's 296th meeting on 23 May 1955.[48] It was not until Sir Gerald himself requested the Commission, at its 368th meeting on 15 June 1956, to express its views on certain questions which he submitted, that the Commission discussed, *inter alia,* whether the draft articles on the *Law of Treaties* should be cast in the form of a code or of a draft convention. Although no vote is recorded, Sir Gerald concluded "that the Commission appeared to be generally agreed that codification of the law of treaties should not take the form of a convention." [49]

However, when the Commission, at its 597th meeting on 26

[47] Yearbook, ILC, 4th Session, 1952, I, 220–222, 224–227 (178th and 179th meetings). Mr. Yepes reminded the Commission that at its 32nd meeting he had suggested dividing the law of treaties among several Rapporteurs because there were a number of "quite distinct and separate subjects" which could conveniently be treated by different members, and this would have "the additional advantage of enabling more members of the Commission to enjoy the honour of acting as special rapporteur." *Ibid.,* 221.

[48] Yearbook, ILC, 7th Session, 1955, I, 75, par. 3.

[49] Yearbook, ILC, 8th Session, 1956, I, 226. Cf. *ibid.,* 216–228.

May 1961, appointed Sir Humphrey Waldock Special Rapporteur for the *Law of Treaties,* in place of Sir Gerald Fitzmaurice, resigned, it agreed to hold a general debate on the subject "with a view to giving Sir Humphrey the necessary instructions." [50] This debate consumed the larger part of two meetings—the 620th and 621st on 28 and 29 June 1961 [51]—and dealt with the following questions: Should the Special Rapporteur be given specific instructions? Should the Commission decide in advance whether it would present draft articles on the *Law of Treaties* in the form of a code or of a draft convention, and instruct the Special Rapporteur accordingly? Should the Commission instruct the Special Rapporteur to preserve the draft articles on the subject tentatively adopted by the Commission at its 11th Session in 1959? Should the Commission itself decide what aspect of the broad subject should first be presented by the Special Rapporteur at its next session?

The practice of the Commission, as correctly noted by Mr. García Amador, had been not to give precise instructions to a Special Rapporteur. The Special Rapporteur was customarily given complete freedom to organize and present his subject as he saw fit and it was only after the presentation of his first report that he received instructions from the Commission.[52] However, as several members noted, the Commission was quite familiar with the problems involved in its long-pending study of the *Law of Treaties* and it was essential to take clear-cut decisions and instruct the Special Rapporteur accordingly. Sir Humphrey Waldock agreed, in general, with views expressed that the Commission's object should be, where possible, to frame rules suitable for incorporation in draft conventions and that he should start with the subject of the conclusion of treaties; however, he believed that the Special Rapporteur should be given considerable latitude in revising the draft

[50] Yearbook, ILC, 13th Session, 1961, I, 99, par. 33.
[51] *Ibid.,* 247–258.
[52] *Ibid.,* 256, par. 24.

articles provisionally adopted by the Commission in 1959.[53]
The Commission thereupon agreed on the following decisions
(in the formulation of the Chairman):

(i) That the draft articles on the law of treaties would be intended to serve as a basis for a draft convention; that decision was
not, of course, a final one;

(ii) To ask the Special Rapporteur to re-examine the articles on
the same topic previously discussed by the International Law Commission;

(iii) To ask the Special Rapporteur to begin with the question
of the conclusion of treaties and then to proceed with the re-
mainder of the subject of the law of treaties with a view to covering the whole subject in two years if possible.[54]

Apparently, it was only with regard to the *Law of Treaties*
that the Commission had felt impelled to give instructions to
a new Rapporteur prior to the presentation of his first report.
When Professor Zourek was elected Special Rapporteur on the
topic of *Consular Intercourse and Immunities* and offered to
outline the topic as he "construed it, with a view to obtaining
the general views of his fellow members of the Commission," [55]
the offer was not accepted. Professor Georges Scelle

viewed the proposed procedure with some apprehension. Special
Rapporteurs had, in the past, always enjoyed absolute freedom in
preparing their reports and there was no call for them to consult
the Commission before they embarked upon their work.[56]

While it is wise to give a Special Rapporteur considerable
latitude in the organization and presentation of a new topic,
the Commission may not wish to grant the same freedom on a

[53] *Ibid.*, 252–253, 257.   [54] *Ibid.*, 258, par. 47.
[55] Yearbook, ILC, 7th Session, 1955, I, 273. (327th meeting, 5 July 1955).
[56] *Ibid.*, 289 (330th meeting, 8 July 1955). Cf. however, the later request of Professor Zourek at the 373rd and 374th meetings for the Commission's views on certain problems involved in preparing a report on
Consular Intercourse and Immunities. Yearbook, ILC, 8th Session, 1956,
I, 249–255.

topic which it has already had under consideration or on which deep policy differences as to the scope and method of treating a topic separate members of the Commission. It was reasons of this character which led to the protracted delays in appointing Special Rapporteurs for the topics of *State Responsibility* and *Succession of States and Governments*. The Commission spent the first two weeks of its 14th Session in 1962 debating the scope and procedural and substantive issues connected with these topics before deciding not to appoint Special Rapporteurs for these topics until sub-committees had presented to the next session reports on which the Commission might base instructions to the Special Rapporteurs.[57] As stated above (see above, p. 233), the Commission, at its 15th Session in 1963 approved the reports of the sub-committees on *State Responsibility* and *Succession of States and Governments* as "guiding principles to be followed by the Special Rapporteur, who, however, will not be obliged to conform to them in his study in every detail." [58] In no other cases has the Commission approved such detailed instructions for a Special Rapporteur prior to his study of a topic. At its 669th meeting on 27 June 1962 the Commission appointed Mr. Abdullah El-Erian as Special Rapporteur for the topic *Relations between States and Inter-Governmental Organizations* without any instructions.[59] The appointment of Professor Milan Bartoš as Special Rapporteur for the topic of *Special Missions* at the 712th meeting of the Commission on 2 July 1963 was preceded by a general debate on the scope of the topic but no specific instructions were given to the Special Rapporteur.[60]

In the nature of things, the Special Rapporteur brings to the Commission in his reports a mastery of his topic which

[57] See 628th to 637th meetings, 24 April–7 May 1962, Yearbook, ILC, 14th Session, 1962, I, 2–45. See above, pp. 232–233.
[58] A/5509, cited, par. 60 and pp. 39–42, for the reports of the sub-committees.
[59] Yearbook, ILC, 14th Session, 1962, I, 273–274.
[60] Yearbook, ILC, 15th Session, 1963, I, 258–267.

not all members of the Commission have had the occasion to acquire. He should therefore be given considerable latitude in the organization and presentation of his special studies. It is useful, however, that he should have a clear general idea of the way in which other members of the Commission envisage the nature and scope of the topic. This can be provided by holding a general debate on the topic at the time the Special Rapporteur is appointed, although it is unlikely that most members will at that time have devoted special study to the topic. Ultimately, of course, it is the Commission which has the final responsibility for the draft.

Since the term of office of all members of the Commission expires at the same time, the problem of planning, in such circumstances, the future work of the Commission has arisen on several occasions.[61] The Commission has correctly based its policy on the conclusion that the Commission, as such, is a continuing body [62] and a program must be planned for the session following an election even though that program is subject to change by the newly elected members. Because of the necessity for preparatory work by a Rapporteur, the likelihood of such a change is perhaps more a theoretical than a practical consideration except where a Rapporteur is not himself re-elected. The possibility that a Rapporteur might not be re-elected has deterred the Commission from undertaking new subjects on more than one occasion. At its 71st meeting, on 19 July 1950, the Commission declined to appoint a Rapporteur for the subject of the "nationality of married women" for that reason, among others. Dr. Ivan Kerno, Assistant Secretary-General, admitting that the inability of the Commission to

[61] Cf. Yearbook, ILC, 2nd Session, 1950, I, 247–255.

[62] At the 71st meeting of the Commission, on 19 July 1950, Dr. Ivan Kerno, Assistant Secretary-General, observed that although the members of the International Law Commission were elected for a fixed term, the "Commission was a permanent body, and it was on that basis that it had drawn up its programme of work and selected fourteen topics for codification." Yearbook, ILC, 2nd Session, 1950, I, 249.

anticipate the re-election of members created a serious problem, thought that "the Commission's uncertainty in that regard should not result in its complete inactivity in the interval between its third and fourth sessions. Provision could be made, for example, for the Commission to hold a very short session after the conclusion of the Sixth General Assembly and adopt whatever decisions it had had to leave in suspense pending the appointment of its members by the Assembly." The Commission was apparently not impressed with the practicality of the suggestion.[63]

At a private meeting of the Commission, held on 8 June 1953, the Commission reached a decision which it confirmed at its 189th meeting, 9 June 1953, in the following language:

2. As to the term of office of the members, the Commission had decided that it should expire on 31 December 1953. A Special Rapporteur who had not been re-elected by the General Assembly would have to cease working on that date; a Special Rapporteur who had been re-elected should, on the other hand, continue his work unless and until the Commission as newly constituted decided otherwise.[64]

The four members who were not re-elected in the 1953 election did not include the Rapporteur of any pending subject, and the newly constituted Commission carried on in 1954 without modification of its previously adopted program. At its 8th Session in 1956, the Commission requested its Rapporteurs on the *Law of Treaties* (Sir Gerald Fitzmaurice), *State Responsibility* (Professor F. V. García Amador) and *Consular Intercourse and Immunities* (Professor Jaroslav Zourek) to continue their work in preparation for future sessions, despite the fact that all terms of office expired that year.[65] All the Rapporteurs were re-elected.

---

[63] *Ibid.*, 254.

[64] Yearbook, ILC, 5th Session, 1953, I, 27–28 and, in slightly different language, *ibid.*, II, 231 (Report, par. 172).

[65] Yearbook, ILC, 8th Session, 1956, II, 301.

At its 597th meeting, on 26 May 1961, Professor Alfred Verdross, observed that since the term of office of all members of the Commission expired in 1961, there would be no certainty of the attendance of any members at the next session except those nominated by permanent members of the Security Council. He, therefore, proposed that Sir Humphrey Waldock be elected Rapporteur on the *Law of Treaties*. Professor Roberto Ago seconded the suggestion, noting that the Commission was in the delicate position of being unable to predict its membership in 1962 and yet was obliged to provide a topic for the work of the 14th Session. Professor G. I. Tunkin, agreeing, said that the Commission was not in a position to propose a new topic for discussion because it could not anticipate its composition in 1962. The appointment of Sir Humphrey as Special Rapporteur for the *Law of Treaties* was agreed upon and the Commission later engaged in the debate referred to above in order to give him, at his request, the necessary instructions.[66]

The Commission's decision of 9 June 1953, instructing a Special Rapporteur who has been re-elected to the Commission to keep on with his work, has not entirely allayed the uncertainties of the Commission in planning for the continuity of its work. Suggestions that Special Rapporteurs who had not been re-elected to the Commission nevertheless be continued as members pending the completion of the subjects entrusted to them have not gone beyond the stage of suggestion.[67] Similarly the suggestion has frequently been made that the Commission should appoint some rapporteurs or assistant rapporteurs from persons not members of the Commission.[68] As Professor Ahmed Matine-Daftary stated:

Some more permanent solution would have to be found for the

[66] Yearbook, ILC, 13th Session, 1961, I, 99.

[67] Yearbook, ILC, 3rd Session, 1951, I, 5 (Hsu); *ibid.*, 13th Session, 1961, I, 213, par. 21 (Pal).

[68] See above, pp. 146 ff.; Yearbook, ILC, 3rd Session, 1951, I, 5 (Hsu); *ibid.*, 13th Session, 1961, I, 211 (Hsu), 215 (Matine-Daftary), 217 (Sandström).

problem of special rapporteurs. One solution might well be to appoint eminent international lawyers from outside the Commission. If necessary, the Statute of the Commission should be amended in order to make that possible. There were some eminent international jurists, qualified to act as special rapporteurs, who were debarred from membership on the Commission because they had the same nationality as one of its members.[69]

While no provision of the Statute would prevent such appointments for codification, as distinguished from progressive development projects, the suggestion has always aroused political and practical objections.[70]

Time Required by the Commission to Complete its Projects

The time required by the International Law Commission to complete a piece of work obviously varies with the nature of the topic and the time left available by other projects. At its 1st Session in 1949, the Commission completed in twenty-two meetings the *Draft Declaration on Rights and Duties of States*, in addition to devoting nine meetings to organizing and planning its future work and parts of ten meetings to other substantive topics.

During its 2nd Session in 1950, the Commission completed three reports: *Ways and Means for Making the Evidence of Customary International Law More Readily Available, Formulation of the Nürnberg Principles*, and *Questions of International Criminal Jurisdiction*. During the same Session the Commission devoted all or part of twenty-eight meetings to other substantive topics: *Offences Against the Peace and Security of Mankind* (12), *Law of the Sea* (8), *Law of Treaties* (5), *Arbitral Procedure* (3). The small amount of time left for the latter three topics was caused by the compliance of the Commission with the requests of the General Assembly for priority reports on topics perhaps more political than legal.

The same difficulty confronted the Commission during its

[69] Yearbook, 13th Session, 1961, I, 215.
[70] Cf. Liang, *ibid.*, 217–218.

3rd Session in 1951 when it completed for the General Assembly three reports on *Reservations to Multilateral Conventions,* the *Question of Defining Aggression,* and the *Draft Code of Offences Against the Peace and Security of Mankind.* These tasks consumed all or part of thirty-six of the Commission's meetings during that Session, in spite of which the Commission managed to devote all or part of eighteen meetings to the *Law of the Sea.*

Commencing with its 4th Session in 1952, the Commission has been able to avoid scattering its attention on up to a half dozen topics a session. During that session, it devoted all or part of thirty meetings to preparing a *Draft Convention on Arbitral Procedure,* fifteen to *Statelessness,* and eleven to the *Regime of the Territorial Sea.*

The Draft Convention on Arbitral Procedure was completed at the 5th Session in 1953 after a total of fifty-one meetings during three sessions. In 1954, the 6th Session of the Commission completed the two draft conventions on *Statelessness,* after fifty-five meetings. In 1956, the Commission, after one hundred and seventy meetings on the topic over a seven-year period, completed its monumental *Draft Articles Concerning the Law of the Sea.* In 1957, the Commission completed in one Session its provisional draft on *Diplomatic Intercourse and Immunities.* That draft and the Commission's *Model Rules on Arbitral Procedure* were both given final form at the 10th Session of the Commission in 1958. The 12th (1960) and 13th (1961) Sessions of the Commission, and much of the 11th Session (1959), were devoted to *Consular Intercourse and Immunities,* the final draft on which was completed in 1961 after one hundred and eleven meetings.

This record of achievement is impressive, considering the brevity of the Commission's annual sessions. Eight of the completed drafts of the Commission—the four on the *Law of the Sea,* the two on *Statelessness,* and the draft articles on *Diplomatic Intercourse and Immunities* and on *Consular Intercourse and Immunities*—have already been submitted to international conferences. In its Report for 1958, the Commission queries whether "even if the Commission were to produce drafts more quickly, Governments and the Assembly itself, would be able to keep pace with them." [71] Such considerations should not deter the Commission from efforts to increase its productivity while maintaining the high quality of its work.

[71] Yearbook, ILC, 10th Session, 1958, II, 109–110, par. 68 (c).

CHAPTER 2

The Annual Reports of the International Law Commission and Dissenting Opinions

ALTHOUGH the Statute of the International Law Commission contains no provision requiring the submission of an annual Report to the General Assembly, the Commission has followed the practice of submitting to that organ a Report of the International Law Commission covering the work of each annual session. Drafted by the Secretariat of the Commission in collaboration with the General Rapporteur elected annually by the Commission, the Reports are nevertheless subjected to careful examination by the full Commission and each paragraph is accepted or modified by vote of the Commission. While certain parts of the annual Reports are standardized— for example, a chapter on the Organization of the Session, indicating membership, officers, and agenda, and a chapter of varied content on "Other Decisions of the Commission"—the inclusion of current substantive drafts, with commentary, provides the opportunity for a third reading of these drafts by the Commission.

Since these annual Reports are an official expression of the views of the International Law Commission as a commission, jealous care is exercised as to their content (see above, p. 223). The fact that decisions of the Commission are taken by majority vote has led to demands that minority views also receive expression in the Commission's Reports.

Practice of the International Law Commission with Regard to the Inclusion of Dissenting Opinions or Reservations in Its Annual Reports

The practice of the International Law Commission during its first seven Sessions reveals controversy and some confusion as to the inclusion in its annual Reports to the General Assembly of dissenting opinions, reservations, or "minority" reports made by individual members of the Commission. The controversy arose from differing views as to the propriety of including personal statements in the Report of the Commission and the confusion was in part traceable to the fact that individual members were not consistent in their attitudes toward the problem. Questions which were debated, decided, and debated again were: Does the individual member of the Commission have a right to the inclusion in the Commission's Reports of personal opinions contesting the "majority" view, explaining his votes (dissenting, concurring, or abstention), making "reservations," or merely noting his dissent, without explanation, but with a cross-reference to his recorded remarks in the Summary Records of the Commission's proceedings? If the view were taken that a member had such a right, what was its legal basis? In particular, could it be derived indirectly from the supposed obligation of the Commission under Article 20 of its Statute to include in the commentaries to its drafts conclusions relevant to divergences and disagreements *within* the Commission? If the view were taken that nothing could be included in the Commission's Reports without its agreement, how far was it desirable for the Commission to go in restricting the length or content of reservations or statements of dissent?

At the 1st Session of the Commission, Mr. Vladimir Koretsky objected [1] to a footnote [2] prepared by the Rapporteur, Mr. Gilberto Amado, for inclusion in the Commission's Report indicating the fact that Mr. Koretsky and Mr. Manley O. Hudson

[1] Yearbook, ILC, 1st Session, 1949, p. 242, (34th meeting, 6 June 1949).
[2] Ibid., 241, n. 5 (n. 4 to par. 23 of the draft Report).

had voted against the *Draft Declaration on the Rights and Duties of States* and summarizing briefly the explanations given by them for their votes with a citation to the pertinent Summary Records. At the 36th meeting of the Commission, Mr. Koretsky submitted for inclusion in the Report a lengthy footnote, ostensibly explaining his vote, but including attacks on "aggressive *blocs* such as the North Atlantic Pact and the Western Union, whose actual aim, despite false professions concerning peace and collective security, was the preparation of new wars," and charging the Commission's draft Declaration with "denying the Sovereignty of States." [3]

Mr. Georges Scelle objected to the inclusion of the footnote, in part because "the new text, which was some forty lines long, in fact constituted a minority report." The members of the Commission had, he thought, a right to their views but the inclusion of such lengthy personal statements in the Commission's Report was not desirable. Mr. Roberto Córdova thought Mr. Koretsky "had the right" to express his views at whatever length he desired, particularly since the Commission's draft Report did not set out with sufficient clarity the grounds on which the majority had approved the various articles of the draft Declaration.

Without further debate, the Commission approved, by a vote of 7 to 3, the insertion in the Report of Mr. Koretsky's proposed footnote.[4] Mr. Ricardo J. Alfaro observed that "in view of the decision taken by the Commission" every member "had the right" to introduce footnotes explaining why he had voted for or against certain articles. Judge Hudson, Chairman, thought "there was a difference between votes on the draft Declaration as a whole and votes on specific articles." Mr. Jean Spiropoulos appeared to think that only those who "voted against the draft Declaration should have the right to expound their reasons for doing so." He agreed that Mr. Koretsky's note was too long, but "had voted for its insertion in the report

[3] *Ibid.*, 258.   [4] *Ibid.* Cf. n. 21 to Report, *ibid.*, 287.

because the views expressed therein were those of a whole group of States." [5]

At the 37th meeting of the Commission, a proposal [6] by Mr. Koretsky to insert in a footnote to the Report his personal criticisms of the Secretariat Memorandum on *Ways and Means of Making the Evidence of Customary International Law More Readily Available* [7] was rejected by the Commission, by a vote of 7 to 1, after Mr. Hudson had threatened to request the inclusion of a footnote countering Mr. Koretsky's criticisms.[8] Mr. Koretsky charged the Commission with "infractions of its own Statute": it "had not respected the right of each and every member to have included in the report any opinions he had expressed in the course of the debate and to which he attached a certain importance." [9]

At the same meeting, requests for the insertion in the Report of footnotes explaining their votes were made by Messrs. Yepes, Scelle, Spiropoulos, and Alfaro. Messrs. Yepes and Scelle agreed to the modification of the phrasing of their draft statements when Chairman Hudson questioned the expression of their personal views. The Chairman ruled that the statements requested would be inserted as footnotes. After Mr. James L. Brierly, noting the draft Declaration had been adopted by a majority of 11 to 2, questioned the desirability of footnotes by members of the majority "prejudicing the draft Declaration," four members of the majority—Messrs. Spiropoulos, Scelle, Alfaro, and Yepes—withdrew their requests.[10]

After approving, somewhat hastily, the long footnote submitted by Mr. Koretsky and rejecting his second request, the Commission approved the inclusion of an additional one-sentence note in which Mr. Koretsky challenged the interpretation placed by the Commission on Articles 18 and 19 of its

[5] *Ibid.*, 258–259, (36th meeting, 8 June 1949).
[6] *Ibid.*, 264, (37th meeting, 8 June 1949).
[7] A/CN.4/6, 7 March 1949.
[8] Yearbook, cited, 264–265.
[9] *Ibid.*, 265.   [10] *Ibid.*, 266–269.

Statute.[11] At the same Session, the Commission also approved inclusion of a one-sentence explanation of his vote against the draft *Declaration on Rights and Duties of States* which, after some hesitation, Mr. Hudson requested; [12] and, at the request of Mr. Scelle, noted the fact of his dissent from a sub-committee draft.[13]

Although several members referred to the "right" of members to have explanatory footnotes included in the Commission's Report, the legal basis for such a "right" was not examined and the record is barren of any recognition by the Commission of such an alleged right. Instead, the Commission considered the texts of draft footnotes explaining votes and decided in each case to accept or reject them for inclusion in the Commission's Report.

The 1950 Report of the International Law Commission, covering the work of its 2nd Session, contains in footnote 3 the following information: Mr. Alfaro explains in 9 lines why he voted in favor of Part III of the Report dealing with the *Formulation of the Nürnberg Principles* with a reservation; Mr. Hudson explains in 15 lines why he abstained from the vote on Part III; and Mr. Scelle explains in 13 lines why he dissented from Part III.[14]

At the 76th meeting on 25 July 1950, the Commission engaged in an inconclusive debate as to the appropriate time for members to submit explanations of their votes for inclusion in the Report; if they were not submitted prior to the second reading, their incorporation in the Report might have to be left to the Rapporteur or the Secretariat.[15]

At the 78th meeting, at the conclusion of the first reading of its draft Report, Mr. Scelle, Chairman, read the statement which later appeared in footnote 3 of the Commission's Re-

[11] *Ibid.*, 267–268. N. 5 of the Report, *ibid.*, 281.
[12] *Ibid.*, 241, 259, 266, 267, 268, 269. N. 21 of the Report, *ibid.*, 287.
[13] *Ibid.*, 250. N. 12 of the Report, *ibid.*, 282.
[14] Yearbook, ILC, 2nd Session, 1950, II, 374.
[15] *Ibid.*, I, 283.

port and Mr. Hudson stated his understanding that "the Chairman was explaining the negative vote he intended to cast." Mr. Scelle agreed "that it was an opposing vote, not an abstention." [16]

At the 81st meeting, Mr. Hudson read the text of a prepared "reservation" and asked his colleagues to comment on it. The Chairman, Mr. Scelle, did not think that members of the Commission were entitled to criticize a reservation—there was no question of "adopting the reservation." Mr. Hudson thought that reservations should be examined by the Commission just as dissenting opinions had been examined by judges of the Permanent Court of International Justice. The Commission proceeded to discuss the text and content of reservations made by Mr. Hudson, Mr. Scelle, and Mr. Alfaro and decided that they should appear as a footnote to Part III of the Report. No question was raised on the point that Mr. Hudson was requesting the privilege to explain an *abstention* instead of a negative vote.[17]

At the 3rd Session of the International Law Commission Mr. Yepes protested strongly against the section of the draft Report of the Commission dealing with *Reservations to Multilateral Conventions*. While not inaccurate, he said, it "did not contain the arguments in support of the procedure followed by the Pan American Union, and a perusal of it would suggest that the Commission regarded that procedure as absurd." He thought the Commission's Report should summarize various viewpoints and the arguments made in their favor, instead of dealing only with the majority conclusion. Mr. Ivan Kerno, Assistant Secretary-General, pointed to the distinction between Reports of the Sixth Committee of the General Assembly and those of the International Law Commission: the former did indeed summarize the various arguments made in its sessions but the Reports of the International Law Commission "had

16 *Ibid.*, 299 (78th meeting, 27 July 1950).
17 *Ibid.*, 315–316 (81st meeting, 29 July 1950).

been differently arranged from the outset, a fact which . . .
had at times led certain members of the Commission to submit
individual comments for insertion as footnotes." Mr. Gilberto
Amado noted that members of the International Law Commission, unlike members of the Sixth Committee, were not representatives of States acting on instructions, and the insertion
of their individual opinions in the collective Report of the
Commission would introduce a note of ambiguity: the Report
"should only record the conclusions reached by the Commission in its corporate capacity." Individual opinions could be
stated in footnotes.[18]

Mr. Yepes stated that he would not care to adopt "such an
offensive procedure," and proposed that the draft Report be
amended to state, *inter alia,* that although "the system followed
by the Pan American Union might be deemed to represent the
existing law on the subject" this view "was not shared by the
majority of the Commission." [19] In the face of objections to his
proposed amendment, Mr. Yepes requested the insertion "on his
sole responsibility" of a 50-line note defending the Pan American system relating to reservations to multilateral treaties.[20]

Mr. Hudson objected that no member could state that any
passage of the Commission's Report was inserted on his sole
responsibility—anything it contained must be approved by
the Commission, and the Report was not a suitable vehicle for
an attack on the Commission. Other members thought that Mr.
Yepes must be granted the same privilege as Mr. Koretsky had
been granted. The Chairman, Mr. James L. Brierly, said "that
there was no question of any right belonging to members" to
insert individual opinions in the Commission's reports: it was

[18] Yearbook, ILC, 3rd Session, 1951, I, 366–367. (125th meeting, 16
July 1951). Cf. Mr. Hudson "that the Commission's proceedings were recorded in detail in the summary records. In his view, the rapporteur
should report only the conclusions reached by the Commission." *Ibid.,*
367.
[19] *Ibid.,* 367, 369.
[20] *Ibid.,* 385–386 (128th meeting, 19 July 1951).

for the Commission to decide on the contents of its Report. Mr. Alfaro thought that Mr. Yepes might be requested to agree with the General Rapporteur and the Secretariat on an abridged version explaining his vote against a part of the Report. Mr. Yepes accepted the suggestion but "considered that he had been treated rather unfairly." [21]

During the discussion, Mr. J. P. A. François called for the reversal of the "disastrous precedent" by which Mr. Koretsky had been permitted to have a long reservation inserted in the Report. He hoped that "the Commission would decide that, from that day on, *it would no longer accept detailed explanations, but merely a statement to the effect that, for the reasons given in the summary records, one member was opposed to the adoption of a particular passage in the report."* [22] Mr. Kerno stressed the fact that the Koretsky precedent "had not recognized the right of any member to insert a note in the report," but, on the contrary, "had implied that the Commission was entitled to refuse permission." After a debate on whether the François proposal should apply to the pending request of Mr. Yepes, the Commission "decided by 7 votes to 5, to adopt for future sessions the proposal by Mr. François." [23]

The revised draft of the note indicating the dissent of Mr. Yepes was approved by the Commission at its 133rd meeting on 26 July 1951.[24] Because some members thought it unfair to apply the new rule to him, Mr. Yepes was permitted to express in a note in the Commission's Report his opinion that the Commission should have adopted the Pan American system as the existing law on the matter of reservations to multilateral treaties. At the same Session, the Commission approved

---

[21] *Ibid.,* 385–387. At the next meeting Mr. Yepes stated that he had come to the conclusion that the Commission had been absolutely right. *Ibid.,* 394.

[22] *Ibid.,* 387, par. 32. Italics added. Cf. also, par. 14, *ibid.,* 386 (128th meeting).

[23] *Ibid.,* 386–388 (128th meeting, 19 July 1951).

[24] *Ibid.,* 422. Cf. Report of the Commission, n. 15, *ibid.,* II, 128.

a one-sentence footnote in which Mr. Hudson explained a negative vote.[25]

At the 4th Session of the Commission, the François formula was applied only after further debate as to its desirability. At the 181st meeting on 6 August 1952, Mr. Hudson asked the permission of the Commission to append to the Commission's Report a footnote explaining his negative vote against the draft on *Arbitral Procedure*. Mr. Hersch Lauterpacht objected that the note drafted by Mr. Hudson "contained a controversial argument to which the majority had no opportunity to reply." Some members called for the application of the François formula; Mr. F. I. Kozhevnikov called for its reconsideration as "not clear." Mr. Faris El-Khouri proposed that Mr. Hudson's request be granted, but that in the future no requests for explanatory footnotes be granted. Both before and after the Commission had approved the request of Mr. Hudson by a vote of 4–3–2, members of the Commission questioned its compatibility with the François formula, and Mr. Hudson therefore redrafted his note to comply with the formula, and the Commission approved its insertion in the Report unanimously.[26]

After further debate, the proposal of Mr. El-Khouri that no future requests for the inclusion of a footnote expressing the attitude of individual members be granted was rejected as too restrictive, by a vote of 5–3–1. The Chairman noted that the Commission would continue to be bound by the François formula.[27]

The next day, at its 182nd meeting, the Commission was confronted with draft footnotes which Mr. Jaroslav Zourek and Mr. Kozhevnikov wished inserted in the Report to explain their votes against the draft on *Arbitral Procedure*. Mr. Lauterpacht thought that, for example, the words in Mr. Zourek's draft note that "he could not accept the new concept of arbi-

[25] *Ibid.,* 131, n. 18.
[26] Yearbook, ILC, 4th Session, 1952, I, 242–243 (181st meeting, 6 Aug. 1952).
[27] *Ibid.,* 243–244.

tration as it emerged" in the Commission's draft did not meet
the François formula because it contained a statement not acceptable to the majority of the Commission who did not agree
that the draft articles were based on a new concept of arbitration. A motion by Mr. Hudson to reconsider the François formula adopted at the previous session was defeated by a vote of
6 to 5, but the members continued to discuss its desirability.
The Commission then rejected, by identical votes of 7 to 4, the
requests of Mr. Zourek and Mr. Kozhevnikov. Mr. Kozhevnikov
branded the rejection of his request as "a flagrant denial of a
fundamental right belonging to all members of the Commission and a direct violation of the Commission's Statute." After
being redrafted in conformity with the François formula the
notes of Mr. Zourek and Mr. Kozhevnikov were unanimously
accepted by the Commission for inclusion in its Report.[28]

At the 183rd meeting on 8 August 1952, Mr. Zourek read
a further draft footnote for inclusion in the Commission's
Report in explanation of his votes in regard to the preparation
of a draft on *Statelessness.* After members of the Commission
had challenged the compatibility of his statement with the
François formula, because it set forth reasons for his votes instead of referring to the Summary Records, the Commission accepted Mr. Zourek's draft note by a vote of 6–4–1.[29]

The reluctance of members of the Commission to give strict
application to the François formula did not arise from its lack
of clarity, but from strongly held views as to its desirability. By
the end of the session, Mr. Lauterpacht had reached the conclusion that the question should be re-examined; although footnotes might be abused, "to deprive members of the right to
express dissent and give their reasons for it was both objectionable in principle and contrary to the dignity of the Commission." [30] Other members thought this argument quite be-

[28] *Ibid.,* 245–248. (182nd meeting, 7 Aug. 1952). Cf. Report of the
Commission, n. 4, *ibid.,* II, 58.
[29] *Ibid.,* I, 252–254. Cf. Report of the Commission, n. 9, *ibid.,* II, 68.
[30] *Ibid.,* I, 254.

side the point: the issue was not a right to express dissent—which would be fully recorded in the Summary Records—but the danger of distorting the Commission's collective Report with a flood of individual opinions.

The debate was resumed at the 5th Session of the Commission, in 1953, when, on the proposal of Mr. Zourek, the Commission added to its agenda an item for consideration of "Provision for the Expression of Dissenting Opinions in the Commission's Final Report on the Work of Each Session." Mr. Yepes supported the inclusion of the item because he believed that "the Commission's Report to the General Assembly ought to reflect accurately, faithfully and impartially the course of debates throughout the session." [31] Mr. Zourek presented a memorandum, with attached draft resolution, the operative part of which called upon the International Law Commission to recognize:

(a) that any member of the Commission may attach a statement of his dissenting opinion to any decision by the Commission, on draft rules of international law, if the whole or part of the said decision does not express the unanimous opinion of the members of the Commission;

(b) that any dissenting member may briefly explain his views in a footnote, if, in cases other than those covered by sub-paragraph (a) above, a decision has been taken on a question of principle affecting the work of the Commission.[32]

In presenting his proposal, Mr. Zourek stated that dissenting statements on questions of international law should appear in an annex to the Commission's Report. The advantages he envisaged were to have the Commission's Report reflect more accurately the views of members, thus aiding governments and the General Assembly in their consideration of the Commission's drafts, and to recognize "the right" of members

[31] Yearbook, ILC, 5th Session, 1953, I, 3 (184th meeting, 1 June 1953).
[32] A/CN.4/L.42, 2 June 1953, reprinted in Yearbook, ILC, 1953, I, 66–68 n. 1.

to have their dissenting opinions expressed in the Commission's Report. This "right" he attempted to establish by analogy with dissents in international arbitral and judicial proceedings and, indirectly, from the presumed obligation under Article 20 (*b*) of the Commission's Statute for the Commission to include in its Report conclusions relevant to divergencies within the Commission.

Although the analogy with dissenting opinions of judges of international tribunals was questioned, there was no discussion of the alleged right of dissent based upon Article 20 of the Commission's Statute. Professor Lauterpacht thought that it was "intolerable to deny the right of freedom of expression to any member of the Commission" and sought to overcome the irrelevancy of this argument by regarding as "mere evasion" the assumption that governments might consult the Summary Records which testified to complete freedom of expression within the Commission. Other members thought that the annex containing individual dissenting opinions would necessarily be longer than the Commission's Report and might distract attention from the agreed decisions and conclusions of the Commission.

Mr. Zourek's proposal was rejected by a vote of 7–3–3. The Commission then rejected two proposals entitling members of the Commission to append to the Report brief explanatory statements of dissent, and the Chairman stated that the previous decision (i.e., the François formula) remained in force.[33]

At the final meeting of the Session, the Commission, on the proposal of Mr. Zourek, decided that the Report should contain reference to this agenda item. Amending the phraseology submitted by Mr. Zourek, the Commission decided unanimously to conclude its reference to this item with the following words:

The existing rule, adopted at the third session, provides that the

[33] Yearbook, ILC, 5th Session, 1953, I, 66–72 (195th meeting, 16 June 1953).

Commission's report should only contain a statement to the effect that, for the reasons given in the summary records, one member was opposed to the adoption of a particular passage in the report.[34]

At the 232nd meeting of the Commission, on 5 August 1953, Mr. Amado, Mr. Zourek, and Mr. Kozhevnikov requested the inclusion of footnotes in the Report noting the fact that they had voted against the draft on *Arbitral Procedure*. No objection was made to the characterization by Mr. Kozhevnikov of the commentary on *Arbitral Procedure* as "one-sided." [35] At the 234th meeting Mr. Kozhevnikov, Mr. Scelle, Mr. Zourek, and Mr. Hsu explained negative votes in relation to the draft on the *Continental Shelf* or some of its articles.[36] Although only Mr. Kozhevnikov is recorded as requesting that his vote "be recorded," the dissents are all noted in footnote 8 to the Commission's Report.[37] Mr. Zourek and Mr. Kozhevnikov asked for notes recording their negative votes against the drafts on *Statelessness* and Mr. Yepes stated that he was "still opposed" to a specified article.[38] All three dissents are noted in footnote 16 of the Report.[39]

All of these notes may be said to comply with the François formula. Although the Summary Records of this Session do not record any vote of the Commission on the requests made for the inclusion of footnotes of dissent, the Chairman asked the General Rapporteur to consider where some of them would best be placed.[40]

It should also be noted that at its 5th Session, the Commis-

[34] *Ibid.*, 384–386, par. 16 (240th meeting, 14 Aug. 1953). Cf. Report, par. 163, *ibid.*, II, 230–231, where a variant of the text adopted includes the words "that detailed explanations of dissenting opinions should not be inserted in the report."

[35] *Ibid.*, 325.

[36] *Ibid.*, 343–344 (234th meeting, 7 Aug. 1953).

[37] *Ibid.*, II, 212.

[38] *Ibid.*, I, 382–383 (239th meeting, 13. Aug. 1953).

[39] *Ibid.*, II, 221. See also n. 9 recording a dissent by Mr. Yepes, *ibid.*, 213.

[40] *Ibid.*, 383.

sion, on the proposal of Mr. Zourek, included in its Report a more detailed summary of minority views on arbitral procedure.[41]

At the 6th Session of the Commission in 1954, the François formula was applied without controversy, but certain procedural changes emerged. After voting on the adoption of drafts on *Statelessness*,[42] *Offences Against the Peace and Security of Mankind*,[43] and the *Regime of the Territorial Sea*,[44] various members explained their votes or abstentions. Some did, and some did not, request the insertion of footnotes recording their votes. Contrary to previous practice, no draft notes were submitted for consideration by the Commission, and the Commission did not vote on any requests. Toward the end of the session, the Chairman, Mr. A. E. F. Sandström, requested members "to submit their reservations to the Secretariat in writing for inclusion in the general report." [45] In the closing minutes of the session, Mr. Zourek resubmitted his proposal entitling a member to have a short dissenting opinion included in the Commission's reports. By a vote of 5–2–2 the proposal was deferred to the next session.[46]

At its 7th Session, the Commission examined at its 322nd and 323rd meetings on 29 and 30 June 1955,[47] a proposal by Mr. Zourek [48] in terms almost identical with paragraph (a) of his proposal which had been rejected at the 5th Session of the Commission by a vote of 7 to 3, with 3 abstentions.[49] The pro-

[41] *Ibid.*, 319, 322–323, and par. 28 and 29 of the Report of the Commission, *ibid.*, II, 203–204.

[42] Yearbook, ILC, 6th Session, 1954, I, 170–171, 176. Cf. notes 2 and 3 to Report of the Commission, *ibid.*, II, 142, 148.

[43] *Ibid.*, I, 195. Cf. n. 6, Report, *ibid.*, II, 151.

[44] *Ibid.*, I, 194, 203. Cf. n. 7, Report, *ibid.*, II, 153.

[45] *Ibid.*, I, 195, par. 17.   [46] *Ibid.*, 204.

[47] Yearbook, ILC, 7th Session, 1955, I, 240–246.

[48] A/CN.4/L.61, 29 June 1955, reproduced in *ibid.*, II, 43.

[49] See above, p. 263. Mr. Zourek incorrectly stated that his previous proposal had been rejected "following a tied vote of 6 votes for and 6 against." *Ibid.*, I, 242. The 1953 Yearbook, ILC, I, 72, records the vote against the proposal as 7–3–3.

posal differed principally in a preambular assertion that because Article 20 of the Commission's Statute required it to specify "the extent of agreement on each point in the practice of States and in doctrine" and the "divergencies and disagreements which exist, as well as arguments invoked in favour of one or another solution," it followed that the Commission should, in its annual Reports to the General Assembly, "record all the views expressed in the Commission and the main arguments invoked" and that the best method of achieving this was to recognize "the right" of members to express their dissenting opinions in an annex to the Commission's Report.

In the discussion which followed, the alleged "right" of members of the Commission, on the basis of Article 20 of the Statute, to insert individual opinions in the Commission's Report was referred to by Mr. Sandström, who observed

that the French text of Article 20 of the Commission's Statute, by referring to *les divergences et désaccords qui subsistent,* was perhaps somewhat misleading. If read hastily, it might be construed as referring to divergences of opinion within the Commission. In actual fact, as was made clear by the English text and particularly by the whole context of the article, the reference was to divergences of opinion which might exist in legal circles generally concerning the issues upon which the Commission was reporting.[50]

Mr. Spiropoulos added "that article 20 of the Commission's Statute referred not to the Commission's general report but rather to the commentary it attached to the drafts prepared by it." [51] The implication of these remarks is that Article 20 of the Statute provided no legal basis for a right to insert individual opinions in the Commission's Reports.

Although Mr. García Amador expressed disapproval of the view that "the Commission itself should exercise control over the recording of dissenting views" and urged that "the right

[50] Yearbook, ILC, 7th Session, 1955, I, 244. For earlier comments, cf. Yearbook, ILC, 5th Session, 1953, I, 323.
[51] Yearbook, ILC, 7th Session, 1955, I, 245.

of members to place their dissenting views on record should be unconditionally recognized," [52] the discussion turned less on the alleged right, and its possible legal basis, than upon the desirability of adopting a practice which, in the view of the majority, would throw the Reports of the Commission out of balance and tend to lessen their authoritativeness. After Mr. Zourek had accepted an amendment requiring a member to consult with the Chairman before exercising his "right" to add his dissenting opinion to a report, the Commission rejected the proposal by a vote of 8 to 5 [53] and, as the Commission's Report states, "reaffirmed the existing rule adopted at the third session." [54]

At the last meeting of the Session, the Chairman invited members "to place their reservations on record before the report as a whole was adopted by the Commission." Mr. García Amador objected that reservations in which Mr. Edmonds, in explanation of his votes, made assertions about the three-mile limit as international law and the utility of the Commission's draft article on fisheries were not in accordance with the rule. The Chairman, Mr. S. B. Krylov, stating that it was undesirable for the Commission's rule to be interpreted too strictly, ruled that Mr. Edmonds' proposed footnotes could be included in the Report because they did not infringe the rule "in any very material way." Mr. Edmonds, nevertheless, modified his reservations to conform to the rule.[55] All reservations made to the Report of the 7th Session conformed to the rule, and the Commission then adopted its draft Report, as amended.[56]

This desirable procedure was not followed at the 8th Session of the Commission in 1956. In its closing meeting, the

[52] *Ibid.* par. 46.   [53] *Ibid.*, 245–246.

[54] *Ibid.*, II, Report, par. 38. At the request of Mr. El-Khouri a footnote was inserted declaring his opposition to the insertion in the Report of any dissenting opinion. *Ibid.*, n. 19.

[55] *Ibid.*, I, 287.

[56] *Ibid.*, I, 287–289 (330th meeting, 8 July 1955). For the reservations, see Report of the Commission, notes 4, 13, and 19, *ibid.*, II, 21, 34, 43.

Commission unanimously adopted its draft Report, which contained no footnotes of reservation or dissent.[57] Mr. Pal stated that "it was clear from the vote that members found that the report gave an accurate account of the Commission's work and of the views of the majority," and he therefore thought it "unnecessary for members to enter reservations to particular articles." The Chairman, Mr. García Amador, nevertheless invited members to hand to the Secretariat "a note of any reservations they might wish to have included in the report." The Session was then closed without opportunity for the Commission to examine notes of dissent.[58] Sir Gerald Fitzmaurice, Mr. Serge Krylov, and Mr. Jaroslav Zourek expressed dissent in notes which appear to conform to the spirit of the François formula, without, however, giving citations to the Summary Records.[59]

The Report of the International Law Commission covering the work of its 9th Session in 1957 contains no notes of reservation or dissent [60] even though Mr. Milan Bartoš and Mr. Grigory I. Tunkin stated at the closing meeting that they had voted for the draft articles and commentary on *Diplomatic Intercourse and Immunities* with reservations.[61] The Reports of the Commission covering its 10th [62] and 11th [63] Sessions in 1958 and 1959 are likewise without notes of reservation even though the Commission at its 10th Session adopted final drafts on *Arbitral Procedure* and *Diplomatic Intercourse and Immunities.* The Report of the Commission covering its 12th Session in 1960 records only one footnote of reservation in which Sir Gerald Fitzmaurice explains in terms which do not comply literally with the Commission's rule, a reservation to one paragraph of the Commission's commentary to one article of its

[57] A/CN.4/L.68 and addenda.
[58] Yearbook, ILC, 8th Session, 1956, I, 290 (381st meeting, 4 July 1956).
[59] *Ibid.,* II, 256, Report, n. 10.
[60] Yearbook, ILC, 9th Session, 1957, II, 131 ff.
[61] *Ibid.,* I, 231 (430th meeting, 28 June 1957).
[62] Yearbook, ILC, 10th Session, 1958, II, 78 ff.
[63] Yearbook, ILC, 11th Session, 1959, II, 87 ff.

draft on *Consular Intercourse and Immunities.*[64] Sir Gerald presented the text of his proposed reservation at the 579th meeting of the Commission with a request that it be incorporated as a footnote to the Commission's Report. The chairman stated "that the reservations would be recorded"; and the Commission's draft Report, "as amended, was adopted unanimously, subject to drafting changes." At the same meeting, three members explained that in voting for the Report they had not abandoned previously expressed views, although they did not ask for the inclusion of any notes to that effect in the Report.[65]

The Report of the Commission covering its 13th Session in 1961,[66] which presents the draft on *Consular Relations,* contains no indication of individual dissents even though the Summary Records reveal divergences of opinion on some texts adopted. The 1962 Report of the Commission covering the work of its 14th Session notes the dissent of Mr. Briggs to three draft articles on the *Law of Treaties,* each of the notes having been formulated to accord with the Commission's practice and having been authorized by the Commission.[67] The 1963 and 1964 Reports covering the 15th and 16th Sessions of the Commission contain no notes of reservations.[68]

The conclusion to be drawn from examination of the practice of the International Law Commission is that the Commission has never recognized that a member has a legal right to the inclusion in the Commission's annual Reports of individual opinions, no matter how emotionally the dissenting opinion may be held. In every case, the Commission has decided what should or should not be included in its Reports. Usually the decision has been express, although, after the Commission

---

[64] Yearbook, ILC, 12th Session, 1960, II, Report, n. 16, p. 165.

[65] *Ibid.,* I, 342 (579th meeting, 1 July 1960).

[66] A/4843, Yearbook, ILC, 13th Session, 1961, II, 88 ff.

[67] A/5209, notes 28, 33, and 48. Cf. Yearbook, ILC, 14th Session, 1962, I, 281, 286.

[68] A/5509 (1963 Report) and A/5809 (1964 Report).

adopted a general rule on the matter, it has been tacitly followed.

The legal basis of the alleged "right" of individual members of the Commission to have their dissenting opinions or reservations inserted in the Commission's Reports has never been thoroughly discussed in the Commission, probably because no cogent legal argument to that effect has ever been presented to it. The argument basing the alleged "right" on an analogy to dissenting opinions of judges of international courts and arbitral tribunals received short shrift in the Commission. As Mr. Spiropoulos observed:

> The Commission was not a judicial body, but an assembly of jurists preparing texts that were usually intended for incorporation in a convention. Surely no precedent existed for annexing dissenting opinions to the draft of an international convention.[69]

Nor have attempts to derive from the Commission's Statute an individual right to insert dissenting opinions in the Commission's annual Reports—which are not even referred to in the Statute—been regarded as worthy of serious attention. The only provision of the Statute on which it has been sought to base such an alleged right is Article 20, particularly sub-paragraph (b)(ii). By this provision "the Commission" is required, in submitting its codification drafts to the General Assembly, to accompany them with "a commentary containing . . . (b) Conclusions relevant to: . . . (ii) Divergencies and disagreements which exist (Fr.: *qui subsistent*), as well as arguments invoked in favour of one or another solution."

Of this provision the following observations may be made:

1. The provision refers to the commentary to a codification draft and not to the Commission's annual Report to the General Assembly.

2. Read in the context of the entire article, the divergencies and disagreements referred to—like the "adequate presentation of precedents" and "the extent of agreement . . . in the

[69] Yearbook, ILC, 5th Session, 1953, I, 71 (195th meeting, 16 June 1953).

practice of States and in doctrine"—are intended to establish a general frame of reference permitting the Commission's codification draft to be viewed in the light of precedent, practice, doctrine, and the reasons for disagreement where it exists. Given the broad purpose of Article 20, it seems unlikely that the obligation of the Commission to present a commentary containing its conclusions on, *inter alia,* divergencies, disagreements, and arguments invoked was intended to refer to divergencies and arguments within the Commission.

3. Even on the contrary assumption that the International Law Commission is required by this provision to present in its commentary to a codification draft conclusions relevant to disagreements and arguments invoked within the Commission, this obligation of the Commission would confer no legal right on its individual members to dictate the inclusion in the Commission's corporate Report to the General Assembly of personal opinions and doctrinal beliefs. The Statute makes it clear that it is "the Commission" which prepares and submits to the General Assembly drafts, commentaries, and recommendations, and not the individual members composing the Commission.

In the absence of any tenable legal argument supporting the alleged right to insert individual dissenting opinions or reservations in the Commission's Report, the Commission has quite properly regarded its own responsibilities as precluding such a right.

This places the claim to have dissenting opinions included in the Commission's Reports in proper perspective: it is a matter of policy, not of legal right.

Against the responsibility of the Commission to see that its measured conclusions, reached after free and comprehensive deliberation, are not submerged by strongly held individual dissents or doctrinal beliefs, may be set the understandable desire of those whose views were, after consideration, rejected by the Commission to dissociate themselves from the collective judgment of the Commission, which they believe to be incorrect.

The minority on any particular point has not been denied freedom of expression or the right to dissent. The Summary Records of the Commission's proceedings are eloquent testimony to this conclusion. The issue is really the more limited one of the method of recording expressions of dissent. The Summary Records of the Commission's proceedings are carefully prepared to record what was said and can be corrected by speakers. The Summary Records suffice to set forth individual opinions. No individual opinions or reservations held by the members composing a particular majority find expression in the Commission's Reports, and the same rule should apply to all.

However, an adherent of the view adopted as the Commission's conclusion has a satisfaction which is denied to a member whose views were rejected, after consideration, by the Commission. Dissenting members, therefore, want their dissents recorded twice: once in the Summary Records and again in the Commission's Reports. In support of this privilege they have argued that the Summary Records were not easily available— a point which is no longer true even if it ever was true as regards public officials and scholars.

A more serious argument for the privilege of inserting dissenting opinions is that the Commission's annual Reports, unlike the Reports of the Sixth Committee to the General Assembly, do not summarize comprehensively all the arguments made and adopted or rejected in the meetings of the Commission. At an early date the Commission decided, perhaps without thorough discussion, that the emphasis of its annual Reports to the General Assembly should be on conclusions reached by the Commission rather than on all arguments debated.[70] The records reveal a reluctance to include in the Reports a summary of proposals rejected or articles deleted from a draft after reconsideration. This policy can be defended on the ground that it is not the hesitations of the Commission but its considered conclusions which are of interest to the General Assembly and

[70] Cf. Yearbook, ILC, 1st Session, 1949, pp. 222 ff.

to the States which compose it. However elaborately proposals or arguments rejected by the Commission might be set forth in its Reports, they would be weakened by the fact that, after consideration, they had been rejected by the Commission. Where minority views have been strongly held, the Commission has, in its most recent Reports, summarized them in more detail. This may account, in part, for the small number of reservations attached to recent Reports. Employed with restraint, this may be a useful compromise.

If one reviews the practice of the Commission with regard to the inclusion of individual dissents and reservations in its Reports, the conclusion seems justified that it has adopted the correct policy. There was little excuse for inserting in the 1949 Report of the Commission covering the 1st Session the diatribe of Mr. Koretsky found in footnote 21 to that Report except perhaps the uncertainty of members at their first session on how to handle the problem. At least the decision was made by the Commission and not by Mr. Koretsky, a point which was emphasized when his second request was rejected.

At its 2nd and 3rd Sessions the Commission felt its way toward the adoption of a general rule in an atmosphere clouded by the Commission's reluctance to come to grips with the assertion that a member had a "right" to the inclusion in the Commission's Reports of his dissenting opinions or reservations. By implication, the Commission rejected such a claim of right and kept in its own hands the decision as to what should be included in its Reports. During these sessions the Commission also exercised the responsibility of modifying the content, form, or length of draft reservations submitted to it for inclusion in its Reports.

The rule adopted by the Commission at its 3rd Session that it "would no longer accept detailed explanations, but merely a statement to the effect that, for the reasons given in the Summary Records, one member was opposed to the adoption of a particular passage in the report" (see above p. 260), is still the governing rule on the subject. At the 4th Session its application was challenged by members who wished to insert brief explanations of their votes and at the 5th and 7th Sessions of the Commission, in 1953 and 1955, determined efforts to repeal the rule in favor of the right to insert dissenting statements in an annex to the Reports were defeated.

Perhaps because the formula adopted by the Commission left little for debate where it was followed, the practice of submitting the text of a draft footnote of reservation for discussion by the Commission gradually declined.

A model procedure was followed at the 7th Session of the Commission in 1955, where, with Mr. Krylov in the Chair, the members were invited to place their reservations on record before the draft Report of the Commission was adopted. Sir Gerald Fitzmaurice, for example, made a carefully phrased statement of reservations to be included in the Summary Record of the 330th meeting and concluded by presenting the text of brief footnotes which he requested be inserted in the Report.[71] Although it might be desirable for the Commission to vote to accept each footnote of reservation submitted, the same effect was achieved by treating them as amendments to the draft Report prior to its adoption.[72] This is more satisfactory than the procedure followed at the 8th Session in 1956, where the Commission as such had no opportunity to consider the texts of reservations submitted to the Secretariat after the closure of the session.

The complete absence of reservations of dissent from the Reports of the Commission covering its 9th (1957), 10th (1958), 11th (1959), 13th (1961), and 15th (1963) Sessions and the few reservations to the 12th (1960) and 14th (1962) Reports are an encouraging sign. It is not entirely the absence of controversy —since the Summary Records include expressions of dissent— but perhaps the fact that the Commission's Reports refer to minority views, which may have made this possible.

[71] Yearbook, ILC, 7th Session, 1955, I, 287–288 (330th meeting, 8 July 1955).
[72] Yearbook, ILC, 7th Session, 1955, I, 287–289.

CHAPTER 3

Recommendations of the International Law Commission to the General Assembly

THE Statute of the International Law Commission provides that when the Commission has completed a final draft on a particular topic the Commission shall submit it to the General Assembly with its recommendations. The pertinent provisions of Article 16, paragraphs (*i*) and (*j*), provide that when the Commission has adopted "a final draft and explanatory report" for the progressive development of international law

(*j*) The Commission shall submit the draft so adopted with its recommendations through the Secretary-General to the General Assembly.

With regard to projects for the codification of international law, Article 22 provides in part that

the Commission shall prepare a final draft and explanatory report which it shall submit with its recommendations through the Secretary-General to the General Assembly,

and Article 23, paragraph 1, reads:

1. The Commission may recommend to the General Assembly:
   (*a*) To take no action, the report having already been published;
   (*b*) To take note of or adopt the report by resolution;
   (*c*) To recommend the draft to Members with a view to the conclusion of a convention;
   (*d*) To convoke a conference to conclude a convention.

Although Article 16 (*j*) does not specify possible recommendations by the Commission to the General Assembly, the possibilities listed in Article 23 with regard to codification drafts are also available for final drafts for the progressive development of international law. The International Law Commission itself observed in paragraph 54 of the Report covering the work of its 5th Session (1953):

So far as recommendations proposed by the Commission are concerned, it seems to matter little whether a final draft falls within the category of development or that of codification. While article 23 of the Statute . . . specifies the kind of recommendations which the Commission may make to the General Assembly on any given subject, article 16 (j) refers to recommendations generally. There seems to be no reason for any differentiation between the two kinds of recommendation. Neither does it appear that any such differentiation was intended.[1]

The recommendations made by the International Law Commission with reference to its completed drafts are set forth below.

I

1. *Draft Declaration on Rights and Duties of States* (1949). The first occasion on which the Commission had to decide what form its recommendation to the General Assembly should take with reference to a formal draft was upon completion of its *Draft Declaration on Rights and Duties of States*. At the 24th meeting of the Commission, on 20 May 1949, its Chairman, Judge Manley O. Hudson, recalled that the Panamanian draft from which the Commission's Draft Declaration was in part derived had been submitted to governments for their comments; and that since governments had thus been consulted before the Commission was instructed by the General Assembly, by resolution 178 (II) of 21 November 1947, "to prepare a draft declaration" on the basis of the Panama draft, taking into consideration the observations submitted by govern-

---

[1] Yearbook, ILC, 1953, II, 208.

ments,[2] the Commission's Draft could be submitted directly to the General Assembly.[3] Professor Koretsky (U.S.S.R.) opposed this view, expressing the opinion that Articles 16 and 21 of the Statute required the publication of the Draft Declaration and its submission to governments for comment prior to its submission to the General Assembly. The debate turned upon whether, in drafting the text of the *Draft Declaration on Rights and Duties of States* pursuant to General Assembly resolution 178 (II), the Commission was engaged in a specially assigned task or whether the differing procedures governing development or codification of international law were applicable.[4] Dr. Ivan Kerno, Assistant Secretary-General, noted that the Commission could not invoke Article 23, presumably because of the General Assembly resolution, and concluded that the Commission "should limit itself to presenting its report and the draft declaration, without making recommendations." [5]

The Report of the Commission covering its 1st Session contains, in paragraph 53, the following passages:

The Commission, with Mr. Vladimir M. Koretsky dissenting, came to the conclusion that its function in relation to the Draft Declaration fell within neither of the two principal duties laid upon it by its Statute, but constituted a special assignment from the General Assembly.

Declaring that in "this connexion, the Commission was guided by the terms of General Assembly resolution 178 (II) and the relevant provisions of its own Statute," the Report continues:

The Commission therefore decided, by twelve votes to one, to submit the Draft Declaration, through the Secretary-General, to the General Assembly immediately and to place on record its conclusion that it was for the General Assembly to decide what further course of action should be taken in relation to the draft Declara-

---

[2] Cf. A/CN.4/4, 2 Feb. 1947, pp. 9–10.
[3] Yearbook, ILC, 1949, p. 175.
[4] *Ibid.*, 175–177, 179–182.
[5] *Ibid.*, 181.

tion and, in particular, whether it should be transmitted to Member Governments for comments.[6]

With regard to the first final draft which it completed, the International Law Commission therefore made no specific recommendation to the General Assembly as to action to be taken in relation thereto.

It is perhaps significant that the General Assembly, in taking note, by resolution 375 (IV), of the *Draft Declaration on Rights and Duties of States* and in commending it to the continuing attention of Member States and jurists of all nations,[7] appeared to accept without question the important thesis enunciated in paragraph 53 of the Commission's Report that it was within the competence of the Commission to adopt procedures for special tasks assigned to it by the General Assembly which differed from procedures set forth in the Statute for development or codification of international law. In the Commission, Professor Koretsky had argued that the Statute gave the Commission "a choice between two procedures," codification or development, and "provided for no exception to the two procedures which it defined." [8] In the Sixth Committee, the International Law Commission was charged with having violated its Statute by departing from these procedures in submitting the Draft Declaration to the General Assembly without consulting governments on its Draft.[9] Professor Koretsky believed "that the General Assembly should make it clear to the Commission that, in future, it should obey its Statute rather than seek to circumvent it." [10] A Polish motion [11] to adjourn discussion on the Draft Declaration until, presumably in accordance with Ar-

[6] *Ibid.*, 290.

[7] GAOR, 4th Session, 1949, Resolutions (A/1251), p. 66. Res. 375 (IV), 270th plenary meeting, 6 Dec. 1949, Cf. *ibid.*, Plenary Meetings, pp. 537-549.

[8] Yearbook, ILC, 1949, pp. 176, 181.

[9] GAOR, 4th Session, 1949, Sixth Committee, Summary Records, pp. 165 (Byelorussian S.S.R.), 168 (Poland).

[10] *Ibid.*, 263.   [11] *Ibid.*, 168-169.

ticles 16 and 21 of the Commission's Statute,[12] it had been referred to governments for comment was voted to be out of order,[13] and the Committee took no stand on the competence of the Commission to vary its procedures. The fact that the General Assembly decided to transmit the Draft Declaration to Member States for their comment and for their advice on the question whether any further action should be taken by the General Assembly on it [14] implies no criticism by the General Assembly of the Commission's view of its own competence to select procedures as indicated in paragraph 53 of the Commission's Report.

II

With regard to the next six completed items submitted by the International Law Commission to the General Assembly, the Commission's recommendations followed an identical form which made no reference to Articles 16 or 23 of its Statute: the Commission merely stated that its reports "are submitted to the General Assembly for its consideration." [15] This was the formula applied to the following topics:

2. *Ways and Means for Making the Evidence of Customary International Law More Readily Available* (1950). The Commission's report on this topic, which is called for by Article 24

[12] The Norwegian representative pointed out that there appeared to be some confusion in the minds of certain representatives as to the nature of the Statute of the International Law Commission: ". . . the Statute was simply a permanent instruction issued to the Commission by the General Assembly, and was therefore binding on the Commission but not on the Assembly itself." *Ibid.*, 171.

[13] *Ibid.*, 171–172.

[14] Res. 375 (IV), par. 3 (cited). In view of the paucity of replies received, the General Assembly, by resolution 596 (VI), adopted at its 352nd plenary meeting on 7 Dec. 1951, decided to postpone consideration of the draft Declaration. GAOR, 6th Session, 1951–52, Resolutions (A/2119), p. 83–84. Cf. also *ibid.*, Sixth Committee, SR., 7–26, (253rd to 256th meetings).

[15] Yearbook, ILC, 1950, II, 366 (par. 14 of its annual Report); *ibid.*, 1951, II, 124 (par. 8).

of its Statute, is found in Part II of its Report for 1950; and in paragraphs 90 to 94 the Commission makes specific recommendations to the General Assembly with reference to the preparation and distribution of publications relating to international law.[16] By resolutions 487 (V) of 12 December 1950, 602 (VI) of 1 February 1952, 686 (VII) of 5 December 1952, 987 (X) of 3 December 1955, 1291 (XIII) of 5 December 1958, 1451 (XIV) of 7 December 1959, 1506 (XV) of 12 December 1960, and 1814 (XVII) of 18 December 1962, the General Assembly took steps to comply with these suggestions of the Commission.

3. *Formulation of the Nürnberg Principles* (1950). The Commission was directed to deal with this topic by General Assembly resolution 177 (II) of 21 November 1947.[17] The Commission's report, containing seven Principles, with comment, is found in Part III of its Report for 1950.[18] The Commission debated the question whether or not it "should ascertain to what extent the principles contained in the [Nürnberg] Charter and judgment constituted principles of international law" but reached the conclusion that its task "was not to express any appreciation of these principles as principles of international law but merely to formulate them." [19] The Chairman, Judge Manley O. Hudson, pointed out "that the Commission was not empowered to draft either a declaration or a convention." [20] The report makes no recommendations.

By resolution 488 (V) of 12 December 1950, the General Assembly invited governments of Member States to comment on the Commission's formulation of the Principles and requested the Commission to take into account these comments and the extensive debate in the Sixth Committee when the Commission prepared a draft code of offences against the peace and security of mankind.[21] In paragraph 57 of the Report covering its 3rd

[16] *Ibid.,* 1950, II, 367–374.   [17] A/CN.4/4, p. 9.
[18] *Loc. cit.,* 374–378.
[19] Yearbook, ILC, 1949, p. 282, par. 26, and *ibid.,* 1950, II, 374, par. 96.
[20] Yearbook, ILC, 1949, p. 132, par. 29.
[21] A/1775, Resolutions Adopted, 5th Session, p. 77. The debate re-

Session, the Commission informed the General Assembly that it had complied with this request.[22]

4. *The Question of International Criminal Jurisdiction* (1950). The Commission's report on this topic, which was assigned to it by General Assembly resolution 260 (III) B of 9 December 1948, is in Part IV of its Report for 1950 and makes no recommendations.[23] By resolution 489 (V) of 12 December 1950, the General Assembly decided to refer the question of preparing draft conventions and proposals for establishing an international criminal court to a special committee.[24]

5. *Draft Code of Offences Against the Peace and Security of Mankind* (1951 and 1954). Prepared at the direction of the General Assembly,[25] this Draft Code in the form of articles is Chapter IV of the Commission's Report for 1951.[26] The Commission "refrained from drafting an instrument for implementing the code." [27] At its 30th meeting, on 31 May 1949, the Commission debated the nature of its task in relation to the General Assembly's directive to it to prepare the Draft Code.[28] Mr. Spiropoulos inquired whether the matter involved progressive development or codification of international law—in which case he believed that the Commission would have to follow strictly articles 16 and 19 and the following of its Statute—or "whether it could be considered as a specific mandate of the Commission as had been decided with respect to the Draft Declaration on Rights and Duties of States," in which case "the Commission would be completely free to discuss the matter as it wished." He believed that the project was clearly

ferred to took place at the 231st–239th meetings of the Sixth Committee, GAOR, C.6, SR., 131–198.

[22] Yearbook, ILC, 1951, II, 134.

[23] Yearbook, ILC, 1950, II, 378–379.

[24] A/1775, pp. 77–78. Cf. also resolutions 898 (IX), 14 Dec. 1954, A/2890, p. 50, and 1187 (XII), 11 Dec. 1957, A/3805, p. 52.

[25] GA res. 177 (II), par. (b), 21 Nov. 1947.

[26] Yearbook, ILC, 1951, II, 133–137.

[27] *Ibid.*, 134; Report, par. 58 (d) (misnumbered 52).

[28] Yearbook, ILC, 1949, pp. 216–219.

one of the progressive development of international law. Professor Koretsky "protested once again against the attitude that if the Commission considered a matter to be referred to it as a specific question, it did not need to apply the provisions of its Statute." A majority of the Commission agreed that Article 16 of the Statute was applicable although no formal vote was taken on the question. The question was reopened at the 89th [29] and 111th [30] meetings of the Commission on 25 May 1951 and 26 June 1951. Despite the views expressed that the Commission should comply with Article 16 of the Statute and transmit the draft to governments for their comments, the Commission voted by 10–0–1 to transmit it directly to the General Assembly.[31] No recommendation as to its disposition was made by the Commission.

The General Assembly twice postponed consideration of the question. At its 7th Session, the President of the General Assembly stated that "this was done on the understanding that the matter would continue to be discussed by the International Law Commission." [32] The Commission therefore reconsidered its draft at its 6th Session in 1954 in the light of observations received from governments, and once again debated the form its recommendation to the General Assembly should be given.[33] Mr. Zourek thought that the Commission should make a recommendation pursuant to Article 23, preferably that the General Assembly should adopt the report by resolution. Dr. Liang, Secretary of the Commission, questioned the applicability of Article 23, since the Commission "had considered the preparation of the Draft Code as a special task which was strictly speaking neither codification nor development of international law." Mr. Zourek thought the Commission's Statute applicable in all cases. Mr. Spiropoulos, observing that experience showed that "the General Assembly rarely adopted the Commission's recommendations," suggested that the Com-

[29] *Ibid.*, 1951, I, 55–57.   [30] *Ibid.*, 248–251.   [31] *Ibid.*, 251.
[32] A/CN.4/72, 13 May 1953 (mimeographed only); A/PV. 382, par. 5.
[33] Yearbook, ILC, 1954, I, 144–146.

mission simply transmit the draft without any specific recommendation. The Commission agreed and its Report contains no recommendation to the General Assembly.[34]

By resolutions 897 (IX) of 4 December 1954 [35] and 1186 (XII) of 11 December 1957,[36] the General Assembly decided to defer consideration of the Draft Code pending its consideration of the question of defining aggression.

6. *Question of Defining Aggression* (1951). Confronted with vaguely worded General Assembly resolution 378 B (V) of 17 November 1950,[37] the International Law Commission considered and rejected at its 3rd Session in 1951 the possibility of defining aggression. Chapter III of the Commission's Report for 1951 informs the General Assembly of the Commission's efforts, without recommendation.[38]

7. *Reservations to Multilateral Conventions* (1951). By General Assembly resolution 478 (V) of 16 November 1950, the International Law Commission was invited "to study the question of reservations to multilateral conventions both from the point of view of codification and from that of the progressive development of international law." [39] The Commission's report on the subject constitutes Chapter II of its Report for 1951.[40] In this report the Commission made certain suggestions of which the General Assembly took note in resolution 598 (VI) of 12 January 1952.[41]

With the exception of the Commission's report on *Ways and Means for Making the Evidence of Customary International Law More Readily Available,* which was made pursuant to Article 24 of its Statute, the other five reports here discussed

[34] *Ibid.,* II, 149 ff.   [35] A/2890, p. 50.   [36] A/3805, pp. 51–52.
[37] A/1775, Resolutions, GA, 5th Session, p. 13.
[38] Yearbook, ILC, 1951, II, 131–133. The General Assembly's further pursuit of this will-o'-the-wisp is indicated in GA resolutions 599 (VI) of 31 Jan. 1952, 688 (VII) of 20 Dec. 1952, 895 (IX) of 4 Dec. 1954, and 1181 (XII) of 29 Nov. 1957.
[39] A/1775, pp. 74–75.
[40] Yearbook, ILC, 1951, II, 125–131.
[41] A/2119, Resolutions, 6th Session, p. 84.

were made at the specific request of the General Assembly. Of the six reports, only those dealing with the *Formulation of the Nürnberg Principles,* and the *Draft Code of Offences Against the Peace and Security of Mankind* were drafted in the form of articles.

III

8 and 9. *Arbitral Procedure* (1953 and 1958). The debate within the International Law Commission which led to its recommendation regarding its *Draft Convention on Arbitral Procedure* is instructive. This was the Commission's first recommendation to the General Assembly on a completed draft the subject of which had been selected by the Commission itself. At its 1st Session in 1949, the Commission, in accordance with Article 18, paragraph 1, of its Statute, selected *Arbitral Procedure* as one of the topics for "codification" of international law which should be given priority.[42] At its 33rd meeting, on 3 June 1949, the Commission appointed Professor Georges Scelle as Rapporteur for the topic and decided to request information from governments pursuant to Article 19, paragraph 2, of its Statute.[43] At its 156th meeting, on 3 July 1952, the Commission decided, in conformity with Article 21 of its Statute, that its draft on *Arbitral Procedure* be issued as a Commission document and submitted to governments for comment.[44] The view of some members that the draft articles "were much more a progressive development than a codification of international law" [45] were countered with the observation that the procedure under Article 21 was likewise in accordance with Article 16, paragraphs (*g*) and (*h*).[46]

The question was raised again by Mr. Kozhevnikov at the

---

[42] Yearbook, ILC, 1949, pp. 50–51, 57–58.

[43] *Ibid.,* 238–239.

[44] Report of the International Law Commission covering its 4th Session, par. 14, Yearbook, ILC, 1952, II, 58; *ibid.,* I, 97–100, 103–105.

[45] Mr. François, *ibid.,* I, 100. Cf. Mr. Yepes, *ibid.,* 104.

[46] Mr. Kerno, *ibid.,* 104.

226th meeting of the Commission, on 29 July 1953, when he alleged that the Commission had "exceeded its terms of reference" by going beyond codification of existing law and practice in its draft on arbitral procedure.[47] However, instead of urging the Commission to make a recommendation under Article 16, dealing with progressive development, Mr. Kozhevnikov first favored a recommendation pursuant to Article 23, paragraph 1 (a) that the General Assembly should "take no action, the report having already been published," and later insisted that it was not mandatory on the Commission to make any recommendation.[48] The Commission voted 8 to 2 that it should make a recommendation to the General Assembly and resumed its debate as to the particular recommendation which should be made.

Mr. Zourek preferred a recommendation under sub-paragraphs 1 (a) or 1 (b) of Article 23, leaving it to the General Assembly to decide whether to take no action on the Commission's draft or to take note of it or adopt it. Mr. Scelle raised the question of the exact purport of the four courses enumerated in Article 23, paragraph 1:

Was the adoption of a report by resolution, the course laid down in paragraph 1 (b), stronger than the recommendation of a draft to States Members, the course laid down in paragraph 1 (c)? And was the latter course in turn stronger than that suggested in paragraph 1 (d), namely, the mere convocation of a conference without any recommendation or adoption of a draft? [49]

Did the choice of sub-paragraph 1 (d) over 1 (c) depend on the urgency of the draft, as Mr. Lauterpacht believed, or was it designed to permit a conference which included States not Members of the United Nations, as Mr. Liang suggested? [50] Mr. Spiropoulos doubted whether its drafters ever intended Article 23 to be analyzed and dissected in the way certain members of the Commission had done.[51]

---

[47] Yearbook, ILC, 5th Session, 1953, I, 281.
[48] Ibid., 306–308 (229th meeting, 1 Aug. 1953).
[49] Ibid., 307.   [50] Ibid., 306.   [51] Ibid., 312.

At the 230th meeting, on 3 August 1953, Mr. Lauterpacht, Rapporteur, submitted the following draft recommendation:

In the opinion of the Commission the draft Code as adopted calls for action, on the part of the General Assembly, contemplated in paragraph (c) of the Statute of the Commission, namely, "to recommend the draft to Members with a view to the conclusion of a convention." The Commission makes a formal recommendation to that effect. It is understood that in recommending the draft to Member States with a view to the conclusion of a convention, the General Assembly would be giving its approval to the draft Code which, after it has been completed by the addition of final clauses, would become a convention approved by the General Assembly and open to signature or accession by Members of the United Nations and, possibly, other States.[52]

Supporting this text, Mr. Scelle expressed the view that a recommendation under sub-paragraph 1 (d) that the General Assembly convoke a special conference would have meant, in effect, a recommendation that the Commission's work be gone over again by that conference, a course he wished to avoid.[53] After further debate,[54] the Commission indicated its preference for a recommendation pursuant to Article 23, paragraph 1 (c) by a vote of 8–2–3, but without the interpretation of the significance of a General Assembly recommendation as approval which is contained in the last sentence of Mr. Lauterpacht's draft.

In paragraph 54 of its Report to the General Assembly covering its 5th Session, the Commission points out that its *Draft Convention on Arbitral Procedure* falls within the categories both of the progressive development of international law and the codification of international law; that it "is probable that the same cumulation of functions must apply, in varying proportions, to other aspects of the work of the Commission"; and that therefore it mattered little whether recommendations were made under Article 23 or Article 16 (j). The Report then states:

[52] *Ibid.,* 309–310.　　[53] *Ibid.,* 310.　　[54] *Ibid.,* 309–316.

55. In the opinion of the Commission the final draft on arbitral procedure as adopted calls for action, on the part of the General Assembly, contemplated in paragraph (*c*) of Article 23 of the Statute of the Commission, namely, "to recommend the draft to Members with a view to the conclusion of a convention." The Commission makes a recommendation to that effect.[55]

After a lengthy debate in the Sixth Committee at its 382nd to 388th meetings, 9 to 18 November 1953, in which the Draft Convention was severely criticized for its advances over existing law,[56] the General Assembly, by resolution 797 (VIII) of 7 December 1953, decided to request governments for further comments on the Draft [57] instead of complying with the recommendation made by the International Law Commission.

The Sixth Committee resumed debate on the Draft, and the comments received, at its 461st to 464th and 466th to 472nd meetings from 22 November to 7 December 1955.[58] Discussion culminated in the issue whether the *Draft Convention on Arbitral Procedure* should be referred back to the International Law Commission for reconsideration or whether an international conference should be convened to consider the conclusion of a convention on arbitral procedure as soon as twenty states had indicated a willingness to participate.[59] By a vote of 26–22–5 the former alternative was preferred.[60] The General Assembly, at its 554th plenary meeting on 14 December 1955, adopted, by a vote of 31–8–16, resolution 989 (X), in accordance with which the General Assembly

[55] Yearbook, ILC, 1953, II, 208.

[56] GAOR, 8th Session, Sixth Committee, Summary Records, 109–140; and below, pp. 349 ff.

[57] A/2630, p. 51.

[58] GAOR, 10th Session, 1955, Sixth Committee, Summary Records, 83–103, 109–144.

[59] A/C.6/L.371, 5 Dec. 1955, joint six-power amendment sponsored by Canada, Egypt, France, Honduras, Sweden, and the United Kingdom. *Ibid.*, Annexes, Agenda item 52.

[60] 472nd meeting, *loc. cit.*, 143, par. 37.

2. *Invites* the International Law Commission to consider the comments of Governments and the discussions in the Sixth Committee in so far as they may contribute further to the value of the draft on arbitral procedure, and to report to the General Assembly at its thirteenth session;

3. *Decides* to place the question of arbitral procedure on the provisional agenda of the thirteenth session, including the problem of the desirability of convening an international conference of plenipotentiaries to conclude a convention on arbitral procedure.[61]

In the preamble to this resolution, the General Assembly noted that "a number of suggestions for improvements on the draft have been put forward" and expressed its belief "that a set of rules on arbitral procedure will inspire States in the drawing up of provisions for inclusion in international treaties and special arbitration agreements."

At its 9th Session in 1957, the International Law Commission examined (in the words of its Report) "the ultimate object to be attained in reviewing," pursuant to the invitation of the General Assembly, "the draft on arbitral procedure and, in particular, whether this object should be a convention or simply a set of rules which might inspire States in the drawing up of provisions for inclusion in international treaties and special arbitration agreements." [62] At its 419th meeting, on 17 June 1957, the Commission abandoned its previous recommendation and decided, by a vote of 10–4–5, against the resubmission of its project in the form of a draft convention.[63]

During its 10th Session in 1958, the Commission redrafted its project as a set of *Model Rules on Arbitral Procedure* and recommended, in accordance with Article 23, paragraph 1 (*b*) of its Statute, that the General Assembly adopt the report by resolution. The Commission's Report indicated clearly that the *Model Rules* were "intended as a guide" and their adoption by the General Assembly would not make them binding

[61] A/3116, pp. 46–47. See A/PV.554, p. 431.
[62] Yearbook, ILC, 1957, II, 143–144. Cf. debate in *ibid.*, I, 172–185.
[63] *Ibid.*, I, 184–185.

on any Member State.[64] In the language of the Commission's Report covering the work of its 10th Session (1958):

17. . . . If, as the Commission, in accordance with article 23, paragraph 1 (*b*), of its statute, now recommends, the Assembly adopts the present report by resolution, the draft articles would become binding on any Member State only in the following circumstances, which indicate the three or four purposes they are now specifically intended to serve:

(i) If they were embodied in a convention between two or more States for signature and ratification *inter se,* intended to govern the settlement of all, or of any specified category of future disputes arising between them;

(ii) If they were similarly embodied in a particular arbitral agreement for the settlement *ad hoc* of an already existing dispute;

(iii) If—which is a variant of (ii)—parties to a dispute which they propose to refer to arbitration, wished to embody the articles, in whole or in part, in their arbitral agreement or in the *compromis d'arbitrage,* or to include clauses based upon them, or for which the articles would serve as a model;

(iv) If, in the same circumstances as (iii), the parties did not wish, or found it difficult, to draw up a detailed arbitral agreement or *compromis,* and preferred simply to declare that the settlement of the dispute and the process of arbitration would be governed by the present articles with or without such exceptions, variations or additions as the parties might indicate.[65]

Once more, after a lengthy discussion in the Sixth Committee,[66] the General Assembly declined to comply with the recommendations of the Commission. The reluctance of some States to have the General Assembly take any action which might be deemed an approval of those features of the draft which sought to plug up the loopholes of traditional arbitral procedures prevented the Assembly from "adopting" the Com-

[64] Yearbook, ILC, 1958, II, 82, par. 17.   [65] *Ibid.*

[66] GAOR, 13th Session, 1958, Sixth Committee, Summary Records, 6, 24–84 (550th, 554th–567th meetings, Sept.–Oct. 1958). Cf. A/3983, 6 Nov. 1958, Report of the Sixth Committee, Annexes, Agenda item 57.

mission's draft. Instead, by a vote of 39–19–13, the Sixth Committee at its 567th meeting on 23 October 1958, adopted a draft resolution which cautiously "takes note" of Chapter II on arbitral procedure of the Commission's Report.[67]

As adopted by the General Assembly, by a vote of 46–17–11 at its 780th plenary meeting on 14 November 1958,[68] resolution 1262 (XIII) reads, in part, as follows:

The General Assembly . . .

Taking note of the comments in that report to the effect, in particular, that the draft articles on arbitral procedure contained therein would have no binding effect on States unless accepted by them and save to the extent that each one is accepted by them in treaties of arbitration or in a *compromis*, . . .

1. *Takes note* of Chapter II of the report of the International Law Commission covering the work of its tenth session; . . .

3. *Brings* the draft articles on arbitral procedure contained in the report of the International Law Commission to the attention of Member States for their consideration and use, in such cases and to such extent as they consider appropriate, in drawing up treaties of arbitration or *compromis;*

4. *Invites* Governments to send the Secretary-General any comments they may wish to make on the draft, and in particular on their experience in the drawing up of arbitral agreements and the conduct of arbitral procedure, with a view to facilitating a review of the matter by the United Nations at an appropriate time.[69]

10 and 11. *Elimination or Reduction of Future Statelessness* (1954). Pursuant to the request of the Economic and Social Council which, by its resolution 319 B III (XI) of 11 August 1950,[70] had requested the International Law Commission to "prepare at the earliest possible date the necessary draft international convention or conventions for the elimination of

---

[67] *Loc. cit.*, p. 83. Mr. Amado (Brazil) thought that the Committee's vote meant that "the question of arbitral procedure would be shelved." *Ibid.*

[68] A/PV. 780, p. 440.   [69] A/4090, p. 53.

[70] A/CN.4/47, Yearbook, ILC, 1951, II, 121–122.

statelessness," the Commission, on 7 August 1953 at its 234th meeting, adopted two provisional draft conventions, one on the elimination of future statelessness and the other on the reduction of future statelessness. Since the Commission had earlier decided [71] that the project involved codification as well as progressive development of international law, the Commission decided, in accordance with both Articles 16, paragraphs (g) and (h), and Article 21, paragraphs 1 and 2 of its Statute,[72] to issue its provisional drafts as Commission documents on which governments were invited to comment. At its 6th Session in 1954, the Commission reconsidered its draft in the light of the comments received, and submitted them to the General Assembly without specific recommendation, but with the observation that the General Assembly "could consider the question whether preference should be given to the Draft Convention on the Elimination of Future Statelessness or to the Draft Convention on the Reduction of Future Statelessness." [73] Since the Commission had included in Article 12 of each draft the provision that "The present Convention, *having been approved by the General Assembly,* shall . . . be open for signature . . . " and "shall be ratified," [74] the Commission appar-

[71] At its 124th meeting, 13 July 1951, the Commission regarded the request from the Economic and Social Council as falling within provisions of Article 17 of the Commission's Statute dealing with progressive development. The Commission decided to relate the project to nationality which it had previously listed as a topic for codification and the topic was listed on its agenda as "Nationality, including Statelessness." Yearbook, ILC, 1951, I, 354–358.

[72] Yearbook, ILC, 1953, II, 221, par. 120 of its annual Report.

[73] Yearbook, ILC, 1954, II, 141, par. 14 of its Report.

[74] *Ibid.*, 145–146. At the 251st meeting of the Commission on 21 June 1954, Dr. Liang, Secretary of the Commission, "pointed out that article 23, paragraph 1 (c), of the Commission's Statute did not mention 'approval.' The General Assembly's approval of a report by the Sixth Committee containing a draft convention did not, *ipso facto,* give rise to any obligations on the part of Member States." Mr. Lauterpacht added that the function of such approval was "establishing a final text and dispensed with the traditional procedure of signature." *Ibid.*, I, 51. Compare the later statement made by Dr. Liang before the Sixth Committee during its consideration of the draft on *Arbitral Procedure* that the

ently deemed it unnecessary to make a specific recommendation in terms of Article 23 of its Statute.

At its 504th plenary meeting on 4 December 1954, the General Assembly, by a vote of 36–7–11, adopted resolution 896 (IX) expressing "its desire that an international conference of plenipotentiaries be convened to conclude a convention for the reduction or elimination of statelessness" as soon as twenty States had communicated a "willingness to co-operate in such a conference." [75]

The United Nations Conference on the Elimination or Reduction of Future Statelessness convened in Geneva on 24 March 1959, with thirty-five States in attendance and with Observers from two other States.[76] The conference adopted the International Law Commission's drafts as the basis of discussion [77] but adjourned without results at its 14th plenary meeting after adopting a resolution that it be reconvened.[78] At the last plenary meeting, the delegate from Switzerland, Mr. Favre, observed in part:

The reasons for the Conference's difficulties were apparent. It had begun its deliberations on the basis of an International Law Commission draft, well-balanced, technically uniform and, so to speak, all of a piece. But discussion had disclosed demographic and political factors for which the Commission's draft had not made sufficient allowance, and that was why the draft had been changed almost out of recognition.[79]

"adoption" by the General Assembly of a report of the International Law Commission would "not mean so much the substance of the individual articles contained in the model rules as the Commission's report in its entirety, including those articles and all the recommendations, limitations, definitions and the like which the Commission had seen fit to express with regard to them." A/C.6/SR.557, 8 Oct. 1958, p. 37, par. 27.

[75] A/2890, pp. 49–50; A/PV.504, p. 362 (item 49).
[76] A/CONF. 9/9, 14 April 1959.
[77] A/CONF. 9/SR. 1, p. 5 (provisional restricted distribution).
[78] A/CONF. 9/SR. 14, 18 April 1959.
[79] *Ibid.*, p. 8 (mimeographed provisional record). Cf. also, A/4132, Annual Report of the Secretary-General, 1958–1959, pp. 93–94.

The Conference reconvened in New York in August 1961 and adopted the text of a draft convention on *Reduction of Statelessness*.[80]

12. *Draft Articles on the Continental Shelf, Fisheries, and the Contiguous Zone* (1953). At its 1st Session in 1949, the Commission selected the *Regime of the High Seas* as a topic for codification. At its 3rd Session in 1951, the Commission decided "to give its drafts the publicity referred to in article 16, paragraph (g) of its Statute, in particular to communicate them to governments so that the latter could submit their comments as envisaged in paragraph (h) of the same article." [81] The drafts were re-examined by the Commission in the light of the comments received, and at its 236th meeting on 10 August 1953, the Commission debated the questions whether its draft articles on the continental shelf were more in the category of progressive development than codification and what recommendation should be made to the General Assembly by the Commission in relation thereto.[82] In his draft report, as Rapporteur of the Commission, Professor Lauterpacht had drawn attention to the dual nature of the articles on the *Continental Shelf* as codification and progressive development, while perhaps emphasizing their character as codification, and proposed that since the articles "constitute a re-affirmation of the traditional principle of the freedom of the seas" in relation to a novel problem, the Commission should recommend, pursuant to paragraph 1 (a) of Article 23 of its Statute that the General Assembly should "take no action, the report having already been published." He was not averse to having the General Assembly "adopt" the report pursuant to paragraph 1 (b), but doubted whether the subject matter of the draft called for the conclusion of a convention under sub-paragraphs (c) or (d).[83]

---

80 A/CONF. 9/15, 29 Aug. 1961.
81 Yearbook, ILC, 1951, II, 139–140, par. 78 of the Commission's Report.
82 Yearbook, ILC, 1953, I, 357–361.
83 *Ibid.*, 357–359, n. 7, for pertinent paragraphs of his draft Report.

Several members of the Commission objected that the views set forth by Professor Lauterpacht in the draft report as the views of the Commission had not been previously discussed. Mr. Sandström, recalling that the Commission had regarded the draft articles on the *Continental Shelf* as progressive development when it had invited comment pursuant to Article 16 of the Statute, proposed that the Commission's Report should recognize their character as progressive development and submit them to the Assembly with a view to the conclusion of a convention. The Commission first accepted Mr. Sandström's proposal by a vote of 4-3-3 and then reversed itself to adopt, by a vote of 7-2-1, a recommendation that the General Assembly adopt the Commission's Report on the subject by resolution (without specifying whether it was acting under Article 16 or Article 23).[84] Paragraph 91 of the Commission's Report reads:

> 91. The Commission recommends to the General Assembly the adoption by resolution of this part of the present report and the draft articles on the continental shelf incorporated therein.[85]

A comparable recommendation, without specification of the pertinent Article of the Statute, was made with reference to the Commission's draft articles on *Fisheries*. The Commission recommended (a) "that the General Assembly should by resolution adopt" that part of its Report relating to fisheries and the draft articles thereon and (b) that it should consult with the United Nations Food and Agriculture Organization "with a view to the preparation of a draft convention incorporating the principles adopted by the Commission." [86] The Commission admitted that its draft articles on *Fisheries,* in their main aspects, "go beyond the existing law and must be regarded to a large extent as falling within the category of progressive development of international law." [87] The Commission believed "that the general importance and the recognized urgency of

---

[84] *Ibid.,* 360–361.   [85] *Ibid.,* II, 217.   [86] *Ibid.,* 219, par. 102.
[87] *Ibid.,* 218, par. 95.

the subject matter of the articles in question warrant their endorsement by a formal act of approval on the part of the General Assembly." The Commission regarded the contemplated adoption of the report and articles by General Assembly resolution as involving an "endorsement" by which "the General Assembly should lend its authority to the principles underlying the articles." [88] This is perhaps a significant interpretation by the Commission of the implications of Article 23, paragraph 1 (b) of its Statute, although the Commission was admittedly dealing here with a subject matter which it regarded as progressive development.

With reference to its single draft article on the *Contiguous Zone,* the Commission made a different recommendation:

114. As the Commission has not yet adopted draft articles on the territorial sea, it recommends the General Assembly to take no action with regard to the article on the contiguous zone, since the present report is already published (article 23, paragraph 1 (a), of the Commission's Statute).[89]

Without examining the substantive content of the Commission's proposed articles,[90] the Sixth Committee of the General Assembly declined in November 1953 to comply with the Commission's recommendations. The Icelandic view that separate action on the continental shelf might prejudice later decisions regarding fisheries and other matters relating to the high seas and the extent of the territorial sea [91] had not been dispelled by a Memorandum submitted by Professor J. P. A. François, Chairman of the International Law Commission, in which he expressed the Commission's view of the desirability of a "prompt solution" of the problem of the continental

[88] *Ibid.,* 219, par. 103.

[89] *Ibid.,* 220, par. 114. Cf. A/CN.4/SR.237, *ibid.,* I, 364–366.

[90] Cf. GAOR, 8th Session, 1953, Sixth Committee, Summary Records, 140–142, 153–161 (389th, 392nd, and 393rd meetings). See also A/2589, 1 Dec. 1953, Report of the Sixth Committee.

[91] A/C.6/SR.392, pars. 18–28, 25 Nov. 1953.

shelf.[92] By a narrow vote of 19 to 14, with 18 abstentions and 9 absences,[93] the Committee adopted the Iceland draft resolution at its 393rd meeting on 25 November 1953. Adopted without change, as resolution 798 (VIII), by the General Assembly on 7 December 1953,[94] the resolution read, in part:

The General Assembly . . .
Having regard to the fact that the problems relating to the high seas, territorial waters, contiguous zones, the continental shelf and the superjacent waters are closely linked together juridically as well as physically,
Decides not to deal with any aspect of the regime of the high seas or of the regime of territorial waters until all the problems involved have been studied by the International Law Commission and reported upon by it to the General Assembly.[95]

This rejection of the recommendations made by the International Law Commission led the Governments of Brazil, China, Liberia, the Netherlands, New Zealand, the United Kingdom, and the United States, later supported by Nicaragua, Honduras, and Bolivia, to sponsor the inclusion in the agenda of the 9th Session of the General Assembly in 1954 of the additional item: "Draft articles on the continental shelf."[96] At its 478th plenary meeting on 25 September 1954, the General Assembly included the item in its agenda after a debate in which representatives of Chile, Iceland, Peru, and Ecuador opposed it, largely because of their special claims relating to high seas fisheries.[97]

The Sixth Committee considered the item[98] at its 430th to

[92] A/C.6/L. 324, 23 Nov. 1953. GAOR, 8th Session, 1953, Annexes, Agenda item 53, pp. 3–4.
[93] A/C.6/SR.393, par. 33 and A/PV. 468, p. 421.
[94] A/PV. 468, pp. 421–423. The vote in the General Assembly was 30–9–11.
[95] A/2630, pp. 51–52.
[96] A/2706, 23 Aug. 1954, and Adds. 1, 2, 3.
[97] A/PV. 478, pp. 63–66.
[98] Agenda item 64, GAOR, 9th Session, 1954.

435th meetings, held from 29 November to 3 December 1954,[99] less on its merits than as a proposal to cause the Committee to reverse the decision taken in 1953 not to discuss the continental shelf or other aspects of the law of the sea until the International Law Commission had completed its study of the entire subject. The resolution approved by the Committee was adopted without change by the General Assembly at its 512th plenary meeting on 14 December 1954, by a vote of 32–0–9.[100] Although labeled resolution "899 (IX) Draft articles on the continental shelf" in the collected resolutions of the 9th Session of the General Assembly, the resolution makes no reference to the continental shelf in its operative paragraphs, but reiterates resolution 798 (VIII) that the law of the sea should be considered as a whole and sets the 11th Session of the General Assembly as a deadline.[101]

13. *Law of the Sea* (1956). Pursuant to General Assembly resolutions 798 (VIII) and 899 (IX), the International Law Commission combined into one draft on the *Law of the Sea* its articles on the *Regime of the High Seas* and *Regime of the Territorial Sea.* At its 374th and 375th meetings on 25 and 26 June 1956, the Commission considered the type of recommendation it should make to the General Assembly with regard to its consolidated draft.[102] Mr. F. V. García Amador

doubted whether it was advisable to recommend that a diplomatic conference be convened for the purpose of concluding a convention on the law of the sea. . . . experience had shown that the vast majority of conventions were ratified by only a handful of States and even their ratifications were as often as not accompanied by reservations. In the case of a convention on the law of the sea, the reservations would most likely be such as to nullify the convention's whole effect.

[99] *Ibid.,* Sixth Committee, Summary Records, 163–180.
[100] A/PV. 512, p. 494. Cf. A/2849, 9 Dec. 1954, Report of the Sixth Committee.
[101] A/2890, p. 50.
[102] Yearbook, ILC, 8th Session, 1956, I, 255–260, 277–279.

2. The Commission should not overlook the new source of international law which was represented by the resolutions and declarations of the General Assembly and the other main international organs. Although they had no binding force, they had great moral force. . . .

13. . . . [A] conference might, for example, wish to adopt a draft convention on the territorial sea, but only a resolution on the subject of the continental shelf.[103]

Mr. Spiropoulos thought "the Commission could be quite sure that the General Assembly would never itself adopt or endorse the rules submitted to it by the Commission." Dr. Liang questioned whether the General Assembly was "an ideal forum for the consideration and adoption of conventions of a technical nature. . . . As had apparently been foreseen in the Statute itself, the General Assembly was not equipped for, and was most reluctant to undertake, the detailed examination of most of the drafts submitted to it by the International Law Commission. . . ."

The view that the Commission's draft should be submitted to an international conference prevailed, and the Commission's Report makes the following observations and recommendation:

25. When the International Law Commission was set up, it was thought that the Commission's work might have two different aspects: on the one hand the "codification of international law" or, in the words of article 15 of the Commission's Statute, "the more precise formulation and systematization of rules of international law in fields where there already has been extensive State practice, precedent and doctrine"; and, on the other hand, the "progressive development of international law" or "the preparation of draft conventions on subjects which have not yet been regulated by international law or in regard to which the law has not yet been sufficiently developed in the practice of States."

26. In preparing its rules on the law of the sea, the Commission has become convinced that, in this domain at any rate, the dis-

103 *Ibid.,* 257, 258.

tinction established in the statute between these two activities can hardly be maintained. Not only may there be wide differences of opinion as to whether a subject is already "sufficiently developed in practice," but also several of the provisions adopted by the Commission, based on a "recognized principle of international law," have been framed in such a way as to place them in the "progressive development" category. Although it tried at first to specify which articles fell into one and which into the other category, the Commission has had to abandon the attempt, as several do not wholly belong to either.

27. In these circumstances, in order to give effect to the project as a whole, it will be necessary to have recourse to conventional means.

28. The Commission therefore recommends, in conformity with article 23, paragraph 1 (*d*) of its statute, that the General Assembly should summon an international conference of plenipotentiaries to examine the law of the sea, taking account not only of the legal but also of the technical, biological, economic and political aspects of the problem, and to embody the results of its work in one or more international conventions or such other instruments as it may deem appropriate.

29. . . . Judging from its own experience, the Commission considers—and the comments of Governments have confirmed this view—that the various sections of the law of the sea hold together, and are so closely interdependent that it would be extremely difficult to deal with only one part and leave the others aside.[104]

After a lengthy and comprehensive debate,[105] the Sixth Committee accepted the recommendation of the International Law Commission in a resolution which was adopted by a vote of 65 to 1 [106] at its 505th meeting on 20 December 1956. At its 658th

[104] Report of the International Law Commission covering the work of its 8th Session, Yearbook, ILC, 1956, II, 255–256. Cf. I, 256, 277.

[105] GAOR, 11th Session, 1956, Sixth Committee, Summary Records, 25–138 (485th to 505th meetings, Nov.–Dec. 1956). Cf. A/3520, 6 Feb. 1957, Report of the Sixth Committee, Annexes, Agenda item 53.

[106] *Loc. cit.*, 136. At the 494th meeting, the representative of Iceland, stating that Iceland considered that "it would be perfectly legal to extend the present four-mile limit considerably, for example to twelve

plenary meeting,[107] on 21 February 1957, the General Assembly, by a vote of 67–0–3, adopted Resolution 1105 (XI), which provided in part as follows:

The General Assembly . . .

2. *Decides,* in accordance with the recommendation contained in paragraph 28 of the report of the International Law Commission covering the work of its eighth session, that an international conference of plenipotentiaries should be convoked to examine the law of the sea, taking account not only of the legal but also of the technical, biological, economic and political aspects of the problem, and to embody the results of its work in one or more international conventions or such other instrument as it may deem appropriate; . . .

9. *Refers* to the conference the report of the International Law Commission as the basis for its consideration of the various problems involved in the development and codification of the law of the sea.[108]

14. *Diplomatic Intercourse and Immunities* (1958). At its 1st Session the International Law Commission selected *Diplomatic Intercourse and Immunities* as a topic for codification and at its 9th Session in 1957 it adopted a provisional draft which it decided, in accordance with Articles 16 and 21 of its Statute, to submit to governments for their observations.[109] The question of what form the draft should be given was debated at the 400th meeting of the Commission on 17 May 1957. Although many members favored developing the project in the form of a draft convention, Sir Gerald Fitzmaurice

---

miles," declared that Iceland saw no need to refer the question to a conference of plenipotentiaries and would vote against the convening of such a conference. A/C.6/SR. 494, pars. 7, 10, p. 70.

[107] A/PV. 658, pp. 1181–1186.

[108] A/3572, p. 54. The documentation of the Geneva Conferences may be found in *United Nations Conference on Law of the Sea, 1958, Official Records,* Vols. I–VII (A/CONF. 13) and *Second United Nations Conference on Law of the Sea, 1960, Official Records* (A/CONF. 19).

[109] Yearbook, ILC, 9th Session, 1957, II, 132, par. 12.

doubted whether a draft convention was the most desirable form. It was most improbable either that the General Assembly would simply approve a draft convention in the form in which it was submitted by the Commission and open it for signature, or that it would convene a special conference to consider it. . . . It would be much more likely to examine it itself, with far less time for careful study of it than the Commission had been able to afford; and, in those circumstances, any changes it made might not be for the better. Moreover, even after the General Assembly had approved the convention and opened it for signature, there was no knowing how many States would ratify it; and difficulties would inevitably arise between those who did and those who did not. There was also the problem of reservations. He was not, therefore, sure that a convention would necessarily be of more value than a model code, which the General Assembly could simply take note of, possibly with some expression of approval.[110]

The Commission nevertheless decided to prepare its draft on the provisional assumption that it would form the basis of a convention.[111] The question was again debated by the Commission during its 10th Session.[112] At the 448th meeting, on 22 May 1958, Dr. Liang pointed to the difference "between the submission of a text in the form of a convention and the submission of a text with a recommendation that the General Assembly take steps to convene a conference with a view to concluding a convention:" [113] the former was merely action in conformity with Article 20 of the Commission's Statute but carried no necessary implication of a recommendation that a convention be concluded pursuant to Article 23, paragraphs 1 (c) or 1 (d), despite the ambiguity of the comment made by the United States on 24 February 1958 that it was "opposed to the suggestion that the draft articles be submitted to the General Assembly in the form of a convention." [114] Sir Gerald Fitzmaurice still preferred a recommendation under Article 23,

110 *Ibid.*, I, 88, par. 67.   111 *Ibid.*, par. 75.
112 Yearbook, ILC, 10th Session, 1958, I, 84–89, 199–200.
113 *Ibid.*, 85–86.   114 *Ibid.*, II, 133.

paragraph 1 (*b*) instead of under paragraph 1 (*c*).[115] However, as the Commission's Report to the General Assembly states:

50. At its 468th meeting, the Commission decided (under article 23, paragraph 1 (*c*) of its statute) to recommend to the General Assembly that the draft articles on diplomatic intercourse and immunities should be recommended to Member States with a view to the conclusion of a convention.[116]

Dr. Liang thought it likely that the General Assembly would convene the type of conference indicated in paragraph 1 (*d*) of Article 23:

Except for the Convention on Genocide, he could recall no case in which the General Assembly had examined a draft convention in detail, article by article, and recommended it forthwith to States. He thought that it was unlikely that the General Assembly would itself examine the draft and commend it to Members for signature. The Assembly had a heavy agenda each year; furthermore many of the delegations did not contain more than a small number of lawyers.[117]

The Sixth Committee of the General Assembly debated the procedures to be followed in dealing with the Commission's draft during its 13th Session at its 568th to 580th meetings from 27 October to 12 November 1958.[118] Although the substantive provisions of the draft articles were not discussed in detail, some provisions were criticized as presenting innovations which went beyond mere codification of existing law. The International Law Commission was criticized for not having drafted final clauses which might have made it possible to open the convention for accession.[119] A proposal by Argentina, Brazil,

[115] *Ibid.*, I, 199. 467th meeting, 19 June 1958.
[116] *Ibid.*, II, 89.   [117] *Ibid.*, I, 199.
[118] GAOR, 13th Session, 1958, Sixth Committee, Summary Records, 86–145 (568th to 580th meetings). Cf. also A/4007, 26 Nov. 1958, Report of the Sixth Committee. Agenda item 56. Cf. below, pp. 353 ff.
[119] Cf. remarks of Mr. Shabtai Rosenne (Israel) at 572nd meeting, 31 Oct. 1958, and reply by Dr. Liang. *Loc. cit.*, 103–105.

Colombia, Costa Rica, Cuba, Mexico, Paraguay, and Peru, the effect of which was to invite the General Assembly itself (or perhaps its Sixth Committee) to formulate and open for signature at its next session a draft convention on the basis of the International Law Commission's draft, was later withdrawn in favor of a resolution which postponed the decision as to what body should formulate a convention.[120]

By a vote of 62–0–9, the General Assembly adopted without change [121] a resolution of the Sixth Committee which provided in part (GA res. 1288 [XIII]):

The General Assembly . . .

Taking into account . . . paragraph 50 of the report of the International Law Commission covering the work of its tenth session wherein it is stated that the Commission decided to recommend to the General Assembly that the draft articles on diplomatic intercourse and immunities should be recommended to Member States with a view to the conclusion of a convention, . . .

2. *Invites* Member States to submit their comments on the draft articles concerning diplomatic intercourse and immunities not later than 1 June 1959. . . .

4. *Decides* to include the item entitled "Diplomatic intercourse and immunities" in the provisional agenda of its fourteenth session with a view to the early conclusion of a convention on diplomatic intercourse and immunities;

5. *Decides* to consider at its fourteenth session the question to what body the formulation of the convention should be entrusted.[122]

At the 14th Session of the General Assembly, the Sixth Committee rejected, by a vote of 54–6–18, a Chilean proposal that the Sixth Committee should itself establish and open for signature the texts of conventions on diplomatic intercourse and immunities, consular intercourse and immunities, and *ad hoc* diplomacy.[123] The Committee adopted, by a vote of 67–1–11, a

---

[120] A/4007, pars. 14–15.   [121] A/PV. 782, 5 Dec. 1958, p. 459.
[122] A/4090, pp. 53–54.
[123] A/C.6/SR.638, 20 Nov. 1959, par. 39. For the preceding discussion,

draft resolution which was approved without change [124] by the General Assembly on 7 December 1959 as resolution 1450 (XIV) by a vote of 67–0–5.[125] In large part, the abstentions came from States which had wished to postpone the convening of the conference until it could discuss consular intercourse and immunities along with diplomatic intercourse and immunities.

General Assembly resolution 1450 (XIV) provided in part:

The General Assembly . . .
Believing that the codification of the rules of international law in this field would assist in promoting the purposes and principles of the Charter of the United Nations
1. *Decides* that an international conference of plenipotentiaries shall be convoked to consider the question of diplomatic intercourse and immunities and to embody the results of its work in an international convention, together with such ancillary instruments as may be necessary. . . .
7. *Refers* to the conference chapter III of the report of the International Law Commission covering the work of its tenth session, as the basis for its consideration of the question of diplomatic intercourse and immunities.[126]

15. *Special Missions* (1960). In paragraph 51 of its Report to the General Assembly covering its 10th Session (1958), the International Law Commission distinguished permanent diplomatic missions, on which it had completed a draft, from " 'ad hoc diplomacy,' covering itinerant envoys, diplomatic conferences and special missions sent to a State for limited purposes,"

---

see GAOR, 14th Session, 1959, Sixth Committee, Summary Records, 168–209, 631st to 638th meetings, Agenda item 56. Cf. also A/4305, 27 Nov. 1959, Report of the Sixth Committee.
[124] By a separate vote of 70–0–8, the Sixth Committee decided that the conference should meet in Vienna. A/C.6/SR. 638, par. 48.
[125] A/PV. 847, 7 Dec. 1959, pp. 645–648.
[126] A/4354, pp. 55–56. For the official records of the Vienna Conference, see *United Nations Conference on Diplomatic Intercourse and Immunities, Vienna, 2 March–14 April 1961, Official Records* (A/CONF. 20).

which it believed should also be studied, at a future session. The same Report, in paragraph 52, referred to "relations between States and international organizations," which like the question of the privileges and immunities of the organizations themselves were largely governed by special conventions.[127] In view of the interest expressed by governments in these questions, the General Assembly, by resolution 1289 (XIII), adopted on 5 December 1958, invited the International Law Commission to give further consideration to these subjects.[128]

At its 12th Session in 1960, the Commission drafted certain articles on *Special Missions* and recommended that the General Assembly refer them to the Vienna Conference on Diplomatic Intercourse and Immunities for consideration.[129] By resolution 1504 (XV), unanimously adopted [130] on 12 December 1960, the General Assembly complied with this recommendation.[131]

The Vienna Conference, after consideration of the draft by a sub-committee, unanimously recommended, at its 4th plenary meeting on 10 April 1961, that the subject of special missions be referred back to the International Law Commission by the General Assembly for further study in view of the importance of the subject and the Commission's own statement that it had not had time to make a thorough study of the question.[132]

At its 16th Session, the General Assembly, by resolution 1687 (XVI), 18 December 1961, requested the International Law Commission "as soon as it considers it advisable, to study further the subject of special missions and to report thereon to the General Assembly." [133] The Commission discussed the

[127] Yearbook, ILC, 10th Session, 1958, II, 89.   [128] A/4090, p. 54.
[129] Yearbook, ILC, 12th Session, 1960, II, 179, pars. 36 ff.
[130] A/PV.943, pp. 1228–1229.   [131] A/4684, p. 59, par. 3.
[132] A/CONF. 20/14, *United Nations Conference on Diplomatic Intercourse and Immunities, Vienna, 2 March–14 April 1961, Official Records,* I, 7, 230; II, 89–90.
[133] A/5100, p. 62. See also A/5043, 15 Dec. 1961, Report of the Sixth Committee on the Question of Special Missions, GAOR, 16th Session, 1961, Annexes, Agenda item 71; and debate, 731st meeting, Sixth Committee, Summary Records.

scope and method of treating the topic at its 711th and 712th meetings, 1 and 2 July 1963,[134] on the basis of a Secretariat working paper [135] it had requested prepared, and decided to appoint Professor Milan Bartoš as Special Rapporteur for the topic. The Commission also decided, in view of its heavy agenda, to hold a special session in Geneva in January 1964 to consider the topic.[136] However, for reasons of economy and the inability of the Secretariat to prepare translations of the Special Rapporteur's Report in time, the General Assembly, at its 18th Session, declined to appropriate the necessary funds for the scheduled meeting. The topic *Special Missions* was placed on the agenda of the 16th Session of the International Law Commission, and at that Session the Commission provisionally adopted an initial sixteen articles on the subject.[137]

16. *Consular Intercourse and Immunities* (1961). At its 1st Session the International Law Commission selected *Consular Intercourse and Immunities* as a topic for codification and at its 12th Session in 1960 it provisionally adopted a draft of 65 articles which, in accordance with Articles 16 and 21 of its Statute, it decided should be submitted to governments for their comment.[138] The Commission devoted practically all of its 13th Session in 1961 to the completion of the topic and unanimously agreed on a draft of seventy-one articles, entitled *Draft Articles on Consular Relations*. At its 624th meeting, on 4 July 1961, the Commission decided, without objection, that it would recommend its draft on *Consular Intercourse and Immunities* to the General Assembly pursuant to Article 23, paragraph 1 (*d*), of the Commission's Statute, with a view to the convoking by the General Assembly of an international

---

[134] A/CN.4/SR.711, 712. See also Report of the International Law Commission covering the work of its 15th Session, A/5509, pars. 62 ff.

[135] A/CN.4/155, 11 March 1963.

[136] Report, cited, pars. 72–73.

[137] Cf. A/CN.4/SR.723–725, 757–758, 760–763, 768–770, and Report, ILC, 16th Session, 1964, Chapter III (A/5809).

[138] Yearbook, ILC, 12th Session, 1960, II, 145, par. 18.

conference to conclude a convention on the subject.[139] The General Assembly at its 16th Session, took a favorable view of the Commission's recommendation, and by resolution 1685 (XVI), 18 December 1961, decided to convene such a conference in Vienna in March 1963.[140]

SUMMARY AND CONCLUSIONS

The hesitations of the International Law Commission in formulating its recommendations to the General Assembly on drafts completed by the Commission are essentially a reflection of a controversy as to the autonomy of the Commission in its selection of working methods and in its judgments as to the results sought to be achieved. The strict constructionists of the Statute, led by the Soviet member, insisted that the Commission had no authority to employ methods other than those set forth in its Statute for codification or development, although they preferred to obliterate any sharp distinction between the two methods by insisting that all projects of the Commission should be submitted in the form of draft conventions. The majority of the Commission insisted not only that the Statute recognized alternatives to the convention method but that special projects submitted to the Commission by the General Assembly frequently required special methods which made irrelevant any determination that the Commission was codifying existing law or developing new law.

No Recommendations for Special Projects

The Commission decided that it was not called upon to make any recommendations pursuant to Article 16 (*j*) or Article 23 of its Statute with regard to such special projects. Such

[139] Yearbook, ILC, 13th Session, 1961, I, 279, par. 114 and *ibid.*, II, 91, par. 27.

[140] A/5100 p. 61. See also A/5013, 7 Dec. 1961, Report of Sixth Committee, GAOR, 16th Session, 1961, Annexes, Agenda item 69 and Sixth Committee, Summary Records, 700th to 712th meetings, pp. 65–117. See also, below, pp. 358 ff. The records of the 1963 Vienna Conference on Consular Relations may be found under the symbol A/CONF. 25.

decisions were made, explicitly or implicitly, with regard to nine of the sixteen projects which the Commission has completed. These are its reports on the *Draft Declaration on Rights and Duties of States, Ways and Means for Making the Evidence of Customary International Law More Readily Available, Formulation of the Nürnberg Principles, The Question of International Criminal Jurisdiction, Draft Code of Offences Against the Peace and Security of Mankind* (on two occasions, in 1951 and 1954), *Question of Defining Aggression, Reservations to Multilateral Conventions, Elimination of Future Statelessness,* and *Reduction of Future Statelessness.*

As noted above, the recommendations of the Commission on *Ways and Means for Making the Evidence of Customary International Law More Readily Available* were made pursuant to Article 24 of its Statute. Of the other projects, all were submitted to the Commission by the General Assembly except the drafts on *Statelessness* which were requested of the Commission by the Economic and Social Council. Certain of these projects, for example, *Reservations to Multilateral Conventions* and the possibility and desirability of defining *Aggression,* obviously did not lend themselves to the preparation of "drafts in the form of articles." Where the Commission did draft some of the special projects in the form of articles—the *Draft Declaration on the Rights and Duties of States,* the *Formulation of the Nürnberg Principles,* the *Draft Code of Offences Against the Peace and Security of Mankind,* and the two drafts on *Statelessness*—the terms of reference by which the projects had been submitted to it were regarded by the Commission as not requiring it to make any recommendations as to the ultimate disposition of the drafts.

With the exception of the report on making the evidence of customary international law more readily available, the General Assembly itself regarded the concern and responsibility of the International Law Commission as having ceased with the performance by the Commission of the task requested of it. The General Assembly has shown intermittent interest in the

Nürnberg Principles, the *Question of Defining Aggression, International Criminal Jurisdiction,* and *Offences against the Peace and Security of Mankind,* but has dealt with them in the Sixth Committee or in special committees. It might be added that the inability of the United Nations to accomplish anything in this field is in no sense attributable to any basic deficiencies in the drafts or reports formulated by the International Law Commission.

Recommendations that the General Assembly "Adopt" a Draft

With regard to the projects initiated by the International Law Commission itself, it is noteworthy that in each case the Commission regarded its work as combining the methods of codification and of progressive development. On two occasions, the Commission has recommended the adoption by resolution of its Reports, in accordance with Article 23, paragraph 1 (*b*) of its Statute. This was true of the Commission's recommendations in its 1953 Report relating to the *Continental Shelf* and to *Fisheries.* The General Assembly rejected the recommendations by declining to deal with any aspect of the law of the sea until the Commission had completed its study of the whole subject (see above, pp. 296 ff.). In 1958, the Commission, after the General Assembly had rejected its previous request that its *Draft Convention on Arbitral Procedure* be recommended to Member States with a view to the conclusion of a convention, made a specific recommendation, in accordance with Article 23, paragraph 1 (*b*) of its Statute, that the General Assembly adopt the Report containing the Commission's *Model Rules on Arbitral Procedure* by resolution. Once again the General Assembly declined to comply, and merely "took note" of the Report, while calling the "draft articles" to the attention of States (see above, pp. 290 ff., and below, pp. 351 ff.).

The reluctance of the General Assembly to "adopt" a Report by resolution may well be based upon doubts as to the precise legal effect of such action. Study of the Commission's documentation appears to justify the conclusion that the Commission would not regard such adoption as conferring legally binding force upon provisions not otherwise obligatory upon States (see, e.g., pp. 289–290). Nevertheless, the approval regarded as implicit in Assembly adoption of a Commission Report has been urged as desirable not only for confirmation of existing law but for progressively developing international law in such fields as the continental shelf, high seas fisheries, and some aspects of arbitral procedure.

The opposition expressed in the General Assembly and its Sixth Committee to having the Assembly "adopt" a proposal may stem in part from those States which dislike certain provisions of existing law and wish to prevent an authoritative confirmation of existing law of which they are critical. Were such a confirmation to be given, it might well be referred to by the International Court of Justice or an arbitral tribunal, as a "subsidiary means for the determination of rules of law" (*per* Article 38, paragraph 1 (*d*) of the Court's Statute), although, by hypothesis, confirmation of existing international law by the General Assembly would be supererogatory insofar as the Court's ability to find that law is concerned. It may, therefore, be the recognition of existing law as law which it is sought to avoid.

The alternative situation in which the General Assembly is asked to "adopt by resolution" a proposal which is admittedly not existing international law raises the same problem in more acute form. Would adoption by the General Assembly of the International Law Commission's proposals regarding the continental shelf have provided the Court with a subsidiary means for the determination of rules of law which could not otherwise be determined? To phrase the question differently, is it likely that the International Court of Justice would regard the mere approval which might be read into Assembly "adoption" of the draft articles as entitling it to rest a decision on this approval without examining the state of the law and the factors which led the International Law Commission to make the proposal?

Observations made in the International Law Commission—

and in the committees which drafted its Statute—suggest that the approval sought through adoption of a Report or a draft by the General Assembly was twofold: (1) with regard to existing law, an authoritative confirmation which would tend to counteract doubts; and (2) with regard to a proposal which admittedly developed—rather than restating the law—an authoritative community expression of the way in which the law should develop. With regard to (2) there is no implication that the International Court of Justice could take the Assembly-adopted draft as ready-made law. The Court knows that the General Assembly has no authority to enact new rules of international law. Adoption by the General Assembly of proposals for the development of international law are directed less to the Court than toward the States which compose the General Assembly. The implicit assumption is that familiarity with a seriously proposed and carefully worked-out suggestion may lead in time to its formal acceptance by international convention. More sanguine, perhaps, is the hope that carefully designed proposals for filling in gaps in international law may influence State conduct and ripen into customary law based upon State practice.

Recommendations to Conclude a Convention

The recommendations made by the International Law Commission with regard to the other projects initiated by it all envisaged the conclusion of a convention. The recommendation made by the Commission in 1960 that its three draft articles on *Special Missions* be referred to the Vienna Conference on Diplomatic Intercourse and Immunities was in the nature of a special recommendation which made no reference to the particular provision of the Statute under which it was made.

After the International Law Commission had combined its draft articles on the Territorial Sea, the High Seas, the Continental Shelf, Contiguous Zones, and Fisheries into one draft on the *Law of the Sea,* it called attention to the fact that the draft comprised both codification of existing law and progressive development of new law and, in its 1956 Report to the General Assembly, recommended, pursuant to Article 23, paragraph 1 (d) of its Statute, that the General Assembly convoke a conference to conclude a convention (see above, pp. 298 ff.). "Only one delegation," says the Report of the Sixth Committee, "dissented from the general view that the matter could not be disposed of by the Sixth Committee itself at the present session, and that the Commission's report would have to be referred to a conference of plenipotentiaries, as indeed the Commission itself had recommended." [141] By unanimous vote, the General Assembly complied with the Commission's recommendation and referred the Commission's draft to the conference as the basis for its work. A similar recommendation by the Commission, pursuant to Article 23, paragraph 1 (d), with reference to its completed draft on *Consular Intercourse and Immunities*, was complied with by the General Assembly in 1961 (see above, p. 308). These are the only two occasions on which the General Assembly complied fully with the specific recommendations made pursuant to Article 23 by the Commission.

On two occasions the General Assembly rejected recommendations of the Commission, pursuant to Article 23, paragraph 1 (c) of its Statute, that the General Assembly "recommend the draft to Members with a view to the conclusion of a convention." The Commission's recommendation to that effect with regard to its *Draft Convention on Arbitral Procedure* was rejected by the Assembly in 1953 because it appeared, in the view of many Members, to change arbitration from a voluntary to a compulsory procedure (see p. 288). A similar recommendation by the Commission with regard to its draft articles on *Diplomatic Intercourse and Immunities* was postponed by the General Assembly in 1958, less, perhaps, from reluctance to approve the substantive content of the draft articles than because of hesitations as to whether a convention on the subject

[141] A/3520, 6 Feb. 1957, par. 11. GAOR, 11th Session, 1956, Annexes, Agenda item 53.

could best be drafted in the United Nations itself or in a specially convened diplomatic conference (see p. 304). In 1959, the General Assembly decided on the latter alternative, thereby indicating its preference for the procedure envisaged in paragraph 1 (*d*) of Article 23 rather than paragraph 1 (*c*). In particular, the General Assembly appears to have given little attention to views expressed at the 448th, 467th, and 468th meetings of the International Law Commission in May and June, 1958, that the draft articles on *Diplomatic Intercourse and Immunities,* being primarily a codification, might be submitted to the General Assembly "in the form of a convention, ready for signature" by representatives of Member States.[142] A possible interpretation of paragraph 1 (*c*) of Article 23 as intended to permit immediate conclusion of conventions based on the Commission's completed codification drafts (with the addition of the necessary final clauses and signatures, but without further reconsideration of its substantive provisions) did not find favor with the General Assembly.

Political preferences aside, difficulties in implementing a recommendation under Article 23, paragraph 1 (*c*) may be attributed in part to the ambiguity or insufficiency of its terms. A mere recommendation by the General Assembly of a draft "to Members with a view to the conclusion of a convention" might provide no initiative for action. The General Assembly would appear to provide a convenient and appropriate forum for supplying that initiative even if the convention were to be concluded by interested States in a conference not convoked by the United Nations. Nor should the absence from paragraph 1 (*d*) of the words "to recommend the draft"—which are found in paragraph 1 (*c*)—prevent the General Assembly from making such a recommendation under paragraph 1 (*d*) when it convokes a diplomatic conference.

It would be premature to conclude that the General Assembly will never "adopt" by resolution a Commission draft or

[142] Yearbook, ILC, 10th Session, 1958, I, 84 ff., 199–200.

submit a completed codification draft of the Commission for signature. Since, however, even a draft which is predominantly a restatement of existing law is likely to modify, however slightly, the understanding of that law, it appears probable that all the Commission's drafts will be examined both for their conformity with existing international law and with a view to the utility of the rules in meeting emergent needs.

CHAPTER 4

The International Law Commission and the Sixth Committee of the General Assembly

RELATIONS between the International Law Commission and the General Assembly are channeled through the latter's Sixth, or Legal, Committee. It was the Sixth Committee which completed the process of drafting the Commission's Statute; and it is the Sixth Committee which gives detailed consideration each year to the Report of the International Law Commission. The President of the International Law Commission, or a member designated by the Commission, attends the sessions of the Sixth Committee during its consideration of the Commission's Report and is regularly invited to introduce the Report and to aid the Committee's deliberations on its contents. There are always several members of the International Law Commission who are designated by their States to serve on the Sixth Committee, and a number of persons who have at some time represented their States on the Sixth Committee have been elected to membership on the International Law Commission. This liaison between the two bodies has provided the opportunity for a close working relationship.

Some of the relations between the Commission and the Sixth Committee—for example, the emoluments and the place of meeting of the International Law Commission and amendments to its Statute—have been considered elsewhere in this study (see Index). On these matters the Sixth Committee has, on the whole, been sympathetic to the problems and recommendations of the Commission and has sided with the Commission against the less understanding positions taken by the Assembly's Fifth Committee and the Advisory Committee on Administrative and Budgetary Questions.

The primary problems to be considered in this chapter relate to (1) the degree of autonomy possessed by the International Law Commission, (2) the attitude of the Sixth Committee toward the selection of topics for codification by the Commission, and (3) the role of the Sixth Committee in relation to the provisional or completed drafts of the Commission.

THE DEGREE OF AUTONOMY OF THE COMMISSION

The first problem—relating to the autonomy of the International Law Commission—underlies the other two but, like all of them, itself derives from a more basic disagreement as to the most appropriate methods for codifying or for developing international law, a disagreement which the compromise set forth in Chapter II of the Commission's Statute has not entirely eliminated.

When the Sixth Committee was considering the Report of the International Law Commission covering its 1st Session (1949),[1] Professor Koretsky (U.S.S.R.) characterized the International Law Commission as "a subsidiary organ of the Assembly, from which it received its instructions." [2] Sir Hartley Shawcross (U.K.), on the other hand, stated that "his Government regarded the International Law Commission as an organ whose authority and independence in international law were second only to the International Court of Justice"; although the "distinguished and independent experts who did not necessarily represent the opinions of their Governments . . . were

---

[1] Yearbook, ILC, 1st Session, 1949, p. 277.

[2] GAOR, 4th Session, 1949, Sixth Committee, Summary Records, 109, par. 65 (159th meeting, 12 October 1949). Cf. the remark of Mr. Tabibi (Afghanistan) that the International Law Commission was the "functional commission" of the Assembly's Sixth Committee. *Ibid.*, 16th Session, 1961, p. 126, par. 26 (714th meeting, 15 Nov. 1961).

responsible in the last analysis to the General Assembly," they "were free to carry out their work as they thought fit," at least as regarded the codification of international law.[3]

Mr. Spiropoulos (Greece) thought that charges which had been made that the Commission "had declared itself autonomous" were exaggerated:

The very existence of the Commission depended . . . upon the will of the General Assembly; the Commission's Statute did not have the force of a constitution but could be revoked by the General Assembly at any time. In the last analysis, it was the General Assembly which took the final decisions on the work of the International Law Commission. It could approve, disapprove, reject and halt the work of that Commission whenever it wished. . . .[4]

This legal and factual dependency of the International Law Commission upon the General Assembly has not prevented general acceptance by the Sixth Committee of the view that the "Commission had been established on the understanding that it would have a certain degree of autonomy and not be subject to constant supervision by the General Assembly"[5] and that the "Sixth Committee would be trespassing on the field reserved to the International Law Commission by Article 19 of its Statute if it tried to impose a plan of work on the Commission"[6] or "to issue directives to the Commission on the conduct of its affairs."[7]

---

[3] Ibid., 4th Session, 105, pars. 26–27. Sir Hartley later added that "it could hardly be asserted that so eminent a body of jurists as the International Law Commission could work only under orders from the Assembly and should confine itself to carrying out those orders, as if they were mere civil servants, without the right to take any initiative regarding the codification of international law." Ibid., 119 (161st meeting, 13 Oct. 1949), par. 7.

[4] Ibid., 115 (160th meeting, 13 Oct. 1949), par. 43.

[5] GAOR, 7th Session, 1952, Sixth Committee, Summary Records, 64, Guerreiro (Brazil), 315th meeting, 30 Oct. 1952.

[6] Ibid., 69, El-Tanamli (Egypt), 316th meeting, 31 Oct. 1952.

[7] GAOR, 12th Session, 1957, Sixth Committee, Summary Records, 18, Rosenne (Israel), 512th meeting, 3 Oct. 1957.

SELECTION OF TOPICS FOR CODIFICATION BY THE COMMISSION

The compromise embodied in the Commission's Statute by which the General Assembly makes to the Commission proposals for the progressive development of international law (Article 16) and the Commission selects topics for codification (Article 18), and the Commission's exercise of this right at its 1st Session in 1949, are discussed elsewhere.[8] At the 4th Session of the General Assembly, the Chairman of the International Law Commission, Judge Manley O. Hudson, called the attention of the Sixth Committee to the decision taken by the International Law Commission, by 10 votes to 3, that it considered itself "competent to carry out its work in accordance with the procedure laid down in Articles 19 to 23 of its Statute, without awaiting the General Assembly's decision on recommendations submitted by the Commission under Article 18, paragraph 2." [9] Mr. Gilberto Amado (Brazil), a member of the International Law Commission, defended the initiative of the Commission and observed that although the Commission "had not lost sight of the fact that it was a subsidiary organ of the General Assembly," particular requests by the Assembly "should not hamper the Commission in the performance of its essential function, which was to seek topics for codification." [10]

On the other hand, the initiative displayed by the Commission was criticized as a violation of its Statute by several delegations; it was asserted that although the task of deciding whether a topic was technically or juridically appropriate for codification belonged to the International Law Commission, the political decision to proceed with codification was solely

---

[8] See commentary on Articles 16 and 18 of the Commission's Statute, above, (pp. 143 ff., 161 ff.).

[9] GAOR, 4th Session, 1949, Sixth Committee, Summary Records, 101 (158th meeting, 11 Oct. 1949).

[10] *Ibid.*, 103–104 (159th meeting, 12 Oct. 1949).

the responsibility of the General Assembly.[11] Professor Vladimir Koretsky (U.S.S.R.), who had earlier led the battle against the right of the Commission [12] to select topics for codification, stated that his delegation had no objection at all to the topics actually selected for codification by the Commission,[13] but that by "deciding that it could pursue its codification work without waiting for the approval of the General Assembly, the International Law Commission had usurped a right not conferred upon it by its Statute; it had therefore violated its Statute." [14]

Nevertheless, the Sixth Committee—as stated above (see pp. 164 ff.)—endorsed the right of the International Law Commission to interpret its Statute as conferring on the Commission the right to select topics for codification. The question thus settled has not arisen again in this form.

General Assembly Requests

The right of the General Assembly or its Sixth Committee to request the Commission to undertake projects not only for progressive development but also for codification of international law has not been doubted,[15] but the advisability of overloading the agenda of the International Law Commission or of pressing for priority treatment has sometimes been questioned. During its early sessions, the International Law Commission was somewhat restive because the number of topics on which the General Assembly had requested it to work left practically no time for its program of codification.[16] At the

[11] Cf. Report of Sixth Committee, A/1196, par. 11, 3 Dec. 1949. GAOR, 4th Session, 1949, Plenary Meetings, Annex, p. 192, Agenda item 49.

[12] See commentary on Article 18, above (pp. 162 ff.).

[13] *The Law of Treaties,* the *Law of Arbitral Procedure,* and the *Regime of the High Seas.*

[14] GAOR, 4th Session, 1949, Sixth Committee, Summary Records, 109 (159th meeting, 12 Oct. 1949). Cf. his further remarks, *ibid.,* 129–130.

[15] Paragraph 3 of Article 18 of the Commission's Statute (dealing with codification of international law) provides: "The Commission shall give priority to requests of the General Assembly to deal with any question."

[16] See commentary on Article 18, above, pp. 176 ff.

226th meeting of the Sixth Committee, on 23 October 1950, Sir Frank Soskice (U.K.) pointed out that although "the codification of international law and its progressive development were the Commission's primary task" (its "essential work") the Commission "had had to devote two-thirds of its time to special tasks assigned to it by the Assembly"; the United Kingdom delegation deprecated sending the Commission any further special tasks which would "distract it from its work of codification." [17]

In fact, the Commission had been confronted at its 1st Session with General Assembly requests for a *Draft Declaration on the Rights and Duties of States,* the *Formulation of the Nürnberg Principles,* preparation of a *Draft Code of Offences Against the Peace and Security of Mankind,* and the *Question of Establishing an International Criminal Court.*[18] At its 2nd Session in 1950, the Commission was still devoting most of its time to these questions (except the first) and was requested by the General Assembly to include the *Regime of Territorial Waters* in the list of topics to be given priority.[19] Two new topics requested by the General Assembly were added to the agenda of the 3rd Session of the Commission in 1951: the *Question of Defining Aggression* and *Reservations to Multilateral Treaties.*[20] To this list should be added the requests made by the Economic and Social Council in 1950 that the International Law Commission undertake and give priority to work on *Nationality of Married Women* and the *Elimination of Statelessness.*[21]

At the 7th Session of the Sixth Committee in 1952, the Yugoslav delegation, complaining of violations of the privileges and immunities of Yugoslav diplomats in other Communist coun-

[17] GAOR, 5th Session, 1950, Sixth Committee, Summary Records, 91.
[18] Yearbook, ILC, 1st Session, 1949, p. 279.
[19] *Ibid.,* 2nd Session, 1950, II, 365.
[20] *Ibid.,* 3rd Session, 1951, II, 124.
[21] *Ibid.,* 4th Session, 1952, II, 67. Cf. Rosenne, "The International Law Commission, 1949–1959," 1960 B.Y.I.L. 104, 133 ff.

tries, introduced a draft resolution under which the General Assembly, noting, in part, that the International Law Commission had included the topic of *Diplomatic Intercourse and Immunities* in its provisional list of topics for codification, and that by Article 18, paragraph 3, of its Statute the Commission was required to give priority to requests of the General Assembly to deal with any question, would request the International Law Commission to undertake the codification of the topic as a matter of priority.[22] Mr. Fitzmaurice (U.K.), supporting the proposal provided that it would not have the effect of disrupting the Commission's work, stated that "although the Assembly was entitled to give directives to the Commission, it should as far as possible refrain from doing so and should leave the Commission to arrange and carry out its own programme of work." [23] In the event, the Sixth Committee adopted a modified draft resolution, omitting any reference to Article 18 (3), and requesting the International Law Commission to codify the topic "as soon as it considers it possible" and "to treat it as a priority topic." [24]

The following year (1953), the Sixth Committee exhibited even greater self-restraint in relation to the International Law Commission. A proposal by Mr. García Amador (Cuba) that the General Assembly request the International Law Commission "as soon as it considers it possible, to undertake the codification of the principles of international law governing *State Responsibility* and to include it among topics to which it accords priority" [25] was not approved by the Sixth Committee

[22] A/C.6/L.250, 29 Oct. 1952, GAOR, 7th Session, Annexes, Agenda item 58, p. 3. Cf. also A/2252, 11 Nov. 1952, Report of the Sixth Committee, *ibid.*, 4; GAOR, 7th Session, 1952, Sixth Committee, Summary Records, 53 ff. (313th meeting, 29 Oct. 1952).

[23] Sixth Committee, Summary Records (cited), 58 (314th meeting, 29 Oct. 1952).

[24] A/2252, Report of the Sixth Committee, *loc. cit.* As adopted by the General Assembly at its 400th plenary meeting, on 5 Dec. 1952, this became res. 685 (VII).

[25] A/C.6/L.311, 2 Nov. 1953, GAOR, 8th Session, 1953, Annexes, Agenda item 53, Italics added.

until its sponsor had accepted the deletion of the request for priority and the substitution of the word "advisable" for "possible." Some delegates thought that these amendments deprived the text of any significance, but the Sixth Committee approved it by a vote of 30–0–16.[26]

Not for five years did the Sixth Committee again request consideration of a topic by the International Law Commission.[27] At the 13th Session of the Sixth Committee in 1958, considerable interest was aroused by a French proposal that the International Law Commission include in its agenda a study of *Relations between States and International Organizations,* distinguishing those aspects which could be codified from those falling within the progressive development of international law.[28] Some representatives questioned what they regarded as the implication of the International Law Commission in paragraph 52 of its 1958 Report that, because the subject was governed by special conventions, it did not require codification.[29] The Sixth Committee, in a vaguely worded draft reso-

[26] *Ibid.,* Sixth Committee, Summary Records, 161–165 (393rd and 394th meetings, 25 and 28 Nov. 1953). As adopted by the General Assembly at its 468th plenary meeting, on 7 Dec. 1953, it became res. 799 (VIII).

[27] GA res. 821 (IX) of 17 Dec. 1954, by which the General Assembly decided to transmit certain documents to the International Law Commission with reference to a Polish charge of piracy in the China Seas and to invite Governments of Member States to send to the Commission "their views concerning the principle of freedom of navigation on the high seas"—a topic already on the Commission's agenda—was not a request by the Assembly to study a new topic. At its 290th meeting, on 12 May 1955, the Commission decided, by a vote of 8–0–2 (with two additional members refusing to vote or to abstain), "that the Commission had no competence to deal with the complaint made by the Government of the Polish People's Republic in its memorandum (A/CN.4/L.53)" of 6 May 1955 to the Commission. Yearbook, ILC, 7th Session. 1955, I, 39. Cf. *ibid.,* II, 1 and 21.

[28] A/C.6/L.427, 27 Oct. 1958. GAOR, 13th Session, 1958, Annexes, Agenda item 56. Cf. debate, *ibid.,* Sixth Committee, Summary Records, 89–145 (569th to 580th meetings); A/4007, 26 Nov. 1958, Report of the Sixth Committee, Annexes, 5.

[29] Yearbook, ILC, 10th Session, 1958, II, 89.

lution, invited the Commission "to give further consideration to the question of relations between States and inter-governmental international organizations at the appropriate time," taking care not to alter the priorities already established by the International Law Commission.[30]

In 1959, during its 14th Session, the Sixth Committee considered several requests for the study of new topics by the International Law Commission. After extensive debate on the desirability of codifying the topic of *Asylum,* the Sixth Committee, on 14 October 1959, adopted, by a vote of 63–1–12, a Salvadorean draft resolution requesting the International Law Commission "as soon as it considers it advisable, to undertake the codification of the principles and rules of international law relating to the *Right of Asylum.*" No request for priority was made.[31] Comparable in this respect—although it did not specifically call for codification—was the Sixth Committee's adoption of a draft resolution requesting the International Law Commission, "as soon as it considers it advisable, to undertake the study of the question of the *juridical regime of historic waters* including historic bays, and to make such recommendations regarding the matter as the Commission deems appropriate." [32]

[30] As adopted by the General Assembly, res. 1289 (XIII), 5 Dec. 1958, A/4090, p. 54.
[31] GAOR, 14th Session, 1959, Annexes, Agenda item 55, pp. 3, 4, 6; *ibid.,* Sixth Committee, Summary Records, 9–61 (602nd to 612th meetings). As adopted by the General Assembly at its 842nd plenary meeting, on 21 Nov. 1959, it became res. 1400 (XIV).
Sir Gerald Fitzmaurice, as Chairman of the International Law Commission, admitted that a resolution requesting the Commission to codify, without requesting priority, a topic already on the Commission's list might appear superfluous, but added that the "Commission would certainly attach much weight to an Assembly resolution" drafted in those terms. *Ibid.,* Sixth Committee, Summary Records, 52 (610th meeting, 12 Oct. 1959).
At its 544th meeting on 20 May 1960, the International Law Commission decided to defer consideration of the topic *Right of Asylum* to a future session. Yearbook, ILC, 12th Session, 1960, I, 111.
[32] Italics added. GAOR, 14th Session, 1959, Annexes, Agenda item 58;

At the same session, the Bolivian delegation introduced, on 5 October 1959, a draft resolution requesting the International Law Commission to take up the codification of the utilization and navigation of international waterways "as the next subject in its programme of work." [33] Several delegations questioned the advisability of overburdening the International Law Commission with topics suggested by the Sixth Committee.[34] Mr. Morozov (U.S.S.R.) called on the Sixth Committee to "exercise restraint by not recommending any changes in the Commission's work programme" unless the topics "were really of exceptional importance." [35] After modifying its draft resolution to permit the International Law Commission to decide when to take up the topic, the Bolivian delegation introduced a third draft which made no request of the International Law Commission but merely called upon the United Nations Secretariat to provide information relating to legal problems involved in the utilization of international rivers.[36]

By 1959, the Sixth Committee had thus come a long way from its earlier tendency to crowd the International Law Commission's agenda with new topics. This self-restraint may have

---

ibid., Sixth Committee, Summary Records, 227–241 (643rd to 646th meetings). As adopted by the General Assembly at its 847th plenary meeting, on 7 Dec. 1959, it became res. 1453 (XIV). At its 544th meeting on 20 May 1960, the International Law Commission discussed the lack of precision of the concept of "historic waters" and decided to defer consideration of the topic to a later session, while requesting the Secretariat to gather further materials on the subject. Yearbook, ILC, 12th Session, 1960, I, 111–116. Cf. A/CN.4/143, 9 March 1962, Secretariat Study of *Juridical Regime of Historic Waters, including Historic Bays.*

[33] A/C.6/L.445, 5 October 1959, GAOR, 14th Session, 1959, Annexes, Agenda item 55.

[34] *Ibid.*, Sixth Committee, Summary Records, 30–69 (606th to 614th meetings).

[35] *Ibid.*, 46 (609th meeting).

[36] Cf. *ibid.*, Annexes, Agenda item 55. As adopted by the General Assembly, res. 1401 (XIV), 21 Nov. 1959. For the valuable Report made by the Secretariat pursuant to this resolution, see *Legal Problems Relating to the Utilization and Use of International Rivers,* A/5409, 15 April 1963, 3 vols. (mimeographed).

resulted, in part, from a growing understanding in the Sixth Committee of the limited amount of careful drafting which could be accomplished by the Commission in an annual ten-week session and, in part, by the importance of the topics already on its agenda.

The 1960 debate of the Sixth Committee on the Future Work of the International Law Commission resulted in no new requests to the Commission; but in 1961, at the 16th Session of the General Assembly, the Sixth Committee recommended that the Commission "continue its work in the field of the *Law of Treaties* and of *State Responsibility* and to include on its priority list the topic of *Succession of States and Governments.*" [37] A proposal by the Colombian representative to add the topic *Right of Asylum* to the priority list of the Commission was withdrawn by its sponsor for lack of support, "on the understanding that his views and those of certain representatives supporting them would be brought to the attention of the International Law Commission." [38] At the same session, the Sixth Committee requested the International Law Commission, "as soon as it considers it advisable," to give further study to the subject of *Special Missions*, pursuant to the recommendation of the Vienna Conference on Diplomatic Intercourse and Immunities.[39]

The 1960 Debate on Future Work in International Law [40]

When the General Assembly met for its 15th Session in 1960,

[37] GA res. 1686 (XVI), 18 Dec. 1961. Cf. A/5036, 15 Dec. 1961, Report of the Sixth Committee on Future Work in the Field of the Codification and Progressive Development of International Law, GAOR, 16th Session, 1961, Annexes, Agenda item 70.

[38] A/5036, par. 36, and A/C.6/SR.729 and 730, GAOR, 16th Session, 1961, pp. 214–220.

[39] GA res. 1687 (XVI), 18 Dec. 1961. Cf. A/5043, 15 Dec. 1961, Report of the Sixth Committee on the Question of Special Missions, Annexes, Agenda item 71; A/C.6/SR. 731, *loc. cit.*, 221–223.

[40] See GAOR, 15th Session, 1960, Sixth Committee, Summary Records, 3–115 (648th to 672nd meetings); *ibid.*, Annexes, Agenda item 65; A/4605, 1 Dec. 1960, Report of the Sixth Committee.

only three of the ninety-two items on its agenda were assigned to the Sixth Committee. The principal item—the Report of the International Law Commission covering the Work of its 12th Session—was primarily an interim report on a provisional draft by the Commission on *Consular Intercourse and Immunities* and called for no action by the Sixth Committee.

Many delegations deplored the paucity of the Sixth Committee's agenda. Some attributed it to a lack of interest by the United Nations in international law at a time when international law had an increasingly important role to play. A few were inclined to blame the International Law Commission for not providing enough work for the Sixth Committee. This view was rejected by most representatives: they expressed appreciation of the work of the Commission and denied that it was under any obligation to provide annual work for the Sixth Committee. If the Sixth Committee had nothing to do, it was suggested that it should itself undertake studies of matters such as the compulsory jurisdiction of the International Court of Justice, the registration of treaties, or the methods of work of the General Assembly. These topics were not regarded by other delegations as meeting current needs; they preferred studies of legal questions connected with peaceful coexistence of States, disarmament, the abolition of colonialism, outer space, or new sources of international law arising from resolutions or decisions of international organizations.

During the Sixth Committee's discussions, irresponsible political attacks were made by Communist representatives against the Office of Legal Affairs of the United Nations Secretariat,[41] the Secretary of the International Law Commission, and the Commission's Special Rapporteur on the topic of *State Responsibility*.

The Special Rapporteur was attacked because his reports

[41] The Office of Legal Affairs was attacked for not including enough staff members from African, Asian, Latin American, or Communist States and for lack of initiative in providing the Sixth Committee with items of work.

to the Commission on the topic of *State Responsibility* dealt
with the legal responsibility of States under international law
for injuries to aliens rather than wandering down political by-
paths to deal with alleged legal responsibility "for violation of
the rights of peoples and nations to self-determination," [42] and
the exploitation of their national resources, and State responsibility for subversive activities, espionage, terrorism, and violations of territorial integrity. The Secretary of the Commission,
Dr. Yuen-li Liang, was attacked for having invited the Harvard
Law School to arrange for a revision of the 1929 draft of the
Harvard Research in International Law on the *Responsibility
of States for Damage done in their Territory to the Person or
Property of Foreigners*,[43] even though the International Law
Commission had later approved his initiative in making the
request.[44] The Czech representative on the Sixth Committee
mistakenly regarded the requested revision as reflecting the
views of the Harvard Law School and as serving "the interests
of the Western countries alone," [45] while the Soviet representative pretended to believe that "such a draft could reflect only
the reactionary views of its parent institution." [46] The Special
Rapporteur, Dr. F. V. García Amador, was falsely criticized [47]
for not complying in his reports on *State Responsibility* with
General Assembly resolution 799 (VIII),[48] with justifying ag-

[42] Sixth Committee, Summary Records, 67, 662nd meeting, par. 2
(Albania). Cf., 651st, par. 10 (U.S.S.R.), 653rd, pars. 10 ff. (Romania),
666th, par. 28 (Romania) meetings.

[43] Cf. 23 American Journal of International Law, Special Number,
131 ff. (April 1929).

[44] Cf. Yearbook, ILC, 8th Session, 1956, I, 228 ff. (370th meeting, 19
June 1956).

[45] Summary Records, Sixth Committee, 27 ff., 655th meeting (Czechoslovakia).

[46] *Ibid.*, 40, 657th meeting.

[47] *Ibid.*, 10, 651st meeting (U.S.S.R.); 20, 653rd meeting (Romania).

[48] By res. 799 (VIII), 7 Dec. 1953, the General Assembly requested the
International Law Commission "to undertake the codification of the
principles of international law governing State responsibility," without
making reference to the scope or content of those principles. A pream-

gression and the claims of colonial powers to exploit the economic resources of underdeveloped countries, and with basing his reports on obsolete principles.

Since the International Law Commission had not yet undertaken a systematic study of the topic and had submitted no draft on the subject to the General Assembly, the discussion in the Sixth Committee was obviously an attempt to influence the future consideration of the topic by the International Law Commission. Although the Netherlands representative, Professor Tammes, called on the Sixth Committee to "abstain from interfering in studies which were not yet ready for submission to the Assembly," [49] and Mr. Sharp (New Zealand) stated that "the Sixth Committee should hesitate to give directives to the Commission, or to interpose itself between the Commission and the Special Rapporteurs," [50] representatives of Hungary,[51] the U.S.S.R.,[52] and Bulgaria,[53] *inter alia,* defended the view that the General Assembly should instruct the International Law Commission as to the manner in which the Assembly wished the Commission to codify the principles of international law governing State responsibility. This view is reflected in the last phrase of paragraph 8 of the preamble of resolution 1505 (XV) printed below.

The debate in the Sixth Committee revolved around the question whether a special committee or the International Law

---

bular passage stating "that it is desirable for the maintenance and development of peaceful relations between States" to codify the law of State responsibility was distorted by his critics into a bludgeon to attack the Special Rapporteur.

[49] Sixth Committee, Summary Records, 50 (659th meeting).

[50] *Ibid.,* 53.   [51] *Ibid.,* 25 (654th meeting).

[52] *Ibid.,* 35–36 (656th meeting).

[53] *Ibid.,* 47. Mr. Todorov believed "that the Sixth Committee had the right, and indeed the duty, to instruct the International Law Commission" that it wished the study of State responsibility to include "such important matters as State responsibility for the violations of State sovereignty, of the rights of peoples of self-determination, of the right of every nation freely to exploit its natural riches and resources and so on"; par. 33 (658th meeting).

Commission itself should be charged with the preparation of a new list of topics for codification. Those favoring reference of the task to the Commission feared that to set up a special committee would reflect lack of confidence in the Commission and duplicate its work. Representatives backing the proposal for the establishment of a special committee stressed the political nature of selecting topics for codification and wished the decisions made by representatives of States rather than by experts in international law. The compromise unanimously adopted by the Sixth Committee at its 672nd meeting, on 21 November 1960 is embodied in operative paragraphs 1 and 2 of resolution 1505 (XV), adopted by the General Assembly at its 943rd plenary meeting on 12 December 1960, as follows: [54]

The General Assembly,

Bearing in mind the purposes and principles of the United Nations,

Considering that the conditions prevailing in the world today give increased importance to the role of international law—and its strict and undeviating observance by all Governments—in strengthening international peace, developing friendly and co-operative relations among the nations, settling disputes by peaceful means and advancing economic and social progress throughout the world,

Recalling its resolutions 1236 (XII) of 14 December 1957 and 1301 (XIII) of 10 December 1958,

Mindful of Article 13, paragraph 1, of the Charter of the United Nations, which provides that the General Assembly shall initiate studies and make recommendations for the purpose of encouraging the progressive development of international law and its codification,

Considering the extent of the progress made by the International Law Commission in the codification of topics listed in paragraph 16 of the report covering its first session,

Expressing its appreciation to the Commission for the work it has accomplished in the field of the codification and progressive development of international law.

[54] Cf. A/4796, 10 July 1961.

Considering that many new trends in the field of international relations have an impact on the development of international law,

Considering that it is desirable to survey the present state of international law, with a view to ascertaining whether new topics susceptible of codification or conducive to progressive development have arisen, whether priority should be given to any of the topics already included in the Commission's list or whether a broader approach may be called for in the consideration of any of these topics,

Deeming it necessary therefore to reconsider the Commission's programme of work in the light of recent developments in international law and with due regard to the need for promoting friendly relations and co-operation among States,

1. *Decides* to place the question entitled "Future work in the field of the codification and progressive development of international law" on the provisional agenda of its sixteenth session in order to study and survey the whole field of international law and make necessary suggestions with regard to the preparation of a new list of topics for codification and for the progressive development of international law;

2. *Invites* Member States to submit in writing to the Secretary-General, before 1 July 1961, any views or suggestions they may have on this question for consideration by the General Assembly.

Replies were received from the Governments of Afghanistan, Austria, Belgium, Burma, Ceylon, Colombia, Czechoslovakia, Denmark, Ghana, Greece, Indonesia, Israel, Mexico, Netherlands, Norway, South Africa, Sudan, Sweden, United Kingdom, Venezuela, and Yugoslavia, the Governments of Greece, Norway, South Africa, and the Sudan stating that they had no observations to make.[55] The topics suggested in these replies will be listed below in connection with topics suggested in the 1961 debate of the Sixth Committee.

The 1961 Debate on Future Work in International Law

At the 16th Session of the General Assembly, the Sixth Com-

[55] A/4796 and Adds. 1–8, 10 July–5 Oct. 1961; reprinted in GAOR, 16th Session, 1961, Annexes, Agenda item 70.

mittee debated Agenda item 70, "Future Work in the Field of the Codification and Progressive Development of International Law" at its 713th to 730th meetings, from 14 November to 13 December 1961.[56] The desirability of reconsidering the program of work drawn up by the International Law Commission at its 1st Session in 1949 was generally conceded, but debate was resumed on the question whether the Commission or the Sixth Committee should draw up a list of topics to be studied by the Commission over the next five or ten years, on whether the Commission should avoid politically controversial topics or, on the contrary, should embrace the opportunity to make a contribution on controversial topics of current interest, and on the Commission's methods of work.

Topics suggested during the debate[57] or prior thereto[58] for submission to the International Law Commission are listed below, with indication of the States expressing preference for such topics.

Law of Treaties	Afghanistan, Argentina, Australia, Austria,[59] Brazil, Bulgaria, Byelorussian S.S.R., Canada, China, Colombia, Czechoslovakia, Denmark, Ecuador, France, Greece, Guatemala, Hungary, India,[60] Indonesia, Iran, Iraq, Ireland, Israel, Italy, Ivory Coast, Lebanon, Liberia, Mexico, Mongolia, Nepal, Netherlands, New Zealand, Nicaragua, Pakistan, Panama, Peru, Philippines, Spain, Sweden, Turkey, Ukrainian S.S.R., U.S.S.R.,

[56] Cf. A/C.6/SR.713–730, GAOR, 16th Session, 1961, Summary Records, Sixth Committee, 119–220; A/5036, 15 Dec. 1961, Report of Sixth Committee, *ibid.,* Annexes, Agenda item 70.

[57] *Ibid.*

[58] A/4796 and Adds. 1–8.

[59] "The law of treaties in respect of international organizations." A/4796, Add. 6.

[60] India suggested several topics to "be added to the subjects already chosen by the International Law Commission." A/C.6/SR.719, *loc. cit.,* 146.

United Arab Republic, United Kingdom, United States, Venezuela, Yugoslavia [61]

State Responsibility   Afghanistan, Argentina, Australia, Austria, Brazil, Bulgaria, Byelorussian S.S.R., Canada, China, Colombia, Czechoslovakia, Denmark, Ecuador, France, Ghana, Greece, Guatemala, Hungary, India, Indonesia, Iran, Iraq, Ireland, Israel, Italy, Ivory Coast, Lebanon, Liberia, Mexico, Mongolia, Nepal, Netherlands, Panama, Peru, Poland, Romania, Spain, Sweden, Turkey, Ukrainian S.S.R., U.S.S.R., United Arab Republic, United Kingdom, United States, Venezuela, Yugoslavia [62]

(NOTE: What was termed a "broader approach" to the codification of the *Law of State Responsibility* was advocated by a few States, viz.: Austria, Bulgaria, Byelorussian S.S.R., Czechoslovakia, Indonesia, Iran, Iraq, Mexico, Poland, Romania, Ukrainian S.S.R., U.S.S.R., and Yugoslavia. On the other hand, the United Kingdom representative warned that "attempts to give it a political content should be firmly resisted." [63] Representatives of Ceylon, Ghana, Greece, New Zealand, and Venezuela advocated codification of the *Status* or *Treatment of Aliens* as a separate topic.)

[61] In addition to the 47 governments whose representatives specifically called for continuation of the International Law Commission's work on the *Law of Treaties,* the following States sponsored draft resolutions for that purpose: Cambodia, Ceylon, Chile, Dahomey, Ghana, Japan, Libya, Mali, Romania. It should also be noted that at its 730th meeting on 13 Dec. 1961, the Sixth Committee unanimously adopted the draft resolution calling in par. 3 (a) for continuation of the Commission's work on the *Law of Treaties.* Cf. A/5036, and GA res. 1686 (XVI), 18 Dec. 1961.

[62] To this list of 46 States advocating continuation of the Commission's work on *State Responsibility* should be added the following States sponsoring draft resolutions for that purpose: Cambodia, Ceylon, Chile, Dahomey, Japan, Libya, Mali, Pakistan. The draft resolution calling in par. 3 (a) for continuation of the Commission's work on *State Responsibility* was unanimously adopted by the Sixth Committee. Cf. A/5036 and GA res. 1686 (XVI).

[63] A/C.6/SR. 717, *loc. cit.,* 136.

Succession of States and Governments	Afghanistan, Austria, Belgium, Brazil, Canada, Ceylon, Czechoslovakia, Denmark, Ecuador, Ghana, Greece, Indonesia, Iraq, Ireland, Italy, Lebanon, Liberia, Mexico, New Zealand, Nicaragua, United Arab Republic, United States, Venezuela, Yugoslavia [64]
Special Missions	Belgium, Brazil, Czechoslovakia, France, Ghana, India, Iraq, Israel, New Zealand, Pakistan, Poland, United Arab Republic, United Kingdom, Yugoslavia [65]
Right of Asylum	Belgium, Ceylon, China, Colombia, Ecuador, Ghana, Guatemala, Nicaragua, United Arab Republic, Venezuela, Yugoslavia
Extradition	Ceylon, Colombia, Ghana

[64] To this list of 24 States should be added the following States sponsoring draft resolutions recommending the inclusion of the topic *Succession of States and Governments* in the priority list of the International Law Commission: Cambodia, Chile, Dahomey, Japan, Libya, Mali, Pakistan, Romania, Turkey. The draft resolution calling for such priority treatment was unanimously adopted by the Sixth Committee (A/5036), although codification of the topic had been opposed by Peru (A/C.6/SR.726, *loc. cit.*, 193) and queried by Israel (*ibid.*, 195). The representative of China thought that if the Commission undertook the study of the topic, succession of States and of Governments should be separately considered (A/C.6/SR. 729, *loc. cit.*, 214), as proposed by Canada (A/C.6/SR. 727, *loc. cit.*, 201).

[65] To this list of 14 States should be added Argentina and Italy, who joined in sponsoring a draft resolution requesting the International Law Commission, "as soon as it considers it advisable, to study further the subject of special missions and to report thereon to the General Assembly." At its 731st meeting, 15 Dec. 1961, the Sixth Committee unanimously adopted the draft resolution. Cf. A/5043, 15 Dec. 1961, Report of the Sixth Committee on the Question of Special Missions, and GA res. 1687 (XVI), 18 Dec. 1961.

Recognition of States and Governments	Czechoslovakia, Denmark, Ghana, Mexico, Nicaragua, Venezuela, Yugoslavia
Pacific Settlement of Disputes	
Means for inducing greater resort to judicial or arbitral methods; Compulsory Jurisdiction	Denmark, Ghana, Liberia, Pakistan, Sweden
Conciliation	Colombia, Indonesia, Ireland
Jurisdiction of International Courts and Organizations regarding Domestic Jurisdiction and Human Rights	Ceylon
Peaceful Coexistence [66]	
State Jurisdiction and Jurisdictional Immunities	
State Jurisdiction	Ghana
Territorial Domain of States	Venezuela
Criminal Jurisdiction	Venezuela
Jurisdictional Immunities	Belgium, Brazil, Ceylon, Denmark, Ghana, Ireland
Acts of State	Belgium, Venezuela
Outer Space or Air Space	Afghanistan, Burma, Ghana, Mexico, Nicaragua
International Rivers	Argentina, Iran, Netherlands

[66] The topic *Legal Aspects of Peaceful Coexistence* was the subject of an extended political debate in the Sixth Committee. While a few States appear to have regarded it as an appropriate topic for reference to the International Law Commission, others opposed such reference, and the Sixth Committee unanimously decided to place on the agenda of the 17th session of the General Assembly the question: "Consideration of principles of international law relating to friendly relations and co-operation among States in accordance with the Charter of the United Nations." A/5036 and GA res. 1686 (XVI), 18 Dec. 1961. See the Report of the Special Committee on that topic, A/5746, 16 Nov. 1964.

Historic Waters and Bays	United Arab Republic
Territorial Sea	Burma, Yugoslavia
International Trade	Yugoslavia
Economic Development	Yugoslavia
Sovereignty over Natural Re-sources [67]	Czechoslovakia, Indonesia
Independence and Sovereignty of States	
Acquisition of Statehood	Austria, Ghana
Self-determination	Austria, Czechoslovakia
"The right of a State, in particular a new State, to determine, to implement, and to perfect its political form, socially and economically in conformity with the professed ideology and to take all necessary steps to accomplish this, e.g., de-colonization, normalization, nationalization" and "to control all its natural resources."	Indonesia
Right to territorial integrity and self-defence	Indonesia
Fundamental Rights and Duties of States	Mexico, Nicaragua, Venezuela
International Court of Human Rights	Colombia, Nicaragua, Venezuela

[67] The representative of Mexico opposed reference of this topic to the International Law Commission because it was being studied by other United Nations organs, A/C.6/SR. 722, *loc. cit.,* 164.

Defence of Democracy	Venezuela
Nationality, including Stateless-ness	Burma, Ghana, Venezuela
Corollaries of Non-Intervention	Czechoslovakia, Mexico, Netherlands
Enforcement of International Law	Ghana
Prohibition of War	Afghanistan
Prohibition of Aggressive War, Mass Weapons of Destruction and Responsibility for Breaches of Peace	Czechoslovakia
Laws of War and Neutrality	Austria
Relations of International Organizations with States (treaties, responsibility, etc.)	Austria, Netherlands, United Arab Republic, Yugoslavia
Sources of International Law in Light of Resolutions of International Organizations	Mexico

At its 730th meeting, on 13 December 1961, the Sixth Committee unanimously adopted the following draft resolution, later approved by the General Assembly as resolution 1686 (XVI) of 18 December 1961:

Future Work in the Field of the Codification and Progressive Development of International Law

The General Assembly,
Recalling its resolution 1505 (XV) of 12 December 1960,
Considering that the conditions prevailing in the world today give increased importance to the role of international law in relations among nations,
Emphasizing the important role of codification and progressive

development of international law with a view to making international law a more effective means of furthering the purposes and principles set forth in Articles 1 and 2 of the Charter of the United Nations,

Mindful of its responsibilities under paragraph 1 (a) of Article 13 of the Charter for encouraging the progressive development of international law and its codification,

Having surveyed the present state of international law with particular regard to the preparation of a new list of topics for codification and progressive development of international law,

1. *Expresses its appreciation* to the International Law Commission for the valuable work already accomplished by it on the codification and progressive development of international law;

2. *Takes note* of chapter III of the report of the International Law Commission covering the work of its thirteenth session; [68]

3. *Recommends* the International Law Commission:

(a) To continue its work in the field of the law of treaties and of State responsibility and to include on its priority list the topic of succession of States and Governments;

(b) To consider at its fourteenth session its future programme of work, on the basis of sub-paragraph (a) above and in the light of the discussion in the Sixth Committee at the fifteenth and sixteenth sessions of the General Assembly and of the observations of Member States submitted pursuant to resolution 1505 (XV), and to report to the General Assembly at its seventeenth session on the conclusions it has reached;

4. *Decides* to place on the provisional agenda of its seventeenth session the question entitled "Consideration of principles of international law relating to friendly relations and co-operation among States in accordance with the Charter of the United Nations."

By unanimously recommending in paragraph 3 (a) of the resolution that the International Law Commission continue its work on the *Law of Treaties* and *State Responsibility*, the Sixth Committee again endorsed the selection of these topics by the Commission itself. The fact that no less than fifty-six States specifically gave preference to the *Law of Treaties* and

[68] Yearbook, ILC, 13th Session, 1961, II, 128.

that fifty-four sponsored *State Responsibility* indicates that the International Law Commission was not out of touch with the needs and preferences of States when it selected those topics. The thirty-three States urging consideration by the Commission of *Succession of States and Governments* endorsed a topic already on the provisional list of the Commission but which it had not yet had time to work on.

The Sixth Committee wisely refrained from recommending priority treatment for any topics other than these three, but requested the Commission to give further study to the subject of *Special Missions* "as soon as it considers it advisable." [69] Mr. Tunkin (U.S.S.R.), prior to the voting, had informed the Sixth Committee that four topics "was a maximum figure, which already almost exceeded the bounds of reason. The Commission's experience had shown that it should consider only one topic at each session so that its members would have time to carry out the necessary preparatory research." [70]

Although the Sixth Committee made no decision on the question whether the International Law Commission should avoid or embrace controversial topics, the endorsement of the topics *Law of Treaties, States Responsibility, Succession of States and Governments,* and *Special Missions* suggests that the Sixth Committee preferred that the Commission should concentrate on legal topics, even if to some extent controversial, rather than on political subjects of little legal content.[71]

No decision was reached by the Sixth Committee on the much debated question whether the Committee or the Commission should draw up a list of topics for the long-range work of the Commission. Instead, by paragraph 3 (b) of the resolution, the Committee requested the Commission to consider its

[69] Cf. GA res. 1687 (XVI), 18 Dec. 1961.

[70] A/C.6/SR.729, *loc. cit.,* 211.

[71] Cf. Mr. Stirling (Australia): "His delegation had no objection to controversial issues, provided that the controversy was of a legal and not of a political nature." A/C.6/SR. 723, par. 6, *loc. cit.,* 167–168.

future program of work in the light of the Sixth Committee's debates of 1960 and 1961 and the suggestions made by States, and to report its conclusions to the 1962 Session of the General Assembly.

As regards the Commission's methods of work, the Sixth Committee's report observes that

some representatives wanted the Commission to speed up its work. They suggested that the terms of office of members should be extended or the sessions should be made longer, that experts who were not members of the Commission should be appointed to assist the special rapporteurs or that a single subject should be entrusted to two rapporteurs so that the study thereof would not be interrupted if the post of rapporteur fell vacant. They also suggested that the Commission should be divided into sub-commissions.

27. However, most representatives considered that the Committee's [*sc.*: Commission's] rate of progress in its work was satisfactory, and that speed was not the most important element, the time devoted to attempting to reconcile opinions, positions or ideas not being time lost; the main consideration, they believed, should be the quality of the Commission's work. . . .[72]

The Sixth Committee made no decisions on these questions; the view again prevailed that the methods of work of the Commission must be left to the Commission.

The debate leading to the adoption of resolution 1686 (XVI) took place in an assemblage representing 104 States of the world and was characterized by Mr. Alberto Ulloa (Peru) as marking "a turning point in the evolution of international law." He added:

There had never before been such a strong affirmation of the three criteria on which the formulation of international law rested: its universality, its human foundation, and the equality of States. The triumph of universality could be seen in the present number of Members of the United Nations and the fact that they represented all the legal systems, forms of civilization and large

[72] A/5036, pars. 26–27.

geographical areas of the world. . . . Having thus attained universality, international law should now develop in depth.[73]

At its 14th Session in 1962, the International Law Commission devoted its 629th to 637th meetings to a detailed discussion of "Future work in the field of codification and progressive development of international law" in the light of General Assembly resolution 1686 (XVI) and the discussion in the Sixth Committee. After reference of the item to a sub-committee for further consideration, the Commission decided at its 668th meeting on 26 June 1962 "to limit the future programme of work for the time being to the three main topics under study," namely, *Law of Treaties, State Responsibility,* and *Succession of States and Governments;* and "to include in the programme four additional topics of more limited scope which had been referred to it by earlier General Assembly resolutions," namely, *Special Missions, Relations between States and Inter-Governmental Organizations, Right of Asylum,* and *Juridical Regime of Historic Waters, Including Historic Bays.*[74]

THE SIXTH COMMITTEE AND THE COMMISSION'S DRAFTS

The Sixth Committee of the General Assembly has from the beginning exhibited some uncertainty as to its proper role in relation to drafts of the International Law Commission. Commencing with the Report covering its 2nd Session in 1950, the International Law Commission has explicitly distinguished items "submitted to the General Assembly for its consideration" from items on which the Commission was continuing to work and on which a progress report—sometimes in the form of a provisional draft—was submitted "for the information of the General Assembly." [75]

[73] A/C.6/SR. 726, meeting of 7 Dec. 1961, *loc. cit.,* 192.

[74] A/5209, par. 60, Report of the International Law Commission, 14th Session, 1962; and Yearbook, ILC, 14th Session, 1962, I, 2–45, 266, 273.

[75] Yearbook, ILC, 2nd Session, 1950, II, 366, pars. 14, 16.

The Sixth Committee and Work in Progress in the International Law Commission

At the 245th meeting of the Sixth Committee, on 28 November 1950, Mr. Ivan Kerno, Assistant Secretary-General in charge of the Legal Department, called the attention of the Committee to this distinction and doubted whether it need devote much time to matters submitted merely for its information. Mr. Morozov (U.S.S.R.) agreed and questioned whether the Commission should even have included in its Report a discussion of work in progress. Mr. Röling (Netherlands), observing that some representatives had questioned whether final drafts of the International Law Commission should be re-examined by the General Assembly, thought that the Sixth Committee might usefully present observations on work in progress which the Commission could take into account. A motion for the closure of debate on Parts V and VI of the Commission's Report— which had been presented merely for the information of the General Assembly—was adopted despite the comment of one member of the Committee "that it was impossible to pronounce the closure of a debate which had not yet begun, and that some representatives would certainly wish to speak on the questions dealt with in parts V and VI. . . ."[76]

At the following session, Mr. Röling (Netherlands) again expressed the view that the Sixth Committee should in the future "hold a general debate on the Commission's work before it was completed," stating in part:

The Committee's function was to give directions and criticisms for the guidance of the International Law Commission in the early stages of the Commission's work on a particular question. It should not introduce changes into the Commission's completed work, but merely adopt it, reject it or refer it back to the Commission. He suggested that in the future it might be more advantageous for the Sixth Committee to discuss the Commission's work while it was in the planning stage or in progress.

[76] GAOR, 5th Session, 1950, Sixth Committee, Summary Records, 243–245, par. 55.

If, he added, the Commission could take account of views expressed by members of the Sixth Committee, its completed drafts "would be more likely to meet with general approval." [77]

This view was challenged by Mr. Abdoh (Iran), who "doubted whether the Assembly was really entitled to give directives to the Commission on the work which had not yet been completed and had been submitted simply for the Assembly's information." [78] The Committee then adopted a draft resolution by which it merely *"Notes* the progress of the Commission's work on those questions." [79]

Although the 1952 Report of the International Law Commission stated in its first paragraph that, "being in the nature of a progress report, [it] is submitted to the General Assembly for its information," [80] some members of the Sixth Committee thought that the Committee "should discuss the substance of the report," including a thirty-two-article provisional draft on *Arbitral Procedure* containing questions which were said to be "extremely controversial." [81] Mr. Spiropoulos (Greece), a member of the International Law Commission, pointed out that the Commission had been under no obligation to submit a report on pending questions and that it would obviously be premature for the Assembly to embark on a detailed discussion of the Commission's provisional draft, which had, however, been submitted to governments for their comments.[82] Dr. Liang, Secretary of the International Law Commission, recalled that the drafters of the Commission's Statute had had a choice between having the Commission

consult the General Assembly each year and ask for directions, or it could submit only its final work, and not its tentative conclusions, to the General Assembly. The General Assembly had chosen

---

[77] *Ibid.*, 6th Session, 1951–52, Sixth Committee, Summary Records, 274–275 (297th meeting, 24 Jan. 1952).

[78] *Ibid.*, 274.   [79] *Ibid.*, 275.

[80] Yearbook, ILC, 4th Session, 1952, II, 57.

[81] GAOR, 7th Session, 1952, Sixth Committee, Summary Records, 48 (312th meeting, 28 Oct. 1952).

[82] *Ibid.*, par. 46.

the latter course, since it had felt that the comments of governments could be better prepared in their own foreign offices than
in the General Assembly, where so many other matters called for
their attention.[83]

Without engaging in debate on the work in progress in the
Commission, the Sixth Committee once again adopted a draft
resolution noting that progress.[84]

The pattern thus established was followed in succeeding sessions of the Sixth Committee. Few representatives on the Committee indulged in substantive discussion of uncompleted work
or provisional drafts of the International Law Commission
until the 12th Session of the Committee in 1957. The Commission's Report for that year contained a provisional draft of
thirty-seven articles on *Diplomatic Intercourse and Immunities*
which had been transmitted to governments for their comments.[85] Although Mr. Zourek, Chairman of the International
Law Commission, informed the Sixth Committee that the
provisional draft had been submitted only for the information
of the Committee,[86] a draft on diplomatic privileges and immunities proved too tempting for diplomats to pass over in
silence. One representative discussed substantively no less than
fifteen articles; [87] others were critical of particular provisions.
The reminders of Senator Henri Rolin (Belgium) that the discussion was premature and "that some representatives were
unable to offer anything but purely personal observations," [88]
and of Mr. Zourek that such comments "might very usefully
be incorporated in the comments of their respective governments," [89] point to the conclusion earlier expressed by Dr.
Liang that the General Assembly, in drafting the Commission's
Statute, had believed that comments of governments on the
Commission's drafts would be more useful if prepared in their
own foreign offices. However, at the close of its debate, the

[83] *Ibid.,* 50, par. 67.   [84] *Ibid.,* 47–51.
[85] Yearbook, ILC, 9th Session, 1957, II, 132.
[86] GAOR, 12th Session, 1957, Sixth Committee, Summary Records, 7.
[87] *Ibid.,* 6–7.   [88] *Ibid.,* 10.   [89] *Ibid.,* 23.

Sixth Committee adopted a draft resolution requesting that its Summary Records on the subject be forwarded to the International Law Commission.[90]

At its 14th Session in 1959, the Sixth Committee largely refrained from detailed discussion of the substantive content of an interim report on aspects of the *Law of Treaties,* but representatives of at least thirty States debated at some length the question whether the subject should be presented in the form of a code or of draft conventions.[91] Making no recommendation on the subject, the Committee took note of the Commission's Report.

The debate on the work of the International Law Commission which dominated the 15th Session of the Sixth Committee in 1960, involved, as stated above, an attempt by a group of States to influence the future work of the International Law Commission on the topic of *State Responsibility* (see p. 329).

The practice of the Sixth Committee in relation to work in progress in the International Law Commission, and even toward drafts provisionally formulated by the Commission, appears to be based on the conception that the Committee should refrain from detailed discussion of the Commission's work until the Commission itself requests such consideration. Individual representatives or groups in the Sixth Committee have suggested the desirability of discussion of work in progress so that the Commission might not lose touch with "political realities." These views have never prevailed in the adoption of resolutions. The prevalent view has been that politics should not dominate the process of stating the law, and that when the International Law Commission has submitted to the General Assembly a completed draft, that draft can then be considered both for its legal and for its political implications.

[90] Cf. GA res. 1185 (XII), 11 Dec. 1957; GAOR, 12th Session, 1957, Annexes, Agenda item 53.

[91] GAOR, 14th Session, 1959, Sixth Committee, Summary Records, 5 ff., especially 601st to 610th meetings, 24 Sept.–12 Oct. 1960; *ibid.,* Annexes, Agenda item 55.

In the meantime, the positions of States on controversial points of law or practice can be better communicated to the International Law Commission in the measured language of documents drafted by their legal advisers than in the oral debates of the Sixth Committee.

The Sixth Committee and the Completed Drafts of the International Law Commission

If it is considered undesirable for the Sixth Committee to discuss the provisional drafts of the International Law Commission because such discussion would be premature, and would tend to inject politics into the technical task of restating the law, is it desirable for the Sixth Committee to engage in a detailed analysis of the final drafts presented by the Commission?

Obviously, the Sixth Committee has the function of advising the General Assembly as to the proper disposition of the Commission's completed drafts. By Article 23 of its Statute, the Commission makes a recommendation and the Sixth Committee may appropriately discuss whether to recommend to the General Assembly acceptance, rejection, or modification of the Commission's recommendation. Should it do more? In particular, if the International Law Commission has recommended that the General Assembly *"adopt* the report by resolution" or *"recommend* the draft to Members with a view to the conclusion of a convention," is it desirable for the Sixth Committee to modify the Commission's draft before endorsing it?

The Sixth Committee has never amended a final draft of the International Law Commission, despite occasional opinions expressed in the Sixth Committee that it should do so prior to adopting or recommending a draft or referring it to an international conference as the basis of discussion.

It appears that the Sixth Committee has itself been uncertain as to its proper role in relation to completed drafts of the International Law Commission. The first completed draft of the Commission was the *Draft Declaration on Rights and Duties of States,*[92] submitted to the 4th Session of the General Assembly in 1949. It was severely criticized by many representatives in the Sixth Committee,[93] some of whom called on the Committee to examine it, article by article, and proposed deletions, additions, and amendments to the Commission's text.[94]

On the other hand, Mr. Harmel (Belgium), although criticizing the Commission's draft as containing contradictions and ambiguities, opposed the submission of any amendments as likely to destroy the integrated structure of the draft.[95] Mr. Fitzmaurice (U.K.) thought that if the Sixth Committee undertook a detailed revision of the Commission's draft it would consume weeks or months and the "resulting draft would probably be inferior." He added that

there was no use in having such a Commission if the General Assembly was to repeat its work. Such a course of action would amount to treating the Commission as a secretariat whose function was to produce working papers. . . . The Commission was a more expert body than the Committee and was more competent to draft international instruments. . . . As a body of experts, it was intended to do creative work. The Sixth Committee or the General Assembly was not bound to approve the draft declaration, but it could not instruct the International Law Commission to produce something different.[96]

After a full debate, in which the Commission's draft was more criticized than praised, its unamended text was attached to a resolution by which the General Assembly took note of

[92] Cf. Yearbook, ILC., 1st Session, 1949, p. 287.

[93] GAOR, 4th Session, 1949, Sixth Committee, Summary Records, 170–272 (169th to 183rd meetings). Cf. above, p. 279.

[94] Cf., e.g., Gomez Robledo (Mexico), *ibid.,* 179–180; Hsu (China), *ibid.,* 185, 187, 189; García Amador (Cuba), *ibid.,* 201–203.

[95] *Ibid.,* 175–176.

[96] *Ibid.,* 197. Cf. the statement of Mr. Spiropoulos at the 297th meeting that a "text of codification submitted to the Committee by the International Law Commission stated what that juridical body considered to be the law; it ought not be altered by the Committee and all directions concerning that text should be given beforehand." GAOR, 6th Session, 1951–52, Sixth Committee, Summary Records, 274.

it, deemed it a notable and substantial contribution toward the progressive development of international law and its codification, commended it for further study, and invited States to make suggestions as to "the future procedure to be adopted in relation to it." [97] The text remains today in the form drafted by the International Law Commission.

During the 5th Session of the General Assembly in 1950, members of the Sixth Committee engaged in an extended but inconclusive debate on the substantive provisions of the International Law Commission's formulation of the *Nürnberg Principles*,[98] but the Committee made no attempt to amend or reformulate the Commission's text.[99] The resolution adopted requested the Commission to take account of observations made in the Sixth Committee, and by Governments, on the Commission's formulation.[100] Since the reports submitted by the International Law Commission to the General Assembly in 1950 on *Ways and Means for Making the Evidence of Customary International Law More Readily Available* and on the *Question of International Criminal Jurisdiction* [101] and in 1951 on *Reservations to Multilateral Conventions* and on the *Question of Defining Aggression* [102] were not prepared in the form of draft articles, the temptation to rephrase them did not arise in the Sixth Committee. On the subject of *Reservations to Multilateral Conventions* the Sixth Committee engaged in an extended substantive debate and adopted a draft resolution which differed in important respects from the recommendations of the International Law Commission.[103] On the other

---

[97] GA res. 375 (IV), 6 Dec. 1949, A/1251, pp. 66–67. See above, p. 279.

[98] Yearbook, ILC, 2nd Session, 1950, II, 374.

[99] GAOR, 5th Session, 1950, Sixth Committee, Summary Records, 131–198 (231st to 239th meetings); *ibid.*, Annexes, Agenda item 52; A/1639, 8 Dec. 1950, Report of the Sixth Committee.

[100] GA res. 488 (V), 12 Dec. 1950, A/1775, p. 77.

[101] Yearbook, ILC, 2nd Session, 1950, II, 367 ff. and 378.

[102] Yearbook, ILC, 3rd Session, 1951, II, 125 ff. and 131.

[103] GAOR, 6th Session, 1951, Sixth Committee, Summary Records, 69–149 (264th to 278th meetings); *ibid.*, Annexes, Agenda items 49 (a) and 50.

three reports the Sixth Committee devoted most of its attention to a discussion of the nature of any further action which
might be desirable, although there was considerable substantive discussion of the possibility of defining aggression.[104]

It is the International Law Commission's drafts on *Arbitral
Procedure* which have been subjected to the most intensive
analysis in the Sixth Committee. When the Commission submitted to the General Assembly its thirty-two-article *Draft
Convention on Arbitral Procedure* in 1953, with the recommendation, pursuant to Article 23, paragraph 1 (c) of its Statute, that
the General Assembly "recommend the draft to Members with
a view to the conclusion of a convention," [105] representatives
of more than thirty States indulged in general debate of its
contents,[106] over a dozen expressing unfavorable views on the
substance of the draft, with a small number defending it. Mr.
Jacob Robinson (Israel) believed the "idea of considering the
draft article by article should be dismissed as being prolonged,
useless and even harmful." He criticized the draft on grounds
of substance, form, and utility. He opposed the recommendation of the International Law Commission that the draft be
submitted to member States with a view to the conclusion of
a convention and preferred to have the General Assembly take
note of the Commission's draft "as representing an expression
of the majority views of a body enjoying authority in the
world." [107] Instead, the Sixth Committee decided to submit
the draft to Governments for their comments and to include
the question in the provisional agenda of the 10th Session of the
General Assembly.[108]

During the 10th Session of the General Assembly, the Sixth
Committee again debated the Commission's draft in the light

104 *Ibid.*, 149–261 (278th to 295th meetings), Agenda item 49 (b).

105 Yearbook, ILC, 5th Session, 1953, II, 201–212.

106 GAOR, 8th Session, 1953, Sixth Committee, Summary Records,
109–140 (382nd to 389th meetings); *ibid.*, Annexes, Agenda item 53. See
above, p. 288.

107 *Ibid.*, 111 (382nd meeting).

108 Cf. GA res. 797 (VIII), 7 Dec. 1953, A/2630, p. 51.

of comments received from the governments of only fourteen of the sixty States then Members of the United Nations.[109] While some representatives questioned the desirability of a detailed debate on the substantive provisions of the Commission's draft,[110] others indulged in analysis of particular articles. The burden of the complaint against the Commission's draft was that, in attempting to provide means of avoiding the unilateral frustration of an agreement to arbitrate, the Commission had infringed the autonomy of the will of the parties.[111] Mr. A. K. Brohi (Pakistan) correctly pointed out that the essence of the concept of arbitration, viz.,

the free consent of the parties to submit a justiciable issue to umpires or to a tribunal chosen by them for decision in accordance with a specified body of law—had been strictly preserved by the Commission. . . . It was, however, stretching the argument too far to regard such autonomy of the will as extending throughout the entire arbitral procedure. To do so would be to authorize States to withdraw at any time, or to reject the award, and would defeat the whole purpose of arbitration. It was only in the initial stage of submitting a dispute to a forum that autonomy could be exercised.[112]

Nevertheless, the Sixth Committee, hinting that the Commission's draft was *too* progressive a development of the international law of arbitral procedure, referred the draft back to the Commission for reconsideration in the light of comments of governments and discussions in the Sixth Committee.[113]

The International Law Commission yielded in the face of

[109] GAOR, 10th Session, 1955, Sixth Committee, Summary Records, 83–103, 109–144 (461st to 464th and 466th to 472nd meetings); *ibid.,* Annexes, Agenda item 52.

[110] Cf., e.g., Perez Perozo (Venezuela), *ibid.,* 84; Chairman Lachs (Poland), *ibid.,* 130.

[111] Cf., e.g., Perez Perozo, *ibid.,* 84–85; Sen (India), *ibid.,* 89; Amado (Brazil), *ibid.,* 95–96; Mme. Bastid (France), *ibid.,* 123–124; and A/3083, Report of 6th Committee, 12 Dec. 1955, pars. 10–14.

[112] *Ibid.,* 121 (468th meeting, 3 Dec. 1955).

[113] GA res. 989 (X), 14 Dec. 1955.

the strongly expressed criticisms of its progressive development of the law of arbitral procedure and, while retaining the major substantive provisions of its *Draft Convention on Arbitral Procedure,* presented it to the General Assembly in 1958 as a set of *Model Rules on Arbitral Procedure* to be adopted by the General Assembly only as model rules upon which States could draw, "to such extent as they might see fit in concluding bilateral or plurilateral arbitral agreements *inter se,* or in submitting particular disputes to arbitration *ad hoc.*" [114]

During the 13th Session of the General Assembly in 1958, the Sixth Committee considered the Commission's draft at its 554th to 567th meetings.[115] Because the *Model Rules* still emphasized means by which a party that had freely accepted a legal obligation to arbitrate might be prevented from violating that agreement and frustrating the arbitral process, a proposal that the General Assembly *commend* the *Model Rules* to the attention of Member States for such guidance as they might deem appropriate in drawing up arbitral agreements [116] was abandoned; it was considered too strong by representatives who wanted no indication that the Assembly approved the rules in any way.

The representative of the Byelorussian Soviet Socialist Republic observed that as a "result of the International Law Commission's stubborn refusal to abide by the views of the General Assembly," and by sending the old draft back "disguised as 'model rules'," the Commission was attempting to secure Assembly approval for provisions departing from the traditional notion of arbitration and transforming it "into a supranational jurisdictional procedure." [117] Mr. Morozov (U.S.-S.R.), praising "traditional arbitration," opposed any expres-

[114] Yearbook, ILC, 10th Session, 1958, II, 80–88. See above, p. 290.
[115] GAOR, 13th Session, Sixth Committee, Summary Records, 24–84; *ibid.,* Annexes, Agenda item 57.
[116] A/C.6/L.422, 17 Oct. 1958 (Greece), Annexes, Agenda item 57.
[117] Sixth Committee, Summary Records, *loc. cit.,* 25 (554th meeting, 2 Oct. 1958).

sion of approval of the *Model Rules* by the General Assembly: that would endow them "with unquestionable moral authority." Nor, he said, could the Sixth Committee congratulate the Commission on its work: "It was a matter not of exercising any pressure on the experts of the International Law Commission, but simply of making them understand that the instructions of the General Assembly too must be considered as a source of international law since they reflected the opinions of the representatives of different legal systems." [118]

Other representatives wanted the Sixth Committee to examine the *Model Rules,* article by article, with a view to amending them and filling in gaps.[119] Mr. Chaumont (France) thought that the Sixth Committee would have to study the *Model Rules* "in order to modify any provisions which it might find unsatisfactory"; [120] without such examination, he added, "it did not appear possible to adopt the proposal of the International Law Commission and to recommend to the States a draft which the Sixth Committee had not considered." [121] Mr. Glaser (Romania), rejecting the view expressed by other representatives, "could not agree that the Sixth Committee had no right to amend a text drawn up by a group of experts." [122]

Although some representatives favored Assembly approval of the *Model Rules*,[123] the Sixth Committee, by a vote of 39–19–13, adopted a draft resolution, the restrained nature of which is indicated by a preambular clause reading:

[118] *Ibid.,* 56–57 (561st meeting).
[119] Cf., e.g., Douc Rasy (Cambodia), *ibid.,* 28.
[120] *Ibid.,* 40 (558th meeting).
[121] *Ibid.,* 55 (561st meeting). Cf. also Venezuela, *ibid.,* 54; Sweden, *ibid.,* 55; Tunisia, *ibid.,* 62; Ethiopia, *ibid.,* 63; Iraq, *ibid.,* 65.
[122] *Ibid.,* 60.
[123] Cf., e.g., the views expressed, sometimes with qualifications, by representatives of Pakistan, *ibid.,* 25; United Kingdom, *ibid.,* 27; Mexico, *ibid.,* 28; New Zealand, *ibid.,* 28; Italy, *ibid.,* 32; Burma, *ibid.,* 33; Portugal, *ibid.,* 33; Malaya, *ibid.,* 34; Yemen, *ibid.,* 34; Belgium, *ibid.,* 35; Greece, *ibid.* 36; El Salvador, *ibid.,* 40; Canada, *ibid.,* 43; United States, *ibid.,* 44; Netherlands, *ibid.,* 45; Indonesia, *ibid.,* 49; Venezuela, *ibid.,* 53–54; China, *ibid.,* 56; Ecuador, *ibid.,* 61.

Taking note of the comments in that report [of the Commission] to the effect, in particular, that the draft articles on arbitral procedure contained therein would have no binding effect on States unless accepted by them and save to the extent that each one is accepted by them in treaties of arbitration or in a *compromis*, . . .

and by the first and third operative paragraphs by which the General Assembly "takes note" of the Commission's 10th Report and

3. Brings the draft articles on arbitral procedure . . . to the attention of Member States for their consideration and use, in such cases and to such extent as they consider appropriate, in drawing up treaties of arbitration or *compromis*.[124]

The recommendations of the International Law Commission that its *Draft Convention on Arbitral Procedure* be submitted to Member States with a view to the conclusion of a convention and its later recommendation that its *Model Rules on Arbitral Procedure* be adopted by the General Assembly were thus both rejected by the Sixth Committee. It is perhaps significant that even in the two cases in which the Sixth Committee has rejected the Commission's drafts, the Sixth Committee resisted the plea that it reformulate or modify the text of the Commission's drafts.

In the same 13th Session in which it disposed of the *Model Rules on Arbitral Procedure,* the Sixth Committee received the completed draft of the International Law Commission on *Diplomatic Intercourse and Immunities* with the Commission's recommendation, in accordance with paragraph 1 (*c*) of Article 23 of its Statute, that the General Assembly "recommend the draft to Members with a view to the conclusion of a convention." [125] The Sixth Committee discussed the draft at its 568th

---

124 *Ibid.,* Annexes, Agenda item 57, p. 7. Cf. GA res. 1262 (XIII), 14 Nov. 1958.
125 Yearbook, ILC, 10th Session, 1958, II, 89.

to 580th meetings in October and November 1958.[126] Although individual articles came in for critical comment, there was no systematic examination of the Commission's draft and the debate turned on the appropriate role of the Sixth Committee in relation to the draft. A large majority favored the conclusion of a convention on the subject but opinions differed as to whether the drawing up of such a treaty should be submitted to an international conference or should be done by the Sixth Committee itself. Mr. Cutts (Australia) preferred the second course because the Sixth Committee, in his view, could not even recommend the Commission's draft to a conference without first considering it in detail.[127] Mr. Zlitni (Libya) thought the preparation of the Convention by the Sixth Committee would "enhance the Committee's standing and entail less expenditure." [128] Mr. Chaumont (France), observing that the Committee was once again faced with a decision on methods, deplored the tendency to avoid detailed discussion of the International Law Commission's draft. He agreed that "without a discussion on the substance of the text, the Committee could not act on the International Law Commission's recommendations and recommend the draft articles to Member States with a view to the conclusion of a convention." [129] The contrary view was expressed by others. Thus, Mr. Evans (U.K.), pointing out that the Commission's draft represented a compromise between conflicting views, questioned whether a detailed discussion in the Sixth Committee was likely to improve the text, and observed that there would be no advantage in such a debate if the text was to be forwarded to a conference.[130]

The resulting General Assembly resolution invited further

---

[126] GAOR, 13th Session, 1958, Sixth Committee, Summary Records, 86–145; *ibid.*, Annexes, Agenda item 56. See above, p. 303.

[127] Sixth Committee, *loc. cit.*, 90 (569th meeting).

[128] *Ibid.*, 131. Cf. Rodriguez (Costa Rica), *ibid.*, 97.

[129] *Ibid.*, 90–91 (569th meeting).

[130] *Ibid.*, 94. Cf. Perez Perozo (Venezuela), *ibid.*, 95; Rosenne (Israel), *ibid.*, 104.

comments from governments on the Commission's draft articles, and postponed to the 14th Session of the General Assembly the question "to what body the formulation of the convention should be entrusted." [131] At the 14th Session, after further debate,[132] a Chilean proposal providing, *inter alia,* "that the Sixth Committee shall be entrusted with the drafting of the conventions on diplomatic intercourse and immunities, on consular intercourse and immunities, on *ad hoc* diplomacy and on immunities of inter-governmental organizations as and when the International Law Commission submits reports on those questions" was rejected by a vote of 54 (against) to 6, with 18 abstentions.[133] In the debate preceding the vote, the arguments that Sixth Committee members were well qualified to draft conventions on international law and that it would be cheaper than convening a diplomatic conference were countered by arguments that some delegations lacked the necessary experts and that the Sixth Committee lacked the necessary time. On request, Mr. Stavropoulos, Legal Counsel, provided information that when the Sixth Committee had itself drafted the Genocide Convention, it had required fifty meetings to adopt a convention of nineteen articles, only nine of which were of a substantive nature, whereas the International Law Commission's draft on *Diplomatic Intercourse and Immunities* contained forty-five substantive articles.[134]

[131] GA res. 1288 (XIII), 5 Dec. 1958.

[132] GAOR, 14th Session, 1959, Sixth Committee, Summary Records, 168–209 (631st to 639th meetings).

[133] *Ibid.,* Annexes, Agenda item 56 (Report of the Sixth Committee, A/4305), pp. 24–25.

[134] Sixth Committee, *loc. cit.,* 175 (633rd meeting, 13 Nov. 1959). At the 711th meeting of the Sixth Committee on 9 Nov. 1961, Mr. Stavropoulos pointed out that the Vienna Conference of 1961 had required seven weeks, at a rate of two meetings a day, to study the 45-article draft on *Diplomatic Intercourse and Immunities* and complete its work. The 71-article draft of the International Law Commission on *Consular Intercourse and Immunities,* he estimated, would take nine weeks unless the work could be expedited by setting up two committees. A/C.6/SR.711, par. 40.

The Sixth Committee, by a vote of 67–1–11, decided to recommend the convocation of an international conference to which should be referred the International Law Commission's draft "as the basis for its consideration of the question of diplomatic intercourse and immunities." [135]

It appears to be of some significance that the argument made during its 13th Session that the Sixth Committee could not recommend International Law Commission drafts to a conference without detailed discussion of their substantive provisions did not prevent such action at the Committee's 14th Session. The implication seems clear that the Sixth Committee does not regard as its proper role any reformulation of a Commission draft prior to its submission to an international conference as a basis of discussion.

This issue had not arisen when the Sixth Committee was considering the submission to international conferences of the International Law Commission's final drafts on *Statelessness* and on the *Law of the Sea*. In the former case, after a short debate in which there was much criticism but no comprehensive substantive discussion of the Commission's draft conventions on the *Elimination of Future Statelessness* and the *Reduction of Future Statelessness*,[136] the Sixth Committee adopted a draft resolution expressing the desire that a conference be convened to conclude a convention on either the reduction or the elimination of future statelessness as soon as at least twenty States had communicated to the United Nations their willingness to participate.[137] Although the resolution did not specifically refer the International Law Commission's two drafts to such a conference, a later memorandum of the United Nations Secretariat observed, in part, "that it has always been

135 Annexes, *loc. cit.,* Agenda item 56, pp. 24, 26, 27. Cf. GA res. 1450 (XIV), 7 Dec. 1959.

136 Yearbook, ILC, 6th Session, 1954, II, 141.

137 Cf. GAOR, 9th Session, 1954, Sixth Committee, Summary Records, 5–31 (397th to 402nd meetings); *ibid.,* Annexes, Agenda item 49; GA res. 896 (IX), 4 Dec. 1954.

anticipated that the Conference would have to choose between the two drafts." [138]

The International Law Commission's draft on the *Law of the Sea* [139] was the subject of discussion at the 481st and 485th to 505th meetings of the Sixth Committee in November and December 1956. Representatives of no less than sixty States participated in the general debate, many of them expressing the views of their governments on the substantive provisions of the Commission's draft. Although there was no systematic reading or adoption of that draft, article by article, the propriety of referring the Commission's draft to the proposed Conference on the Law of the Sea without such action by the Sixth Committee was not questioned.[140] Mr. Jorge Castañeda (Mexico) observed that the reference of the Commission's Report as the "basis" of consideration by the Conference did not mean "that the General Assembly had sanctioned or approved the report of the International Law Commission." [141] If by this statement he meant that the General Assembly had not formally adopted the Commission's draft on the *Law of the Sea,* or any of its articles, one may agree. It was clearly understood that the provisions of the Commission's draft would be subject to discussion and reformulation at the proposed conference. On the other hand, resolution 1105 (XI), unanimously adopted by the General Assembly on 21 February 1957, clearly indicates

[138] A/CONF.9/3, 13 Feb. 1959, United Nations Conference on the Elimination or Reduction of Future Statelessness, Secretariat Memorandum concerning the Method of Work, etc., par. 7. In fact, the Conference adopted the International Law Commission's draft convention on the *Reduction of Future Statelessness* as a basis for discussion. Cf. A/CONF.9/12, 9 Aug. 1961, par. 5, Secretariat Note on Organization and Work of the Conference during the Period from 24 March to 17 April 1959, and A/CONF.9/15, 29 Aug. 1961.

[139] Yearbook, ILC, 8th Session, 1956, II, 254.

[140] GAOR, 11th Session, 1956, Sixth Committee, Summary Records, 25–138; *ibid.,* Annexes, Agenda item 53, including A/3520, Report of the Sixth Committee, especially pars. 70, 77 and 78.

[141] *Ibid.,* Summary Records, *loc. cit.,* 125 (502nd meeting).

Assembly approval of the Commission's draft as a basis of discussion in stating that the General Assembly

9. *Refers* to the conference the report of the International Law Commission as the basis for its consideration of the various problems involved in the development and codification of the law of the sea, and also the verbatim records of the relevant debates in the General Assembly for consideration by the conference in conjunction with the Commission's report;

10. *Requests* the Secretary-General to transmit to the conference all such records of world-wide or regional international meetings as may serve as official background material for its work; [142]

From 20 October to 14 November 1961, the Sixth Committee, at its 700th to 713th meetings,[143] discussed the recommendation of the International Law Commission, pursuant to Article 23, par. 1 (*d*) of its Statute, that its final draft on *Consular Intercourse and Immunities* be submitted to an international conference of plenipotentiaries.[144] During the debate, few representatives engaged in discussion of the substantive provisions of the Commission's draft and a number opposed a proposal to hold such a discussion at the 17th Session of the General Assembly in 1962. Mr. Nisot (Belgium) stated:

The Committee need not evaluate the Commission's text, except to note that it could, in its present form, be regarded as the culmination of the preparatory studies and as a suitable working basis for a settlement of the question. Such a settlement was outside the Committee's institutional competence. The relevant decisions would ultimately have to be taken by Governments themselves, in the context of international law in general, at a diplomatic conference.[145]

[142] A/3572, p. 54.

[143] GAOR, 16th Session, 1961, Sixth Committee, Summary Records, 65–119; A/5013, 7 Dec. 1961, Report of the Sixth Committee, 16th Session, Annexes, Agenda item 69.

[144] Cf. Yearbook, ILC, 13th Session, 1961, II, 91.

[145] Sixth Committee, Summary Records, cited, 69 (702nd meeting) and 88 (706th). A similar position was taken by representatives of Romania, *ibid.*, 88 (706th), Ceylon, *ibid.*, 89 (707th), U.S.S.R., *ibid.*, 94–95

Despite this view, the Committee decided to recommend inclusion of the item "Consular relations" on the provisional agenda of the 17th Session "to allow further expressions and exchanges of views concerning the draft articles on consular relations." [146] Such an exchange, it was suggested,[147] would give advance notice to the conference to be convened of controversial items, although the Soviet representative believed that detailed discussion of the draft should be avoided and "comments of a general nature would be of no practical interest." [148]

At its 712th meeting on 13 November 1961, the Sixth Committee unanimously adopted a draft resolution complying with the recommendation of the International Law Commission. Requesting the Secretary-General to convoke an International Conference of Plenipotentiaries on Consular Relations at Vienna at the beginning of March 1963, the resolution not only referred to the Conference the Commission's Report "covering the work of its thirteenth session, together with the records of the relevant debates in the General Assembly, as the basis for its consideration," but specifically noted "with satisfaction" that the International Law Commission's draft articles on *Consular Intercourse and Immunities* "constitute a good basis for the preparation of a convention on that subject." [149]

CONCLUSIONS

The complementary nature of the relationship between the International Law Commission and the Sixth Committee is the most striking feature of this survey. In execution of its obligation under Article 13, paragraph 1 (a) of the Charter to "initiate

(708th), Liberia and Greece, *ibid.*, 99, 100 (709th), Bulgaria and Spain, *ibid.*, 111 (711th), among others.

146 GA res. 1685 (XVI), 18 Dec. 1961, par. 11, A/5100, p. 62.
147 Blix (Sweden), 710th meeting, *loc. cit.*, 105.
148 Morozov (U.S.S.R.), 708th meeting, *loc. cit.*, 95.
149 GA res. 1685 (XVI), 18 Dec. 1961.

studies and make recommendations for the purpose of . . . encouraging the progressive development of international law and its codification," the General Assembly created the International Law Commission to perform the substantive task and has selected its members primarily because of their professional competence in international law, but with a view to assuring in the Commission as a whole representation of the main forms of civilization and of the principal legal systems of the world. These policy determinations are supplemented by the provision that the General Assembly makes the final decision as to the disposition of the Commission's completed drafts.

However, the General Assembly has come to recognize that the Commission requires a substantial degree of autonomy to perform its work of codification and development of international law. This has meant in practice that, despite occasional contrary tendencies, the Sixth Committee has learned to exercise some restraint in proposing topics for consideration by the Commission, has refrained from close and constant supervision over the methods of work of the Commission, or the precise content of its provisional drafts, and has carefully resisted the temptation to modify the Commission's completed drafts even when they did not command the support of a majority of the States represented on the Sixth Committee. The view has prevailed that it is better to reject or defer action on a Commission draft which is politically unacceptable than to tamper with the phraseology or principles of a draft prepared by highly skilled international lawyers.

The most successful work of the International Law Commission has been on topics originally selected by itself—*Law of the Seas, Diplomatic Intercourse and Immunities,* and *Consular Intercourse and Immunities,* although priority treatment was recommended on the latter two topics by the Sixth Committee. An apparent exception is the Commission's draft on *Arbitral Procedure.* Although the selection of this topic by the Commission was approved by the General Assembly, it is currently the fashion in some quarters to decry its selection and treatment as an indication of lack of political sense in the Commission. In fact, the Commission's *Model Rules on Arbitral Procedure* are a superior piece of professional work whose excellence and practical utility may yet come to be recognized. Care should be exercised in drawing conclusions from the fact that the members of the International Law Commission, unlike the members of the Sixth Committee, are not representatives of States. Members of the Commission are sensitively alive to the political implications of their work and have exhibited statesmanship as well as legal acumen.

Appendix

Statute of the International Law Commission[1]

Article 1

1. The International Law Commission shall have for its object the promotion of the progressive development of international law and its codification.

2. The Commission shall concern itself primarily with public international law, but is not precluded from entering the field of private international law.

CHAPTER I. ORGANIZATION OF THE INTERNATIONAL LAW COMMISSION

Article 2 *

1. The Commission shall consist of twenty-five members who shall be persons of recognized competence in international law.

2. No two members of the Commission shall be nationals of the same State.

3. In case of dual nationality a candidate shall be deemed to be a national of the State in which he ordinarily exercises civil and political rights.

Article 3

The members of the Commission shall be elected by the General Assembly from a list of candidates nominated by the Governments of States Members of the United Nations.

Article 4

Each Member may nominate for election not more than four candidates, of whom two may be nationals of the nominating State and two nationals of other States.

[1] Text from A/CN.4/4/Rev.1 (1962).
* Text amended by GA res. 1647 (XVI) of 6 Nov. 1961.

Article 5

The names of the candidates shall be submitted in writing by the Governments to the Secretary-General by the first of June of the year in which an election is held, provided that a Government may in exceptional circumstances substitute for a candidate whom it has nominated before the first of June another candidate whom it shall name not later than thirty days before the opening of the General Assembly.

Article 6

The Secretary-General shall as soon as possible communicate to the Governments of States Members the names submitted, as well as any statements of qualifications of candidates that may have been submitted by the nominating Governments.

Article 7

The Secretary-General shall prepare the list referred to in article 3 above, comprising in alphabetical order the names of all the candidates duly nominated, and shall submit this list to the General Assembly for the purposes of the election.

Article 8

At the election the electors shall bear in mind that the persons to be elected to the Commission should individually possess the qualifications required and that in the Commission as a whole representation of the main forms of civilization and of the principal legal systems of the world should be assured.

Article 9 †

1. The twenty-five candidates who obtain the greatest number of votes and not less than a majority of the votes of the Members present and voting shall be elected.

2. In the event of more than one national of the same State obtaining a sufficient number of votes for election the one who obtains the greatest number of votes shall be elected and if the

† Text amended by GA res. 1647 (XVI) of 6 Nov. 1961.

votes are equally divided the elder or eldest candidate shall be elected.

Article 10 ‡

The members of the Commission shall be elected for five years. They shall be eligible for re-election.

Article 11

In the case of a casual vacancy, the Commission itself shall fill the vacancy having due regard to the provisions contained in articles 2 and 8 of this Statute.

Article 12 §

The Commission shall sit at the European Office of the United Nations at Geneva. The Commission shall, however, have the right to hold meetings at other places after consultation with the Secretary-General.

Article 13 ||

Members of the Commission shall be paid travel expenses, and shall also receive a special allowance, the amount of which shall be determined by the General Assembly.

Article 14

The Secretary-General shall, so far as he is able, make available staff and facilities required by the Commission to fulfil its task.

CHAPTER II. FUNCTIONS OF THE INTERNATIONAL LAW COMMISSION

Article 15

In the following articles the expression "progressive development of international law" is used for convenience as meaning the preparation of draft conventions on subjects which have not yet been regulated by international law or in regard to which the law has

‡ Text amended by GA res. 985 (X) of 3 Dec. 1955.
§ Text amended by GA res. 984 (X) of 3 Dec. 1955.
|| Text amended by GA res. 485 (V) of 12 Dec. 1950.

not yet been sufficiently developed in the practice of States. Similarly, the expression "codification of international law" is used for convenience as meaning the more precise formulation and systematization of rules of international law in fields where there already has been extensive State practice, precedent and doctrine.

A. *Progressive Development of International Law*

Article 16

When the General Assembly refers to the Commission a proposal for the progressive development of international law, the Commission shall follow in general a procedure on the following lines:

(*a*) It shall appoint one of its members to be Rapporteur;

(*b*) It shall formulate a plan of work;

(*c*) It shall circulate a questionnaire to the Governments, and shall invite them to supply within a fixed period of time data and information relevant to items included in the plan of work;

(*d*) It may appoint some of its members to work with the Rapporteur on the preparation of drafts pending receipt of replies to this questionnaire;

(*e*) It may consult with scientific institutions and individual experts; these experts need not necessarily be nationals of Members of the United Nations. The Secretary-General will provide, when necessary and within the limits of the budget, for the expenses of these consultations of experts;

(*f*) It shall consider the drafts proposed by the Rapporteur;

(*g*) When the Commission considers a draft to be satisfactory, it shall request the Secretary-General to issue it as a Commission document. The Secretariat shall give all necessary publicity to this document which shall be accompanied by such explanations and supporting material as the Commission considers appropriate. The publication shall include any information supplied to the Commission in reply to the questionnaire referred to in subparagraph (*c*) above;

(*h*) The Commission shall invite the Governments to submit their comments on this document within a reasonable time;

(*i*) The Rapporteur and the members appointed for that purpose shall reconsider the draft taking into consideration these comments and shall prepare a final draft and explanatory report which they shall submit for consideration and adoption by the Commission;

(*j*) The Commission shall submit the draft so adopted with its recommendations through the Secretary-General to the General Assembly.

Article 17

1. The Commission shall also consider proposals and draft multilateral conventions submitted by Members of the United Nations, the principal organs of the United Nations other than the General Assembly, specialized agencies, or official bodies established by inter-governmental agreement to encourage the progressive development of international law and its codification, and transmitted to it for that purpose by the Secretary-General.

2. If in such cases the Commission deems it appropriate to proceed with the study of such proposals or drafts, it shall follow in general a procedure on the following lines:

(*a*) The Commission shall formulate a plan of work, and study such proposals or drafts, and compare them with any other proposals and drafts on the same subjects;

(*b*) The Commission shall circulate a questionnaire to all Members of the United Nations and to the organs, specialized agencies and official bodies mentioned above which are concerned with the question, and shall invite them to transmit their comments within a reasonable time;

(*c*) The Commission shall submit a report and its recommendations to the General Assembly. Before doing so, it may also, if it deems it desirable, make an interim report to the organ or agency which has submitted the proposal or draft;

(*d*) If the General Assembly should invite the Commission to proceed with its work in accordance with a suggested plan, the procedure outlined in article 16 above shall apply. The questionnaire referred to in paragraph (*c*) of that article may not, however, be necessary.

B. *Codification of International Law*

Article 18

1. The Commission shall survey the whole field of international

law with a view to selecting topics for codification, having in mind existing drafts whether governmental or not.

2. When the Commission considers that the codification of a particular topic is necessary or desirable, it shall submit its recommendations to the General Assembly.

3. The Commission shall give priority to requests of the General Assembly to deal with any question.

Article 19

1. The Commission shall adopt a plan of work appropriate to each case.

2. The Commission shall, through the Secretary-General, address to Governments a detailed request to furnish the texts of laws, decrees, judicial decisions, treaties, diplomatic correspondence and other documents relevant to the topic being studied and which the Commission deems necessary.

Article 20

The Commission shall prepare its drafts in the form of articles and shall submit them to the General Assembly together with a commentary containing:

(a) Adequate presentation of precedents and other relevant data, including treaties, judicial decisions and doctrine;

(b) Conclusions relevant to:

(i) The extent of agreement on each point in the practice of States and in doctrine;

(ii) Divergencies and disagreements which exist, as well as arguments invoked in favour of one or another solution.

Article 21

1. When the Commission considers a draft to be satisfactory, it shall request the Secretary-General to issue it as a Commission document. The Secretariat shall give all necessary publicity to the document including such explanations and supporting material as the Commission may consider appropriate. The publication shall include any information supplied to the Commission by Governments in accordance with article 19. The Commission shall decide whether the opinions of any scientific institution or individual ex-

perts consulted by the Commssion shall be included in the publication.

2. The Commission shall request Governments to submit comments on this document within a reasonable time.

Article 22

Taking such comments into consideration, the Commission shall prepare a final draft and explanatory report which it shall submit with its recommendations through the Secretary-General to the General Assembly.

Article 23

1. The Commission may recommend to the General Assembly:

(*a*) To take no action, the report having already been published;

(*b*) To take note of or adopt the report by resolution;

(*c*) To recommend the draft to Members with a view to the conclusion of a convention;

(*d*) To convoke a conference to conclude a convention.

2. Whenever it deems it desirable, the General Assembly may refer drafts back to the Commission for reconsideration or redrafting.

Article 24

The Commission shall consider ways and means for making the evidence of customary international law more readily available, such as the collection and publication of documents concerning State practice and of the decisions of national and international courts on questions of international law, and shall make a report to the General Assembly on this matter.

CHAPTER III. CO-OPERATION WITH OTHER BODIES

Article 25

1. The Commission may consult, if it considers necessary, with any of the organs of the United Nations on any subject which is within the competence of that organ.

2. All documents of the Commission which are circulated to Governments by the Secretary-General shall also be circulated to such organs of the United Nations as are concerned. Such organs

may furnish any information or make any suggestions to the Commission.

Article 26

1. The Commission may consult with any international or national organizations, official or non-official, on any subject entrusted to it if it believes that such a procedure might aid it in the performance of its functions.

2. For the purpose of distribution of documents of the Commission, the Secretary-General, after consultation with the Commission, shall draw up a list of national and international organizations concerned with questions of international law. The Secretary-General shall endeavour to include on this list at least one national organization of each Member of the United Nations.

3. In the application of the provisions of this article, the Commission and the Secretary-General shall comply with the resolutions of the General Assembly and the other principal organs of the United Nations concerning relations with Franco Spain and shall exclude both from consultations and from the list, organizations which have collaborated with the nazis and fascists.

4. The advisability of consultation by the Commission with inter-governmental organizations whose task is the codification of international law, such as those of the Pan American Union, is recognized.

Index